The Animal Desk Reference

Essential Oils for Animals

Melissa Shelton DVM
Holistic Veterinarian

Copyright April 2012
Melissa Shelton DVM

www.AnimalDeskReference.com

Copyright 2012. All rights reserved. No part of this text may be reproduced or transmitted in any form or by any means, electronic or mechanical, including photocopying, recording, or by any information storage and retrieval system, without permission in writing from the author.

The information contained within this book is for educational purposes only, and only represents a guideline for your use of essential oils and products for animals. The author will assume no liability for any loss or damage of any nature, by the use of any information contained within this publication.

As medical knowledge is constantly changing, new information becomes available. Treatment recommendations and suggestions may change and techniques advance with time. The author has taken care as far as possible, to ensure that the information given in this text is accurate and up to date. However, readers are strongly advised to work in cooperation with a veterinarian, and to use common sense in how to proceed with any illness or administration of natural remedies.

Dedication:

This book is dedicated to my incredible family; my husband Winston, my daughter Ramie, and my son Reiker. I love you all as big as the sky. Their wonderful understanding of the importance of this book, made its creation possible. And with their help; even Fairies, Unicorns, Squids, and Octopuses can benefit from the wonder that is Essential Oils.

And to Norma, we could never have done it without you!

You fill my heart with love and joy,
Mom (otherwise known as Melissa)

TABLE OF CONTENTS

PREFACE 5
ACKNOWLEDGEMENTS 12

INSTRUCTIONS FROM THE AUTHOR 13
THE SAFE USE OF OILS 18
OILS & REPRODUCTION 21
SENSITIVITY TO OILS 23
ESSENTIAL OIL AVERSIONS 25

METHODS OF APPLICATION 27
    DIFFUSION 28
    ADDING OILS TO DRINKING WATER 32
    MIXING OILS INTO FOODS 36
    ORAL ADMINISTRATION 39
    TOPICAL APPLICATIONS 41
    ESSENTIAL OILS & EYES 49
    ESSENTIAL OILS & EARS 52
    RECTAL INSTILLATION 56

HOW MUCH, HOW OFTEN 58
RAINDROP TECHNIQUE 60
EMOTIONAL WORK WITH OILS 67
ADVANCED TECHNIQUES 72
INTO THE FUTURE 76

TABLE OF CONTENTS

ESSENTIAL OIL SINGLES 77

EMOTIONAL USE OF BLENDS 171
PHYSICAL USE OF BLENDS 174
ESSENTIAL OIL BLENDS 177

SUPPLEMENTS & PRODUCTS 203

ESSENTIAL OILS: AVIAN 250
    AVIAN CONDITIONS 255
ESSENTIAL OILS: FERRETS 288
ESSENTIAL OILS: RABBITS 294
ESSENTIAL OILS: EXOTIC ANIMALS 303

ESSENTIAL OILS: FELINE 321
    KITTY RAINDROP TECHNIQUE 325
    FELINE CONDITIONS 327

CANINE RAINDROP TECHNIQUE 373
CANINE CONDITIONS 376

EQUINE RAINDROP 463
EQUINE CONDITIONS 471

LARGE ANIMAL TECHNIQUES 522

INDEX 534

PREFACE

It was the year 2001. I had graduated from veterinary school in 1999, was newly engaged to my high school sweetheart Winston, and was ready to begin a new life and career. As my wedding date approached, there was a problem. My husband-to-be had warts all over his hands, and being a typical bride, I wanted beautiful pictures of our hands showing our new wedding rings. Horrible, ugly warts did not fit into this plan. We had done everything that traditional medicine offered. We had cut off the warts, frozen off the warts, painted on medicines, and even applied duct tape to the warts.

Nothing had worked and we were running out of time. Our minister recommended that we try using the essential oil of clove to get rid of the warts. Thankfully, she recommended using Young Living Essential Oils, and with this truly therapeutic grade oil we saw results. Within 3 months, Winston's hands were completely clear of warts and our wedding pictures were gorgeous.

One would think that this experience would have propelled me into using essential oils on a regular basis, but it did not. The clove oil was placed into a cabinet, and sat there for another 7 years. We were young and healthy and had no children at that point. The motivation for natural and powerful remedies was not a priority in my life or in my career. As a new graduate of veterinary school, it felt as if I knew it all. I had all of this great new knowledge – and could fix any case that came my way. Of course, life teaches otherwise. As time went on, veterinary cases for which I had no answers began to frustrate me. Even though I was continually seeking and learning new information, and I had begun to incorporate many holistic healing modalities into my practice, there were still those frustrating cases for which there appeared to be no answers.

It would be my own family that would drive me back into the realm of essential oils. In 2002, we were blessed with our daughter Ramie. My husband Winston is challenged with a Tourette's-like syndrome, as well as his father, his brother, and my own brother. When Ramie was 2 ½ years old, we recognized that she too, was developing some tics. Then in 2005, our son Reiker was born.

When my son was a newborn baby, we noticed what we were told were "normal" skin issues. Classic cradle cap, baby eczema, and baby acne were conditions described by everyone who saw our son. However, when he was a few months old, he developed the coordination to scratch at his own head. Unfortunately, this showed us that his skin was in fact itching, and he would scratch until the skin was damaged and bloody. No longer were we dealing with skin that just looked bad. We would be up all night with our little baby, having him wear mittens, hats – you name it – trying to keep him from destroying his delicate skin. It was terribly stressful; resulting in many sleepless nights and tears.

As a veterinarian – I knew that this was NOT normal. I was never really comfortable with him having the other "normal" skin conditions either, as it didn't really make sense to me for a fresh, perfect new baby to have skin problems. With our new found horror of his itching, I had to find answers. We went to pediatricians, allergy specialists, naturopaths, homeopaths, chiropractors, kinesiologists, Shamans, and Reiki Masters. I wanted to find someone with an answer – but alas, no one did.

I started to look at the situation as I would for a dog. I had started to notice a direct correlation with breast feeding and the itching. However, I was assured that he had tested negative for all food allergies by the traditional allergist, and even the kinesiologist (using what would commonly be called muscle-testing) could not find a direct correlation with diet and the reaction.

So, I did what I would do for any pet in my hospital – A DIET TRIAL. Since he was breast feeding, it was really a diet trial for me. My diet consisted of eating only plain chicken and water for 2 weeks. And, low and behold, my son was normal. I had my answer. He was definitely reacting to something I was eating, and it was passing through my breast milk and causing an allergic reaction in him.

Next, I introduced foods one at a time to see where the reaction would rear its ugly head. I kept a very exact diet log documenting everything I ate or drank, what time I ate or drank it, when our son was breast fed, and if he had a reaction to the feeding. After a while, it became incredibly confusing to figure out which items were causing the problem. He would react when I had eaten yogurt, but not to milk. He would react if I had ketchup on a hamburger patty, but not to chili with hamburger and tomatoes. He even

PREFACE

seemed to react to me having a soft drink! Every time I thought I found an answer – dairy, tomatoes, beef, citrus… something else would prove that to be wrong. I didn't give up though. I had 2 weeks of diet logs and poured over them to find the answer.

Thankfully, a friend of mine came over and was telling me of her "disgust" of corn syrup. It was in so many foods, was certainly causing health problems, and it was almost impossible to buy anything that didn't contain it. LIGHT BULB!!! I grabbed my diet log – and guess what. Corn syrup was in every item that my son reacted to. Yogurt sweetened with corn syrup, white bread sweetened with corn syrup, ketchup sweetened with corn syrup! However, I was assured by multiple medical doctors that there was no way that a baby could react to corn syrup, and especially not through the mother's breast milk. Tell that to my 4 month old son, scratching his face and head until it bled!

Corn syrup and its derivatives are found in almost every commercial food item today. Bread, soda, popsicles and freezies, ice cream, yogurt, fruit snacks, canned fruits, ketchup, hot chocolate mix, crackers, graham crackers, cereals, chocolate milk, tomato soup, hot dogs, lunch meat; the list goes on and on.

We drastically changed our whole family's diet for our son. We faithfully read ingredient labels and purchased only wholesome foods that did not contain corn syrup, high fructose corn syrup, corn syrup solids or anything else related to corn syrup. We saw amazing changes, and my son was normal again. We hadn't realized that he was also having quite a bit of digestive problems, which also disappeared with the new changes.

However, as we changed all of this – we noted something else. My husband and my 4 year old daughter improved significantly in THEIR tics and symptoms. More importantly, we found another amazing correlation. When we would have a "dietary break" – and they would eat something with corn syrup or chemicals in it – their symptoms would escalate, usually within 24 hours.

Of course, once you clean up your diet – it becomes easier and easier to recognize items that cause a problem. What I have found for our family – has encouraged me to teach others what diet can do for their health concerns. As more and more people eliminate corn syrup, food dyes, artificial sweeteners, preservatives, MSG, and other food chemicals – the results are remarkable. Children that had their diets changed did not need medications or needed much less of them. Adults found that they were having much less skin problems, such as eczema. Children's behavior in general (even in children that didn't have behavioral challenges) – seemed much more easy going and pleasant.

Over and over again, there were significant improvements for children and adults when corn syrup and chemicals were removed from their life. Conditions including Attention Deficit Disorder (ADD), Attention Deficit Hyperactive Disorder (ADHD), Tourette's syndrome, Asperger's, Obsessive Compulsive Disorder (OCD), Anxiety disorders, Autism, Pediatric Autoimmune Neuropsychiatric Disorders Associated with Streptococcal Infections (PANDA's), and multiple other behavioral and neurologic issues; all had major connections with what we were putting into our bodies.

So what does this have to do with my journey towards using essential oils? This whole experience opened my eyes to the fact that a seemingly small thing, can indeed matter. Something as small and supposedly unimportant as corn syrup or a food chemical, *can* cause incredibly profound "side effects" in life and health.

However, I believe that small things can also enact life changing good as well.

As I was starting to comprehend the consequences that un-natural chemicals could bring into our human lives, we were starting to acknowledge some very interesting cases in our veterinary hospital. We encountered dogs that would become very ill when household odor-eliminating sprays were used. We documented cats with elevated liver enzymes from eating on kitchen counters cleaned with a certain polishing compound. We witnessed chronic ear infections and allergies completely disappear when households changed to all natural cleaning products. Use of air fresheners, fabric softeners, and perfumes now appeared on the differential list as a contributor to frustrating chronic illnesses. The horrible effects of everyday household toxins were showing up everywhere – once you knew to look for them.

In good consciousness, I could no longer use these products in my veterinary hospital. If these products were harmful for the animals in my care – what were they doing to my family? I threw out all of my air fresheners, plug in devices, and sprays. Odor control became an issue, as my veterinary hospital is within my home. I felt rather stuck – but I would rather have bad odors than hurt an animal or my loved ones.

We had already started to look toward natural medicines and a holistic approach to life and health for our family. My children's challenges demanded it. As part of this exploration, I attended a class through our local community education program. The class was on natural remedies for all sorts of things; from colds and flu to ADD/ADHD. When I walked into the class, there was a wonderful smell coming from a diffuser. I had found my answer for natural health care for my family, and I was transported back to Young Living Essential Oils once again. But, could the essential oils be safely used for odor control in my vet clinic? The instructor of the class said she knew of many people using Young Living Essential Oils on animals, but of course, I am not one to take one person's word for it. I have to research everything for myself.

I devoured information on essential oils. I perused the Internet. I bought book upon book, and read each one cover to cover. I attended every local class on essential oils that was offered. Inevitably at these classes, people would find out that I was a veterinarian, and they would proceed to share all of their stories on how the oils had been used to treat their dog or cat, horse or goat. I was intrigued. Then as my research and learning turned to my veterinary community – I received a completely different response.

DANGER, DANGER, DANGER... Do NOT use essential oils in pets, and don't even diffuse them around cats. Here were the top names in holistic veterinary medicine, and they were largely against the use of essential oils. How could it be that hundreds and thousands of Young Living members were using their oils safely on their pets, but in general the veterinary community believed that essential oils could be very harmful and recommended avoiding them?

I am not one to allow a mystery to go unsolved. My trek continued, and I was determined to find out the truth about oils and animals. Obviously, I would have to do the research and gather the proof myself. I had already been using Young Living oils for my human family for some time. I was diffusing in almost every room of my own home, and my cats seemed actually drawn to the rooms with diffusers in them. Kittens were born in rooms with diffusers running, and cats routinely slept inside my case of essential oils – they loved the oils. People commented on how intelligent our kittens were, how they looked into the eyes of humans, and how they seemed so much older than they actually were.

I started using oils directly on my own cats, dogs, horses, chickens, and cow. After all, if I did not believe I could use the oils for my own animals, why should I ever recommend them for a patient? All of my animals get routine blood and urine tests, so they were a great model for monitoring against any potential side effects from essential oils. With over 10 animals being exposed to essential oils almost 24 hours a day through diffusion, topical application, and ingestion – there was a definite ability to document their health and responses to essential oils.

Then in my veterinary hospital, patients presented that were close to euthanasia or for which I had no answers to offer traditionally – I now began offering essential oil therapies. This is where I started. In the hopeless cases, that had nothing to lose. I was coming up with the same amazing results that so many pet owners had already communicated to me. There were situations where traditional medicine offered NOTHING – and I was getting responses with essential oils.

The cases with the animals in my practice and Young Living Essential Oils, were nothing less than amazing. Although it may seem like a fast progression, to go from novice essential oil user, to being known internationally in veterinary aromatherapy in under 2 years...you would just have to know me. I never do anything "lightly".

Considering that Veterinary College is only 4 years, and covers every subject in medicine and surgery – 2 years of intense study and medical use of essential oils in animals is really very significant. I throw myself into everything I do, and essential oils had immediately become a passion for me. I condensed 10+ years of essential oil education and experience, into a 1 year adventure.

I have lost count of how many essential oil books I own – and I have read each one, cover to cover. I have listened to almost every CD and recorded educational call that is available – and I don't just listen to them, I memorize them. I have purchased every reference I could find about oils and animals, and I feel proud of the fact that I have found books that even my teachers did not know about.

But with all of the classroom learning and book smarts – nothing compares to actually using essential oils to treat animals. On our 15 acre farm, there is a variety of animals which have included around 20 rescued cats, 13 pet cats, 5 dogs, 3 horses, 1 pony, 2 cows, 1 goat, a flock of chickens, rats,

PREFACE

hermit crabs, fish, and more. My wonderful collection of strays, misfits, injured and ill animals – allow me a great opportunity to "play with the oils". Many of the animals that we took on were hopeless cases. They had no options in life, except to be adopted by a vet, who would go to extraordinary measures to try to make them comfortable and to try to save their lives.

We are now fortunate enough to have clients demanding treatments with essential oils in our practice. Every single case in our hospital benefits from the use of essential oils, even if it is only from basic diffusion. By using oils every day in our veterinary clinic, I have been blessed with an amazing opportunity to witness the powerful effects of truly therapeutic essential oils.

It has always been a passion of mine to educate and share what I have learned; from which diets work the best for my clients to which suture material pit bulls tolerate. I am fortunate that essential oils are combining all of my passions into one; helping animals, teaching, and writing.

The Animal Desk Reference is the progression toward allowing all creatures to benefit from Nature's amazing healing benefits. This first edition grows from my first book *Essential Oils for Natural Pet Care*, and I am excited to bring it to you.

Melissa Shelton DVM

ACKNOWLEDGEMENTS

I would first like to begin by thanking D. Gary Young for his commitment to creating and providing the world's best essential oils – with only the highest of therapeutic qualities. Without this dedication, none of the miracles that I have witnessed would have occurred. By sharing his knowledge on essential oils, he educated those who initially taught me how to use essential oils. Gary has withstood countless criticisms and hardships from "mainstream" healthcare, and yet has remained dedicated to the wondrous powers that essential oils hold for our health. For that, I commend and thank him.

Next, I would like to thank Angela and Mark Meredith for their community education class that started it all. I couldn't have been more fortunate to "fall" into a society of essential oil users who are so devoted to education. The tremendous support that I have received from them is unmatched.

I also wish to thank Cherie Ross and her entire organization. Cherie teaches so many classes, and truly dedicates her life to helping others. She is passionate about saving lives, and has seen and participated in many miracles in her "career" using Young Living Essential Oils. Without her vast knowledge and experience, I would have never learned what I needed to know to start utilizing oils medically.

My acknowledgements would not be complete without also mentioning two wonderful animal aromatherapists – Sara Kenney and Leigh Foster. Their ground breaking work and innovative ideas – created the techniques and recipes which have advanced the world of essential oils and animals 100 fold. Many of my techniques, experiences, and recipes – as well as the courage to try new things – have been inspired by the sharing of their knowledge.

Finally, it is important to recognize the importance of Young Living members. What a vast resource to have this incredible community of people, who share a common passion and mission. The majority of the members, share their lives and oils with animals, thereby contributing greatly to the data that can be pooled together to show the safety and efficacy of Young Living Essential Oils to the veterinary world.

INSTRUCTIONS FROM THE AUTHOR

It is important as you look toward using this book that you see it as an extension of the Essential Oils Desk Reference – currently being published by Life Science Publishing. Information on this publisher can be found at their website www.LifeSciencePublishers.com.

The Essential Oils Desk Reference (EODR) contains valuable and important information regarding the history, art, and science that encompasses the French model of aromatherapy. Duplicating this valuable information would be wasteful. Therefore, I direct you specifically to this book to gather additional information on essential oils, blends, and products.

The Animal Desk Reference (ADR) will outline the basic information specific toward essential oil use in animals. However, you are encouraged to learn more about all of the various concepts that will be presented.

The recommendations in this book are in no means the only protocols that will work or that can be used for various conditions. However, I will recommend those items that are the most friendly to that particular species, as well as have good results. If you encounter a condition that is not responding to the initial recommendations, it is important to use something different. However, it may be best to consult with an experienced animal aromatherapist or veterinary aromatherapist if you are "breaking new ground" in treatment philosophies or oil usage.

As much as possible, I encourage people to start with protocols that have been used in a particular animal species before. Medical Aromatherapy use in many species is relatively new to our society, even though animals have used aromatherapy throughout the ages, through natural exposures. Be sure to learn the most common ways oils are used in your individual species of interest, and if you are faced with a condition that is not yet listed in the ADR, or need to modify your oil usage, continue to use the oils in "species friendly manners."

For Example: You have a cat with a condition that is not yet listed in the ADR. You look up the condition in the EODR, and find a list of recommended oils. Firstly – examine the list of oils, and formulate which oils you believe are the most "cat friendly." I often think of cats as if they were human babies; considering which oil would be gentle or well tolerated. So if Lemongrass and Palo Santo were listed, I would consider Palo Santo to be milder topically and in odor. And, therefore would consider it to be more appropriate for use on a cat.

Next – I would look at the methods in which cats "like" oils applied. We know that cats greatly enjoy the Kitty Raindrop Technique, and that we can modify this technique to include other oils. So one option may be to add Palo Santo into the Kitty Raindrop, and then apply that. Another favorite method of oil application for cats is "Petting the Cat". So, it would be acceptable to place Palo Santo (neat or diluted) onto the palms of your hands, rub them together, and then pet the area of the cat that is of concern. And yet one more option would be to add Palo Santo to the Litteroma Technique.

As you can appreciate, there are many ways that we could use an oil within methods that the species finds acceptable. I urge you to fully learn the methods that are recommended for a particular species. There is good reason why Kitty Raindrop Technique is continually used for cats. Cats love it, owners love it, and it is easy, safe, and effective.

Some of the sections and concepts described in this book may start to sound like a "broken record". Repetition of important concepts and fundamental skills may be noted throughout this book. I find that most people learn better by encountering the same concepts several times. So if you feel like you have "read this before" – you may have – and take it to heart that you will absorb the concept more fully!

How To Use This Book:

I would like to describe to you how I best see you utilizing this book. I would like to encourage you to read the entire book, each section, even those for animals that you do not have or do not wish to ever have contact with! It is not about which animal you will see, but often more about the knowledge to be flexible for individuals. If you can gain a clear understanding of how we modify the use of essential oils for animals such as birds, you will easily be able to modify your use of oils for a particularly sensitive dog or horse. Each animal is an individual, and you will

INSTRUCTIONS

encounter a dog someday, that needs to be treated more like a cat! For those of you who are squirming thinking of a snake or lizard right now, have no fear! The descriptions of the use for exotic species are not explicit, and you should not be plagued by nightmares upon reading it!

There are several different sections to this book that you may find helpful. Reading basic instructions will give you a foundation for how we use oils in animals. Reading about each and every oil, blend, supplement, or product will give you information on each individual item. Then, the conditions listings for each species, will recommend items that are indicated for each condition. If you find a condition listed for one species of animal, but not for another – you can rest assured that the same recommendations will apply for your species. So as Vestibular Disease is not listed in the Feline Conditions, but it is in the Canine Conditions – you can easily refer to the oils and products that are recommended and learn how to best use them for a cat instead of a dog.

As you navigate through the conditions listings, you will also want to reference basic instructions as well as species specific instructions and comments. For example, if a Kitty Raindrop Technique is recommended, you will want to read the basic information on Raindrop Technique and also the feline specific recommendations and description of the Kitty Raindrop Technique. These feline specific instructions will be found at the beginning of the Feline Conditions listings. It won't take long, but after you master the concept of creating and using a Kitty Raindrop Technique, you will be able to see the recommendation, and know exactly what to do.

Also single oils, oil blends, supplements, and products will be recommended in each condition listing. You will want to go to that product section of the book – and read more about how to use that particular item, for your particular species of animal. The oils and products are listed in alphabetical order. Preferences as to which oils and supplements are chosen first, are the most effective, have the most use and data behind them, or are the most user friendly for that species are made within the First Line Recommendations.

FIRST LINE RECOMMENDATIONS:

There will be First Line Recommendations made for each individual condition. These are the things that I will generally select first for a specific condition and for a specific species. These recommendations are made based on what is widely accepted and tolerated by my patients, as well as have good results. In some conditions, you may only see these First Line Recommendations listed, as I felt it was more important to give you a start to what you could use, than to exclude a subject from the conditions listings if I was unable to include the full information on the listing at this time. In future editions of the ADR, these conditions will be expanded on.

It is greatly important to recognize that not every FIRST LINE RECOMMENDATION should be added or used immediately for an animal. Certainly in critical situations we can use more suggestions, however if all of the recommendations were used all at once, without a slow introduction and increase, it is likely that intestinal upset or detoxification responses will be noted.

Single Oils and Blends:

These will be listed in the conditions listing in alphabetical order. It is important that you go to the product description for each oil that you choose to utilize, and read more about its use in your species. For example, for a feather picking bird, Thieves Essential Oil Blend may be included on the list of blends that can be used. However, I would like for you to recognize that this recommendation is less likely to be made as a topical application. Since this is a "hot" oil, considering in what way it would be best used for a bird is important. By reading the product description for Thieves, and specifically exploring the species specific recommendations for birds, you would find that in fact, Thieves would most likely be used orally as an antibiotic or diffused in a water-based diffuser.

Once you have determined which oils you will be using, and have read the methods of how to use them for your species, you can gather more detailed information in the specific chapters at the beginning of this book. So, if you have determined that you would be adding Thieves to the food of a bird, please read the chapter "Mixing Oils into Food", to gain a wider understanding of how we use this method.

Supplements & Products:

In this section, various supplements and products will be listed that may be helpful to that condition, and that are also generally accepted by that type of animal. Not every supplement needs to be given, and a slow introduction to supplements is recommended. When you have a very difficult case, or one that is not responding as you would like, selecting additional supplements from the listing is an important thing to do. You can go to the product listings for more information on how to use particular products in animals, and reading How Much, How Often will give you a better understanding on how to introduce and evaluate responses.

THE SAFE USE OF OILS

To completely understand the safe use of essential oils, it is recommended that you read Chapter 3 of the Essential Oils Desk Reference (EODR). This human based information is significant towards having a complete understanding and working concept of the use of essential oils in all species. In this chapter of the ADR, all of the concepts as they pertain to animals will be discussed.

The great controversy encircling the use of essential oils in animals has always intrigued me. How could there be people doing great things with essential oils and animals, while others report dangerous toxicity? The answer lies not only in the safe use of essential oils, but in the quality and purity of the essential oil used. For this reason, I have felt most comfortable in recommending the exclusive use of Young Living Essential Oils in my work with animals. Every bit of educational information contained within this book – is shared with this rule in mind.

The information provided within this book, is intended as a starting point or guideline. Every animal is an individual, and some have more intricate health concerns than others. The base foundation of use for all animals that you will note – is to start light and increase the amounts used as tolerated.

This is wise with any regimen you wish to start. Just as you should not change a dog's diet quickly, you should not "blast" an animal with twenty different essential oils and five supplements all on the first day. Starting with diluted oils and a light touch is wise when you are gaining experience in animal aromatherapy.

There are exceptions to all rules however, and when dealing with more urgent or critical situations, I am not one to "go lightly". What one needs to remember is that you can give one diluted drop of an essential oil to your dog now, and then if tolerated well, you can give more – even if it is minutes later.

It is certainly "okay" to start with a light approach, but then use more and more oils if indicated or warranted. The guidelines in this book will often give the average amounts or "end point" amounts that I often consider for an animal. This by no means, assures that this is the proper amount for every animal. Some animals may need more, and some animals may need less.

I once was demonstrating Raindrop Technique on two dogs during a class in California. One dog was a very large Great Dane and the other a small Papillon. The Great Dane had a history of "not liking oils" – so I was curious to see what his response would be. As I started to balance him with Valor Essential Oil Blend – only 2 drops in each hand – he showed me what I needed to see. He started to rub his face on the ground.

Although this was perceived as trying to "rub the oils off of himself" and thus the dislike of oils, I saw another picture. When I have encountered dogs trying to "rid themselves" of an odor, they rub the area that smells. This dog should have been rolling on his back, trying to wipe off the oils that were applied to his shoulder and rump area, not rubbing his face. In all actuality, this dog had a detoxification effect of the oil (Valor) that was applied. He had some pre-existing skin irritations, and I feel that the essential oils created a response in the affected skin, that for all intents and purposes, became uncomfortable to the dog. The only way he had to convey this information was to rub at his face.

Now, it would have been foolish for me to overlook the fact that if this 150 pound (68 kg) Great Dane could not handle 4 drops of Valor – almost completely absorbed into my own hands – how would he ever tolerate a full Dog Raindrop Technique?

While it certainly would have been okay for an oil user to call it "quits" for the Dane and not apply more oils, as a veterinarian and with my experience with oils, I chose to move forward with a Raindrop Technique. However, this dog did not get a regular Dog Raindrop. No indeed. He received five drops of a Kitty Raindrop Technique! He did remarkably well with this dilution of oil, and the owner reported apparent benefits to him as well.

His classmate – a tiny Papillon – did get a full Dog Raindrop Technique. Not only did this 7 pound (3 kg) dog get 4 drops of Valor during balancing, but 3 drops of each Raindrop Oil were applied NEAT! This little dog barely batted an eyelash at the application.

The point of this story is that it is important that you use common sense and do not feel compelled to use full amounts or recommendations when an individual animal may show you clues that a lighter approach may be necessary.

When you are new and just starting out in oil use, it is advisable to start lighter than recommended and gradually build up your amounts until you are confident in reading the signs from the animals you are working with.

After many cases and blood work studies, I am convinced that the majority of so-called "oil reactions" - are truly a detoxification response. The more oils that are used, the more detoxification occurs. The detoxification is what made the Great Dane's face feel funny or itchy – not the Valor essential oil coming in contact with the rump and shoulders. The oils traveled through the body and went where they were needed most, to the irritated and infected skin on the chin and face. This makes complete sense to me, but to an inexperienced oil user or veterinarian unfamiliar with using essential oils, likely this case would have been interpreted as a toxic reaction or irritation to the essential oils.

Remember, just because you gave your dog a diluted form of a Raindrop Technique at noon today; there is no rule that says you can't repeat it at 5 pm, or repeat it with stronger oils. Just like learning to drive a race car – you often don't drive at 200 miles per hour your first day of earning your driver's license. Learn your skills at slower speeds, and you'll soon be navigating all the corners with the greatest of ease!

OILS & REPRODUCTION

I am commonly asked if essential oils can be used for breeding animals, during pregnancy, and during lactation. I have found that not only can oils be used during these times, but are indeed helpful instead of harmful. We have used essential oils in many reproductive situations. Birds and eggs have been exposed to water-based diffusion of many types of oils, laying hens have ingested essential oils consistently in their drinking water, and drops of essential oils have been placed into the nest boxes of chickens. Pregnant and nursing cats (as well as babies) have received Kitty Raindrop Techniques, used Litteroma, and have also been exposed to water-based diffusion of almost every essential oil, and at quite high concentrations. The oils have always been well accepted and never appear to influence milk flavor, nursing drive, or cause harm the fetus or neonate in any manner.

Certainly, we need to use common sense and avoid hot and potentially irritating oils directly in the areas of the nipples. However, full dog Raindrop Techniques have been administered to nursing moms, and the puppies just seem to reap the benefits of having a "diffuser mom" or by coming into contact with the residual oils on the mother's back.

Horses, Cows, Goats, and many other animals have received regular Raindrop Techniques, topical essential oils, and even oral essential oils throughout their entire reproductive period. I have never been concerned about the use of essential oils for mother, father, or offspring.

In the case of rabbits and other exotics, water diffusion of almost every form of essential oil has been used. Tiny newborn rabbit babies were noted to be far healthier when the owner started to disinfect her hands with a drop or two of neat Thieves oil, prior to handling the still wet babies. Although the Thieves was completely absorbed into her hands, the residual benefits were absorbed by the baby rabbits. Even such a light exposure to essential oils can be extremely powerful and beneficial.

Some oils may provide a cautionary statement within the EODR, regarding using caution during pregnancy and with children under 18 months of age. With any pregnant animal, it is a good recommendation to use oils without any warning statements regarding its use during pregnancy. However, in practice, we have not noted any ill effects in any pregnant animal from the use of essential oils at this time. As for the use of oils with this recommendation in young animals, there are often other oil selections that can be made. Since animals have different age relationships than humans – I would suggest that this recommendation would apply to animals 6 months of age and less.

SENSITIVITY TO OILS

It is important to recognize that an animal's sense of smell is incredibly more sensitive than humans. This does not mean that they cannot be exposed to intense smells, it merely means that anything that may smell strongly to us, smells infinitely stronger to them. For example, a search and rescue dog sniffing from the bow of a boat, can actually smell and detect a dead body underneath the water! A bloodhound can smell traces of your body cells that exfoliate and fall off of you as you walk!

It is no wonder that many people interpret an animal's response to an essential oil as "dislike." What I find in my work with hundreds of cases, is that animals that project a dislike of essential oils, have usually been introduced to them in an overly aggressive way. Holding a bottle out for an animal to sniff, may well be like shoving your head into a rotten smelling garbage can. Surely you could smell the rotten garbage from across the room. But, burying your head inside the garbage can is a whole new level of intensity. And, likely if anyone came at you with a garbage can in the future, you would have an aversion to ever smelling it again. It didn't hurt you, but it was an episode you soon won't forget.

We also need to remember that recent studies have suggested that hair follicles enhance the transdermal absorption of essential oils. As animals are covered in hair follicles, this makes complete sense why some would appear more sensitive to oils than humans or even other animals. A cat has more hair follicles per square inch of skin, and a finer coat than a dog or a horse. And with an animal such as a chinchilla, with the densest amount of hair follicles of any land animal, one can see why exotic pets may be perceived as much more delicate. I have seen strong and clear responses to mere diffusion alone, convincing me that the hair follicles aid in the absorption of air borne essential oils.

It is likely that species such as chinchillas and rabbits can absorb therapeutic and systemic levels of essential oils, purely via diffusion.

ANIMAL DESK REFERENCE

This scenario also raises incredible insight into the dangers of exposure to household chemicals and toxins in an animal's life. The cleaning chemicals on our floors, fabric softener on our sheets and blankets, odor eliminating sprays on our couches, and air fresheners in our homes; may also be exponentially absorbed by the hair follicles of our furry companions.

Many people have expressed to me the concern that to apply essential oils effectively, we would have to part the fur and ensure that the oils come in direct contact with the skin of an animal. In practice, this theory has been shown to be untrue. I find that a broader "petting" application of an essential oil over a large area of fur or hair, is actually more effective, and certainly less potentially irritating, than one drop applied directly onto the skin.

If you would encounter a situation where the skin, paws, or animal became irritated from an essential oil application, it is important to apply a diluting oil, or carrier oil, to the site. Do not use water or attempt to wash off offending essential oils with water-based soaps or shampoos, as this can act to drive or spread the essential oil only further into and onto tissues. V-6 Enhanced Vegetable Oil Complex is my first recommendation as a carrier oil, but in a "pinch" any sort of fatty vegetable oil or substance containing fats can be used. It is wise to plan ahead, and to always have V-6 with you if you intend to be using oils. However, as I have found with my children, they sometimes need dilution of oils when you least expect it. In cases of urgent need – items like whole fat milk, creamers from restaurants, and butter can be used to calm down a "hot" response to an essential oil or an accidental contact with sensitive tissues (especially in or around eyes.)

The act of diluting an essential oil application basically involves applying the carrier oil (V-6) to the site of irritation. For skin irritations it is tempting to apply another essential oil, which may be known for soothing effects, to a site. I never recommend "fixing an oil problem, with another oil." Since the majority of issues seem to occur from too much detoxification, instead of the actual reaction of the skin to an essential oil; the act of applying additional essential oils may only serve to increase the amount of detoxification and thus discomfort at the site.

ESSENTIAL OIL AVERSIONS

By far one of the most common concerns I hear is that an animal or pet does not like oils. What I usually find in these circumstances is that there has been some sort of event in the animal's history of using essential oils too aggressively for that individual. For example, actions such as dripping peppermint onto the hips of a cat, dropping oils directly into the mouth, tipping the ears with oils, applying oils to the feet or foot pads, or applying oils near the face or nose of an animal, have resulted in certain aversions.

Although these applications can be well tolerated by many, sensitive animals seem to hold a grudge to certain experiences. This is very similar to traditional veterinary medicine where a cat will hide under the bed and not come near you after a few "pilling" episodes.

It is worthwhile when exploring routine and non-critical use of essential oils for animals, to note which methods are best tolerated. Once a mild method is used successfully, I find that amounts can be gradually increased and tolerance of the application is easier and easier.

For example; I often don't dilute my oils – and leave them neat on my hands to pet my animals. For certain cats, diluting these oils or waiting until they are basically absorbed completely into my hands, is tolerated just fine. However, if I were to have a heavier amount of essential oils present on my hands, or be holding the bottle while I approach them, they may move away from the situation. After a few very light applications – I find I can gradually expose them to more and more oils on my hands, because they have never had an over-experience.

Food aversions are well documented in the animal kingdom. A pet nauseated from kidney disease may avoid a food that was fed during that time frame. The pet relates the particular food to the feeling of illness. An aggressive exposure and bad experience with an essential oil, can make an animal leery of all essential oil exposure.

If you look at it like cooking, it can make more sense. Let's say every time your Grandma offered you a taste of soup it was over-seasoned, you would quickly want to avoid tasting Grandma's soup. Too strong makes an impression!

Now, this is not to say it is dangerous to use these oils or that we can't use the oils neat for animals. This is a common misconception. This technique of starting light is just about being respectful of what animals "like" – and to make administration (and life) with an animal easier!

METHODS OF APPLICATION

There are many ways to expose animals to essential oils. The pros and cons of each method, as well as the species they best match with will be described. You will hear me say often – use a "Species Specific" oil application. This refers to the fact that if you are researching a specific condition in humans, and find an oil that you may like to try for an animal, you will consider the type of animal in which you are applying the essential oil to, to determine the best application route.

DIFFUSION

FORMS OF DIFFUSION:

There are several ways in which diffusion of essential oils into the air can occur. Mechanical diffusion utilizes a machine or propulsion of some sort to mobilize essential oil particles into the air. Passive diffusion is what I consider the evaporation of essential oils into the air on their own accord.

Within the mechanical category, three main styles can be considered. One is what I will refer to as water-based diffusion, the other an air-style diffusion, and the third utilizes a spritzer bottle. I do not recommend any type of diffusion that involves heating or "burning"– as this can damage the essential oil.

Passive diffusion can include the placement of essential oils onto cotton balls, tissues, cage papers, and even humans – allowing the oils to passively waft into the area around the animal.

WATER-BASED DIFFUSION:

The Aria Ultrasonic Diffuser is an example of a water-based diffuser. Water is added to the machine along with varying drops of essential oil(s). The beauty of a water-based diffuser is the variable diffusion concentrations that can be achieved. The teeniest dip of a toothpick, one drop of essential oil, or even 20 drops of essential oil can be added to a batch of water in a diffuser; allowing the utmost control in levels of exposure. Although hardly necessary – one drop or less can be added to a diffuser.

STARTING POINTS:

For most water-based diffusers – 1 to 4 drops of essential oil(s) can be added to the machine when close contact with a diffuser and an animal is planned. This includes placing a diffuser close to a caged animal, tenting an animal with the diffuser vapor, and for animals that have not had much "mapping" in essential oil use or whom are considered fragile or exotic. In this category, I would include animals such as insects (honey bees, tarantulas), Chinchillas, Sugar Gliders, etc...

Dilution of the essential oil(s) is accomplished by varying how much oil is added to the water within the diffuser. The need for dilution of essential oils with a carrier oil, is not necessary for water-based diffusion - and could actually be harmful to the diffuser.

I always recommend smelling the diffuser vapor yourself prior to introducing it to an animal. I hadn't considered 4 to 5 drops of Purification to be a very intense concentration, until I put my face directly in the vapor for a few minutes. As I was intending to place this vapor into a cage with a dog – I wanted to know how it felt. It was actually quite intense.

When starting to diffuse for an animal – start with a light amount, start diffusing in an open area, and stay with the animal for the first five to ten minutes or more of the diffusion. If an individual animal can only tolerate 5 minutes of diffusion in an open room – they would likely not tolerate a tenting situation. In emergency situations, you may need to move towards more intense diffusion right away, but these situations are hopefully few and far between.

Another method of water-based diffusion is to add essential oils into water contained in a glass spray bottle – also referred to as a water spritzer. This solution is shaken to disperse the essential oils within the water, and then sprayed into the air. This method is also incredibly flexible, as anywhere from a toothpick dip to 20 or more drops of essential oil(s) can be added to varying amounts of water – allowing for incredible flexibility in the concentration of essential oils that are put into the environment.

WATER DIFFUSION – OPEN ROOM:

In this situation, water-based diffusion is used in an average household room with the animal. The animal may or may not be able to leave the room, but is generally over 5 feet away from the diffuser. This method is appropriate for all animals including birds, reptiles, exotic species, and cats.

WATER DIFFUSION – SMALL CLOSED ROOM:

This situation may include using a water-based diffuser in a much smaller room, such as a bathroom, with an animal. This allows for greater exposure to the essential oil vapor.

WATER DIFFUSION – CAGING:

With this method, I would be directing the diffuser vapors into a cage or kennel of an animal. Basically placing a diffuser in close proximity with an animal who otherwise cannot move away from the vapor.

WATER DIFFUSION – TENTING:

This method is more intense and concentrated than directing diffusion vapor into an otherwise open cage. With tenting, I cover an animal's enclosure to effectively trap the diffusion vapors around the animal, and ensure a higher level of inhalation and exposure. Placing plastic wrap, plastic sheeting, or towels over both the cage and diffuser, creates a situation where generally the animal will be enveloped in a misty cloud of essential oil vapors. This method must be monitored much more intensely.

AIR-STYLE DIFFUSION:

An example of an air-style diffuser would be the TheraPro Premium Diffuser. Diffusing into an open room would be the main method recommended for use around animals with air-style diffusers. Air diffusers eject pure "neat" essential oils into the air. The concentration of essential oil is thus much higher than water-based diffusers. This method of diffusion is best reserved for larger rooms, barns, stalls, chicken coops, etc... The more "sensitive" the animal may be to essential oils, the larger the room and the farther away an air diffuser should be placed and used.

Only rarely would a tenting situation be used with an air-style diffuser. The closest to tenting would be enclosing a stall with solid walls or plastic over the doors and windows and diffusing for a horse or other large animal. This method can be particularly beneficial for Heaves and other respiratory concerns. Plastic "drop sheets" for painting can be hung over the entrance to a lean-to or run-in shelter and a horse can be held inside with a diffuser to administer essential oils in this manner.

MONITORING DURING DIFFUSION:

Can diffusion cause detoxification and "discomfort"? Certainly. What might an animal show if they are not tolerating the level of diffusion you are exposing them to? Lethargy, increased breathing rate, panting, drooling, change in breathing pattern, squinting eyes, or any other change that you would consider to be "detrimental" or out of the ordinary.

If an animal exhibits signs of distress during diffusion, simply turn off the diffuser and increase access to plain fresh air.

ADDING OILS TO DRINKING WATER

Whenever considering adding essential oils to an animal's water supply – several considerations must be made.

Oil Selection:
Of course, there are some oils that are more friendly for use in drinking water than others. Adding "hot" oils such as Oregano would obviously not be as appetizing as Citrus Fresh. Strong tastes and flavors must be a consideration in selection. Starting with items that you find pleasant to drink is a good idea.

Water Containers & Storage:
Many exotic pet water containers are made of plastic or have plastic components. As essential oils may degrade these plastics, care must be taken only to use glass, ceramic, or stainless steel water containers with the use of essential oils. In the situation of horses and large animals, troughs are commonly made of hard plastic or galvanized metals. It is difficult to avoid these materials, and in practice, it appears to cause no detrimental effects. If given a choice, I do prefer the hard plastic troughs or old ceramic bath tubs over galvanized materials when possible. Stainless steel troughs would be even more ideal.

Exposure of the Animal:
Care must also be taken in how the animal may interact with its water source. For snakes who often soak in their water dishes to birds who may bathe in them – considerations must be made to the strength, oil selection, and property of the oil added to the water. Peppermint is a nice oil to drink on a hot day, however a snake soaking in water with peppermint added may find "cold irritation" from the sensation and contact.

Ensuring Adequate Water Intake:

One of the worst things we could do is to cause an animal to avoid drinking by making an essential oil solution too strong or by choosing an essential oil that the animal dislikes. Although many animals actually prefer water with essential oils – it is always wise to provide a plain water source while you offer the new water – until you are certain that the animal is drinking the essential oil water well, and in adequate amounts.

Concentrations:

Unless a situation is critical, it is wise to start with small amounts of oil added to high quality water, and gradually increase the oils over the course of a week. A concentration that is often used for animals is one drop per liter of distilled, reverse osmosis, or good quality spring water. An empty NingXia Red bottle is perfect for mixing and storing your essential oil water – and the current size of the bottle just happens to be one liter.

For highly sensitive or fragile animals – such as certain species of fish, insects, snakes, and amphibians – starting with a toothpick dipped into the essential oil, then into the NingXia Red bottle (1 Liter) of water is a conservative starting point.

In critical situations - adding essential oils to water is typically not a route that would be used – as often times these animals may not be drinking properly.

Species Specific Recommendations:

Birds: Birds generally have a very poor sense of taste, and it is quite easy to add essential oils to their drinking water. Care must be taken for birds who bathe in their water, and careful monitoring of water intake is important. In general, 1 drop per liter of water is commonly used.

Chickens & Poultry: Chickens are much less able to bathe in their drinking water based on the water dispensers used by most farms. Many more "hot" oils have been given via drinking water to flocks for various conditions. This is likely the easiest method for administration to flocks of chickens, turkeys, pheasants, and so forth. Care must be considered when adding the oils to drinking water systems, as high concentrations may damage plastics or certain components of automated systems. Starting with low amounts, and gradually increasing the concentrations is recommended. Knowing how much water your flock generally consumes on a daily basis – BEFORE adding essential oils to the water supply is crucial. After you know how much water should be consumed, you will be able to compare if the same amount of water (or more) is being consumed after the addition of essential oils. Purification is commonly added to the water of poultry.

Exotics: For oils recommended for use in drinking water, the general starting point is to add 1 drop per liter of water. Of course, it is always advisable to start with even more dilute concentrations (such as a toothpick dip), and gradually work your way up to the desired amount of oil.

Cats: Cats are less likely than other animals to consume essential oils within their water, although there certainly are cats that do, and sometimes with surprising oil selections. The key with cats is to start with extremely small amounts (toothpick dips), to always offer an alternate water source for drinking, and to very gradually increase concentrations. It is important to note that just because a cat may refuse to drink one particular essential oil, it does not guarantee the refusal of others. Most cats are unlikely to progress to a concentration stronger than a 1 drop per liter of water.

Dogs: Dogs are much easier to work with. Starting with small amounts and gradually increasing the concentration is still advisable, along with careful monitoring of acceptance and water intake. While 1 drop per liter of drinking water is average, there are many dogs who drink from horse troughs with much higher concentrations of essential oils added to the water.

Horses & Larger: These animals almost prefer essential oils in their water. Often many drops can be added to a trough. Start with 5 drops, and gradually increase based on responses. Agitating the water's surface after the addition of oils can help to disperse them.

Examples of the Use of Essential Oils in Drinking Water:

Birds:

As an antihistamine, antiviral – 1 drop of Melissa Essential Oil in one Liter of water. Shake well and use as drinking water.

Chickens:
1 drop or more of Purification Essential Oil Blend per liter of drinking water – improves health, immune system, replaces medicated feeds.

Guinea Pigs:
1 drop of Citrus Fresh, Orange, Tangerine, or other citrus oils per liter of drinking water.

Snakes:
Toothpick of Purification per liter of water used as drinking and soaking water, gradually working up in concentration.

Dogs:
Peppermint, Citrus Oils, Melissa: start with 1 drop per liter, then gradually increase if needed and tolerated.

Cats:
Cats may refuse oils in drinking water more than other species. Start with toothpick amounts, then gradually increase the concentration. Use mild, "cat friendly" oils such as Citrus Fresh or possibly Melissa – when selecting oils to add to their drinking water. Which oils are tolerated and accepted by our feline friends, will certainly be made clear by the individual cat.

Horses:
Peppermint, Lemon, and other oils are enjoyed. Three to Five drops or more can be added per 50-100 gallons of water. Often with horses and other large animals, we cannot avoid plastic or other materials in the troughs. The hard plastic troughs commonly available, do not appear to become degraded by the essential oils.

Cattle & Large Animals:
Peppermint on hot days is greatly enjoyed.

MIXING OILS INTO FOODS

Some species do very well with this method of using essential oils.

Birds:
Birds have very little taste buds and will accept many oils (even "hot" ones) in their foods. Most bird owners will recognize a favorite food that their bird loves. Often times something such as warm oatmeal is great to add oils to. Starting with a tablespoon of warm (not hot) mushy favorites – mix in a "toothpick dip" of the essential oil. Make sure the bird likes to eat the food item already, and it is wise to make sure they are hungry when you plan to introduce the "therapeutic" item of food. Gradually increase the amounts given as needed, unless the situation is critical. Birds have even ingested oils such as Oregano, Clove, Basil, Copaiba, ImmuPower, Thieves, and Melissa in their favorite foods.

Ferrets:
Ferrets will often easily consume oils in chicken baby food, mashed banana, coconut oil, or another squishy treat or favorite food. Again, starting with small amounts added into a favorite food, and gradually increasing the amount given is recommended. NingXia Red is also a favorite of ferrets, and oils can be added to this juice for administration as well.

Rodents, Reptiles, and Other Exotics:
Just as described for birds and ferrets, it is a good recommendation to start with very small amounts of essential oils added to foods initially. The "name of the game" with the various species, is to find something they enjoy and consume to mix the oils into. For most of these animals, moving towards oral administration of an essential oil is often reserved for more critical cases and conditions. However, there are certain oils that certainly will benefit animals to consume on a regular basis (such as antitumoral oils for rodents).

Ideas for ingestion: For animals who eat crickets and mealworms, these critters can be "gut loaded" by being fed NingXia Red (with extra essential oils added in if desired), prior to them becoming a meal. For rodent-eating exotics, small amounts of essential oils (toothpick dip) can be applied or inserted into a meal prior to serving. With rodents, they may also consume various mushy foods or treats that can have essential oils added to them. For animals who eat fruits, vegetables, sprouts, or leafy greens – a water mister of essential oils can be used to spray the food items with the essential oils. Often exotic animals require a creative approach to the use of essential oils, and it can be fun as well as rewarding.

Rabbits, Guinea Pigs, Chinchillas:
Care with hindgut fermenters such as Rabbits, Guinea Pigs, and Chinchillas should be taken. Exotic animals such as these, rely on gut flora for normal digestive function. Since essential oils can have strong antibacterial action – the oral routes of essential oils are often avoided unless absolutely necessary. Many times there are many other routes of application and exposure that can be used very effectively. However, in critical situations or with severe cases that are not responding to other methods of use, adding very small amounts of essential oils into fruit or vegetable baby foods and syringing them into the mouth, can be quite effective.

Dogs:
It depends on the dog as to if they will eat essential oils in their foods or not. My own dogs routinely consume Longevity, Frankincense, and Copaiba oils mixed into their moistened foods.

Cats:
Cats are unique. They will tell you that themselves. Not many cats are interested in eating essential oils in their food, however there are some that will. Diluted Copaiba mixed in with canned food has been accepted by several cats.

Horses:

Horses easily ingest essential oils in their foods. Mixing oils into applesauce, maple syrup, agave, NingXia Red, oats, molasses, feed, and even onto hay is well tolerated. Almost any oil can be given in this manner. Diffusing with an air-style diffuser into an enclosed hay storage room can permeate the hay with beneficial essential oils for ingestion and also for mold prevention within the hay itself.

Cattle, Others:

Cattle, small ruminants, and other forms of livestock can easily ingest essential oils within feeds. Using the suggestions for horses works well for these animals.

ORAL ADMINISTRATION

This method is generally used in debilitated animals or in more severe situations. For example; animals with hives, internal bleeding, pain, allergic reaction, cancer, internal parasites, etc... Oral use of essential oils is generally not used immediately in most situations, unless it is the easiest route of administration for that particular oil or species of animal.

It is also important to recognize that oral administration may create an aversion to essential oils in some animals. Animals will know when you open the cabinet or grab the oil bottle which was last associated with a very intense oral exposure to oil. The memory of a negative experience with oils will remain stronger than a positive experience, and may lead them to avoidance behavior to any essential oil application.

Via Capsules:
Oils can be added to empty gel capsules and given to dogs by mouth. Smaller gel capsules can be found through health food or medical supply stores and pharmacies, and are helpful for use in cats and smaller dogs.

Via Buccal Route:
The buccal route refers to absorption of the essential oil through the mucous membranes of the cheek or lip area of an animal. Horses do very well with oils dripped into the bottom lip. Dogs also tolerate drops inside the cheek area fairly well.

Via Oral Drops:
Cats often get drips of oils into the mouth for pain or post-operative recovery. With this method, little care is placed as to where the oil drop lands, just getting it into the mouth is the main goal. Cats often drool and salivate from strong odors or tastes. It is common for them to drool from any oral administrations – even traditional antibiotic medications. Do not be alarmed.

Via Gums:

This can be an effective way to get small amounts of essential oil into the oral cavity of dogs. Often a light coating of oil is placed on the fingers, then rubbed onto the gums. Oils can be neat or diluted for this application.

Via Sublingual Administration:

While recovering from anesthesia, drops of essential oils are easily placed under the tongue of animals for easy and fast absorption.

Via Grooming:

Cats will ingest small amounts of essential oils that have been "pet" onto their fur. This may be enough of an ingestion to reach therapeutic levels in some cats.

Via a Carrier:

Essential oils can be mixed into Agave, Honey, Coconut Oil, NingXia Red, and other carriers and offered orally. Follow the directions for mixing oils into foods, for further instructions and details.

TOPICAL APPLICATIONS

There are many different methods to apply oils topically to animals. Each species has methods that are more suitable to their particular needs.

Direct Application:

This involves applying drops of oil directly to the skin or fur of an animal – often in a "drop" form. This includes neat or diluted oils. Raindrop Technique is a form of direct application to an animal – since the oils are dripped directly onto the animal. Another example of direct application would be dripping PanAway directly onto a dog's knee, for a lameness condition.

This method certainly has great benefits when used in the Raindrop Technique, and is used quite often. However, in the case of the dog's knee – a lighter application that covers the entire knee area instead of a one drop location, will likely be better tolerated by the skin and the dog, and may be more effective as it spreads the essential oil over more hair follicles and enhances the absorption of the oil.

This application form is mostly used in the Raindrop Techniques, but may also be used in applications such as dripping oils directly into a wound or abscess, onto a site where acupuncture is to be performed, onto a hoof, or onto another site of intense need.

Animals such as dogs, horses, cows, goats, and other large animals accept this form of application the best. For cats and smaller, when direct application of oils is used, it is generally in a diluted form, such as the Species Specific Raindrop Techniques.

Petting Applications:

This method involves applying essential oils (neat or diluted) to your hands. Your hands are then rubbed together, and a varying amount of essential oil is allowed to remain on your palms. This may vary from completely absorbed (for say a rabbit) to an obviously light coating of oil spread out over your hands. Your hands are then used to pet the animal in question. This technique could also involve petting a specific location – such as the knee of a dog.

This method is well tolerated by almost every form of animal. The technique can be modified for small rodents, amphibians, or animals that may be difficult to handle, simply by having the oils absorbed into your hands, and then "cupping" and holding the animal within your hands.

Even the largest horse or even elephant, will benefit from this method of application. The larger the animal, the more film of essential oil is allowed to remain on our hands prior to petting. Remember, that just because an animal is very large, it may still require a diluted application of essential oil. This is very much an individual variation, and if you are ever in question as to how to proceed, start with the diluted oil, see how the animal does, then use more concentrated oils later.

Tipping the Ears:

This method is a variation of the petting technique to some extent. It involves applying varying amounts of neat or diluted essential oils to your fingertips, then stroking the animal's ear. Although it has often been considered a superior location to apply oils due to increased ability for absorption, I do not believe this to be accurate. Many animals' ears are a bit sensitive to touch and to oil application, and as I have seen obvious responses to petting the body surfaces with oils, I have quickly found that I prefer the petting method – as do many of my patients.

Applying to Pads & Feet:

I have heard varying thoughts on this method of application. On one hand, some say that pads of feet are meant to be "impermeable" to substances, so applying essential oils here would be useless. Other opinions report this location as the safest to use. I have also heard that we will drive more toxins into the feet by applying essential oils to them. I believe the truth lies somewhere in between.

I initially started with applications of oils to the feet and pads of my patients. While applying on the pads themselves often did not result in irritation, it also was a difficult location that pets often disliked cooperating for, and owners quickly wanted to "give up." Applying essential oils to the skin and surfaces of the foot – often the areas between the foot pads – seemed like an easy location – however many dogs created detoxification responses from this application.

What I believe to be true and accurately demonstrated in my veterinary patients, is that there are better methods to apply oils to our pets. What I see often, is that owners have a difficult time applying oils to feet, whether pads or skin. And, when skin application is used, a skin detoxification response may occur more often. I believe there are a couple of factors that may contribute to more skin reactions in the paws of animals. First, animal feet are in contact with far more environmental and household toxins than humans' are. Secondly, many animals (especially dogs) are plagued with inflammation, secondary infections, and skin irritations of the paws due to poor diets, processed foods, and inappropriate ingredients that feed allergies and inflammation.

Water Misting Applications:

This method involves diluting an essential oil, generally in distilled water, shaking well, and spritzing the mixture onto the animal, wound, location of injury, or application site. This method can also be used to spritz leafy greens, vegetables, fruits, sprouts, and other foods when we would like an animal to ingest certain essential oils.

Although we are taught that essential oils and water do not mix, this is an effective way to disperse a light and even amount of essential oil over a large area or onto an animal that is difficult to apply oils to. This method will generally include various bug repellant recipes as well as the Feather Spray for birds.

The oils should be added to a glass spray bottle, especially if they are to be stored for more than a day or two. Essential oils can degrade plastics, so the least amount of contact an oil can make with plastic, the better. The plastic tube and sprayer components seem to do just fine, however, I try to avoid entirely plastic spray bottles.

There are various recipes that will recommend the addition of Bath & Shower Gel Base or Thieves Household Cleaner to the essential oil and water mixture. These items act as a dispersal agent, and help the essential oil to mix with the water more completely and for a longer period of time, before separating. These items are always optional – and I find that a good shake of the bottle before use, is quite effective in mixing plain solutions.

We are also taught that if we want to drive an oil into the skin, that applying a water compress can help to do that. Additionally, we are told that if you need to "take the heat away" from an oil, or "rinse" it from an eye – to not use water and use a diluting carrier oil. Many people have expressed concern that by applying a spray application of essential oils in water, that we would make them more intense. I'll set your mind at ease. Because we are applying these oils with the idea of absorption in mind – it would actually be beneficial for the water to drive the oils "into the animal." Furthermore, the oils are generally being used at quite a low concentration, so water enhancing the absorption is actually a good thing!

As for concerns of intensity, we are simply applying the oils in this manner, not trying to calm an irritated location. So, we do not need to avoid water. For example, if a dog had reddened skin from a Raindrop Technique – it would be completely inappropriate to use a water spritzer on the area – whether there were oils in it or not. In this situation, dilution of the essential oils with V-6 is the correct choice. Likewise – if an essential oil accidentally came in contact with eye tissue – spritzing it with water would be the wrong choice!

When spritzing an animal such as a bird, I have found that they blink their eyes very effectively. When I first used spritzers in birds, I tried to avoid their head and eyes, and aimed only for their feet. The birds quickly showed me who was in control of where the spray landed, and they often made sure that it came in contact with their head, face, and mouth. Unless there is neurologic damage or functional issues with the blink reflex, normal misting towards an animal would rarely, if ever, result in eye irritation.

Situations in which Water Misting is highly useful include the following: misting birds with the Feather Spray, misting large proud flesh wounds in horses, misting wounds (such as hot spots in dogs) in which ointments would provide too much moisture, misting into the air when diffusion is needed, misting bedding, fabrics, or other areas in need of odor control, and the list goes on and on.

When selecting the oils to add to a spritzer – you should consider which oils are the best choices for this use. Certainly, for a horse with proud flesh, any of the oils indicated for this condition could be applied with this technique, and in a fairly high concentration; 20-40 drops or more in 4 ounces (120 mL) of water. However, if we plan to spritz a bird with a water mist – selecting an oil such as Oregano would not be a good idea. When spritzing a bird or small animal, I would consider what it would feel like if I sprayed myself in the face or eyes with the mist, and I often do just that, to test out what I have created. After all, I would never expect that I should be able to spritz a bird with a solution, that I cannot spray directly into my own face.

It would always be the wisest to start with very low concentrations of oils in the water mist. 1 drop of essential oil in 4 ounces (120 mL) of water is a very low concentration, one that is unlikely to cause discomfort or a detoxification response in even the most sensitive of species. You can always start with this concentration for a few applications, and then add an additional drop into your solution – ending up with 2 drops in 4 ounces (120 mL) of water. Then apply this concentration for a few more applications. Increase the concentration again by adding another drop of essential oil to your 4 ounces (120 mL) of water, and so on, and so on. This is how we "titrate" a concentration to a specific animal or species.

A great rule of thumb to remember is "While you can always use more, you can never take away what you have already applied!"

Swimming Pools, Ponds, Soaking Water, and Aquariums:

Any animal entering water containing essential oils will absorb the oils topically. Dispersing agents can be utilized if desired and appropriate – such as adding essential oils first to sea salts, Thieves Household Cleaner, or Animal Scents Shampoo – which will help spread the essential oils throughout the water, instead of just floating on the surface. Adding the oils to salts or cleaner, would be most appropriate for soaking a horse's hoof, for example. Dogs especially enjoy having a few drops of Peppermint oil added to their "wading pools" in the heat of the summer. Not only to they lay in it, but they also drink it. Many owners have reported incredible improvements in arthritis pain when their older dogs soaked in a Peppermint pool!

Certainly oils can be added to any body of water from Koi ponds, habitats for Hippopotamus, ponds for Tigers in zoos, glass aquariums and fish bowls, dolphin holding tanks, dog wading pools, physical therapy pools, underwater treadmills, and more. The key is to start with small amounts of oils, agitate the water's surface to disperse the oils when possible, and to gradually increase the level of concentration of the essential oil exposure. Even when very small amounts of oils are used, there will be benefits to the exposure.

Shampoos, Ointments, and Other Products:

We shouldn't forget how convenient it is to add additional essential oils to products that are routinely used for our animals. If you plan to bathe your dog with Animal Scents Shampoo, why not add a few extra drops of Frankincense oil to the shampoo for Cognitive Dysfunction, or add a few drops of Copaiba oil for Arthritis. Including essential oils into other items can be an easy and wonderful way to provide preventive measures to your animal. I marvel at the idea that if every time you gave your dog a bath, by adding Frankincense to the shampoo, you may be preventing cancer in the future. I for one, will always support prevention over treatment, any day of the week!

Adding additional essential oils to Animal Scents Ointment is also a wonderful technique. For example, adding 1 drop of Idaho Balsam Fir to 1 tablespoon of ointment, and mixing it together, can be a wonderful way to apply the Idaho Balsam Fir onto the feet of a chicken or bird. When using Animal Scents Ointment on animals, it is important to not overuse it, especially with our feathered friends, where we could get them too "greasy." With animals such as Dogs, Horses, and other Large Animals, many more drops can be added to the Animal Scents Ointment, especially when a neat direct application of an oil could be indicated. The technique is incredibly flexible.

Oil Misting Application:

This is similar to water misting, however in place of the water V-6 Enhanced Vegetable Oil Complex is used. I have found that this complex will spray through certain misting bottles, and results in a longer contact time and "oil presence." Situations where I use this method the most, is to repel insects and for topical parasites such as lice.

For example, I have found that by mixing up strong bug recipes in V-6 instead of water for my cow, that I am more effective and have a longer lasting repellant action. For the horses and cows, we have also used Ortho Ease Massage Oil as a base to mix up our bug recipes. This is also a great way to mix and spray on recipes for lice.

This application could be used for any large area that you would like to apply diluted oils to and have a longer contact time, with less evaporation of the essential oils. Avoiding an oil spray may be warranted in conditions where you desire the skin to stay dry (rain rot in a horse, hot spots in a dog, or scabs that are healing up).

Diffusion:

Although this method is not often considered as a topical application, I would beg to differ. Dr. Edward Close has made us well aware of the ability for diffused Thieves Essential Oil Blend to kill toxic molds in the environment, including in and on surfaces of walls and other materials. This is most certainly a topical application.

Since animals absorb oils through hair follicles, diffusion alone can indeed create a topical application of the essential oils. Situations such as Ringworm can be contained and certainly aided by the diffusion of anti-fungal oils that will contact the hairs and skin. Although diffusion may not be the only technique we would utilize for a certain condition, it is certainly not to be excluded in a layered approach to the use of essential oils.

When diffusing for an animal, it is important to select appropriate oils and concentrations in which to diffuse. The instructions discussed in this book for diffusion should still be followed, even if topical exposure to the oils is the goal in mind.

Indirect Applications:

Indirect application of oils topically is considered to be situations such as rubbing essential oils (neat or diluted) onto a perch or onto your hands, and allowing the animal to come in contact with it. A bird perching on a wooden branch would naturally be exposed to small amounts of essential oils found within the tree. When we rub essential oils onto perches or branches, we recreate this indirect transfer of essential oils to the body.

ESSENTIAL OILS & EYES

Although this chapter is sure to meet with some controversy, there is much good that has come from certain uses of essential oils in and around eyes. Since many people are in fact using this method, and many people and animals have reaped benefits from it, I feel it is an important topic to cover.

We are taught continually, to avoid getting essential oils into our eyes. This as a whole, is advice well headed. However, there are many cases in which the proper use of essential oils can benefit various eye conditions.

I urge you to only use these common and well-tolerated methods, and to always err on the side of caution when considering use of this method. I also recommend that before applying any essential oil spray to an animal's face or eye area, that you try it on yourself first. After all, one should never do something to an animal that they wouldn't do first on themselves.

The most common start of the use of what I will term a "water spritzer" for the eyes, I believe started in people with dry eye, most commonly associated with Lasik Surgery. Someone apparently placed 4 drops of Lavender in 4 ounces (120 mL) of distilled water, misted this into their eyes and found amazing comfort. Not only was comfort found, but increased healing as well.

Upon witnessing someone spraying their eyes with a mister – I was immediately curious. Wondering what they were misting, I investigated further. It turns out they were spraying this very diluted lavender solution into their eyes. Well, since her eyes were not red, swollen, watering, and she was not writhing on the ground in pain...I had to try it! It was wonderful. Very soothing and moisturizing.

As time passed on, I would use this eye spritzing technique for my own children during a pink eye scare, for one of my dogs with a corneal abrasion, for friends and patients with dry eye, for eye infections, and so much more. The application has not only become a way to use oils for the eye itself, but for the delicate tissues surrounding the eyes. Styes, conjunctivitis, eyelid tumors, blocked tear ducts, lacerations or surgeries of tissues near the eye – all became accessible to oils via this "mister."

Misting the eye and eye area, has quickly become a favorite tool of mine. It has been used in many animals and humans, however, I would still urge you to use caution and common sense, and never risk any individual's safety, if you do not feel comfortable using this method.

Always have V-6, or another carrier oil, on hand when planning to use essential oils near the eyes, face, or head. Especially when you intentionally plan to use oils for the eye area. If any discomfort would ever be noted, please flush the area with the V-6 Enhanced Vegetable Oil Complex until the area is comfortable. Signs that an animal may be experiencing discomfort with an eye application could be; pawing at the face or eyes, blinking or tearing, increased reddening of eyes or surrounding tissues, squinting, whining, or any other behavior that is out of the ordinary. It is worthy to mention, that these responses have not been noted at this time.

Since cats have different views of the world, unique to being a feline, they often do not appreciate any form of a spritzer being used on them. The use of this method for cats will have to be considered with individual personality and acceptance in mind. I do not recommend "traumatizing" a cat by forcing the spray into their face, unless a critical eye situation demanded the attempt. If any animal greatly dislikes this misting procedure, I recommend finding less stressful ways to expose them to the essential oils. Even water diffusion, via caging or tenting, can be effective in exposing the eye's surface to beneficial essential oils.

Tried & True Recipes:

I will present for you several recipes that have been used repeatedly and with great success. I do not encourage anyone to go outside of these recommendations without the advice of a veterinary aromatherapist or very experienced medical aromatherapist. The only alterations that should be made to these recipes are ones of greater dilution – i.e. adding less essential oils to the water.

Lavender Eye Spritzer:

This is the basic eye recipe, and has been used for several years or more in humans and animals. It is the recipe I recommend starting with, then only if results are not seen with this recipe, moving onto others. This spritzer can be misted into the eyes even 4 or more times per day. Long term use has not been evaluated, but many have used this spritzer for 2 months or more, without harm. Do not aggressively attempt to squirt this mixture directly into the eye, the goal is to lightly mist the area, and if possible hold the eye open slightly while doing so. Even the mist contacting the areas directly next to the open lids, will be beneficial.

- Add 4 drops of Lavandula angustifolia to 4 ounces (120 mL) of distilled water. Use a glass spray bottle. Shake well, mist into eyes or surrounding eye tissues.

Therapeutic Eye Spritzer:

This recipe is wonderful for many reasons. It adds the many other benefits of Copaiba, Frankincense, and Helichrysum Essential Oils to Lavender. This recipe is a powerhouse for situations such as eyelid tumors, inflammation, corneal ulcers, corneal abrasions, post-surgical sites, and more. I still recommend starting with the basic Lavender Eye Spritzer, but this recipe is being used more and more, with wonderful results. This spritzer is recommended to be used up to 4 times per day. Long term use has not been evaluated, but we have used this particular spritzer for 2-3 week intervals without harm. Do not aggressively attempt to squirt this mixture directly into the eye, the goal is to lightly mist the area, and if possible hold the eye open slightly while doing so. Even the mist contacting the areas directly next to the open lids, will be beneficial.

- Add 4 drops of Lavandula angustifolia, 2 drops of Copaiba, 2 drops of Frankincense (Boswellia carteri), and 2 drops of Helichrysum to 4 ounces (120 mL) of distilled water. Use a glass spray bottle. Shake well, mist into eyes or surrounding eye tissues.

ESSENTIAL OILS & EARS

Like eyes, ears also carry a bit of controversy and warning associated with essential oils. Similarly, I have found that there are again some ways we can use essential oils in and around ears, and there are ways we should not. Contacting the ears, and specifically the ear drum or tympanic membrane, with an essential oil can be excruciatingly painful.

Even with these precautions, the veterinary market is flooded with ear washes, flushes, cleaners, treatment solutions, and ointments containing essential oils. Many holistic veterinarians will get negative feedback when knowingly adding an essential oil to an animal product, but yet, when it is "snuck" into the ingredient list as a fractionated and un-natural constituent within a mainstream veterinary product, nobody raises concern.

What I have found to be true is that in the proper ways, in the proper dilutions, and in the proper methods essential oils can be incredibly helpful for ear conditions of all sorts. Ear infections that are resistant to traditional veterinary drugs are often completely eliminated with the use of essential oils in our veterinary practice. Many times these dogs are facing surgical removal of the ear (Total Ear Canal Ablation or TECA) to deal with the resistant and chronic infection. Certainly, the use of essential oils within the ear canal, is a far better solution than the surgical removal of the problem area.

Described will be various methods in which essential oils are used in animal ears, and for which animal each method is recommended for. It is important to note, that most animal's ear canals are "L" shaped, especially dogs. This means that the tunnel that runs from the outside of their ear, to the ear drum, takes a sharp turn near the bottom. This also provides a level of "security" from essential oils being able to drip directly onto the ear drum. Before an essential oil could reach this sensitive surface, it would have to get past a long track of skin without becoming completely absorbed first. Thankfully, this is actually a fairly difficult task.

METHODS OF APPLICATION – EARS

The basic rules that I follow for ears are:
- Always consult with a veterinarian concerning ear related problems. Situations, such as ruptured ear drums are common, and even a veterinary ear cleaner without essential oils can cause damage in this situation.
- Never place neat essential oils directly into the ear canal.
- Never "drip" neat oils or concentrated oil solutions into the ear with the intention of "reaching the bottom."
- Monitor the skin of the ear canal and of the ear flap for irritation to essential oil use.

Cotton Ball Application:

This method involves placing a drop or two of an essential oil (neat or diluted) onto a non-colored, 100% pure cotton, cotton ball. This cotton ball is then inserted into the ear canal of the animal, and left in place for a varying amount of time – usually 12-24 hours. Many animals dislike the cotton ball in their ear, and readily shake it out – so it is not a favorite method of mine. Care must be taken that the cotton ball does not travel too far down into the ear canal of a large dog or horse, which could require extraction by a veterinarian. Cats and small animals do not enjoy this method much. Overall, it is only a method I use when I absolutely have no other options.

Essential Oils in Carrier Oils:

Essential oils can be mixed into Coconut Oil, V-6 Enhanced Vegetable Oil Complex, or Animal Scents Ointment and then be applied to the ears. The focus of this application is not to fill the ear canal with the diluted essential oil, but to allow a coating of the ear tissues with the diluted mixture. Coconut Oil and Animal Scents Ointment are hard at most room temperatures, and will melt and become liquid once in contact with the animal's warmer body temperature inside of the ear and on the tissues. Coconut Oil carries its own antibacterial, antifungal, and anti-inflammatory actions, making it a wonderful tool for cleaning ear debris as well as carrying the essential oils to their place of need.

Sara Kenney's Ear Spray:

This is by far my favorite ear recipe. I have slightly varied it from Sara's original recipe which was included in her book *Natural Health Care For Your Four-Legged Friends*. I mainly recommend this recipe for use in dogs, and I generally would not use it for cats. Dogs are the main animal that experience ear infections that require this sort of remedy.

- Add the following ingredients to a 1 ounce (30 mL) glass spray bottle.
- 7-8 mL of Thieves Spray
- 1 Tablespoon of V-6 Enhanced Vegetable Oil Complex
- 3 drops of Lemongrass Essential Oil
- 4 drops of Copaiba Essential Oil
- 5 drops of Purification Essential Oil
- Then fill the rest of the bottle with Distilled Water.

Shake well and spray 1-3 pumps into the ear(s), once to twice a day. You are not trying to saturate the ear canal or drip this solution into the ear canal directly. Coating the infected outer surface area of the ear and upper part of the exposed ear canal, will result in the "traveling" of this solution to deeper parts of the ear. Monitor the ear tissues for any signs of irritation. This recipe has been used long term, for several months at a time or more. However, if irritation occurs, the solution may be diluted further or discontinued and other methods used. Irritation seems rare with this formulation, however the alcohol present in the Thieves Spray could be drying or irritating to sensitive dogs.

Ear Cleaning Solutions:

Plain Coconut Oil, or Coconut Oil mixed with small amounts of essential oils, make a wonderful ear cleaning concoction. Placing a "glob" of Coconut Oil into the ear canal, and allowing it to soften wax and debris, creates a gentle cleaning action. Gently wiping the ear clean with a cotton-tipped swab, works wonderfully after the Coconut Oil has been instilled into the ear.

A diluted solution of the Thieves Household Cleaner or Animal Scents Shampoo can also be used as an ear cleaning solution. One teaspoon of either can be added to 4 cups of water. The solution can be made stronger or weaker if needed. If the ear becomes too sudsy or foamy, dilute the solution more.

RECTAL INSTILLATION

Rectal suppositories of essential oils are quite effective for several situations. The lining of the rectum and colon are rich in blood supply, and items which are absorbed rectally, happen to get carried to the lungs first and foremost in their travels. This is exceedingly excellent news for conditions such as lung cancer, bronchitis, pneumonia, and various lung infections. Essential oils which are ingested, pass through our liver and are metabolized to varying degrees. This "first pass metabolism" of the essential oil when ingested is still debated somewhat, however, it is certain that less essential oil is available to reach the lung tissue following ingestion, than is available after rectal insertion.

Rectal insertion of essential oil suppositories has been reported to be very helpful in prostatic conditions. There are several methods in which to instill essential oils rectally, and generally these application methods must take into account the ability to administer them to the individual animal. Animals such as dogs, horses, cattle, and other large animals will obviously be easier to administer to than say a cat. Ferrets are commonly affected with prostatic issues, and using the indicated oils externally (over the prostate area) first, is a wise decision. However, if the protocols are not revealing enough results, one can attempt rectal instillation as well.

Effective methods of rectal instillation include diluting the essential oil within V-6 (generally starting with 1 drop of oil in 20 drops or more of V-6), and using a needle-less syringe to introduce the liquid into the rectum. Ample lubrication of the syringe with V-6 or a lubricating jelly is highly recommended. For small animals such as ferrets, cats, or small dogs (less than 20 pounds), instilling 0.5 mL or less of the diluted solution is a recommended starting point. For larger dogs, between 1-3 mL of the dilution could easily be instilled. Exact dosing amounts for rectal administration is less known, and starting with small amounts and increasing the concentration is recommended. Too frequent administration of oils rectally, can lead to irritation of the anus and mucus membranes. In general this therapy is recommended for short term use, usually no more than twice a day. However, for severe cases that respond well to this remedy, more frequent and longer term use can be considered.

Suppositories can also be made for rectal instillation. Raw organic Coconut Oil will generally be liquid in form at most room temperatures, melting at over 76 degrees Fahrenheit (24 degrees Celsius). Essential oils can be mixed into the liquid raw Coconut Oil at approximately 5 drops per tablespoon. The solution is thoroughly mixed, and then placed into a refrigerator or freezer temporarily to start the hardening of the coconut oil. Once the coconut oil mixture is a bit solid, a teaspoon or more of the mixture can be formed into a "bullet shape" on a piece of plastic wrap. You may have to return your bullet to the cold environment several times to perfect your suppository, but once it is in a form that you feel you could insert in to a rectum, place the suppository into the freezer until it is completely frozen and solid. It is this frozen suppository that will be inserted into the rectum. Insertion with a gloved and lubricated finger is generally the easiest method.

For larger animals, there is no set guideline for how much or how we instill the essential oil. Starting with amounts suitable for oral ingestion is suggested, however there are no hard and fast rules. Dilution of the essential oil is recommended (approximately 10-20 drops per tablespoon), and any carrier can be utilized. Larger volumes of liquid are sometimes easier to instill in horses or cows, and the removal of large amounts of fecal material from the rectum is recommended prior to instillation.

HOW MUCH, HOW OFTEN

No matter what the application method, one common question that is constantly raised, always focuses on the questions "how much do I give?" and "how often do I give it?" My best answer is to teach you a common sense approach to empower you to be able to navigate these questions for yourself. As every animal is an individual, you will be far better equipped to logically evaluate a situation and make reasonable changes, if you first understand how to evaluate the situation.

Whether you are starting to use an oil orally, topically, via diffusion, or by administering a Raindrop Technique – the basics are all the same. We can start with a small amount and gradually increase the amounts that an animal is exposed to.

Start by using a small amount of the recommended oil. Did you see a response? How long did it last for? Did the animal show some sort of detoxification response? I never use an essential oil with the immediate goal of using it twice a day, three times a day, or four times a day. How often I use an application method, will largely hinge on how long the animal received comfort from that application. This idea also holds true for determining the correct amount or concentration of an oil application. Starting with a lesser amount, and seeing if there were any results, allows me to decide whether the next application be stronger, the same, or less concentrated.

If I have administered too little oil, I may see no response at all. In this situation, I can repeat the same dose or increase the amount given. It often depends on how critical the situation is as well. More critical health concerns may need to have larger amounts given faster than in other situations.

It is possible to have also administered too much oil. Seeing a detoxification effect, will tell me that I should use less of the essential oil or vary my approach for the future. Various signs of detoxification could include soft stools, poor appetite, scratching or rubbing at the site of application, reddened skin, rolling on the ground, running around the room, sneezing, coughing, squinting, or other behaviors that are out of the ordinary. We must remember that we never have to make an animal uncomfortable through the use of essential oils, to have them be effective! In some situations, I may accept a runnier nose as an acceptable response to a treatment, however if the animal appears to be breathing with difficulty, this would not be satisfactory.

Another consideration, is if the animal caretaker is able to dose the animal once a day, twice a day, or more. Sometimes human factors will dictate how often essential oils will be used. Possibly, a farmer can only access a certain animal once a day. Then, this will be the frequency of the treatments.

It is wise to give a little time to evaluate each change you make to a protocol. If you decided to increase an oral essential oil administration by one drop, then waiting approximately 3 days to evaluate the response to that increase is suggested. Of course in critical situations, waiting 3 days is usually not possible nor recommended.

How we time the next dose being given, is related to how long the treatment lasted for. For example, if a dog gets a Raindrop Technique and itches less for 3 days; however, on day 4 the itching has recurred, then repeating the Raindrop Technique every 3 days would be suggested. This allows for the comfort and benefits to continue, at an interval that is dictated by the body's own needs.

For an animal who is not showing benefits long enough – it is not always true that more oils will equal a longer lasting result. Sometimes the use of more oil, still results in the same length of response. In this situation, it becomes wasteful to give more oils than you need. Increasing the frequency of the use of the essential oil is often the correct choice in these situations.

Most importantly, whether you are using an essential oil or a supplement, start with one thing at a time, use them in very low amounts initially, and wait 3 days between each increase or addition. Do not overwhelm an animal with 20 different oils or supplements all at once.

RAINDROP TECHNIQUE

Please do study and read the Chapter on Raindrop Technique in the Essential Oils Desk Reference. This will allow you to have a greater understanding of the entire Raindrop Technique and philosophy. I will describe the general technique in this chapter – however, it is always best to obtain a greater understanding of all aspects of such a profound application.

For Raindrop "rookies" – fear not! Many of you may feel overwhelmed when you first are exposed to this technique, but I assure you, these methods are very easy, and you cannot "do it wrong." Allow me to introduce you to what I will term "The Down & Dirty" Raindrop Technique! But first, let's learn the basic philosophy and procedure.

The Raindrop Technique was initially created by D. Gary Young for humans. The technique combined the use of essential oils with Lakota and ancient Tibetan healing methods. The oils used with the Raindrop Technique have powerful properties – each unique on their own, but also synergistic when combined. By applying these oils together – a spectacular healing tool can be provided.

The oils within a standard Raindrop Technique are usually as follows: Oregano, Thyme, Basil, Cypress, Wintergreen, Marjoram, and Peppermint. Each of these oils are dripped up the spine area, from about 6 inches above the animal – from the tail to the head.

In cats and smaller animals – generally all of these oils are combined into a single diluted solution. Although each individual oil could be diluted then applied in the same individual manner as for humans – small creatures tend to not sit still for very long periods of time. So it can be more difficult to complete the technique in this manner. Mutually beneficial is the fact that this Raindrop Solution seems to be very effective for these animals. So for convenience, and because it works, why make things harder on ourselves.

Basic Raindrop Procedures:

Balancing:
Prior to dripping the seven main Raindrop oils up the spine, a balancing step can be performed. This step can be optional, however Valor Essential Oil Blend does act as a "primer" of sorts for all of the other oils. Valor is helpful in aligning the energies within the body, and all of the other oils will work better and in greater harmony – thus having a bigger overall effect. Balancing is performed by placing Valor into each hand. Depending on the species of animal you are working with, you may work with the oil from a Valor Roll-On, neat oils directly on the palms of your hands, diluted oils directly on the palms of your hands, neat or diluted oils rubbed into your hands but leaving a light film, or oils absorbed completely into your hands. There are many variations in intensity of oil application. Starting with a light amount, and gradually increasing the amounts your animal is exposed to, is a wise choice.

With the appropriate oils on the palms of your hands, you will then hold each hand over the shoulder and rump area of the animal (some species may have different recommendations for balancing.) As you hold your hands in these locations – breathe deeply and meditate with your companion. If you are experienced in energy work, such as Reiki, this is a perfect time to insert this method into the Raindrop Technique. Continue for as long as this feels comfortable for you and the animal. Often times, you will feel a release of tension in both yourself and the animal, and deep sighs are often noted. If you feel a difference in hot or cold, or tingling between right and left hands, you may hold the balancing step until both hands feel equal.

Do not be alarmed if you feel nothing at all. Many of us experience this. Just strive for relaxation, and holding the position for a few minutes or as you feel guided. There is no perfect or specific way this is meant to feel. This step has also been omitted without detriment when time constraints or ability to handle a certain animal makes it necessary. The medical benefits that can be had with the Raindrop Technique are still present.

I like to teach my students that "There are no Raindrop Police." We need to relax and recognize that a modality can grow with us. Starting with a method that is easiest for us, and gradually adding "skills" into it, makes the most sense in how we actually learn things. Many times in my busy life, I have forgotten a step, modified a step "accidently on purpose," or just plain old messed up. Never fear – I have researched this enough and can guarantee you that the Raindrop Police will not come knocking on your door! And trust me, I've tested them.

What about the feet?

In humans, applying the Raindrop oils to the feet with Vita Flex is a huge component of the technique. With animals, I most commonly found that the application of oils to the paw was either difficult for my clients to perform or that it was less tolerated by the animal. Due to these elements, I mainly began performing Raindrop Technique excluding the use of oils onto the paws or pads. The main exception to this recommendation lies with horses, especially if they are exhibiting any signs of lameness, hoof, or leg issues. For these animals, applying the oils to the hoof and/or leg area is a definite benefit – and is described best in the species specific discussion of their Raindrop Technique. Regardless, I have found that the exclusion of application of oils to the feet, has not affected the efficacy of the Raindrop Technique. And, by making the technique the easiest on my clients and patients, it was performed more often, resulting in better compliance and health.

Applying Oils:

If balancing has been done, the next step is applying the Raindrop oils. Please be sure to consult the section for your particular animal species – as each species may have recommendations specific to their individual needs.

Application of the Raindrop Technique oils will generally be on the spine, from the start of the tail to the base of the head. In most animals, the feet are often excluded from the Raindrop Technique. Please read more about applying oils to feet and pads, as well as the recommendations for your species, for complete understanding of variations.

When applying oils to the spine, dripping from approximately 6 inches above the animal is recommended. In very small animals such as rats, 3 inches or less may be adequate. Again, do not fret if you do not drip the oils directly on the spine, or if your spacing above the spine is not ideal. There are many situations that have to be modified when we work with animals.

The dripping of the oils from a distance above the animal, allows the drops to pass through the animal's energetic field. There are many benefits to this occurrence, ones that science will likely not be able to explain or document for some time.

Each individual oil, or if indicated Raindrop Technique Solution, is dripped up the back in this fashion. Be cautious as you drip oils up the neck, nearing the base of the head. I have many cats and dogs that choose to "look up" and discover what I am doing - right as an oil drop falls towards them. Since animals are often moving targets, I may stop the location of the drip a bit farther down the neck to avoid accidently dripping an oil droplet onto their face or near their eyes.

Although it might seem necessary, shaving the back or parting the fur is not needed for Raindrop Technique to be effective in animals. Some care givers have found it beneficial to shave a strip up the back of long haired dogs, just for sheer ease of administration, but this is not necessarily required or needed. As discussed in the chapter "Sensitivity to Oils" – hair follicles are likely involved with enhanced absorption of essential oils.

Stroking in the Oils:

After oils are dripped up the back, they are stroked into the animal. Various feathering techniques can be used, and you are welcome to use whichever ones you choose. Some choose to stroke with 3 inch strokes, some choose 6 inch strokes, some choose full length strokes, and certainly combinations of each are also okay. There are no hard and fast rules. One cautionary statement – please be aware that while stroking short coats in the opposite direction of the way the hair lies – you may create a flicking of the oils into the air. Altering your technique by using a lighter touch, less aggressive stroke, or in some circumstances a more "full contact" stroke can often eliminate this flicking action.

In general, the stroking of each oil application up the back, is repeated three times. Again, it is not important if you cannot complete three cycles of stroking on a particular animal. Striving for ideal is nice, but with animals, we often have to make concessions.

Applying V-6 Diluting Oil:

V-6 Enhanced Vegetable Oil Complex is the carrier oil I recommend for use with animals. It has a thin and absorbable quality that works well with fur and hair, as well as feathers (although we try to avoid oil on feathers as much as possible). V-6 should be used as the carrier oil for the various Raindrop Technique Solutions (i.e. Kitty Raindrop), and also as the diluting oil in any of the animal Raindrop Techniques. Another benefit to the use of V-6, is that it does not leave as much of an oily residue on fabrics, dog beds, couches, etc… which is important in most households.

Certainly, if you do not have V-6 on hand, a good quality vegetable oil can be used – such as Olive Oil or Coconut Oil. However, planning ahead to make sure you have V-6 on hand, is well worth while.

In general, after the application of Oregano and Thyme, most Raindrop Techniques for animals will involve applying V-6 along the spine. This provides a calming effect to the "hot" oils, and provides a platform for all of the other oils to be applied. There are many ways that we can dilute the essential oils for their use – and it is important to use the method that is most comfortable for you or for your individual animal.

Due to the variety of animals and their individual needs, I have seen multiple scenarios of dilution work incredibly well. V-6 can be utilized after the Oregano and Thyme application, prior to any oil application what-so-ever, at any step of the Raindrop Technique, after the entire Raindrop Technique is completed, or used to dilute the essential oils prior to application. The choice is really up to you, and should hinge more on the needs of the animal receiving the Raindrop, than any human need to teach one specific way or another.

For example, just because a horse is a horse, does not mean that it can tolerate neat oils. If it became apparent that a particularly sensitive horse needed oils pre-diluted, then this should be what is done for that horse.

Modifications of the Raindrop Technique:

One important aspect of using the Raindrop Technique, is the ability to modify it. This can mean a number of things including performing the Raindrop with completely different oils than the standard "Raindrop Oils," to omitting or adding various essential oils from the technique.

Let's say you wish to do a Raindrop Technique on a dog that has cancer. Several other oils for cancer are recommended to be inserted into a modified Dog Raindrop Technique in the conditions listing. In this situation, you would perform the Raindrop Technique as you see fit for that individual dog, but also include several of the recommended oils within the technique. Generally these oils are added around the step of the Wintergreen and Marjoram applications. Do not fret if you forget the exact sequence, you will become more and more comfortable with the technique the more you do it. So, if we had wanted to insert Frankincense and Idaho Balsam Fir into this particular Raindrop – the progression of oil application may appear like this: Oregano, Thyme, V-6, Basil, Cypress, Wintergreen, Frankincense, Idaho Balsam Fir, Marjoram, Peppermint. All of these oils being dripped on, and stroked in, in a similar manner.

There is no right or wrong in how we go about adding or inserting these essential oils into the Raindrop Technique. However, in general I do stop at the insertion of about three additional essential oils into the technique. If I would like to use more than three oils, then I just wait until the next Raindrop Technique is administered, and rotate to using the other additional oils at that time. There are just so many powerful essential oils within the Technique already, that if we were to add in seven more – it may just be too overwhelming for a system.

Another form of Raindrop modification is to create a Raindrop Technique with completely different oils all together. This might be used in a situation such as an emotional release or for respiratory disease. We can pick only the oils that we wish to administer – and apply them in a "Raindrop Fashion."

This version of Raindrop modification was clearly dramatic for an Australian horse that I was consulted about. He had been a rescue horse, and clearly had some health issues as well as traumatic behavioral concerns from his past. He could not tolerate a traditional Raindrop Technique easily; his back produced an abundance of welts, he started to sweat profusely, he would breathe very heavily, created nasal discharge, and he wanted to roll on the ground after each oil application. Although some of these signs are an indicator that we were effecting great changes in the body, which did result in health benefits, we did not have to make the Raindrop an uncomfortable event for this horse.

Since the horse was quite stable, and didn't "have to have" the traditional Raindrop Technique for reasons I felt were medically important, I asked the owners what other oils they had on hand. They had a lovely assortment of emotional oils and blends. I decided to recommend that they use about 6 of those oils without any of the traditional Raindrop oils, however still apply them with the Raindrop Technique. The results were beautiful. No over detoxification causing discomfort, great emotional response, no welts, and we actually saw respiratory symptom improvement as well! In the future, it is very likely that this horse could return to the use of a "full" Raindrop Technique once his body had healed a bit further, and show no over detoxification response at all.

EMOTIONAL WORK WITH OILS

Emotional work with animals is an area that has been neglected for far too long. In an age of rescue dogs, puppy mills, hoarders, and over-run rescues...the emotional health of our animal population is tragic. My patients have taught me so many things once I started to use essential oils. It wasn't that I didn't recognize how important their emotional health was – but just that I never saw how powerful it could be to correct it, until I started using essential oils.

Essential oils are the most holistic modality that I know of. Not only can I get powerful health benefits and responses by the body – but even without trying, I see behavioral and emotional benefits in patients. Essential oils treat mind, body, and spirit – and with this – we can change the face of how animals will benefit from medical treatments in the future. No longer will a pill of amoxicillin be shoved down a cat's throat, creating distrust, upset stomachs, and hiding behaviors. My dream is to incorporate aromatherapy into medical treatments that make everyone happy – as well as healthy.

It is important to recognize that there is no "wrong way" in working with essential oils and emotions. If you feel guided to do one thing versus another – then please do so. However, I will guide you on a few recommendations that are worthy of notice.

First, it is always recommended to separate an animal from others when working on emotional clearing. This would mean separating a dog from other dogs or cats in the household, or separating a horse away from herd mates. Imagine yourself going through an emotional release. We usually are not very comfortable doing this in front of others. In the animal kingdom – the odd ball is often shunned, rejected, or even attacked for bringing attention to the pack, herd, or flock. We would not want to create this experience for any animal we are working with.

Magnify Your Purpose

A word of caution should be placed with the use of this blend for animals. Not for safety or concern for the animal, but for the sheer fact that an animal's "purpose" may not be our own. A show dog who is unhappy being a show dog, may Magnify His Purpose, by leaving the show ring or sitting down! We as humans, often project our feelings and desires onto our animals, without concern of their own wishes. So, although it may be controversial in nature, I will say that there are not many owners willing to accept their own animal's desire for what their purpose should be.

Mixing of Emotional Blends:

There is no law that says that you cannot mix emotional blends. Everyone can also take heart in the fact that you will not create something harmful, if you do choose to mix blends together. What does hold true, is that the energy and frequency that was intended in the original recipe of an emotional blend, will be changed by the comingling. Sometimes this can result in a beautiful thing, and sometimes it results in an unattractive odor. The basic idea of not blending blends, truly exists in the fact that you will lose the intention of the original blend if you combine them.

Quite often in our veterinary hospital, we will add one drop of Trauma Life to a water-based diffuser that is already diffusing Purification (for example.) We have found this to be a beautiful and effective way to emotionally support hospitalized patients, while still ensuring good odor control and reduction of transmissible agents. Any combination could be used in this manner. The intent is not to change the effects of either oil being used, however, we are enhancing the situation ever so slightly, and it has worked wonderfully for our patients.

Common Methods for Emotional Work

Again, there are no right or wrong methods. However, these are the ones that we have found most useful. It is important to recognize, that the humans administering the emotional blends to the animals, will often benefit as well. It may be fair warning to alert the humans in the household of this fact.

Nightly Diffusion: While this can be done with air or water diffusion, I find that water diffusion is much more accepted by the entire household. Often, if an emotional blend is used more intensely than a human in the household "can stand," the emotional work goes by the wayside, and no one benefits. Emotions are powerful things, and the resistance of a human to the use of a certain odor, can be strong when emotions come into play. Nightly diffusion is just that, the diffusion of a selected oil during the night, while animals and humans sleep. The diffuser is generally set up in the same room as the animal, and allowed to run all night. Between 1-4 drops is generally added to a diffuser. Diffusion can occur every night, once a week, once a month, or whatever is deemed necessary by the situation. The same oil can be diffused, or a rotation of different oils can be selected for each new diffuser batch. Many times, the diffuser would be left running all night long, but shorter time frames can also be used.

Rotational Diffusion: We have had situations in our veterinary hospital, where a dog rescued from a puppy mill would benefit greatly from emotional support. However, it is a common situation that we will only have the dog in the hospital for 2 days or less. In these situations, or in others where emotional work is desired to occur on a faster schedule, a different emotional selection can be diffused every hour or two. There is no set recipe, but one scenario may include diffusing one selection for 20 minutes, then in 2 hours, a different blend is selected and diffused for 20 minutes. One could rotate through as many blend selections as they like, but in general, a magic number of around 7 seems to be a golden suggestion. Do not throw out a batch of diffuser water, just because you want to change essential oils. Store the oily water in a covered glass bottle, and use it later.

Example of Rotational Diffusion: A dog was rescued from a puppy mill, and had never seen the light of day, nor had touched grass with her feet. Emotionally and physically, this dog would freeze up and refuse to move. The oils of Release, Trauma Life, Acceptance, Forgiveness, SARA, Present Time, Grounding, and Into the Future were selected for this dog and were diffused in this order. 3 drops of the selected oil were placed within a water-based diffuser, and was diffused for 20 minutes, right next to the cage of the dog. The liquid still containing the essential oil was saved in a glass bottle for future use, instead of just throwing it away and wasting it. Then, 2 hours later, the next oil was diffused for 20 minutes for the dog in the same manner. This was repeated until all of the oils were diffused. It is fine to have variation in when the diffusion is repeated as well. So, one oil could have been initially diffused for 30 minutes, then the next oil diffused for 20 minutes one hour later, then the third oil may have been diffused for 40 minutes three hours later. Flexibility is fine, and we often had to embrace the schedule of the clinic, to determine what our actual intervals would be.

Petting Application: This technique can be performed with any frequency you desire. Nightly, hourly, daily, or monthly; the choice is purely individual. Several drops of an essential oil blend are placed into your hand. Depending on your species of animal, this oil may be diluted or used neat. Also depending on the species of animal, you may have a fair amount of the oil still "wet" on your hand (as for horses and dogs), or you may have the oil completely absorbed into your hands (as for birds, rodents, and exotics) prior to Petting them. It is always amazing how much an animal will smell like the essential oil after Petting, even when the oils have seemingly been completely absorbed into your hands.

Locations of Petting: This too is a completely subjective matter. Yet, there are some oils that just seem to call to application at various sites. Common locations that people are drawn to apply to include over the heart area, over the shoulder area, and over the brain stem area. Any location is fine, and you will not do any harm by applying a "heart" oil over the "liver." Remember, any suggestions on location are purely opinion, and if you feel drawn to apply an oil in a certain location, then by all means, please do!

Emotional Raindrop Technique

This is an amazing technique for using the emotional blends. Single oils can certainly be included as well, so never feel that a single has to be excluded from any form of emotional work.

Basically, between 6-8 emotional blends are selected for an animal (sometimes less), and they are applied over the spine in a Raindrop Technique style of application. None of the Raindrop Oils are used within this method typically, just the emotional oils that have been selected. This has been a phenomenal technique for many animals and situations. Any oils can be used, and in any order.

Example of an Emotional Raindrop: A horse had been rescued and arrived at the new sanctuary farm with a bit of emotional baggage, as well as a respiratory concern. When the horse was given a traditional equine Raindrop Technique it welted significantly, rolled on the ground between applications of oils, started to breathe harder, and created nasal discharge. Since this horse was not in a position to adequately handle the aggressive detoxification of the full Raindrop Technique, the new owners were asked what other oils they had on hand. Quite an assortment of emotional blends were on hand, and it was decided that those would be used in the

Raindrop Fashion. As an example, the oils of Peace & Calming, Believe, Valor, Grounding, Joy, and Frankincense could be applied up the spine and stroked in. The horse did not have any aggressive detoxification response to these oils, and tolerated everything beautifully. The new owners reported not only significant behavioral improvement, but medical improvement as well. Respiratory symptoms were significantly less and the horse had more "get up and go" when coming in from the pasture.

Favorite Oils and Properties

There are a few favorite oils that contribute greatly to emotional work with animals. Palo Santo is helpful in cleansing negative energies, White Angelica provides protective effects, Valor can evoke a sense of bravery, and Trauma Life is a basic all around oil to use for any traumatic event. There are descriptions of each individual oil and blend within the EODR, and in this book, and you are encouraged to read more about each one. Many animal caretakers find a connection with a certain essential oil after reading the descriptions of it, and this is often the perfect selection for that particular household or situation.

ADVANCED TECHNIQUES

There are so many ways we can use essential oils in animals, that are even more advanced than what will be recommended for basic use in this book. Future editions will likely include more specifics on these topics.

Essential oils can be combined with techniques such as Acupuncture, Acupressure, Massage Therapy, Chiropractic Adjustment, Electro-stimulation, Homeopathy, Flower Essences, Reiki, Animal Communication, Neuro Auricular Technique, Vita Flex, Reflexology, and more. I find that every modality that is used in the animal world today, is greatly enhanced by the addition of essential oils.

There are a few techniques that are worthy of discussion and explanation – as they provide additional benefits to the way we can administer essential oils to animals.

Neuro Auricular Technique:

There is sometimes a bit of confusion as to which technique this name refers to. I will define the Neuro Auricular Technique (NAT) as the technique that I was first introduced to at the Dallas Raindrop Training in 2010. This method utilized an auricular probe, Roll-On essential oil applicators, and a series of essential oils applied to the upper neck, spine, and to the back of the skull. At the base of the skull is a little "divot" or depression which has been termed the LC or Locus Ceruleus. The LC is not truly at that external location – but is actually a nucleus within the pons of the brain (part of the brain stem). The LC is involved in physiological responses to stress and panic.

The technique can really be used to apply any essential oil, in any of the locations, and with any of the techniques described. So do not feel that you cannot improvise the use of various essential oils (especially for brain conditions) to include some of these application techniques. But, I'll describe the basic traditional protocol for you.

1. Balance with Valor Essential Oil Blend, as described for your species within the Raindrop Technique discussion.
2. Apply Sacred Frankincense to the LC and along the Occipital Ridge of the skull, generally in a petting application. Then starting at one ear, apply circular pressure with an auricular probe or your finger, to various points along the occipital ridge until you reach the LC. Apply circular pressure at the LC as well, then repeat the process starting from the other ear. The circular motion can be clockwise or counter-clockwise. Clockwise motions are most commonly used for physical work, and counter-clockwise motions are most commonly used for emotional work.
3. Next, starting at Cervical Vertebrae 8 – use the Deep Relief Roll-On in a "crow-bar" or prying motion, in between each vertebrae, until you reach the LC again. Finish with circular pressure at the LC with the Deep Relief Roll-On.
4. Starting at Cervical Vertebrae 8 again – use the Stress Away Roll-On to apply circular pressure in a "cross-stitch" pattern – on either side of the vertebrae. Again working up to the LC location, and finishing with a circular pressure at the LC.
5. Next, starting at the LC, use the RutaVaLa Roll-On to "paint" along the occipital ridge – from the LC to the ear.

You have just completed a Neuro Auricular Technique! You can use any portion of the application methods, with any oil, and with fingers, auricular probes, or roll-ons. The NAT is particularly excellent for brain and neurologic conditions, seizures, senility, anxiety, emotional work – you name it. Any of the oil recommendations for a condition, such as seizures, could be applied in any of the manners described above, for added benefits.

Auricular Adjustment:

If you have taken a CARE Intensive class, you may be familiar with this technique. It basically involves shoving your essential oil-covered fingers into someone's ears, then maneuvering the ear around with your finger. I know, it is an elegant description – however, quite accurate. This technique is helpful in getting essential oils in and around the ear area, as well as functionally opening the ear canal, providing acupressure, as well as a massage of sorts to the ear. I use this technique most often in animals with hearing concerns and neurologic conditions, but the uses are endless.

Although any essential oil can be used (use common sense on selection), favorites for me are Helichrysum, RutaVaLa, Frankincense, Melrose, and Purification. For example, I will coat my fingertips (nails trimmed short), with diluted or neat Helichrysum and then gently insert my fingers into my dog's ears. Cats don't particularly appreciate fingers in their ears, birds only have small ear holes, and snakes don't have external ears at all – so you will want to select your animals for this technique carefully! Once my fingers are inserted into the ear canals, I gently move my fingers in a rhythmic motion, causing the entire ear canal to shift and move.

Motions used in this technique include lifting in a pulsing manner with your fingers upwards, pushing downwards, pulling back with your fingers towards the tail end of the animal, pushing forward with your fingers towards the nose of the animal, and also combinations that include side to side or alternating motions (right, left, right, left, right, left.)

For the most part you are pulsing the motions; applying pressure in a certain direction then returning to a relaxed position of the ear canal. For large animals such as horses, donkeys, and goats – the essential oils can still be applied into the ear canal with your fingertips, but I find it much easier to manipulate the entire ear instead of trying to keep my fingers inside their ear canal. Basically, I grab the ears like they are the handle bars for a motor cycle – and then maneuver the ears gently in various directions. They love it!

Vita Flex Technique:

You can read more about this technique in the Essential Oils Desk Reference. It is an important form of reflexology, and a wonderful way to enhance any application of essential oils, even if you are not applying them to specific reflexology points. Vita Flex almost acts like a spark plug, "firing" energy into the area being treated. This "energy" seems to enhance the absorption and action of the essential oils applied at the site. Whether it is due to massage, acupressure point stimulation, or actual electrical impulses – once you have experienced a proper Vita Flex Technique – you will understand the value of this method 100 fold. I use this technique in all sorts of animals, and in all sorts of locations. It does not matter if we do not know actual reflexology points for stimulation on an animal. Just the act of performing Vita Flex adds value to the essential oil application.

As an example, if I were to pet Idaho Balsam Fir onto the leg of a horse for a bone injury – I would greatly enhance the effects by applying the Vita Flex Technique over the entire application area.

Acupuncture:

To use essential oils with acupuncture in animals, we can use several methods. Some acupuncturists will dip the acupuncture needle into a clean and dedicated bottle of essential oil, coating the needle prior to insertion. Others choose to apply the essential oil of choice (neat or diluted) to the skin at the site of needle insertion. While still others may only have the option of applying an essential oil to the acupuncture site after the needles are withdrawn. Whichever method is used, the essential oils enhance all aspects of acupuncture.

INTO THE FUTURE

The future of essential oil use in animals is profound in my eyes. Not only is there a modality that can replace the use of traditional pharmacology, but likely we will witness a modality that far surpasses the use of traditional pharmacologic chemicals.

I am incredibly excited to be a part of this new frontier. I have a grand vision of a specialized veterinary center, devoted to medical aromatherapy for all animals. One that will provide holistic training to veterinarians and animal caretakers alike. Good health and knowledge should not be limited to those with a medical license. Although there are some things that I can do as a licensed veterinarian that others cannot – like diagnose, prescribe, inject, and perform surgeries – the foundational tools for good health and prevention of disease should be available to everyone. I truly believe this is the only way we can change our current world from one that focuses on sickness, instead of wellness.

The near future will show us that we can correct disease with the intravenous use of essential oils, inject tumors with essential oils and have resolution, replace commercial pharmacology, and heal a broken and emotionally corrupt animal care system. However, the far future is much more exciting. Prevention of disease, for all animal kind. If these modalities can do so much in the face of disease, think about what can happen if we were all privileged to experience their benefits BEFORE the dis-ease ever occurred! That is my goal. I hope that you will share it with me!

ESSENTIAL OIL SINGLES

Within this chapter, the single essential oils that are available from Young Living will be discussed. I will mainly discuss the oils that are commonly used for animals – however all of the essential oils have, and can generally be used with animals. For full information on the chemical constituents, historical data, medical properties, and research references for these oils, please see the Essential Oils Desk Reference.

In this section, I will list if, how, and why each oil is used for animals. This is by no means a complete representation of what each oil can do, or how it can be used – however, it will provide you with a current knowledge of how we are using these oils in the animal kingdom.

Angelica (Angelica archangelica)
Angelica is a photosensitizing oil; do not apply to areas that will be exposed to direct sunlight or full spectrum UV lights for 24 hours. Angelica is not commonly used as a single in animals at this time. Angelica is contained and used in many emotional blends such as Awaken, Forgiveness, Grounding, Harmony, and Surrender.

Anise (Pimpinella anisum)
Anise is very good for digestive concerns. It is not available as a single oil at this time. Anise is excellent for Inflammatory Bowel Disease, and is most commonly used in Di-Gize. It is also found in Awaken, ComforTone, Detoxzyme, Dream Catcher, Essentialzyme, ICP, ParaFree, Polyzyme, and Power Meal.

Balsam Fir (Idaho)
Idaho Balsam Fir is an incredible oil that is worthy of much use. Great for bone conditions, muscle and joint conditions, respiratory conditions, emotional work, inflammatory conditions, lowering cortisol levels, and more. It is an oil that you would never be wrong in including in an animal protocol.

Birds & Exotics: Commonly water diffused, mixed with Animal Scents Ointment and applied topically, included in Species Specific Raindrop Technique, diluted and applied topically via petting.

Cats: Used in all of the methods listed for Birds & Exotics, as well as added to Kitty Raindrop Technique, applied via petting (neat or diluted), or added to Litteroma.

Dogs & Larger: Used in all of the mentioned methods, as well as air diffusion, insertion into Raindrop Technique (neat or diluted), direct topical applications (neat or diluted), Petting applications (neat or diluted), and by oral administration. For oral use in dogs – dilute 1 part Idaho Balsam Fir with 3 parts V-6 – use up to 4 drops of this solution, for each 20 pounds (9 kg) of body weight. Some dogs may require more or less of this solution. For horses and others, starting with 1 drop per 100-200 pounds (45-90 kg) of body weight, given orally twice a day is a good starting point. Monitor responses with a veterinarian, and adjust according to individual need. For reduction in cortisol levels, Idaho Balsam Fir is most commonly given at night before bed.

Basil (Ocimum basilicum)

This oil is one of the Raindrop Oils – and you can rest assured that oils with this status have something large to "bring to the table." As a single oil, we mainly use Basil for anti-histamine properties in animals. There is a cautionary statement in the EODR against the use of Basil in those with epilepsy. Although this precaution is wise to adhere to, in practice many animals who are afflicted with seizures receive Raindrop Techniques (including Basil) on a regular basis, with no ill effects. Basil can be omitted from the Raindrop Technique where there is concern for an animal who has experienced seizures in the past.

Birds & Exotics: Commonly used with water diffusion, added to drinking water for anti-histamine actions (1 drop per liter of water), added to foods (starting with a toothpick dip), used in Species Specific Raindrop Technique.

Cats: Basil can be used in the methods mentioned for Birds & Exotics, with cats being less likely to consume the oil in water or foods. With cats it is most commonly used within the Kitty Raindrop Technique. It could also be mixed into Animal Scents Ointment (1 drop or more mixed into 1 tablespoon), diluted in V-6 (4 drops in 30 mL), applied via Petting, or added to Litteroma.

Dogs & Larger: Basil can be used in all of the mentioned ways, within the Raindrop Technique, direct topical applications, Petting applications, adding to drinking water, and oral administration. For oral use in dogs – dilute 1 part Basil with 3 parts V-6 – use approximately 2 drops of this solution, for each 20 pounds (9 kg) of body weight. Some dogs may require more or less of this solution. For horses and others, starting with 1 drop per 300 pounds (135 kg) of body weight, given orally twice a day is a good starting point. Monitor responses with a veterinarian, and adjust according to individual need.

Bergamot (Citrus bergamia)
Bergamot is generally a photosensitizing oil, however recently, fractionation of this oil is removing the causative constituent. This oil is very good for easing the chiropractic adjustment of animals, and is also wonderful for emotional concerns such as depression and anxiety. It is less commonly used as a single for animals and it is contained within many beneficial blends including Awaken, Clarity, Dragon Time, Dream Catcher, Forgiveness, Gentle Baby, Harmony, Joy, and White Angelica.

Birds & Exotics: Commonly used via water diffusion, added to drinking water, added to foods, used within a water spritzer.

Cats: Most commonly used via water diffusion.

Dogs & Larger: Commonly used in all of the mentioned ways, as well as inserted into a Raindrop Technique, direct topical application, Petting applications, sprayed on via water spritzer, and air diffused.

Cardamom (Elettaria cardamomum)
Not commonly used as a single in animals at this time.

Carrot Seed (Daucus carota)
Not commonly used as a single in animals at this time.

Cassia (Cinnamomum cassia)

Cassia is a beautiful oil is part of the Twelve Oils of Ancient Scripture collection, it is a "hot" oil with powerful anti-bacterial properties. It is mainly used within the blends Exodus II, and EndoGize for animals. Its use as a single for difficult abscesses in Horses and Large Animals could be considered.

Cedar, Western Red (Thuja plicata)

Not commonly used as a single in animals at this time.

Cedarwood (Cedrus atlantica)

Cedarwood is an oil that is extremely high in sesquiterpene content, supporting the body with increased ability to oxygenate. It is commonly used to increase circulation and support the body when oxygenation needs will be higher such as work at higher altitudes, support prior to anesthetic events, increased athletic performance, and increased brain function. Cedarwood is often used in insect repellant recipes available on the commercial market, and could be included in any insect repelling spray or recipe you would like to create. It is also contained within many blends used for animals such as Australian Blue, Brain Power, Cel-Lite Magic Massage Oil, Egyptian Gold, Grounding, Highest Potential, Inspiration, Into the Future, Sacred Mountain, and SARA.

Birds & Exotics: Water diffusion, especially starting 2 weeks prior to anesthesia events.

Cats: Used as mentioned, as well as added to Kitty Raindrop Technique, applied via Petting (neat or diluted), and added to Litteroma.

Dogs & Larger: Used as mentioned, as well as with air diffusion, direct topical application, insertion into a Raindrop Technique, and via Petting applications (neat or diluted).

Celery Seed (Apium graveolens)

Not commonly used as a single oil in animals at this time. It is beneficial for the liver and to increase milk production. This oil is contained within GLF and Juva Cleanse.

Chamomile, German (Matricaria recutita)

Not commonly used as a single oil in animals at this time, purely based on its previous unavailability as an individual oil. This oil has wonderful promise for fatty liver disease, hepatitis, liver, and digestive issues, emotional concerns, and skin conditions. The below mentioned ways to use German Chamomile have not been widely used yet at this time, and are general suggestions of what would be considered starting techniques. German Chamomile is found within ComforTone, EndoFlex, JuvaTone, and Surrender.

Birds & Exotics: This oil can likely be used via water diffusion, added to a Species Specific Raindrop Technique, and may show promise in the future with use in water-based spritzers for feather and skin conditions. Use via oral or water administration is likely as well, especially for liver and digestive concerns.

Cats: This oil can be used via water or air diffusion, added to the Kitty Raindrop Technique, applied via Petting (dilute or neat), or added to Litteroma.

Dogs & Larger: This oil can be used in all of the mentioned methods as well as direct topical application (neat or diluted), insertion into a Raindrop Technique, applied via Petting, administered orally, or air diffused.

Chamomile, Roman (Chamaemelum nobile)

While not as commonly used as a single in animals, Roman Chamomile has wonderful properties indicated for behavioral concerns and anxieties, skin conditions, nerve regeneration, and detoxification of the blood and liver (such as detoxification from vaccination insult.) This oil is found in many products and blends commonly indicated for use in animals such as Gentle Baby, Harmony, Joy, Juva Flex, K&B Tincture, and Rehemogen. The below mentioned ways to use Roman Chamomile have not been widely used yet at this time, and are general suggestions of what would be considered starting techniques.

Birds & Exotics: This oil can be used via water diffusion. Other likely methods of use include adding the oil to a Species Specific Raindrop Technique, adding to drinking water or food, application via Petting techniques (diluted), and Roman Chamomile may show promise in its use within water-based spritzers for feather and skin conditions. Oral use within products such as K&B Tincture and Rehemogen has been established for exotics such as ferrets, rodents, large cats, wildlife, and other zoo animals with less data on birds, rabbits, guinea pigs, chinchillas, sugar gliders, and reptiles. The use of tinctures is largely avoided in some exotic and avian species, due to alcohol content.

Cats: Roman Chamomile can be diffused via water diffusion, added to a Kitty Raindrop Technique, added to Litteroma, or applied via Petting (neat or diluted). The oral use within K&B Tincture is well established in cats.

Dogs & Larger: Roman Chamomile can be used easily in many methods for these animals. Water or air diffusion, insertion into Raindrop Technique, direct topical application (neat or diluted), via Petting, and administered orally.

Cinnamon Bark (Cinnamomum verum)

Cinnamon oil contains a moderate level of Eugenol, which is often implicated in toxic situations in animals and especially cats. Although quite a hot oil and rarely indicated for direct single use in animals, there are actually many situations in which Cinnamon oil is used successfully, and without ill effects. The blends of Abundance, Christmas Spirit, and Thieves contain cinnamon and are often water diffused in households with cats, birds, and other exotics. Also, the blends of Thieves, Exodus II, Highest Potential, Egyptian Gold, and Gathering contain cinnamon, and are often used in many species. Many cat owners regularly report the use of Egyptian Gold on their feline friends. Products such as Thieves Household Cleaner, Thieves Spray, Dentarome, Dentarome Plus, and Dentarome Ultra are also widely used for animals.

Care must be taken with Cinnamon oil in animals who are bleeding, have a tendency to bleed, or are on any sort of anti-coagulant therapy. The over use of essential oil(s) that have anti-coagulant actions, especially in oral administration, can produce a temporary and dose dependent, increases in bleeding and reduction of clotting.

Birds & Exotics: As a single oil, this oil would rarely be used.

Cats: As a single oil, this oil would rarely be used.

Dogs: As a single oil, cinnamon would likely only be indicated for severe abscesses that were resistant to other first line therapies.

Horses & Large Animals: Cinnamon oil is well indicated for large abscesses, applied neat or diluted, directly to the site. Cinnamon is a wonderful oil for hoof abscesses, and other conditions such as Canker, Thrush, warts, or other lesions which do best with a "burning" sort of action to eliminate them from the body. Cinnamon is often implicated in the balancing of blood sugars – and used diluted could be given (especially to horses) orally for this effect. However, since there are many other oils which also perform this action, their use may be better indicated.

Cistus (Cistus ladanifer)

Cistus is also known as Labdanum, Rose of Sharon, or Rock Rose. Cistus is contained within the Twelve Oils of Ancient Scripture collection. The most common use for Cistus in the veterinary field is for conditions of blood clots and hemorrhage. Cistus is by far the leading oil indicated in conditions of internal hemorrhage (bleeding). This oil has been successfully used in many cases of internal hemorrhage and weeping after an Ovariohysterectomy or Spay surgery.

Birds & Exotics: Cistus would likely only be used in emergency situations of hemorrhage or of blood clots. 1 drop of Cistus diluted in 2 mL of V-6, would be used for oral administration. 1 drop of the diluted solution would be given orally, and repeated every 20 minutes or more until internal bleeding was controlled. Cistus can be applied neat or diluted directly to a bleeding toe nail, or broken blood feather to help stop the bleeding. Water diffusion could also be utilized, especially in situations where lung penetration is desired.

Cats: Cistus would commonly be used by adding it to a Kitty Raindrop Technique, applying via Petting (dilute or neat), added to Litteroma, or in emergency situations given orally. Depending on the severity of the bleeding, Cistus could be used orally either neat or diluted with an equal part of V-6. Whether diluted or neat, the Cistus would be given orally, one drop at a time, repeating every 20 minutes or more until the bleeding was controlled. Cistus would also be well indicated for situations of blood clots in cats, such as Saddle Thrombus. Water diffusion could also be used, especially in situations where lung penetration is desired.

Dogs & Larger: Cistus can be used in many ways; air or water diffusion, insertion into a Raindrop Technique, direct topical application (neat or diluted), via Petting (neat or diluted), and orally. In situations of internal hemorrhage approximately 3 drops per 20 pounds (9kg) of dog is given under the tongue or directly into the mouth. This can be repeated if necessary, usually about every 20 minutes. However, the frequency is usually based upon the severity of the situation. A maximum dosage has not been determined, but after repeat dosing, dogs have received approximately 7-10 drops per 20 pounds (9kg) in total oils, without concern.

Citronella (Cymbopogon nardus)

This essential oil has been widely used for insect repellant properties in animals and humans. Citronella is contained within Purification and Animal Scents Shampoo, and is now available as a single oil through Young Living. The single oil has not been used as widely, and the majority of the use of this oil has been within the products that contain it. The single oil could be added to any insect repellant recipes, and will likely be a great single oil for ear mites, mange, and other forms of external parasites and insects.

Birds & Exotics: Citronella has mainly been used within Purification.

Cats: Citronella has mainly been used within Purification with cats. If needed, Citronella could be added to the Kitty Raindrop Technique. Petting with the single oil (either diluted or neat) will likely be well tolerated, however the majority of information on the use of this oil with cats has been through its use within the blend of Purification.

Dogs & Larger: Citronella has mainly been used within Purification, however it can likely be used as a single in these animals with very little caution. Diffusion (air or water), insertion into a Raindrop Technique, direct topical application (neat or diluted), Petting applications (neat or diluted), and additions into spritzer and sprays is very appropriate.

Clary Sage (Salvia sclarea)

Clary Sage is most commonly thought of for hormonal balancing. This oil can be used in both male and female animals, and would be indicated for any condition where hormones are the suspected culprit. Situations where we use Clary Sage include excessive egg laying, poor egg production, lack of singing in Canaries, hormonal and cranky mares, excessive stud behavior in stallions, lack of cycling, false pregnancies, cystic ovaries, and more. Basically anything that is hormonally driven, Clary Sage is indicated for.

Birds & Exotics: Water diffusion is the most indicated and well used method of administration at this time. We are just beginning to use Clary Sage in water spritzer applications – generally at a dilution of 4 drops per 4 ounces (120 mL) of distilled water – misted onto the bird or animal directly. Oral administration has not been widely used at this time.

Cats: Cat friendly methods of use include water diffusion, Petting, adding to Kitty Raindrop Technique, and adding to Litteroma. Rarely would we use this oil orally in a cat.

Dogs & Larger: Water or air diffusion, direct application, Petting application, insertion into Raindrop Technique, oral administration. With oral administration – a starting amount of 1 drop per 20 pounds (9 kg) of dog, and 1 drop per 200 pounds (91 kg) of larger animals can be used. Careful monitoring for response will allow you to adjust the amounts up or down for the individual needs of the animal.

Clove (Syzygium aromaticum)

Clove oil contains a very high level of Eugenol, which is often implicated in cases of toxicity reported in small companion animals, especially in cats. Many times I have been asked to evaluate animal products which contain Clove oil. I consistently find that these products are poorly designed, and that the creator of the product has very little understanding of essential oils or of animal physiology. It seems that many companies jump on the "natural" band wagon, produce a flea and tick spray, label it for use in cats, then add poor quality, fractionated, or synthetic constituents of Clove or other essential oils. Clove oil is clearly not the enemy, as it is used successfully in the animal kingdom every day. However, the quality level of the Clove oil used, and its appropriate use for an individual species, are the most important factors with any sort of toxicity issue.

Clove oil is one of the highest (if not the highest) anti-oxidant substances on earth. Its health benefits are quite amazing. Clove is commonly used in the animal kingdom for conditions such as warts, canker, abscesses, dental disease, gastric ulcers, preventing blood clots or thinning the blood, and deworming. Clove oil is most commonly used in blends and products such as the Dentarome Toothpastes, ImmuPower, K&B Tincture, En-R-Gee, Longevity, Longevity Softgels, Melrose, PanAway, ParaFree, Thieves, Thieves Household Cleaner, Thieves Spray, and Transformation.

Diffusion of Clove oil in a home will greatly reduce human and animal responses to airborne allergens. Diffusing for a few hours prior to a "sensitive" human visitor, can leave them wondering if you even have the pets they are usually allergic to. Diffusion of the Clove containing Thieves, also imparts this wonderful benefit.

Care must be taken with Clove oil in animals who are bleeding, have a tendency to bleed, or are on any sort of anti-coagulant therapy. The over use of essential oil(s) that have anti-coagulant actions, especially in oral administration, can produce a temporary and dose dependent increase in bleeding and reduction of clotting.

Birds & Exotics: Clove is used most often within blends and products in these animals. Please see the individual product listing for more detailed information. Clove oil has been used as a single in birds with severe Papillomatosis (warts). The Clove oil was mixed into soft foods, and gradually increased in concentration. This method was used with the theory that the essential oil would come into contact the lining of the gastrointestinal tract that was affected with the papilloma. As bird digestive systems are quite different from others, the essential oils are capable of contacting the internal linings of certain parts of the digestive tract.

Cats: Clove oil is rarely used as a single oil in cats.

Dogs: Clove oil is most commonly used within other products and blends for dogs. Clove oil can be used topically (neat or diluted) for difficult abscesses or dental abscesses and pain. Clove can also be given orally for anti-coagulant actions and can also be added to various pain protocols.

Horses & Large Animals: Clove oil is used most commonly in these species, and can be used as a single or within blends. Direct topical application (often in the neat form) is used for abscesses, thrush, hoof conditions, canker, warts, and other similar conditions. Oral use of Clove oil is common in horses, and is very well tolerated. Oral Clove aids in healing and health through its massive anti-oxidant effects, and appears to decrease pain significantly when used orally. Starting with 5 drops dripped into the lip, is a fine starting point. Evaluate the response, and determine when to repeat the administration or if increased amounts are needed. Some horses have received 20 or more drops of Clove oil orally to aid with severe pain. Use caution with high oral amounts, if other anti-inflammatory drugs are being used which may decrease clotting ability.

The use of Clove, and other oral essential oils, have been used at the same time as traditional medications with no apparent interactions.

Copaiba (Copaifera reticulate/langsdorfii)

Copaiba has to be one of my favorite oils. With barely any scent or flavor, it is a powerhouse in the animal world. One of the highest anti-inflammatory oils, it replaces Non-Steroidal Anti-Inflammatory Drugs (NSAID's) in my practice regularly. The beauty of this oil is that it can be given simultaneously with the NSAID's until symptoms improve and a weaning of the NSAID can begin. Since inflammation is a component of any dis-ease, Copaiba is always indicated in a protocol.

Copaiba is wonderful to use in many conditions; arthritis, gastric ulcers, skin conditions, inflammation, gastro-intestinal disorders, pain, cystitis, urinary incontinence, urinary disorders, and more. Copaiba also appears to magnify the effects other essential oils that it is used with. This could be a direct synergistic effect, but also since all dis-ease contains inflammation, the act of the Copaiba to reduce the inflammation is a considerable contribution to healing.

Birds & Exotics: Copaiba is used in many, many ways, and is an oil that I consider an important addition to any regimen. Water diffusion can be used in open rooms, small rooms, in caging, and tented. Often 3-4 drops are added to a water-based diffuser to start. Copaiba can also be added to drinking water, starting with 1 drop in 1 liter of water, and gradually increasing as needed. Copaiba is also added to foods quite easily. Beginning with a "toothpick dip" of the essential oil added to a tablespoon of food, the amount can gradually be increased based on response. Please see the chapter How Much, How Often for a more complete explanation of how to monitor and increase or decrease amounts of essential oils used. Copaiba has also been used topically – 1 drop mixed into a tablespoon of Animal Scents Ointment, 1 drop mixed with 5 or more drops of V-6, 4-5 drops added to 4 ounces (120 mL) of distilled water and misted onto the bird or animal, added to soaking water for reptiles, as well as added to fish tanks. Application by Petting (often diluted) and transfer from perches or hands is also used. Copaiba can also be added to any Species Specific Raindrop Technique with amazing benefits and results.

Please also see the Myrrh essential oil description for more information on a Pain Recipe, which combines Copaiba, Helichrysum, and Myrrh.

Cats: Again, Copaiba is a worthy addition to any feline regimen. Situations where Copaiba is especially indicated: Cystitis, FLUTD, Inflammatory Bowel Disease, Pancreatitis, and Arthritis. Copaiba can be used in all of the previously mentioned ways for cats. Some cats may or may not drink Copaiba in their water – so this option may not work for everyone. Also, when adding Copaiba to the food of a cat, this may also be rejected. Starting with very small "toothpick" amounts, and gradually increasing the amounts they are exposed to, seems to work well for most cats, effectively getting them used to the flavor or smell that surely they detect. The most well accepted and common ways to use Copaiba for cats is with diffusion, addition to the Kitty Raindrop Technique, via Petting (neat or diluted), or by adding to Litteroma.

Dogs & Larger: All of the previously mentioned techniques and benefits apply to dogs and larger animals as well. With these animals however, we can often easily use Copaiba, and with a more direct approach. Air diffusion can also be an included method, as well as direct neat application. Dilution for these animals is needed much less often. Adding Copaiba into the Raindrop Technique is a wonderful idea.

For horses, Copaiba is an important essential oil for the replacement of harmful NSAID's which are known to promote gastric ulcer formation. Not only is Copaiba highly anti-inflammatory, but it also protects against the formation of gastric ulcers, eliminating the need for expensive ulcer guarding medications.

The following are recommendations for the oral use of Copaiba, however remember that some individuals may require more or less.
- For dogs up to 20 pounds (9 kg): 1 part of Copaiba oil can be mixed with 3 parts of V-6, and 1-2 drops of this dilution can be given twice a day, either mixed with food, given directly in the mouth, or even applied topically.
- For dogs 20-50 pounds (9-22 kg): 1 part of Copaiba oil can be mixed with 1 part V-6, and 1-2 drops of this dilution can be given twice a day.
- For dogs over 50 pounds (23 kg) generally 1 drop of undiluted Copaiba oil can be used twice a day.
- For Horses and other Large Animals: Copaiba can be used orally undiluted either directly or mixed with foods or water. Approximately 1 drop of Copaiba can be used per 100-200 pounds (45-90 kg) of animal body weight. With horses, starting with approximately 5 drops twice a day is typical.

Coriander (Coriandrum sativum)

Coriander is a lovely oil that is mainly used for diabetes, blood sugar control, metabolic syndromes, and supporting pancreatic function. It is most commonly used in horses with Cushing's, Insulin Resistance, and Metabolic Syndromes. It would also be indicated for Ferrets with insulinoma.

Close monitoring with a veterinarian is important when using any essential oil with animals receiving Insulin or oral hypoglycemic drugs. As correction of the body occurs, there may be less need for the Insulin, and a dangerous situation can occur when more Insulin is given to an animal than they currently need. The veterinarian needs to be aware that natural remedies are being used that may reduce your animal's need for diabetic medications. Even the pure action of dietary improvement in cats, has eliminated the need for Insulin in many patients. So, taking a slow and careful position with animals on these medications is important.

Birds & Exotics: Coriander oil has not been used extensively in these animals at this time. Water diffusion, and the oral use of Coriander either mixed with foods or added to water would be recommended starting places.

Cats: Coriander has not been used extensively in cats at this time. However Coriander would likely best be used via water diffusion, addition of the oil to Kitty Raindrop Technique, within Litteroma, and/or by Petting applications (dilute or neat).

Dogs: Coriander has not been used extensively in dogs at this time, however all of the methods mentioned previously can be used for dogs. Oral use of Coriander directly or in food, could start with 1 part Coriander mixed with 3 parts V-6 – with 1 drop of this solution, being given twice a day, for each 20 pounds (9 kg) of body weight. Insertion into the Raindrop Technique, Petting, and Direct Applications (neat or diluted) would also be appropriate.

Horses & Large Animals: Coriander is most commonly used in horses for blood sugar balancing. Direct topical application, insertion into Raindrop Technique, adding to food or water, and direct oral administration are most common. Starting with 1 drop per 100-200 pounds (45-90 kg) of body weight, given orally twice a day is a good starting point. Monitor with a veterinarian, and adjust accordingly based on need and response.

Cumin (Cuminum cyminum)

Cumin is not available as a single oil at this time. It is most commonly used within Detoxzyme.

Cypress (Cupressus sempervirens)

Cypress is one of the Raindrop Technique oils. It is mainly used to increase circulation in animals, and aids every condition with this quality. Resorption of bruises, improvement of circulation, and circulatory disorders are main reasons to use this oil.

Birds & Exotics: Most commonly used within Species Specific Raindrop Technique. 1 drop could also be mixed with 1 tablespoon of Animal Scents Ointment or V-6 for topical application.

Cats: The previous methods could also be used for cats, although use in cats is most commonly used within Kitty Raindrop Technique. Petting (neat or diluted), topical application (diluted 4 drops to 30 mL of V-6), and Litteroma could also be used. Ingestion of Cypress is most likely to occur from grooming after Petting or Kitty Raindrop applications.

Dogs & Larger: Any method of use of Cypress is acceptable. Insertion into Raindrop Technique, Petting (neat or diluted), air or water diffusion, direct topical application (neat or diluted), adding to drinking water, adding to foods, and direct oral use are acceptable application methods. For oral use in dogs – dilute 1 part Cypress with 5 parts V-6 – use 1 drop of this solution twice a day, for each 20 pounds (9 kg) of body weight. For horses and others starting with 1 drop per 300 pounds (135 kg) of body weight, given orally twice a day is a good starting point. Monitor responses with a veterinarian, and adjust according to individual need.

Cypress, Blue (Callitris intratropica)

This oil has mainly been used within the blends of Australian Blue, Brain Power, and Highest Potential for animals. It only recently became available as a single oil, and the anti-viral potential of this oil seems high. Conditions such as warts (papilloma), herpes, and other viral situations will likely benefit from this oil. This oil is extremely thick and takes forever to drip from the bottle. Have patience. At this time there is no information on the oral use of this oil in animals.

Birds & Exotics: 3-4 drops in a water-based diffuser is recommended.

Cats: The addition of 1 drop of Blue Cypress to the Kitty Raindrop Technique is an excellent starting point for cats. The addition to Litteroma could also be used.

Dogs & Larger: All of the previously mentioned methods can be used. Dilution of this oil by using 1 part (or drop) to 5 parts of V-6 is recommended for initial use. This dilution may then be inserted into a Raindrop Technique, applied via Petting, or applied topically.

Dill (Anethum graveolens)

Dill is used mainly for diabetes, blood sugar and insulin regulation, and for pancreatic conditions in animals. Due to the "pickle" smell associated with this oil, it is not often applied topically to animals. Dill is indicated especially in horses with Cushing's, Insulin Resistance, or Metabolic Syndrome, and is used most commonly in the oral route.

Close monitoring with a veterinarian is important when using any essential oil with animals receiving Insulin or oral hypoglycemic drugs. As correction of the body occurs, there may be less need for the Insulin, and a dangerous situation can occur when more Insulin is given to an animal than they currently need. The veterinarian needs to be aware that natural remedies are being used that may reduce your animal's need for diabetic medications. Even the pure action of dietary improvement in cats has eliminated the need for Insulin in many patients, so taking a slow and careful position with animals on these medications is important.

Birds & Exotics: Dill can be added to drinking water at 1 drop per liter, and can also be added to foods. Dill can also be added to Species Specific Raindrop Techniques. Water diffusion of dill is also acceptable, as long as the occupants of the home find it pleasant.

Cats: Dill would mainly be used by adding it to the Kitty Raindrop Technique, as long as cat and caretaker find it satisfactory. One could start by adding only one drop to the Kitty Raindrop Solution, and increasing the content slowly.

Dogs & Larger: Any method of use of Dill is acceptable, as long as the smell is not offensive to the animal caretaker. Insertion into Raindrop Technique, Petting (neat or diluted), air or water diffusion, direct topical application (neat or diluted), adding to drinking water, adding to foods, and direct oral use are acceptable application methods. For oral use in dogs – dilute 1 part Dill with 3 parts V-6 – use 1 drop of this solution twice a day, for each 20 pounds (9 kg) of body weight. For horses and others starting with 1 drop per 100-200 pounds (45-90 kg) of body weight, given orally twice a day is a good starting point. Monitor responses with a veterinarian, and adjust according to individual need.

Dorado Azul (Hyptis suaveolens)

Dorado Azul has only recently been introduced into the essential oil world. Information on the uses of this oil will likely expand as time goes on. Less information is available on the use of this oil in animals at this time, however it is likely that all properties shown in humans will also follow suit in animals. Currently Dorado Azul is found to have actions for all sorts of respiratory conditions, hormonal issues, and cancers. Conditions where Dorado Azul is especially indicated include asthma, bronchitis, pneumonia, heaves, lung cancer, and hormonal concerns.

Birds & Exotics: Recommended uses would be via water diffusion, addition into Species Specific Raindrop Technique, or by adding 1 drop into 1 tablespoon of Animal Scents Ointment or V-6 for topical application. With birds applying to perches (neat or diluted) would be an acceptable application method.

Cats: The previously mentioned application methods could be used for cats as well. The most common methods for use in cats would be via Petting (diluted or neat), addition to Kitty Raindrop Technique, or via Litteroma. For cats with asthma water diffusion with caging or tenting methods may prove helpful.

Dogs & Larger: All of the mentioned application methods can be used. Other methods of use would include air diffusion, direct topical application (neat or diluted), insertion into Raindrop Technique, adding to drinking water or food, and direct oral administration. For oral use in dogs – dilute 1 part Dorado Azul with 3 parts V-6 – use 1 drop or more of this solution twice a day, for each 20 pounds (9 kg) of body weight. For horses and others starting with 1 drop per 100-200 pounds (45-90 kg) of body weight, given orally twice a day is a good starting point. Monitor responses and adjust according to individual need.

Elemi (Canarium luzonicum)

Often described as "poor man's Frankincense", Elemi is an often overlooked essential oil. It has not been used as extensively in the animal kingdom as it likely should. More information is definitely needed on this oil, but reports have been very favorable for respiratory concerns and symptoms of Feline Herpes Virus. It is also reported to have benefits for cystitis (FLUTD), urinary issues, muscle and nerve pain, scar tissue, and the reduction of sebaceous secretions from skin. It is likely that this oil would be indicated for animals with sebaceous cysts, seborrhea oleosa (greasy flakey skin), excessive skin oil production, proud flesh, and scarring.

Birds & Exotics: Although this oil has not been used with many exotic pets at this time, it is likely that water diffusion, addition into Species Specific Raindrop Techniques, Petting with diluted oil (1 part to 3 parts), Perch applications, and similar methods are reasonable.

Cats: All of the previous methods of application can be used for cats. The most common ways to use this oil in cats would be addition to Kitty Raindrop Technique, water diffusion including tenting and caging, Petting (neat or diluted), and Litteroma.

Dogs & Larger: All of the previous methods can be utilized for these animals. The most common ways to use this oil would include water and air diffusion, insertion into Raindrop Technique, Petting (neat or diluted), and direct topical application. It is likely that oral administration of this oil is suitable for these animals as well.

Eucalyptus Blue (Eucalyptus bicostata)

This eucalyptus comes from Ecuador, and is much milder than most eucalyptus oils. It can be used more easily with asthmatics and those who are more sensitive to the respiratory responses that eucalyptus oils can produce. In animals, Eucalyptus Blue has been found to be incredibly helpful for respiratory infections and conditions, especially when there is a viral component. Eucalyptus Blue is also reported to have good insect repellant properties, however it has not yet been used extensively in animals for that purpose. This oil should not be consumed or ingested.

It is worthy to note that Eucalyptus Blue does have a "top note" that reminds many people of cat urine. This can be an unpleasant thing, and has tricked some people into thinking that their cat had been urinating in the house! An easy solution to this problem is to not diffuse the oil alone. I usually just add 1-2 drops of Eucalyptus Blue to 3-4 drops of Thieves, Purification, or another single oil that I will be diffusing in a water-based diffuser. I find these combinations to be especially remarkable for respiratory concerns of all sorts.

Birds & Exotics: Water diffusion with the mentioned recipe via open room, small room, caging, and tenting. Addition into Species Specific Raindrop Technique could also be used. Application to perches and by indirect diffusion is also possible.

Cats: Use of water diffusion as stated above is highly used. Although it is likely that Eucalyptus Blue can also be added to the Kitty Raindrop Technique or applied via Petting, a cat's grooming nature will result in the oil being ingested to some extent. Frequent use of these methods with Eucalyptus Blue may be best avoided in cats. Eucalyptus Blue can also be added to Litteroma.

Dogs & Larger: Eucalyptus Blue can be used via water or air diffusion, insertion into Raindrop Technique, Petting (neat or diluted), direct application, and mixed into various insect repelling recipes (water misting and oil misting).

Eucalyptus Globulus (Eucalyptus globulus)

Eucalyptus Globulus is indicated for use in respiratory conditions, asthma, bronchitis, fungal conditions, insect repellant, internal parasites, and flu conditions. Care should be taken when exposing an asthmatic to this oil for the first time, as it may be quite intense for them initially. Eucalyptus Globulus is very beneficial for purifying and cleansing the air.

Birds & Exotics: Water-based diffusion in an open room, small room, caging, or tenting can be used, and is especially indicated to help cleanse the air in quarantine situations. Addition into Species Specific Raindrop Technique, Petting (diluted or neat) in non-avian exotics, Indirect Diffusion, and Perch applications for birds are appropriate methods of use.

Cats: Methods of use include water-based diffusion, addition into the Kitty Raindrop Technique, Petting (neat or diluted), and Litteroma. Eucalyptus globulus has been used orally in cats for urinary tract infections, however extensive documentation for this is not available.

Dogs & Larger: All of the previously mentioned techniques can be used as well as: air diffusion, direct application (neat or diluted), insertion into Raindrop Technique, and addition into insect repellant recipes. At this time Eucalyptus Globulus has not been used extensively by the oral route in animals.

Eucalyptus Polybractea (Eucalyptus polybractea)
This oil is especially indicated for urinary tract infections, Herpes infections, respiratory conditions, and also has insect repellant properties.

Birds & Exotics: Water-based diffusion in an open room, small room, caging, or tenting can be used. Addition into Species Specific Raindrop Technique, Petting (diluted or neat) in non-avian exotics, Indirect Diffusion, and Perch applications for birds are also acceptable.

Cats: Water-based diffusion, addition into the Kitty Raindrop Technique, Petting (neat or diluted), and Litteroma can also be used.

Dogs & Larger: All of the previously mentioned techniques can be used as well as: air diffusion, direct application (neat or diluted), insertion into Raindrop Technique, and addition into insect repellant recipes. At this time Eucalyptus Polybractea has not been used extensively by the oral route in animals.

Eucalyptus Radiata (Eucalyptus radiata)
This oil is especially indicated for vaginitis, Herpes infections, asthma, bronchitis, viral respiratory conditions, and sinusitis. It is especially effective against Herpes when combined with Bergamot. Eucalyptus Radiata is also beneficial for purifying and cleansing the air.

Birds & Exotics: Water-based diffusion in an open room, small room, caging, or tenting can be used, and especially to help cleanse the air in quarantine situations. Addition into Species Specific Raindrop Technique, Petting (diluted or neat) in non-avian exotics, Indirect Diffusion, and Perch applications for birds are also acceptable.

Cats: Water-based diffusion, addition into the Kitty Raindrop Technique, Petting (neat or diluted), and Litteroma can also be used.

Dogs & Larger: All of the previously mentioned techniques can be used as well as: air diffusion, direct application (neat or diluted), and insertion into Raindrop Technique. At this time Eucalyptus Radiata has not been used extensively by the oral route in animals.

Fennel (Foeniculum vulgare)

Fennel essential oil is commonly used in animals for diabetes, blood sugar balancing, hormone balancing, intestinal parasites, urinary tract infection, stimulating milk production, and for gastrointestinal concerns. It is most commonly used within the blend Di-Gize, and is also found in Dragon Time, ICP, Juva Flex, K&B Tincture, Mister, ParaFree, Power Meal, and SclarEssence. There is a cautionary statement in the EODR against the use of Fennel in those with epilepsy. Although this precaution is wise to adhere to, in practice many animals with seizure conditions have used the products and blends that contain Fennel. The use of Fennel as a single oil or in an aggressive manner, is best avoided in animals with seizure conditions.

Birds & Exotics: Fennel has most commonly been used within Di-Gize in these animals. Fennel can be used by water diffusion, addition to drinking water (1 drop per liter of water), addition into foods, and addition to Species Specific Raindrop Technique. 1 drop of Fennel can be added to 1 tablespoon of Animal Scents Ointment or V-6 and applied sparingly to feet, skin, or mammary areas. Perch applications could also be used for birds.

Cats: Fennel can be used as stated previously. Methods most commonly used for cats would be addition to Kitty Raindrop Technique, Litteroma, and Petting (neat or diluted). Oral use in cats is commonly accomplished by the use of Di-Gize, and not with Fennel as a single oil.

Dogs & Larger: Fennel can be used in all of the ways stated, as well as direct application (neat or diluted), insertion into Raindrop Technique, and by oral administration. For lactating animals, Fennel can be included in various udder washes and teat dip recipes for easy and routine exposure to the oil and to increase milk production. Large animals can easily accommodate more concentrated applications of Fennel oil. Unless milk is contaminated with the essential oil itself, residual flavor of the essential oil does not transfer into the milk. For oral use in dogs – dilute 1 part Fennel with 10 parts V-6 – use 1 drop or more of this solution twice a day, for each 20 pounds (9 kg) of body weight. For horses and others starting with 1 drop per 500 pounds (225 kg) of body weight, given orally twice a day is a good starting point. Monitor responses and adjust according to individual need.

Frankincense (Boswellia carteri)

Frankincense of the carteri variety is often referred to as "regular Frankincense" as opposed to Sacred Frankincense. Frankincense is likely one of the most important and well used oils in the animal world. It has been used with every species, in almost every way imaginable. It is incredibly safe, well tolerated, versatile, and effective. Major conditions in which Frankincense is used include all forms of cancer, tumors, cysts, behavioral conditions, depression, brain disorders, seizures, immune system stimulation and regulation, autoimmune disorders, DNA repair, and more. Frankincense is considered a "life force" oil and has been used extensively in critical cases in our veterinary hospital. The use of Frankincense in times of transition and death is incredibly helpful to animal and caretaker.

Often times with cases of cancer, animals present to my practice at a point we would refer to as "end-stage." This means that the cancer is so progressed, that it is unlikely that the body can recover from the dis-ease. When owners desire to try everything, and to use aggressive methods in an attempt to reverse the cancer, the use of Frankincense oil is high. For these often terminal animals, even if the Frankincense was unable to aid their body in a complete reversal of the condition, it is always reported by the animal caretaker to have eased the transition tremendously.

Frankincense has been used in newborns of every species, even when they are only minutes old. We have literally had Frankincense on the towels and hands of those who are handed a puppy from a C-Section procedure – making Frankincense one of the first things they are exposed to once they are removed from their mother's womb. It is purely magnificent to be able to change an abnormal birth situation, into a thing of beauty. Anointing the umbilical cords of kittens, puppies, foals, calves, and chickens has become routine for our farm. Diffusing Frankincense can be performed around eggs, nests, and birthing areas to further expose animals. It is a general guideline for me, that if it is a baby of any sort, Frankincense should be included in its life!

Frankincense also appears to magnify and enhance the effects of other essential oils when they are used concurrently. Frankincense is also found in many essential oil blends and products, which can be utilized in animals: 3 Wise Men, Abundance, Acceptance, Awaken, Believe, Brain Power, ClaraDerm, CortiStop Women's, Exodus II, Forgiveness, Gathering, Gratitude, Harmony, Highest Potential, Humility, ImmuPower, Inspiration, Into the Future, KidScents Tender Tush, Longevity, Longevity Softgels, Progessence Plus Serum, Transformation, Trauma Life, and Valor. The most noteworthy blends that are used to gain the medical benefits of Frankincense are 3 Wise Men, Brain Power, ImmuPower, Longevity, and Longevity Softgels.

Birds & Exotics: Frankincense has been used in many, many ways in all animals: butterflies have dipped their feet into it, honey bees have had cotton ball diffusers placed within their bee hives, birds have been misted with water-based solutions, fish have had it added to their aquariums, it has been ingested in large amounts in many species, rabbits and guinea pigs have been pet with it, and it has been diffused in a variety of ways.

Common ways to use Frankincense in Birds & Exotics are: adding 1 drop (or more) to 1 liter of drinking water, adding 1 drop (or more) to 1 tablespoon of food, adding to a Species Specific Raindrop Technique, water misting with 4 drops (or more) added to 4 ounces (120 mL) of distilled water, via Petting (neat or diluted), direct application (neat or diluted), indirect diffusion, and water diffusion. Frankincense remains an incredibly safe essential oil, that can be used in high amounts in these species, however, it is still advisable to start with lower amounts and gradually increase the amount of Frankincense that the animal is exposed to. For example, start with diffusing 3-4 drops in a water-based diffuser in an open room. If the exotic animal tolerates that, you can either increase the amounts of drops added, increase the length of exposure, or move towards a caging or tenting situation of diffusion. Likewise with a water spritzer, begin with 4 drops in a recipe, and you can gradually increase to 5-6 drops in the recipe if the condition warrants it.

Cats: All of the previous methods can be used with cats. The most common ways Frankincense is used with cats are: Addition into the Kitty Raindrop Technique, via Petting (neat or diluted), Litteroma, water diffusion including caging and tenting, mixing into foods, giving orally via capsule, giving directly in the mouth (they enjoy this less), direct application to tumors (neat or diluted), direct application to skin (neat or diluted), and ingestion via grooming after application of Petting. For oral use of Frankincense in cats, you will likely start with very small amounts of oil (toothpick dip) mixed into canned or moist foods. As the cat accepts the lesser amount, you can gradually increase how much is added to the food. Smaller empty gel capsules can be obtained from health food stores and pharmacies, and can be filled with Frankincense to be "pilled" into the cat. Directly dripping the Frankincense into the mouth of a cat can be done, however they often drool and salivate profusely. With most cats, the act of "pilling" or dripping an essential oil into their mouth, is not likely to be greeted with joy for long.

For cats who need a more chronic and consistent exposure to Frankincense, we may need to use methods that they find friendly, or you will soon have your cat continually hiding under the bed when they see you coming. In severe conditions, such as cancer, layering your methods of application can be the best way to ensure higher levels of "cat friendly" exposure. For example a cat could have water diffusion, Petting, Litteroma, Kitty Raindrop with Frankincense, tolerated amounts mixed into foods, and topical applications. That being said, when the situation calls for it, I will gladly force a capsule of Frankincense "down my cats throat" whether they like it or not. Yet, if I can achieve results with multiple cat friendly methods, eliminating the need to use the "pilling route" for my cat, all the better.

For oral use of Frankincense in cats, start with very low amounts if you are planning to mix it into food or drinking water, and gradually increase amounts as your cat tolerates it. When placing into a capsule or directly dripping into the mouth, start with 1 drop (neat or diluted), once or twice a day. Depending on the severity of the situation, more Frankincense may be chosen to be given straightaway. Many cats enjoy eating raw organic coconut oil, and we have been successful in mixing some essential oils into this for direct ingestion or by mixing it into foods for consumption. Maximum levels for Frankincense use has not been established at this time, however working up to a level of 10 drops (or more) per day of ingested Frankincense would be acceptable in severe cases of cancer. It is ideal to split the daily amount into 3-4 doses throughout the day. Administering these levels of oral Frankincense is most likely to be achieved only with capsule administration.

Dogs & Larger: All of the previous methods discussed can be used for dogs, horses, and large animals. Air diffusion in all methods including caging and tenting can also be used. Dogs are much more likely to eat higher levels of Frankincense within their foods, and are much easier to give a capsule to. Horses can have their bottom lip pulled out, and the oil dumped into the little pocket that is created. Frankincense is well used when inserted into the Raindrop Technique, and direct neat application of the oil to tumors and skin is generally tolerated in large amounts.

With tumors, it is important to recognize that many will look much worse before they look better. Tumors such as Sarcoids in horses or Mast Cell Tumors in dogs may go through stages of death and irritation before they resolve. For the most part, I am comfortable with this happening, however it solely depends on if the animal itself is comfortable with the event. Tumors growing, itching, weeping, burning, or being chewed at may warrant a lighter approach until the body can catch up with the rejection of the cancer. Though, this decision is best made on an individual basis and with veterinary advice regarding the severity of the condition at hand.

For oral use of Frankincense, extremely large amounts have been consumed safely in dogs and larger animals. I often determine the amount of Frankincense that will be ingested based more on the owner's financial budget, and less on the actual maximum amount that can be consumed. For dogs with cancer, a general guideline would be to strive towards ingestion of at least 10 drops per 20 pounds (9 kg) of body weight twice a day. Although, there have been many dogs who have easily consumed over 5 times this amount without toxicity. This sort of aggressive protocol is of course mainly used for severe cases of cancer. With more stable and less aggressive forms of cancer or tumors, starting with low amounts and gradually increasing the amounts given until effects are seen is suggested. Although very large volumes of Frankincense can be administered, some situations respond to quite low amounts, and it would be wasteful to use excessively more essential oil than is actually needed for an animal.

For oral use of Frankincense in large animals – the sky is the limit. I doubt that we could reach a maximum amount that could be given. A general guideline would be to strive to have 10 drops per 100-200 pounds (45-90 kg) of body weight ingested per day for severe cases of cancer. Thankfully, we see responses in animals with much less being administered, so please never feel that being able to give only one or two drops per day is not a worthwhile endeavor. I have been amazed at what only one drop of Frankincense can do for a huge animal such as a horse. Never underestimate the power of a drop of oil.

Frankincense, Sacred (Boswellia sacra)

Sacred Frankincense is relatively new to the world of Frankincense oil, but has already been used quite extensively in animals. This version of Frankincense seems to be a bit more powerful than "regular" Frankincense Carteri and certainly much more emotionally and spiritually connecting. For some animals, it can be a bit overwhelming and we will turn to the use of Frankincense Carteri for these individuals. For budgetary reasons, we often select Frankincense Carteri instead of Sacred Frankincense when large amounts of Frankincense are anticipated to be used. In birds and exotic pets, Carteri has had more extensive use – so for these animals it is often chosen first. There is much research being done with Sacred Frankincense oil, and the future holds great promise in many ways. Sacred Frankincense has been used in all of the methods and doses mentioned for Frankincense Carteri, please see those instructions for more detailed use information.

Galbanum (Ferula gummosa)

This essential oil has not been used extensively as a single oil in animals. It is most commonly used in the blends Exodus II, Gathering, Gratitude, and Highest Potential. Water diffusion of this oil would be acceptable for all animals.

Geranium (Pelargonium graveolens)

Geranium is an oil which can be used for many purposes in the animal kingdom. Hepatitis, Fatty Liver Disease, skin conditions, ringworm, Herpes infections, hormone balancing, liver and pancreas stimulation, and dilation of bile ducts for liver detoxification. Emotionally it helps to release negative memories and eases nervous tension. Used less as a single it is widely used in blends and products such as Acceptance, Animal Scents Ointment, Animal Scents Shampoo, Awaken, Clarity, EndoFlex, Envision, Gathering, Gentle Baby, Harmony, Highest Potential, Joy, Juva Flex, JuvaTone, K&B Tincture, Release, SARA, Trauma Life, and White Angelica.

Birds: In birds, Geranium by itself has not been used widely at this time, however in conditions such as Fatty Liver Disease, Geranium is likely to be of aid. Birds have been more consistently exposed to Geranium through the water-based diffusion of blends and with the topical use of Animal Scents Ointment. The following methods are suggestions for use in birds, however, please note that these methods have not been used in high numbers of birds at this time. For birds water-based diffusion of Geranium

(1-4 drops in a diffuser) or the addition of 1 drop to 1 tablespoon of Animal Scents Ointment or V-6 for the application to feet or perches would be very appropriate. It is also likely that this oil can be used in drinking water (1 drop per liter) or mixed into foods. The use of Geranium within a water spritzer is likely to be very successful. Starting with only 1 drop of Geranium to 4 ounces (120 mL) of distilled water, or with adding 1 drop of Geranium to the Feather Spray Recipe would be recommended starting points. The addition of Geranium to an Avian Raindrop Technique would also be appropriate. Before using Geranium in birds, it is first recommended to have explored the use of other more commonly administered oils.

Exotics: All of the previously mentioned methods could be used with exotic pets as well. Exotic pets have certainly been exposed to Geranium in much higher levels than birds, and have a wider range of options for its use. These methods are recommended: water-based diffusion, addition into Species Specific Raindrop Technique, Petting (neat or diluted), addition into drinking water (1 drop per liter), addition into foods, direct application (neat or diluted – especially in cases of ringworm), water spritzers, and adding to aquariums and soaking water. Where oral ingestion is considered, dilute 1 drop of Geranium oil to 2 mL of V-6 or Coconut Oil. Using the diluted solution, give 1 drop once to twice a day, starting with very low amounts, and gradually increasing to the recommended amount. This can be mixed into foods or given directly when possible.

Cats: All of the previously mentioned techniques could be used with cats. The most common ways Geranium would be used for a feline are: water diffusion, addition into the Kitty Raindrop Technique, Petting (dilute or neat), Litteroma, and direct application (neat or diluted) especially in cases of ringworm. Oral administration could be used in severe cases of Fatty Liver Disease, and would begin with the same recommendations as stated above, however working up to an amount of 5 drops (or more) of the diluted solution, given 2-4 times a day. Oral administration of Geranium has not been used widely in cats at this time, and careful monitoring with a veterinarian is recommended.

Dogs & Larger: All of the previously mentioned methods can be used for these animals as well. Stronger concentrations of Geranium can easily be used for direct topical application, especially in cases of ringworm where neat application is recommended. Insertion into Raindrop Technique and oral administration is recommended for Herpes infections and other severe conditions. For oral use in dogs – dilute 1 part Geranium with 10 parts V-6 – use 1 drop or more of this solution twice a day, for each 20 pounds (9 kg) of body weight. For horses and others starting with 1 drop per 500 pounds (225 kg) of body weight, given orally twice a day is a good starting point. Monitor responses and adjust according to individual need.

Ginger (Zingiber officinale)

Ginger is most commonly used within the blend of Di-Gize in animals. The single oil is most commonly used for nausea (especially car sickness) in dogs. It is important to note that Ginger also contains anti-coagulant properties. Care must be taken with Ginger oil in animals who are bleeding, have a tendency to bleed, or are on any sort of anti-coagulant therapy. The over use of essential oil(s) that have anti-coagulant actions, especially in oral administration, can produce a temporary and dose dependent, increase in bleeding and reduction of clotting.

Birds & Exotics: Ginger is mainly used within the blend Di-Gize.

Cats: Ginger is mainly used within the blend Di-Gize.

Dogs: Ginger is mainly used within Di-Gize for dogs, however Ginger as a single oil is used commonly for Car Sickness, and appears to have a stronger effect for this condition that Di-Gize alone. Most commonly Ginger is either applied to the stomach via Petting (neat or diluted), diffused directly or indirectly (for example placing a few drops on a cotton ball inside of the transport crate), or by direct oral administration. Dripping the oil directly into the mouth (neat or diluted) seems to be the most effective method for nausea. For oral use in dogs – dilute 1 part Ginger with 2 parts V-6 – use 1 drop or more of this solution, for each 20 pounds (9 kg) of body weight. For dogs who are approximately 50 pounds (23 kg) and larger, generally one neat drop is given orally. Oral administration can be repeated multiple times as needed for nausea, generally every 10-20 minutes. Due to the anti-coagulant potential of Ginger, a maximum dose of 3 neat drops per 20 pounds of dog should likely be followed. Needless to say, if you have approached this recommended maximum of drops, and your dog is still nauseated, a different oil is well indicated!

Horses & Larger: Ginger is most commonly used within the blend Di-Gize in these animals, however can be used as a single when desired. Ginger would most commonly be used by addition to drinking water, addition to foods, insertion into Raindrop Technique, Petting (neat or diluted), direct topical application, and direct oral ingestion. For ingestion, 1 drop per 500 pounds (225 kg) of body weight, given orally twice a day is a good starting point. Monitor responses and adjust according to individual need.

Goldenrod (Solidago Canadensis)

Goldenrod is not commonly used for animals at this time. However, its properties indicate it may be helpful for Fatty Liver Disease, liver conditions, urinary tract and bladder conditions, hypertension, and as a diuretic. Although the use of other more commonly used oils would be recommended first, Goldenrod is an oil that could be called upon for difficult or non-responsive cases. Working closely with a veterinarian to monitor blood work and responses, when using uncharted essential oils is wise.

Birds & Exotics: Goldenrod has not been used extensively in these species at this time. In cases where other essential oils have not yielded sufficient results, or where the severity of the case calls for the addition of this essential oil, the following methods would be appropriate to use: addition of 1 drop into Species Specific Raindrop Technique, water-based diffusion, addition to drinking water (1 drop per liter), addition to foods, and Petting (diluted) in non-avian exotics. Where oral ingestion is considered, dilute 1 drop of Goldenrod oil to 2 mL of V-6 or Coconut Oil. Using the diluted solution, give 1 drop once to twice a day, starting with very low amounts, and gradually increasing to the recommended amount. This can be mixed into foods or given directly when possible.

Cats: The same comments as noted for Birds & Exotics is true for cats as well. The following methods would be most suitable for use in cats when needed: adding to the Kitty Raindrop Technique, Petting (neat or diluted), water diffusion, and Litteroma. Oral administration can also be attempted with the same directions as noted for Birds & Exotics, however working up to 5 drops of the diluted solution twice a day is reasonable. There may be some cats who will consume the diluted oil within food or coconut oil, and some may tolerate direct oral administration, however it is likely that capsule administration will be necessary.

Dogs & Larger: Although Goldenrod has not commonly been used in these animals, we are fortunate that dogs and larger animals can easily be transitioned into the use of more novel oils, by scaling their usage to match human recommendations. Insertion into Raindrop Technique, Petting (neat or diluted), adding to foods, adding to drinking water, and oral administration can be used. For oral use in dogs – dilute 1 part Goldenrod with 10 parts V-6 – use 1 drop or more of this solution twice a day, for each 20 pounds (9 kg) of body weight. For horses and others starting with 1 drop per 500 pounds (225 kg) of body weight, given orally twice a day is a good starting point. Monitor responses and adjust according to individual need.

Grapefruit (Citrus paradisi)

Grapefruit oil is indicated for use in animals for conditions such as tumors, fatty tumors (lipomas), cancer, obesity, detoxification, diuresis, fluid retention, liver conditions, cognitive dysfunction, senility, and anxiety. Grapefruit is a photosensitizing oil, so application is recommended to sites that will not be exposed to direct sunlight or full spectrum UV lights within 24 hours. For example, in horses, the use of Grapefruit oil can be designated to the underside of the belly – or in the poetic words of Cherie Ross, "Put it where the sun don't shine." Because of fur and feathers, we have yet to witness a photosensitive side effect with the use of these oils, but that is not to say it cannot happen. We are better off to heed the warning, than to regret it later.

Another common question regarding Grapefruit oil is if it interacts with medications. Many people are told to avoid drinking grapefruit juice or eating grapefruit while they are on prescription medications. It does appear that the Grapefruit Essential Oil is different in action than the meat or juice of the fruit itself, and I have known many humans and animals who use the oil right alongside of other medications with no ill effects. In veterinary medicine, it is actually a recommended practice to strategically use grapefruit juice to effectively reduce the amounts of prescription drugs that are needed for a patient. If there are other essential oils that will yield the same benefits as Grapefruit oil, we can certainly use the alternative oil choices first, for those who are concerned. However, if indicated, I have no reservation on using Grapefruit oil together with prescription medications. Working with a veterinarian and monitoring the condition closely is advisable.

Birds & Exotics: Grapefruit oil is used in the following ways: water diffusion, addition to drinking water (1 drop or more per liter), addition to foods, addition into Species Specific Raindrop Technique, adding to aquarium or soaking water, water misting (4 drops or more in 4 ounces (120 mL) of distilled water, application to perches (avian), Petting (neat or diluted, non-avian), direct application (neat or diluted, especially to fatty tumors), and direct ingestion when desired (rodents, ferrets, and such licking the oil off of our hands). For oral ingestion, there really has not been a maximum amount witnessed. For most animals, the strong taste of the essential oil will be the limiting factor on how much we add to food or water. Starting with small amounts (toothpick dips) and gradually increasing the amount based on taste preference and response is recommended.

Cats: All of the methods mentioned for Birds & Exotics can be used for cats, and some cats may drink or ingest Grapefruit oil as well. Cat friendly methods for the use of Grapefruit oil include: addition to Kitty Raindrop Technique, Litteroma, Petting (neat or diluted), and water diffusion. Keep in mind that with the Petting method, cats will ingest certain levels of the essential oil when they groom.

Dogs & Larger: All of the methods discussed can be used as well as; insertion into Raindrop Technique, direct application (neat or diluted), air diffusion, and oral administration. Higher concentrations of Grapefruit oil are likely to be tolerated, and generally can easily be given in drinking water, foods, or NingXia Red. For oral use in dogs – 1 drop or more can be given twice a day, for each 20 pounds (9 kg) of body weight. Start with a smaller amount, and gradually increase as needed. For horses and others starting with 1 drop per 100-200 pounds (45-90 kg) of body weight, given orally twice a day is a good starting point. Monitor responses and adjust according to individual need.

Helichrysum (Helichrysum italicum)

Helichrysum is one of my favorite oils. It truly is miraculous and worthy of use in almost every condition. You will never be wrong selecting Helichrysum, and it has been used in many ways, in all forms of animals. Helichrysum is indicated in cases of blood clots as an anticoagulant, but is also used in cases of hemorrhage, bleeding, and bruising. This is the interesting thing with many natural remedies, is that they tend to bring the body to a point of homeostasis. Whatever is needed within the body appears to be honored. Much like eating food that nourishes certain aspects of health, we are merely providing the body with the tools it needs for health, and the body mainly decides on what to do with those tools, and when.

In animals, Helichrysum is especially indicated for nerve regeneration and neurologic conditions, hearing impairment, circulatory and blood vessel disorders, heart disease, blood clots, liver disease, hypertension, chelation of chemicals, toxin exposure, poisoning, vaccination detoxification, healing of lacerations and wounds, for control of pain, and as a topical anesthetic. There is not much that Helichrysum does not contribute to, and it falls into a category of "must have" oils in my opinion. It is worthy to note that Helichrysum is found in blends and products such as Aroma Life, Awaken, Brain Power, ClaraDerm, Forgiveness, GLF, Juva Cleanse, Juva Flex, M-Grain, PanAway, and Trauma Life. When the single of Helichrysum is not at hand, the use of PanAway for example, is an excellent way to gain access to the healing power of Helichrysum.

Helichrysum is the primary oil used orally for pain control in animals. Often, its use alone is adequate, however combining it with Copaiba and/or Myrrh creates an enormous synergistic effect for pain management, and is well tolerate by many species.

Diffusing Helichrysum in situations of lung bruising or trauma (pulmonary contusions), such as in animals who have been hit by a car, has proved incredibly helpful in recovery. Caging or Tenting with an air diffuser to gain penetration of the lung tissues, works wonderfully. Combining this diffusion with oils that also aid in oxygenation, reduction of inflammation, and healing (Cedarwood, Copaiba, Frankincense) provides nothing short of near miraculous results in our veterinary hospital. I have witnessed severe lung trauma reverse in 12 hours, where typically bruising of the lungs would continue to worsen for the first 24 hours.

Birds & Exotics: Helichrysum has been used in many ways in all species. Water-based diffusion (with caging or tenting), addition to Species Specific Raindrop Technique, in drinking water (1 drop or more per liter), in foods, directly oral, in water spritzers (starting with 1 drop per 4 ounces (120 mL) of distilled water, and working up to 4 or more drops), mixed into Animal Scents Ointment (1 or more drops in 1 tablespoon), adding 1-4 drops into the Feather Spray Recipe, adding 1-5 drops into 2 mL of V-6 and using for topical application, via Petting (neat or diluted for non-avian species), via Perches and indirect exposure, in soaking water and aquariums, and directly topical (neat or diluted). For oral consumption, often 2 drops is added to 2 mL of V-6, and 1 drop or more of this diluted solution is given orally, usually 2-3 times a day. This diluted solution can also be mixed into foods as well. The animal is monitored for response, and given repeated doses as needed. The concentration of the solution can be increased as needed as well. Many respond to this initial dilution, and maximum limits of Helichrysum ingestion have not been determined. It does appear that there is an extremely wide range of safety with this oil.

Case Example: A bird with a broken wing was given a solution of 2 drops of Helichrysum, 1 drop of Copaiba, and 1 drop of Myrrh in 2 mL of V-6 for pain management. Approximately 1 drop of this solution was administered by syringe, directly into its mouth, 2-3 times a day. The bird experienced so much comfort from this remedy, that traditional pain medications were not needed, and the little bird was difficult to keep quiet and rested! Please also see the Myrrh essential oil description for more information on this Pain Recipe.

Cats: All of the previously mentioned techniques can be used with cats as well. Helichrysum does appear to be best tolerated when diluted for direct topical use in cats. Petting (neat or diluted) will result in some ingestion of the oil while grooming. Litteroma is well tolerated, as is addition into the Kitty Raindrop Technique. When pain management is needed for cats, often 1 neat drop is given orally for an average sized cat. Even kittens weighing less than 1 pound (0.5 kg) have received 3 drops of neat Helichrysum orally at one time, with no ill effects and showing only wonderful pain control and healing. Cats will generally salivate in response to the oral administration of the oil. This is fairly expected, although not all cats do this.

Case Example: A cat who had eaten a poisonous plant, had 1 drop of Helichrysum given orally, every 3 hours. The cat had previously been hospitalized at a veterinary clinic with severe kidney failure, and after 1 week with no response to intensive treatments, was sent home to die. The cat not only received Helichrysum, but also NingXia Red, K&B, and Sulfurzyme – and made a complete recovery!

Dogs & Larger: Helichrysum can be used in all of the ways mentioned previously as well as insertion into Raindrop Technique, direct topical application (neat or diluted), and oral administration. For oral use in dogs – 1 drop or more can be given twice a day, for each 20 pounds (9 kg) of body weight. Start with a smaller amount, and gradually increase as needed. For horses and others starting with 1 drop per 100-200 pounds (45-90 kg) of body weight, given orally twice a day is a good starting point. Monitor responses and adjust according to individual need.

Hyssop (Hyssopus officinalis)

Hyssop has many indications for use in animals, and is generally regarded as a purging oil. A psalm in the Bible states "Purge me with hyssop, and I shall be clean: wash me, and I shall be whiter than snow." This certainly helps many to remember the power and cleansing activity of Hyssop oil, obviously recognized since ancient times. Hyssop tends to be a mild oil topically, but when taken internally can be quite aggressive.

Hyssop is indicated whenever you would like to "expel" something from the body – whether it is a toxin, poison, respiratory mucus, parasites, viruses, or bacteria. Common conditions that would call for the single oil of Hyssop include snake bites, tick paralysis, poisoning, parasites, and viral infections. There is a cautionary statement in the EODR to avoid the use of Hyssop with epilepsy. Although we have not witnessed any problems with the use of Hyssop containing blends in animals known to have seizures, it may be best to avoid the single in these animals when possible.

Hyssop is most commonly used within the blends of Awaken, Egyptian Gold, Exodus II, GLF, Harmony, ImmuPower, Relieve It, and White Angelica.

Birds & Exotics: Hyssop as a single has not been used commonly in these species. The most recommended uses of Hyssop would be to include the oil in a Species Specific Raindrop Technique or to diffuse in a water-based diffuser. In cases of severe need, water misting (1 drop to 4 ounces), adding to drinking water (1 drop per liter), adding to foods (diluted), Petting (diluted), and diluted topical application would be appropriate methods to try – however it is important to recognize that these techniques have not been used commonly for these animals at this time, and close veterinary monitoring would be important. For use in food, diluting 1 drop of Hyssop into 2 mL of V-6 would be advised, and using a toothpick dip or more in 1 tablespoon of food, twice a day would be recommended.

Cats: The most common ways to use Hyssop in cats is by addition to the Kitty Raindrop Technique, Petting (neat or diluted), water diffusion, and by Litteroma. In cases of severe need (poisonous snake bites…) oral use of Hyssop can be considered if other methods are not yielding enough results.

For oral use 5 drops of Hyssop are added to 2 mL of V-6, and 1 drop or more of this dilution is given orally, twice to three times per day. Careful veterinary monitoring is suggested.

Dogs & Larger: The most common ways to use Hyssop in these animals is by insertion into Raindrop Technique, Petting (dilute or neat), direct topical application (dilute or neat), air or water-based diffusion, direct oral administration, adding to drinking water, or adding to foods.

Generally topical methods are used first, followed by oral administration only for severe and unresponsive cases. For oral use in dogs – 5 drops of Hyssop are diluted in 1 mL of V-6. 1 drop or more of this dilution can be given twice a day, for each 20 pounds (9 kg) of body weight. Start with a smaller amount, and gradually increase as needed. For horses and others, starting with 1 drop per 500 pounds (225 kg) of body weight, given orally twice a day is a good starting point. Monitor responses and adjust according to individual need.

Jasmine (Jasminum officinale)

Jasmine is an absolute and not a true essential oil. It can be water diffused for all animals and is most commonly used within the blends of Awaken, Clarity, Dragon Time, Forgiveness, Gentle Baby, Harmony, Highest Potential, Inner Child, Into the Future, and Joy. It is most commonly used for anxiety, depression, and hormonal behavioral issues, such as cranky mare syndrome.

Birds: As a single oil, Jasmine is used via water-based diffusion in an open room. It is most commonly used within the blends that contain it.

Exotics: Jasmine as a single oil is most commonly water diffused in an open room. Applying via Petting (diluted 1 drop in 10 drops of V-6) has also been used. Jasmine is most commonly used within the blends that contain it.

Dogs & Larger: Jasmine as a single oil is most commonly water or air diffused in an open room. Petting (neat or diluted) can also be used for these animals. Jasmine is most commonly used within the blends that contain it.

ESSENTIAL OIL SINGLES

Juniper (Juniperus osteosperma and J. scopulorum)

Juniper is indicated as a digestive cleanser and stimulant, for liver conditions, kidney conditions, to promote the excretion of toxins, promote nerve regeneration, for fluid retention, and for urinary infections. Juniper is commonly used in the following blends and products; 3 Wise Men, Awaken, Cel-Lite Magic Massage Oil, Di-Gize, Dream Catcher, En-R-Gee, Grounding, Hope, Into the Future, K&B, and Ortho Ease Massage Oil.

Birds: Juniper has not been used widely in birds at this time. Water diffusion in an open or small room is the recommended method of exposure.

Exotics: Juniper has been used via water diffusion, Petting (neat or diluted), and by addition to Species Specific Raindrop Technique. Oral use of Juniper has not been established in exotic animals at this time.

Dogs & Larger: Juniper has been used via water and air diffusion, addition into Raindrop Technique, Petting (neat or diluted), direct topical application (neat or diluted), added to drinking water, added to foods, and by oral ingestion. In general, oral ingestion is reserved for when topical applications have failed to yield sufficient results. For oral use in dogs – 1 drop of Juniper is diluted in 5 drops of V-6. 1 drop or more of this dilution can be given twice a day, for each 20 pounds (9 kg) of body weight. Start with a smaller amount, and gradually increase as needed. For horses and others, starting with 1 drop per 500 pounds (225 kg) of body weight, given orally twice a day is a good starting point. Monitor responses and adjust according to individual need.

Laurus Nobilis (L. nobilis)

Laurus Nobilis is also known as Bay Laurel. Laurus Nobilis is indicated for nerve regeneration, loss of appetite, gingivitis, viral infections, as an anticonvulsant, for respiratory infections, and especially for bacterial infections with Staphylococcus, Streptococcus, and E. Coli. Laurus Nobilis is also used orally for cases of Tetanus infection. Laurus Nobilis is most commonly used in animals within the oral use of ParaFree.

Birds & Exotics: Laurus Nobilis has not been used extensively in birds or exotic animals at this time. The use of other essential oils with more extensive documentation, would be recommended prior to moving towards the use of Laurus Nobilis. A method that has been used currently is water diffusion (3-4 drops added to a diffuser, in an open room, small room, via caging, or tented). The following techniques have not been used widely, but could also be considered for use: addition to a Species Specific Raindrop Technique, addition to foods – adding a toothpick dip into 1 tablespoon of food, 1 drop per liter of drinking water, 1 drop added into the Feather Spray recipe (birds), water misting - 1 drop per 4 ounces (120 mL) of distilled water, and Petting (dilute or neat – non-avian exotics). Laurus Nobilis is likely to be helpful in cases of crop infections – both bacterial and fungal (yeast) in nature – however use of more commonly used essential oils would be advised first.

Cats: All of the methods for birds and exotics, can and have been used in cats. Other methods of feline use include oral administration (direct or in a capsule), Litteroma, and addition to Coconut Oil to rub gums affected with gingivitis. The most cat friendly methods are likely to be addition to Kitty Raindrop Technique, Litteroma, and Petting. Laurus Nobilis is most commonly used within ParaFree in cats. Laurus Nobilis has been used orally as an antibiotic for cats with urinary tract infections, is commonly applied to abscesses directly (neat or diluted), and has been used topically and orally in cases of severe autoimmune disease. The oral use of this oil is reserved for difficult and critical cases, and would be started very slowly, with less than one drop given per day, and gradually increasing in amount. 5 drops or more per day have been administered orally. Veterinary monitoring with blood work and other laboratory tests (urinalysis), is advised before, during, and after administration.

Dogs & Larger: The use of Laurus Nobilis can be much more widely used for these animals. All methods of application can be used. The most common methods include air and water diffusion, insertion into Raindrop Technique, direct topical application (dilute or neat), oral administration, use in ParaFree, addition into foods, and Petting.

For oral use in dogs – 1 drop of Laurus Nobilis can be diluted with 3 drops of V-6. 1 drop or more of this dilution can be given twice a day, for each 20 pounds (9 kg) of body weight. Start with a smaller amount, and gradually increase as needed. For horses and others, starting with 1 drop per 200 pounds (90 kg) of body weight, given orally twice a day is a good starting point. Monitor responses and adjust according to individual need.

For severe infections and conditions such as Tetanus, Laurus Nobilis has been given at a rate of 3 drops orally, 6 times per day, for animals 50 pounds (23 kg) and larger.

Lavender (Lavandula angustifolia)

Lavender is one of the most adulterated and synthetically created essential oils on the market today. Very few available Lavender oils are pure enough to be called medical grade, or qualify for use in animals. Lavender is incredibly mild and well suited for use in all species of animal. It has been used extensively in even the most fragile of creatures. Lavender is especially indicated for skin conditions, ringworm and other fungal skin infections, for muscular concerns, for calming effects, for burns and frostbite, and high blood pressure.

Birds & Exotics: Lavender can be used in many ways including; water diffusion (including caging and tenting), addition to Species Specific Raindrop Technique, in water spritzers (up to 20 drops per 4 ounces of distilled water), in soaking waters, pools, and aquariums, Petting (dilute or neat in non-avian species), applied to perches (avian), added to water (1 drop or more per liter of water), added to foods (1 drop or more per tablespoon), applied by direct topical application (dilute or neat), added to Animal Scents Ointment (1 drop or more per tablespoon), and by indirect diffusion on cotton balls and cage papers. The Feather Spray Recipe is by far the most common way to apply Lavender to birds, and is often used as the first line exposure technique for Lavender oil.

Cats: All of the mentioned methods can be used for cats. The most cat friendly methods include addition to Kitty Raindrop Technique, Petting (neat or diluted), and Litteroma.

Dogs & Larger: Lavender can be used in any method, and also is used by air diffusion and direct oral administration. The amounts of Lavender that can be applied are much higher for these animals, and often 5-10 drops (or more) will be applied topically at a time. Starting with smaller amounts, and even pre-diluted oil, is still recommended as many animals respond to lesser amounts. However, if needed, much larger quantities can be applied safely.

For oral use in dogs – 1 drop of Lavender can be diluted with 2 drops of V-6. 1 drop or more of this dilution can be given twice a day, for each 20 pounds (9 kg) of body weight. Start with a smaller amount, and gradually increase as needed. For horses and others, starting with 1 drop per 200 pounds (90 kg) of body weight, given orally twice a day is a good starting point. Monitor responses and adjust according to individual need.

Ledum (Ledum groenlandicum)

Ledum is often used in animals for it benefits to the liver. Conditions such as hepatitis, elevated liver enzymes, fatty liver disease, vaccinosis, ascites, liver cancer, and fluid retention are benefited by Ledum. Ledum is also found in GLF and Juva Cleanse.

Birds & Exotics: Ledum has not been used extensively in birds or exotic animals at this time. A method that has been used currently is water diffusion (3-4 drops added to a diffuser, in an open room, small room, via caging, or tented). The following techniques have not been used widely, but could also be considered for use when a situation calls for Ledum: addition to a Species Specific Raindrop Technique, addition to foods – adding a toothpick dip or more into 1 tablespoon of food, 1 drop per liter of drinking water, 1 drop added into the Feather Spray recipe, water misting - 1 drop per 4 ounces (120 mL) of distilled water, Petting (dilute or neat – non-avian exotics). Ledum is likely to be helpful in many forms of liver disease. Monitor cases closely with a veterinarian. It is advisable to only move towards other methods in which to use Ledum, only after water diffusion has not yielded adequate results.

Cats: Cats can use Ledum in all of the ways mentioned for Birds & Exotics. The most cat friendly methods of use include addition into Kitty Raindrop Technique, Petting (dilute or neat), and Litteroma. Oral use can be considered in severe cases, and may require direct or capsule use of the oil. Some cats may ingest Ledum in food or water, and cats will ingest the oil while grooming after Petting application. For oral use, monitoring liver values with a veterinarian is important to evaluate how much essential oil is needed. Start with a very small amount, and work your way up to 1-2 drops per day. Adjust the amount according to the individual needs and responses.

Dogs & Larger: Ledum can be used by any application method for these animals. The most common methods of use are addition to the Raindrop Technique, Petting (neat or diluted), direct topical application (neat or diluted), addition to foods, addition to water, and direct oral administration by any technique. For oral use in dogs – 1 drop of Ledum can be diluted with 2 drops of V-6. 1 drop or more of this dilution can be given two or more times a day, for each 20 pounds (9 kg) of body weight. Start with a smaller amount, and gradually increase as needed. For horses and others, starting with 1 drop per 200 pounds (90 kg) of body weight, given orally twice a day is a good starting point. Monitor responses and adjust according to individual need.

Lemon (Citrus limon)

Lemon oil is widely used in all species, and in many routes. It has a very wide safety margin. Lemon is particularly used in animals for anti-tumoral properties, immune stimulation, to increase white blood cells, for obesity and lipomas (fatty tumors), for gentle cleansing and detoxification, for anti-bacterial properties, to cleanse the air and reduce disease transmission, for urinary tract infections, hypertension, digestive issues, and anxiety. Lemon oil is also used to remove sticky substances from animals such as tree sap, medical adhesive tape, or chewing gum. I have found that by applying Lemon oil diluted in V-6 to these items, they are easily removed from an animal. Lemon is a photosensitizing oil; avoid applying to skin that will be exposed to sunlight or full spectrum UV light within 24 hours. This oil is used commonly in the Feather Spray for birds, and we have not noted a photosensitizing issue for fully feathered birds at this time. However, I would still advise caution, as many birds using the Feather Spray Recipe are missing feathers and have fully exposed skin. Caution with full and natural sunlight is more likely needed, than with the full spectrum indoor lighting commonly used for birds and reptiles.

Birds & Exotics: Lemon oil has been used in many, many ways: water diffusion (including caging and tenting), added to Species Specific Raindrop Technique, within the Feather Spray Recipe, added to drinking water (1 or more drops per liter), added to foods (1 or more drops per tablespoon), addition to Animal Scents Ointment, water spritzers (up to 20 drops per 4 ounces), Petting (diluted non-avian), and allowed to be directly ingested when animals chose to lick the oil off of hands and other items.

Cats: Lemon oil has been used for cats in all of the mentioned methods. The most cat friendly methods of use include adding to the Kitty Raindrop Technique, water diffusion, Petting (diluted), Litteroma, and direct topical application (usually diluted). Some cats will ingest Lemon oil in foods or water as described for Birds & Exotics. We have not noted photosensitivity issues for cats who are fully furred, however the recommendation to apply the oil where the sun will not contact the skin (stomach), is a wise recommendation.

Dogs & Larger: Lemon oil can be used very easily and in all methods of application for these animals. Common methods of use include insertion into Raindrop Technique, addition into foods, addition into drinking water (1 drop or more per liter for dogs), direct topical application (diluted), Petting (diluted), water and air diffusion, and direct oral administration. The amounts and concentrations of Lemon that can be applied and administered are much higher for these animals, and often 5-10 drops (or more) will be applied topically at a time.

Lemon oil applied directly to the skin, is usually best diluted (at least 1 drop per 1 drop) in V-6, Coconut Oil, Animal Scents Ointment, Cell-Lite Magic Massage Oil, or another carrier of some sort. Starting with smaller amounts or more diluted oil, is still recommended as many animals respond to lesser amounts. However, if needed, much larger quantities can be applied safely.

For insertion into Raindrop Technique, Lemon oil could be applied to the underside of the belly of Goats, Horses, and other Large Animals who may be exposed to the sun. Photosensitivity has not been noted in furred areas, but caution is still a wise idea.

For oral use in dogs – 1 drop of Lemon can be diluted with 2 drops of V-6. 1 drop or more of this dilution can be given twice a day, for each 20 pounds (9 kg) of body weight. Start with a smaller amount, and gradually increase as needed. For horses and others, starting with 1 drop per 200 pounds (90 kg) of body weight, given orally twice a day is a good starting point. Monitor responses and adjust according to individual need.

Lemongrass (Cymbopogon flexuosus)

Lemongrass is used in animals for a variety of conditions. It has powerful antifungal action, regenerates connective tissue and ligaments, improves circulation, promotes lymph flow, is anti-inflammatory, antibacterial, and anti-parasitic. It is specifically useful for bladder infections, respiratory and sinus infections, cruciate injuries, muscle injuries, Salmonella, MRSA (Methicillin Resistant Staphylococcus Aureus), fluid retention and edema, digestive issues, and parasites. Lemongrass is a rather "hot" oil when applied to animals topically, and is generally used diluted. Lemongrass is yellow in color, and will stain light and white colored animals temporarily. Lemongrass is often used in Di-Gize, En-R-Gee, ICP, Inner Child, MultiGreens, Ortho Ease Massage Oil, Ortho Sport Massage Oil, Purification, Super C, and Super Cal.

Birds: Lemongrass can be used via water-based diffusion (starting with 2 drops added to the diffuser), including caging and tenting techniques. Lemongrass can be ingested, and is generally added to foods, with one or more toothpick dips of oil being added into 1 tablespoon of soft foods. Starting with a small amount, and gradually increasing is recommended. Careful monitoring with a veterinarian, with blood work and laboratory monitoring is wise. Oral use of Lemongrass can kill normal flora of the gastrointestinal tract, and repopulation with Life 5 probiotic may be necessary after heavy use. Lemongrass is most commonly used in Purification blend with birds, and in this way has even been water misted topically. Di-Gize and MultiGreens also contain Lemongrass and are commonly used orally in birds.

Exotics: All of the methods in which we use Lemongrass for birds, can also be used for other exotics. With most non-avian exotic animals, Lemongrass can be used in many more ways. Caution is used with exotics who are "hind-gut fermenters" – as the powerful antibacterial action of Lemongrass may overwhelm their natural intestinal flora. Use of gentler essential oils is recommended for Rabbits, Guinea Pigs, and Chinchillas. Lemongrass is most commonly used within Di-Gize, Purification, and MultiGreens in exotic species (even for hind-gut fermenters). The use of these blends, or other more mild essential oils, is often suggested for exotic animals. When the use of Lemongrass is deemed necessary, the following methods would be appropriate: addition of 1 drop into Species Specific Raindrop Technique, dilution of 1 drop in 30 mL (1 ounce) of V-6 for topical application or Petting, and oral administration in foods. The same methods used for birds, should be used when diluting and adding Lemongrass to foods for exotic animals.

Cats: Lemongrass is most commonly used in Di-Gize, Purification, MultiGreens, Ortho Ease Massage Oil, and Ortho Sport Massage Oil in cats. Individual use of Lemongrass can include water diffusion, Petting (diluted), addition of 2 drops to Kitty Raindrop Technique, Litteroma (some cats may refuse this), and oral administration via capsule. For oral administration 1 drop of Lemongrass is diluted in 10 drops of V-6. Give 1 drop of the diluted solution in a small gel capsule, twice a day. Monitor responses and increase the amount given as needed for the individual. Oral administration of Lemongrass as a single oil is generally reserved for when other oils have not been effective.

Dogs & Larger: Lemongrass is commonly used in the mentioned blends and products, but is also used as a single oil commonly in these animals. The most common methods of use include; air and water diffusion, insertion into Raindrop Technique (occasionally pre-diluted), direct topical application (often diluted), Petting (neat or diluted), water and oil misting, addition into Animal Scents Ointment, and oral ingestion. For oral use in dogs – 1 drop of Lemongrass can be diluted with 3 drops of V-6. 1 drop or more of this dilution can be given twice a day, for each 20 pounds (9 kg) of body weight. Start with a smaller amount, and gradually increase as needed. For horses and others, starting with 1 drop per 200 pounds (90 kg) of body weight, given orally twice a day is a good starting point. Monitor responses and adjust according to individual need.

Marjoram (Origanum majorana)

Marjoram is one of the Raindrop Oils. Marjoram is well known as one of the "muscle" essential oils, but it is also indicated for body and joint discomfort, arthritis, respiratory conditions (expectorant and mucolytic), ringworm, muscle spasms, muscle conditions, increasing motility of the gastrointestinal tract (promotes intestinal peristalsis), fluid retention, lowering blood pressure, vasodilation, circulatory disorders, and nerve pain. Marjoram carries effects for menstrual problems and PMS in humans, which likely carries over into hormonal issues in animals. Marjoram is most commonly used in Raindrop Technique and is also found in Aroma Life, Aroma Siez, CardiaCare, Dragon Time, M-Grain, Ortho Ease Massage Oil, R.C., and Super Cal.

Birds: Marjoram is most commonly used in birds by water diffusion (including caging and tenting), in the use of Avian Raindrop Technique, by addition to water (1 drop per liter), addition to foods (1 toothpick dip to 1 drop added per tablespoon of food), Perch applications, indirect diffusion, and by mixing 1 drop into 1 tablespoon of Animal Scents Ointment for light application to non-feathered areas. Marjoram is especially helpful for crop infections, crop stasis, respiratory conditions, excessive egg laying, excessive sexual drive, and hormonal issues in birds. Starting with diffusion alone, is often enough to give benefits. Advancing to more intensive exposure is generally used after diffusion has not proven to be effective enough. Marjoram has not been added to a water spritzer at this time.

Exotics: Marjoram can be used in all of the methods discussed for birds, as well as by Petting (dilute or neat), and direct topical application (generally diluted, except for ringworm where neat application is more likely). It is likely that Marjoram could be added to the soaking water of reptiles, turtles, and other zoo animals for muscular concerns, fungal infections, and to promote intestinal activity. Starting with very small amounts (a toothpick dip) of Marjoram added to the water would be advisable, then gradually increasing the amount of exposure.

Cats: Marjoram is most commonly used within the Kitty Raindrop Technique. Other cat friendly methods of use include Petting (dilute or neat), addition to Animal Scents Ointment, Litteroma, water diffusion, and direct topical application (generally used diluted first, but may increase to neat application as in cases of ringworm).

It is unlikely to be necessary to administer Marjoram orally, but it can be done. If a cat was willing to ingest Marjoram in food, this is an option. Starting with small amounts, as described for birds and exotics, is recommended. It is likely that the cat will refuse eating the Marjoram far before a problematic dosage could ever be reached. For direct oral administration via capsule, 1 drop of Marjoram can be diluted in 10 drops of V-6. 1 drop of this diluted solution can be given in a small gel capsule, twice a day. Monitor responses and increase the amount given as needed for the individual. Oral administration of Marjoram would generally be reserved for when other application methods or other oils have not been effective.

Dogs & Larger: Marjoram can be used in all of the previously mentioned methods. In dog and larger animals, Marjoram is most commonly used within the Raindrop Technique, by Petting (neat or diluted), by water or air diffusion, by direct topical application (neat or diluted), by adding into Animal Scents Ointment, Animal Scents Shampoo, or into other carriers, by adding into soaking or swimming water, and by oral administration when other methods have not been adequate or it is deemed necessary. For oral use in dogs – 1 drop of Marjoram can be diluted with 3 drops of V-6. 1 drop or more of this dilution can be given twice a day, for each 20 pounds (9 kg) of body weight. Start with a smaller amount, and gradually increase as needed. For horses and others, starting with 1 drop per 200 pounds (90 kg) of body weight, given orally twice a day is a good starting point. Monitor responses and adjust according to individual need.

Melaleuca Alternifolia (Melaleuca alternifolia)

Melaleuca is likely to be the most controversial essential oil used in animals. Also known as Tea Tree Oil, this oil became popular quickly, which spurred an abundance of poor quality, contaminated, and synthetically created "oils" to flood the consumer market very quickly. It is true that poor quality Melaleuca "essential oil" has indeed killed cats. Cases of toxicity that have enough data to trace and research the events at hand, have always revealed very poor grade and synthetic essential oils or their gross misuse. In one case, a bottle of essential oil was spilled, and a cat came into contact with the spillage. The cat seizured the next day and died. The brand was a basic "over-the-counter" variety that can be purchased in most health food stores.

In contrast, a feline patient presented to our veterinary clinic for evaluation prior to an essential oil protocol being started. Blood work was obtained, and this cat proceeded to receive 4 drops of Young Living Melaleuca Alternifolia, directly into its mouth, twice a day. Blood work was re-evaluated after one week of administration and was completely normal. This is not to say that every cat could handle an administration of this intensity; however, it is a very interesting contrast medically.

Melaleuca is also contained within several blends and products, to which many cats are exposed to on a very regular basis: Animal Scents Ointment, ClaraDerm, Melrose, ParaFree, Purification, Rehemogen, and Rose Ointment. No toxicity has been noted from use of these products.

ESSENTIAL OIL SINGLES

A note regarding toxicity versus detoxification: I am of the firm belief that when quality, natural essential oils are used some "reactions" are purely symptoms of detoxification. Occasionally, the over-use or inappropriate use of an oil can cause soft stools, poor appetite, respiratory signs, skin irritations, redness of the skin, or hair loss. When used correctly, Melaleuca alternifolia can indeed be used in cats, and other animals successfully.

Melaleuca Alternifolia is antibacterial, antifungal, antiviral, antiparasitic, and anti-inflammatory. It is indicated for yeast infections of the skin, ringworm, candida, sinus and lung infections, hypertension, deworming, and skin conditions.

Birds: Melaleuca oil of any species must be of the utmost quality for use in birds. Methods of use include water diffusion (generally 3-4 drops added to a diffuser – caging and tenting can be used), use within Animal Scents Ointment, additional drops mixed into Animal Scents Ointment (1 drop per tablespoon), and by indirect diffusion. The topical use of Melaleuca is often accomplished and recommended through the use of Purification, which has even been sprayed onto birds via water misting.

Exotics: Methods mentioned for birds can be used for exotic animals, as well as addition to Species Specific Raindrop Technique, Petting (usually diluted), and use within blends and products mentioned. Purification and Animal Scents Ointment are the most commonly used products that contain Melaleuca. When the use of Melaleuca is desired in these animals, often it is accomplished through their use.

Cats: Some people will feel more comfortable taking a cautious approach to the use of Melaleuca for felines, and this is completely fine. There are so many other essential oils to choose from, that the use of Melaleuca in cats is likely unnecessary. However, it is nice to know that if a case seems to be completely unresponsive to other remedies, or if Melaleuca seems like the perfect oil to use – this is still a viable option to consider. Veterinary monitoring and pre-exposure blood work is always recommended, and especially so that the documentation of the safe use of Melaleuca in cats can be further demonstrated. The use of Melaleuca within the common products and blends mentioned, is highly recommended and has been well documented. The most cat friendly methods of use of the single oil of Melaleuca alternifolia include; addition into Kitty Raindrop Technique (starting with 1 drop added), water diffusion, Litteroma, addition into Animal Scents Ointment, direct topical application (usually diluted), and

Petting (usually diluted). Oral administration is reserved for only the most severe of conditions, and it is likely that other essential oils could be used instead of Melaleuca.

Dogs & Larger: Melaleuca alternifolia can be used in all of the methods of application, with the most common forms being insertion into Raindrop Technique, direct topical application (diluted or neat), Petting (dilute or neat), air or water diffusion, addition into various carriers or ointments, and when deemed necessary by the oral route. It may be less likely for Melaleuca to be consumed in water or food due to its strong flavor, however some animals seem to enjoy it. For oral use in dogs – 1 drop of Melaleuca Alternifolia can be diluted with 5 drops of V-6. 1 drop or more of this dilution can be given twice a day, for each 20 pounds (9 kg) of body weight. Start with a smaller amount, and gradually increase as needed. For horses and others, starting with 1 drop per 300 pounds (135 kg) of body weight, given orally twice a day is a good starting point. Monitor responses and adjust according to individual need.

Melaleuca Ericifolia (Melaleuca ericifolia)

Melaleuca Ericifolia is a slightly milder form of Melaleuca, when compared to Alternifolia. Its properties include antibacterial, antifungal, antiviral, anti-parasitic, and anti-inflammatory actions. It is indicated specifically for Herpes Virus and respiratory and sinus infections. Melaleuca Ericifolia can be used in all of the ways mentioned for Melaleuca Alternifolia – however Ericifolia has been used much less commonly in animals. In cats, exotics, and birds the use of Melaleuca Ericifolia should start cautiously as the use of this oil has not been widely documented.

Melaleuca Quinquenervia (Melaleuca quinquenervia)

This essential oil is also known as MQV and Niaouli. This oil is most commonly used within the blend of Melrose in animals. Extensive use of this oil as a single has not been documented. Properties suggest this oil would be indicated for hypertension, urinary tract infections, respiratory and sinus infections, allergies, and enhancement of male hormones. At this time, the use of MQV is suggested to be used via the use of the blend Melrose. Water diffusion is generally the method selected when use of an "un-documented" essential oil is initiated in animals. Careful monitoring and gradual increases in exposure intensity is recommended.

Melissa (Melissa officinalis)

Melissa is also known as Lemon Balm. Melissa essential oil falls into the category of a "must-have" oil for me. Although it can be considered expensive, the massive benefits from very small amounts of this oil make the investment well worthwhile. Melissa is a powerful oil with a very high vibrational energy. Melissa is most likely the highest anti-viral substance available, and it is especially indicated with Herpes Viruses. Melissa also has very high anti-histamine type actions. Melissa is used for many conditions including depression, anxiety, viral infections, pruitis (itching), hives, seizures, as a replacement for anti-histamines, and for anaphylaxis. Melissa oil is one to try when you have tried everything else! I am continually amazed at reports of what Melissa oil has helped with, and the possibilities seem quite endless.

Birds: The most common use of Melissa has been by addition to drinking water (1 drop per liter). This is widely accepted, and when needed 2 drops per liter can be used. Other common methods of use include water diffusion and addition into foods (starting with a toothpick dip per tablespoon). 1 drop could be added to the Avian Raindrop Technique for severe viral situations, where other methods have not yielded results.

Exotics: All of the methods for birds can be used for exotics. Other methods of use include addition of 1 drop of Melissa into Species Specific Raindrop Technique, and Petting (diluted). In severe viral situations addition into soaking waters and aquariums can also be used, starting with adding a toothpick dip, and gradually increasing the amount used. Melissa is quite a powerful and intense oil, and many times portions of the drinking water solution (1 drop per liter) will be added to aquariums, soaking water, and foods to reduce the intensity.

Cats: All of the methods listed for birds and exotics can be used in cats. The most cat friendly methods include the addition of 1 drop of Melissa to the Kitty Raindrop Technique, water diffusion, Litteroma (often only 1 drop), and via Petting (diluted). If a cat will ingest the oil in foods or in drinking water, this is great, especially in viral situations. The oral use of Melissa can be considered, especially with severe viral situations, hives, allergic reactions, or anaphylaxis.

For oral use in cats, diluting 1 drop in 1 liter of water, and administering this solution by syringe or dropper can be used. No maximum amount has been reached with this method, and typically 3-5 mL of "Melissa water" would be administered, 2-6 times a day. Cats are likely to refuse the administration of the water before you could ever "give too much." This water solution, or even the essential oil, can also be mixed with NingXia Red or other foods for oral administration. In emergency situations, I do not worry about being "cat friendly" and will gladly force an oral dose. 1 drop of Melissa can be added to 2 ounces of NingXia Red as well, and this solution can be administered as needed. Generally 1-3 mL is given 2-6 times a day. Starting with smaller amounts and gradually increasing is recommended.

1 drop of Melissa can also be diluted in 20 drops of V-6, and 1 or more drops of this dilution can be given directly in the mouth or via capsule. This dilution can be given twice a day or more, as needed for the severity of the condition. For chronic viral infections, a much slower introduction to the oil can be followed. Melissa is especially indicated for Feline Leukemia, FIP, Feline Corona Virus, FIV, Feline Herpes Virus, Feline Distemper, other viral conditions. Melissa has also been used successfully for seizures.

Dogs & Larger: Melissa can be used in all application methods, but is generally pre-diluted for use in the Raindrop Technique, for Petting, direct topical application, and for oral use. The dilution rate of Melissa is often determined by the severity and chronicity of the condition, and sometimes by budgetary concerns. Diluting the Melissa oil at least 50:50 with V-6 is a good starting point (equal amounts of Melissa and V-6 added together.) If the condition has been somewhat chronic or we have limited financial access to the Melissa oil, then I will often dilute 1 part Melissa to 5-10 parts V-6. These dilutions are then used in most of the methods of application, except for diffusion. One or more drops of Copaiba and/or Frankincense can also be added to these diluted batches of Melissa oil. The magnifying and synergistic effects of these oils, when combined with the Melissa, will also intensify the remedy.

For oral use in dogs, 1 drop of Melissa can be diluted with 10 drops of V-6. 1 drop or more of this dilution can be given twice a day, for each 20 pounds (9 kg) of body weight. Start with a smaller amount, and gradually increase as needed. For horses and others, starting with 1 drop per 500 pounds (225 kg) of body weight, given orally twice a day is a good starting point. Monitor responses and adjust according to individual need.

Melissa oil can also be added to NingXia Red for oral administration to these animals. Simply combine the desired amount of Melissa oil, with the desired amount of NingXia Red that will be given throughout the day.

Divide up the total amount into several doses. Horses and Large Animals easily take this mixture by mouth, syringe, or mixed with foods. Some dogs greatly enjoy NingXia Red and will drink any essential oil that is added to it, while others need syringe administration, or enjoy the solution mixed into some yummy food.

Mountain Savory (Satureja Montana)

Mountain Savory is often used as a gentler version of Oregano. Its actions are similar and include strong antibacterial, antifungal, antiviral, anti-parasitic, anti-inflammatory, and immune stimulating properties. It is especially indicated for spinal and back conditions as well as viral infections (such as Herpes and FIV.) Mountain Savory is often used in ImmuPower and Surrender.

Birds & Exotics: Mountain Savory has not been used extensively at this time, however it seems likely that it can be used similarly to Oregano, and may be a more mild selection to utilize. Please see Oregano for a description of methods of application.

Cats: Mountain Savory has not been used extensively in cats at this time, however it seems likely that it can be used similarly to Oregano. It would be most indicated in cases of Feline Herpes Virus and FIV (Feline Immunodeficiency Virus.) Please see Oregano for a description of methods of application.

Dogs & Larger: Mountain Savory can be used in all of the ways that Oregano is used and recommended. Please see Oregano for a description of methods of application. Mountain Savory would be especially indicated for use with viral infections, Equine Herpes Virus, spondylosis, and other back conditions.

Myrrh (Commiphora myrrha)

Myrrh is used in many ways in animals. Its medical properties make it well indicated for use in diabetes, cancer, hepatitis, fungal infections, tooth and gum infections, skin conditions, and as an analgesic. Myrrh is commonly used in blends and products such as Abundance, Animal Scents Ointment, ClaraDerm, Egyptian Gold, EndoGize, Exodus II, Gratitude, Hope, Humility, Rose Ointment, Thyromin, and White Angelica. Myrrh is also supportive for many endocrine and hormonal conditions including support of the thyroid, growth hormone production, pituitary gland function, and hypothalamus function.

One of the more common uses of Myrrh in animals is for pain management. Myrrh is often given in combination with Copaiba and Helichrysum in an oral form, with very effective results. We have seen this combination replace the use of many traditional pain medications in the veterinary hospital. Topically, Myrrh has also been helpful in controlling pain and aiding in the healing of post-surgical sites.

Birds: Myrrh is most commonly used within Animal Scents Ointment and ClaraDerm spray (these are not applied to feathered areas). For pain management 1 drop of Myrrh, 2 drops of Helichrysum, and 1 drop of Copaiba are added to 2 mL of V-6. Approximately 1 drop (or 0.05 mL) of this solution is given orally, to a bird up to 100 grams in weight. For larger birds, starting with one drop is still advisable; however it is likely that increased amounts could be used if needed. The dose was repeated every 8 hours for a particular individual, however the judgment on when to re-dose should be placed more on response than on a specific time frame. This blend was very effective in controlling the discomfort associated with a broken wing in our veterinary hospital, and the bird required no further pain medications or injections. Certainly Myrrh alone could also be administered in this concentration orally.

Myrrh can also be used by addition into Avian Raindrop Technique, addition to Animal Scents Ointment (1 or more drops per tablespoon), by Perch application, by addition of 1 drop to the Feather Spray Recipe, by water diffusion, and by direct topical application (diluted, 2 drops in 2 mL V-6).

Exotics: Myrrh can be used in all of the ways mentioned for birds. Oral use of Myrrh would follow the same recipes to start with, however it is likely that the concentration of the Pain Recipe could be increased to 2-3 drops of each oil added into 2 mL of V-6. This solution would be given orally or mixed with foods at a rate of 1 or more drops per 5 pounds (2 kg) of body weight. For most exotics, starting with one drop and judging response and duration of the response, is the best way to establish a dosing regimen.

Myrrh can also be used by Petting (generally diluted), addition to soaking water (starting with 1 toothpick dip into 1 liter of water), and by addition into Species Specific Raindrop Technique.

Cats: Myrrh is especially indicated for hyperthyroidism, pain management, ringworm, use after declaw surgeries, hepatitis, diabetes, and skin conditions. Cat friendly methods of use include addition in Kitty Raindrop Technique, Petting (dilute or neat, especially over the neck or thyroid gland area), Litteroma, water diffusion, and oral administration. For cats a Pain Recipe can start with 5 drops each of Myrrh, Helichrysum, and Copaiba per 2 mL of V-6. This solution can be given orally directly, by capsule, or within foods or NingXia Red if the cat is willing. 5 drops or more of this dilution can be given, 3 or more times per day. Cats will often salivate when given any essential oil orally, and this is an expected and harmless event. This solution can also be used to apply near surgical incisions and onto paws that have been declawed. Direct application to a surgical incision is rarely necessary, and application directly next to the incision works well.

Dogs & Larger: Myrrh can be used in all of the application methods for these animals. The most common methods include insertion into Raindrop Technique, Petting (dilute or neat, especially over the neck or thyroid gland area), direct topical application (neat or diluted), addition into Animal Scents Ointment, and by oral administration. For oral use in dogs, 1 drop of Myrrh can be diluted with 5 drops of V-6. 1 drop or more of this dilution can be given twice a day, for each 20 pounds (9 kg) of body weight. Start with a smaller amount, and gradually increase as needed. For horses and others, starting with 1 drop per 500 pounds (225 kg) of body weight, given orally twice a day is a good starting point. Monitor responses and adjust according to individual need.

An effective Pain Recipe for dogs is 1 drop of Helichrysum, 1 drop of Myrrh, 1 drop of Copaiba, and 10 drops of V-6 placed within a gel capsule and given orally. This is generally used for dogs approximately 50 pounds (23 kg) in weight, and can be dosed 2-3 times a day. This blend is generally used for more severe pain situations such as an injury, trauma, or surgery. The patient should be monitored closely, ideally in cooperation with a veterinarian, and amounts and dosing frequency adjusted based on the individual.

Myrtle (Myrtus communis)

Myrtle is used mainly in animals for liver, prostate, thyroid, and respiratory concerns. It is most commonly used within the blends and products such as EndoFlex, Inspiration, JuvaTone, Mister, Purification, R.C., Super Cal, and Thyromin.

Birds: Myrtle is not commonly used as a single in birds, and is most commonly used within EndoFlex, Purification, and R.C.. Water diffusion of Myrtle as a single oil is appropriate. Topical application of Myrtle is generally accomplished through the use of Purification.

Exotics: Myrtle has also not been commonly used as a single for exotic animals, but has been used within EndoFlex, Purification, and R.C. on a more extensive basis. Myrtle as a single can be considered for use by addition into Species Specific Raindrop Technique, Petting (diluted), and water diffusion. More extensive use of Myrtle is often accomplished through the use of the blend Purification.

Cats: Cat friendly methods in which to use Myrtle include water diffusion, addition into Kitty Raindrop Technique, Petting (often diluted), and Litteroma.

Dogs & Larger: Myrtle is also more commonly used within the products and blend that were previously mentioned. Myrtle is often indicated for dogs with hypothyroidism, liver disease, and prostate disease. Myrtle can be used in all of the application methods for these animals and is most commonly used via insertion into Raindrop Technique, by Petting (neat or diluted – especially over the thyroid or neck area), or by water or air diffusion. Rectal Instillation of Myrtle can be used for cases of prostatic disease (see that chapter for more details). Oral administration can also be considered, although is not commonly used.

For oral use in dogs – 1 drop of Myrtle can be diluted with 10 drops of V-6. 1 drop or more of this dilution can be given twice a day, for each 20 pounds (9 kg) of body weight. Start with a smaller amount, and gradually increase as needed. For horses and others, starting with 1 drop per 500 pounds (225 kg) of body weight, given orally twice a day is a good starting point. Monitor responses and adjust according to individual need.

Neroli (Citrus sinensis)

Neroli is an absolute and not a true essential oil. It has not been used as a single oil extensively in animals at this time. It is mainly used within the blends of Acceptance, Awaken, Humility, Inner Child, and Present Time. Water diffusion is likely to be acceptable for all animal species. Medical properties indicate it may be useful for anxiety, depression, and hypertension.

Nutmeg (Myristica fragrans)

Nutmeg is a magnificent oil with many supportive properties including anti-inflammatory, anticoagulant, antiparasitic, analgesic, liver protecting, stomach protecting against ulcers, circulatory stimulation, adrenal support and stimulation, muscle relaxation, and the increase of growth hormone and melatonin production. Conditions in animals that are aided by Nutmeg include; arthritis, heart disease, hypertension, liver disease, gastric ulcers, digestive disorders, parasites, nerve pain and neuropathy, and Addison's Disease. Nutmeg is found in blends and products such as EndoFlex, En-R-Gee, Magnify Your Purpose, ParaFree, and Power Meal.

Care must be taken with Nutmeg oil in animals who are bleeding, have a tendency to bleed, or are on any sort of anti-coagulant therapy. The over use of essential oil(s) that have anti-coagulant actions, especially in oral administration, can produce a temporary and dose dependent increase in bleeding and reduction of clotting.

Birds: Nutmeg is commonly used within EndoFlex, ParaFree, and Power Meal in birds. In birds the most common administration of Nutmeg essential oil is by addition to drinking water (1 drop per liter), by adding into foods (starting with 1 toothpick dip per tablespoon), and by water diffusion. Although it has not been used in this way yet, addition into Avian Raindrop Technique is likely to be well tolerated.

Exotics: Nutmeg can be used in all of the methods described for birds as well as by addition to Species Specific Raindrop Technique, Petting (diluted), addition into Animal Scents Ointment (1 drop per tablespoon), and oral administration. Oral use is generally only moved towards when other methods of use have failed to be effective. For oral use 1 drop of Nutmeg is diluted in 2 mL of V-6, and 1 drop or more of this dilution can be added to foods or given orally, twice a day. Monitor for responses and adjust according to individual need.

Cats: Cats can use Nutmeg as described for exotics and birds. Cat friendly methods of using Nutmeg include addition into Kitty Raindrop Technique, Petting (generally diluted), and Litteroma. It is unlikely that most cats will be willing to consume Nutmeg, and it is most commonly used within ParaFree for oral consumption.

Dogs & Larger: Nutmeg can be used in all of the methods of application with the following methods being the most common: insertion into Raindrop Technique, Petting (neat or diluted, especially over the adrenal gland area), direct application (neat or diluted), addition to foods or water, and by direct oral administration.

For oral use in dogs, 1 drop of Nutmeg can be diluted with 20 drops of V-6. 1 drop or more of this dilution can be given twice a day, for each 20 pounds (9 kg) of body weight. Start with a smaller amount, and gradually increase as needed. For horses and others, starting with 1 drop per 500 pounds (225 kg) of body weight, given orally twice a day is a good starting point. Monitor responses and adjust according to individual need. See the cautionary statement regarding bleeding and anticoagulant activity.

Ocotea (Ocotea quixos)

Ocotea is a relatively new essential oil, although the tree itself has been used for over 500 years. Ocotea stands out as the oil of choice for Diabetes and pancreatic disorders. Medical properties reveal that Ocotea is also useful for high blood pressure, anxiety, fungal infections, inflammation, and parasites. Ocotea also appears to have anti-histamine sort of responses in many animals and humans.

Caution and careful monitoring with a veterinarian is recommended whenever Ocotea is used in animals receiving Insulin or oral hypoglycemic medications. Ocotea can correct and lower the need for these medications, so much so, that continued administration of the "pre-Ocotea" dosages, may prove dangerous. It is not that Ocotea appears to interfere with the medications, however, quite the opposite. Ocotea appears to be correcting the need for these medications, leading to a situation where the animal could be over-dosed with the prescription medication. When working with a veterinarian, it is helpful to describe that you will be using a natural remedy that has been shown in humans to reduce the required levels of Insulin or other diabetic medications. Most veterinarians are familiar with the careful monitoring and adjusting of Insulin doses in diabetic animals – especially when we are first introducing the therapy. In the case of Ocotea, we basically monitor "in reverse," slowly exposing the animal to Ocotea, while performing the same careful monitoring and blood glucose curves, at intervals determined by the veterinarian. Over time, Insulin and medication requirements may lessen, and a reduction in dosage can be made with your veterinarian.

It is important to use very small amounts, and avoid multiple methods of application initially in animals on Insulin. We start extremely slowly when Insulin is being given. Animals who are not receiving Insulin and have been diagnosed with Diabetes, are much more able to utilize Ocotea in a more aggressive manner. Since we are not giving potentially dangerous injections of Insulin or medications that lower the blood sugar levels, we are able to expose the animal to more Ocotea, without fear of correcting their condition "too quickly."

Birds: Ocotea has been used in water diffusion, in drinking water (1 drop per liter), and has also been added to foods (starting with 1 toothpick dip or more per tablespoon). It is commonly used to replace anti-histamines, for crop infections (fungal/yeast), with suspected Diabetes, anxiety, and for various internal parasitic conditions.

Exotics: Ocotea has been used in the ways described for birds and is also commonly used by addition into Species Specific Raindrop Technique, water diffusion, Petting (diluted), addition into Animal Scents Ointment (1 drop per tablespoon), direct topical application (generally diluted, and especially applied topically in the case of ringworm), and by oral administration. For oral use 2 drops of Ocotea is diluted in 2 mL of V-6, and 1 drop or more of this dilution can be added to foods or given orally, twice a day. Monitor for responses and adjust according to individual need.

Cats: Ocotea is the first oil choice for Diabetic cats. Although the most effective way to utilize Ocotea for Diabetes in humans seems to be by the direct dripping of the oil under the tongue, this is unlikely to occur in cats, especially for the continued administration that will be necessary. In cats that are not on Insulin, we can layer many "cat friendly" methods of application to increase the cat's exposure to the oil. Since cats groom, it is likely that we can achieve oral levels of Ocotea after various topical applications. For cats who are receiving diabetic medications, starting with only one mild application method, monitoring carefully with a veterinarian, and gradually introducing more and more exposure to Ocotea is recommended. It may take several months to safely work with cats who are on medications.

Cat friendly methods of Ocotea use include insertion into Kitty Raindrop Technique, water diffusion, Petting (diluted initially, and increasing concentration slowly), and Litteroma. Ocotea has been suggested for Heartworm Prevention (and as a replacement for the use of ParaFree) in cats by giving 3 drops of Ocotea with 3 drops of Copaiba by mouth, twice a week. It is likely that much less than this amount is needed, nevertheless, this is the quantity currently being used. Heartworm prevention remains a bit more controversial and harder to document, due to the odd nature of heartworm infection in cats. Nevertheless, the antiparasitic properties of Ocotea are encouraging. See the discussion within ParaFree, for more information on Heartworm Prevention.

Dogs & Larger: With Diabetic dogs, it is much more likely that we can use Ocotea orally as we would in humans. The same precautions need to be followed for dogs who are on Insulin as is recommended for cats. Ocotea can be used in all application methods for dogs and larger, with the most common methods being insertion into Raindrop Technique (often diluted 50:50), Petting (dilute or neat), direct topical application (neat or diluted), addition into Animal Scents Ointment or Shampoo, water or air diffusion, addition into foods, addition into water, and direct oral administration.

For oral use in dogs, 1 drop of Ocotea can be diluted with 5 drops of V-6 (for non-Insulin receiving dogs) or with 20 drops of V-6 (for dogs on Insulin.) 1 drop or more of these dilutions can be given twice a day, for each 20 pounds (9 kg) of body weight. Start with a smaller amount, and gradually increase as needed. Again, carefully monitor with your veterinarian when working with Diabetics. It is likely that much higher amounts can be used for deworming purposes.

For horses and others, starting with 1 drop per 500 pounds (225 kg) of body weight, given orally twice a day is a good starting point. Monitor responses and adjust according to individual need. It is likely that much higher amounts can be used for deworming purposes.

Orange (Citrus sinensis)

Orange oil has been used extensively in all species of animals, and in almost every way imaginable. With a high Limonene content, Orange oil is well indicated for antitumoral benefits. Orange oil is commonly used for cancer, depression, and for health in general.

Orange is a photosensitizing oil; avoid applying to skin that will be exposed to sunlight or full spectrum UV light within 24 hours. This oil is used commonly in the Feather Spray for birds, and we have not noted a photosensitizing issue for fully feathered birds at this time. However, I would still advise caution, as many birds using the Feather Spray Recipe are missing feathers and have fully exposed skin. Caution with full and natural sunlight is more likely needed than with the full spectrum indoor lighting, commonly used for birds and reptiles.

Birds & Exotics: Orange oil has been used in many, many ways: water diffusion (including caging and tenting), added to Species Specific Raindrop Technique, within the Feather Spray Recipe, added to drinking water (1 or more drops per liter), added to foods (1 or more drops per tablespoon), addition to Animal Scents Ointment, water spritzers (up to 20 drops per 4 ounces), Petting (diluted non-avian), and allowed to be directly ingested when animals chose to lick the oil off of hands and other items.

Cats: Orange oil has been used for cats in all of the mentioned methods. The most cat friendly methods of use include adding to the Kitty Raindrop Technique, water diffusion, Petting (diluted), Litteroma, and direct topical application (usually diluted). Some cats will ingest Orange oil in foods or water as described for Birds & Exotics. We have not noted photosensitivity issues for cats who are fully furred, however the recommendation to apply the oil where the sun will not contact the skin (stomach), is a wise recommendation.

Dogs & Larger: Orange oil can be used very easily and in all methods of application for these animals. Common methods of use include insertion into Raindrop Technique (often neat), addition into foods, addition into drinking water (1 drop or more per liter for dogs), direct topical application (generally diluted), Petting (diluted or neat), water and air diffusion, and direct oral administration. The amounts and concentrations of Orange that can be applied and administered are much higher for these animals, and often 5-10 drops (or more) will be applied topically at a time.

Orange oil applied directly to the skin, is usually best diluted (at least 1 drop per 1 drop) in V-6, Coconut Oil, Animal Scents Ointment, Cell-Lite Magic Massage Oil, or another carrier of some sort. Starting with smaller amounts or more diluted oil, is still recommended as many animals respond to lesser amounts. However, if needed, much larger quantities can be applied safely.

For insertion into Raindrop Technique, Orange oil could be applied to the underside of the belly of Goats, Horses, and other Large Animals who may be exposed to the sun. Photosensitivity has not been noted in furred areas, but caution is still a wise idea.

For oral use in dogs, 1 drop of Orange oil can be diluted with 2 drops of V-6. 1 drop or more of this dilution can be given twice a day, for each 20 pounds (9 kg) of body weight. Start with a smaller amount, and gradually increase as needed. For horses and others, starting with 1 drop per 200 pounds (90 kg) of body weight, given orally twice a day is a good starting point. Monitor responses and adjust according to individual need.

Oregano (Origanum compactum)

Oregano is generally the first oil of the Raindrop Technique. High in phenols, it is a powerful oil. Properties of Oregano include antiaging, antiviral, antibacterial, antifungal, antiparasitic, anti-inflammatory, and immune stimulation. Oregano can almost be indicated for every condition through its use in the Raindrop Technique. Oregano is also used very commonly within ImmuPower, Inner Defense, and Ortho Sport Massage Oil. Oregano is known as a "hot" oil, and care must be taken to monitor the skin of animals exposed to it, and to also use caution if diffusing.

Birds: Oregano has mainly been mixed into foods and used within the Avian Raindrop Technique. With addition into foods, 1 toothpick dip is mixed into 1 tablespoon of food, and gradually increased to even 1 drop per tablespoon of food. This can be used as a powerful antibiotic, but has also been used to contact papillomas (warts) within the digestive tract. Within the Avian Raindrop Technique, Oregano is likely to benefit any condition, however, this technique is not always easy to administer to every bird and is reserved mainly for severe cases and conditions. The use of Oregano within ImmuPower is also utilized in birds. Water diffusion of this oil could be considered in extremely low amounts (1 drop mixed with another oil or blend), however ImmuPower is most commonly diffused for birds.

Exotics: Oregano is also mainly used within the Species Specific Raindrop Technique, and by addition into foods. The same protocols as described for birds can be used for exotics. Care must be taken with Rabbits, Guinea Pigs, and Chinchillas as they are considered "hind-gut fermenters." The aggressive use of a powerful antibacterial agent like Oregano, could damage their delicate intestinal flora. Please make sure to see the sections for these animals specifically, for more information on their individual needs and recommendations. Water based diffusion of Oregano is also mainly accomplished through the use of ImmuPower. Topical application of Oregano is generally in the form of the Raindrop solution or with the Ortho Sport Massage Oil. For cases of severe warts, stronger solutions of Oregano can be considered for topical application directly to the wart. Rabbits are the most likely exotic species to get warts, so caution must be used if Oregano is considered for them. Please see the Rabbit section for specific recommendations for this species.

Cats: Oregano is most commonly used within the Kitty Raindrop Technique, within ImmuPower and Ortho Sport Massage Oil, added to Animal Scents Ointment (1 drop per tablespoon), or diluted and directly applied to areas of fungal infection (ringworm – 4 drops or more in 30 mL V-6). Please see comments in Birds and Exotics for information on water based diffusion of Oregano. The oral use of Inner Defense in felines has recently come to light in the veterinary field. See ImmuPower, Inner Defense, and Ortho Sport Massage Oil for more information on their specific uses in various animals.

Dogs & Larger: Oregano can be used much more aggressively in these animals. The most common methods of application are within the Raindrop Technique, direct application (neat or diluted), addition into Animal Scents Ointment, addition into bug sprays and recipes, addition into massage oils and bases, addition into Animal Scents Shampoo, addition into Thieves Household Cleaner (for soaking or bathing Large Animals), addition into foods, and by direct oral administration. In horses, the bottom lip can be "squeezed out" to create a little pocket, and even neat Oregano is very well tolerated in this manner. Cattle and other large animals will often ingest Oregano in grain, hay, or feeds. Oregano can be mixed with NingXia Red, Honey, Maple Syrup, Agave, Apple Sauce, or other items and can be delivered orally with a syringe.

Oregano is most commonly used orally for antibiotic properties and is often used in cases of severe bacterial infection (mastitis, tendon infections, bacterial diarrhea, etc...). Topical application of Oregano is useful for warts, sarcoids, mastitis, canker, abscesses, and fungal infections.

In dogs, the product Inner Defense is often used for oral antibacterial effects. For oral use of Oregano in dogs – 1 drop of Oregano oil can be diluted with 2 drops of V-6. 1 drop or more of this dilution can be given twice a day, for each 20 pounds (9 kg) of body weight. Start with a smaller amount, and gradually increase as needed. Some dogs will lick a more diluted Oregano solution off of your hand, or greatly enjoy the flavor mixed with foods. On average, approximately 1 drop of Oregano per 20 pounds (9 kg) of dog body weight is given per day. Some dogs may need less, and some dogs may need more, careful monitoring and adjusting for the individual dog is important. For Oregano delivered orally by capsule, generally the desired amount of Oregano is added to the empty capsule (and other oils if indicated), and the capsule is filled the rest of the way with V-6 prior to administration. Special consideration should be made of the gut flora of dogs receiving oral Oregano, and Life 5 should be given after any oral administration of powerful antibacterial essential oils. See the Life 5 description for more information.

For horses and others, starting with 1 drop per 200 pounds (90 kg) of body weight, given orally twice a day is a good starting point. Monitor responses and adjust according to individual need. In cases of mastitis and more severe infections – even 10 drops of Oregano have been given orally twice a day. Special care should be considered of the gastrointestinal flora, and it is a good idea to follow the use of oral Oregano with probiotics. Life 5 can be used, but often times a specific large animal product is more cost effective.

Palmarosa (Cymbopogon martini)

Palmarosa has not been used extensively as a single oil in animals at this time. It is most commonly used within the blends and products of Animal Scents Ointment, Awaken, Clarity, Forgiveness, Gentle Baby, Harmony, Joy, and Rose Ointment. Properties suggest its use to be excellent for conditions such as fungal infections, sebaceous cysts, cardiovascular disease, oily skin conditions (seborrhea oleosa), wound healing, skin cell regeneration, and nervous system support.

Palo Santo (Bursera graveolens)

Palo Santo is sometimes referred to as the "South American Frankincense." Highly regarded as a spiritual oil, it is no mistake that these oils often carry many powerful medical benefits with them. Medical properties show that Palo Santo is indicated for conditions such as cancer (especially lung), cartilage repair, joint conditions, tendon and ligament repair and health, as an insect repellant, for skin tags, depression, emotional cleansing, pain control, healing of broken bones, fungal infections, skin conditions, immune stimulation, gout, reducing airborne contaminants, and even antibacterial and antiviral actions. It is likely that this oil may be helpful for almost any condition. It is a fairly mild oil in scent, and with skin application making it well suited for use in animals.

There is a cautionary statement in the EODR regarding using caution during pregnancy and with children under 18 months of age. Certainly with any pregnant animal, it is a good recommendation to use oils without any warning statements regarding its use during pregnancy. However, in practice, we have not noted any ill effects in any pregnant animal from the use of essential oils at this time. As for use of Palo Santo in young animals, there are often other oil selections that can be made. Since animals have different age relationships than humans – I would suggest that this recommendation would apply to animals 6 months of age and less.

Birds & Exotics: In birds, Palo Santo is a powerhouse for its uses. Water diffusion in quarantine areas or areas with multiple birds is likely to reduce airborne transmission of disease while simultaneously providing emotional and health benefits. Currently, Palo Santo has mainly been used in birds via water diffusion, including caging and tenting. The following methods are also likely to be well tolerated in birds, and yield excellent results: addition into Avian Raindrop Technique, addition to Animal Scents Ointment (lightly applied to non-feathered areas), adding 1 drop or more into the Feather Spray Recipe, water misting (starting with 1 drop per 4 ounces (120 mL) of water and increasing gradually to 4 drops), adding 1 drop or more to other water misting recipes, and application via Perches and Hands (neat or diluted). Although it has not been used extensively at this time, for severe cases the addition to drinking water (1 drop per liter) or to foods is likely to be extremely beneficial, especially for cases of gout and cancer. When oral use of an essential oil is first initiated, especially when there has not been widespread use of an oil in this manner, it is important to start with very small amounts (such as a toothpick dip within 1 or more tablespoons of food), to monitor responses closely, and to very gradually increase the consumption of the novel oil.

Exotic animals can use Palo Santo in all of the ways discussed for birds, however they are likely to also benefit from application via Petting (neat or diluted). It is also likely that exotic animals can tolerate much larger amounts of Palo Santo orally, and although starting with a toothpick dip mixed into foods is wise, they are likely to ingest ½ drop or more of oil per day. Ideally, these amounts are divided into several meals throughout the day.

Cats: Cats can use Palo Santo in all of the ways mentioned for birds and exotics. The most cat friendly methods of use include addition to Kitty Raindrop Technique, Petting (neat or diluted), direct topical application (generally diluted), water diffusion, and Litteroma.

Dogs & Larger: Palo Santo can be used in all of the application methods for these animals. The most common methods of use include insertion into Raindrop Technique, direct application (neat or diluted), addition into Animal Scents Ointment, Shampoo, Massage Oils, and the like, adding to wading pools and soaking water, application via Petting (neat or diluted), by water or air diffusion (including caging and tenting), addition into foods, addition into drinking water, and by direct oral administration.

For oral use in dogs – 1 drop of Palo Santo can be diluted with 2 drops of V-6. 1 drop or more of this dilution can be given twice a day, for each 20 pounds (9 kg) of body weight. Start with a smaller amount, and gradually increase as needed. For horses and others, starting with 1 drop per 100-200 pounds (45-90 kg) of body weight, given orally twice a day is a good starting point. Monitor responses and adjust according to individual need.

Patchouli (Pogostemon cablin)

Patchouli is a wonderful oil that has been used widely in animals. It is especially indicated for nausea, vomiting, hypertension, any form of skin condition, and for general calming effects. It is found in Animal Scents Ointment, Di-Gize, Magnify Your Purpose, Peace & Calming, and Rose Ointment.

Birds & Exotics: Patchouli is mainly used within the products and blends of Animal Scents Ointment, Di-Gize, Peace & Calming, and Rose Ointment. Patchouli as a single oil, has mainly been used in birds via water diffusion, however the following methods are also likely to be well tolerated in birds and yield excellent results: addition into Avian Raindrop Technique, addition to Animal Scents Ointment (lightly applied to non-feathered areas), adding 1 drop or more into the Feather Spray Recipe, water misting (starting with 1 drop per 4 ounces (120 mL) of water, and increasing gradually to 4 drops), adding 1 drop or more to other water misting recipes, and application via Perches and Hands (neat or diluted). Although it has not been used extensively in an oral manner as a single, for some cases the addition to drinking water (1 drop per liter) or to foods is likely to be extremely beneficial, especially for cases of regurgitation and nausea. When oral use of an essential oil is first initiated, especially when there has not been widespread use of an oil in this manner, it is important to start with very small amounts (such as a toothpick dip within 1 or more tablespoons of food), to monitor responses closely, and to very gradually increase the consumption of the novel oil. The use of Patchouli orally, is generally best recommended through the use of Di-Gize.

Exotic animals can use Patchouli in all of the ways discussed for birds, however they are likely to also benefit from application via Petting (neat or diluted). It is also likely that exotic animals can tolerate much larger amounts of Patchouli orally, however the use of Patchouli in this manner is best documented through its use within Di-Gize.

Cats: Cats can use Patchouli in all of the methods discussed for birds and exotics. The most cat friendly methods of use will be addition into Kitty Raindrop Technique, Petting (dilute or neat), addition into Animal Scents Ointment, water diffusion, Litteroma, and the addition into Animal Scents Shampoo, other products, or carriers. The oral use of Patchouli has been used for situations of severe nausea and vomiting, however oral administration is less likely to make a cat want to eat afterwards. Cats have even received 2 neat drops of Patchouli directly into their mouth, twice a day, with no ill effects (except for a grumpy cat.) Again, the most common use of Patchouli in cats is through the use of Di-Gize, Peace & Calming, Animal Scents Ointment, and Rose Ointment.

Dogs & Larger: Patchouli can be used in all of the application methods for these animals. The most common methods of use include insertion into Raindrop Technique, direct application (neat or diluted), addition into Animal Scents Ointment, Shampoo, Massage Oils, and the like, adding to wading pools and soaking water, application via Petting (neat or diluted), by water diffusion, addition into foods, addition into drinking water, and by direct oral administration.

For oral use in dogs, 1 drop of Patchouli can be diluted with 2 drops of V-6. 1 drop or more of this dilution can be given twice a day, for each 20 pounds (9 kg) of body weight. Start with a smaller amount, and gradually increase as needed. For horses and others, starting with 1 drop per 100-200 pounds (45-90 kg) of body weight, given orally twice a day is a good starting point. Monitor responses and adjust according to individual need. Certainly much larger amounts of Patchouli have been administered to these animals orally, and considering that even cats have received up to 4 drops total per day, it can be extrapolated that larger animals could easily consume much more.

Pepper, Black (Piper nigrum)

Black Pepper is not used commonly in animals, but when it is, it packs a punch. Used most commonly in the "Flea Bomb Recipe", Black Pepper is also indicated for obesity, stimulating metabolism, for digestive problems, nerve and muscle pain, arthritis, and fungal infections. With animals it is mainly used within the blends of Awaken, Dream Catcher, En-R-Gee, and Relieve It.

Flea Bomb Recipe: This recipe is so powerful, that it is recommended that humans, animals, and fish tanks be removed from the home while administering this treatment. If the area to be treated can be confined, some people have been successful in treating one room at a time, moving their diffuser from room to room, and evacuating to a distant part of the home. If you have fragile animals, it is likely best to have them leave the home completely. Diffusion with an air diffuser is mandatory for this application. I prefer the TheraPro Diffuser for this technique, as it is much more exact.

- In a 15 mL glass essential oil bottle:
- Add approximately 70 drops each of Black Pepper, Peppermint, Oregano, and Orange essential oils.
- Set the dials on the TheraPro to full strength, and non-stop diffusion.
- Diffuse for at least 2 to 4 hours.
- The more severe the flea problem, the more you should desire to penetrate the room with these oils.
- Moving furniture and bedding, and vacuuming thoroughly is important. The entire home must be treated.

Birds & Exotics: Black Pepper is only used within the previously mentioned blends.

Cats: Black Pepper is only used within the previously mentioned blends.

Dogs & Larger: Black Pepper is mainly used within the previously mentioned blends. However for severe obesity, arthritis, nerve and muscle pain, or fungal infections (especially in Large Animals), Black Pepper could be used. For Dogs, I would mainly recommend the use of the blends. However, oral administration is likely very possible, and would mainly be used with obesity. For oral use in dogs – 1 drop of Black Pepper can be diluted with 20 drops of V-6. 1 drop or more of this dilution can be given twice a day, for each 20 pounds (9 kg) of body weight. Start with a smaller amount, and gradually increase as needed.

For horses and others, topical use of Black Pepper is much more likely to be tolerated, and would be indicated generally when the blends or other essential oils have failed. Situations that would warrant the use of Black Pepper as a single would include severe and unresponsive nerve and muscle pain, obesity, metabolic syndrome, and fungal infections. Dilution for topical use should likely start at 1 drop Black Pepper in at least 5 drops of V-6. This would most likely be applied within a Raindrop Technique, or via Petting. For oral use, use of the diluted solution is also recommended. Then giving 1 drop per 500 pounds (225 kg) of body weight, orally twice a day would be a recommended starting point. Monitor responses and adjust according to individual need.

Peppermint (Mentha piperita)

Peppermint is one of the Raindrop Oils. It is generally applied last in the sequence of oil applications as it is a "driving" oil, which means that it appears to enhance the penetration of other oils. Often Peppermint will be applied after layering several other oils in a topical application. Peppermint's medical properties include anti-inflammatory, antitumoral, antiparasitic for worms, antibacterial, antiviral, antifungal, gall bladder and digestive stimulation, pain relief, and appetite suppression. It is indicated for conditions such as arthritis, obesity, Herpes infections, papilloma (warts), candida, diarrhea, nausea, vomiting, and colic. As part of the Raindrop Technique, it is likely helpful to every situation. Peppermint is found in many products and blends which are used regularly in animals. Items that are used most frequently include Aroma Siez, Dentarome Toothpastes, Di-Gize, MightyZyme, Mineral Essence, Ortho Ease Massage Oil, Ortho Sport Massage Oil, PanAway, R.C., Raven, Relieve It, and Thyromin.

Young children have had respiratory reactions to the Menthol in Peppermint, and so its use is not recommended for human children under 18 months of age. This condition has not been witnessed in animals, but it would be wise to be cautious with the use of neat Peppermint oil in very small puppies or kittens. Many foals and calves have gotten Raindrop Technique with neat oils, as early as 1 day of age, and it does not appear that large animals have this tendency for respiratory sensitivity.

Birds & Exotics: Peppermint is used less often as a single in these animals. With birds the most common use is by mixing into foods, starting with a toothpick dip and increasing to 1 drop within 1 tablespoon. Adding to water can be considered, however for birds that bathe in their water, this may not be a good choice, as it could feel very "cold" and sting the eyes. It is used within Avian Raindrop Technique, and can be water diffused - generally added to the diffuser with other oils or blends. Peppermint is most commonly used in Aroma Siez, Di-Gize, and R.C. for birds. Peppermint could also be added to Animal Scents Ointment for topical application to non-feathered areas (1 drop or less to 1 tablespoon.)

With other exotics, Peppermint is also most commonly used within the Species Specific Raindrop Technique, and by addition to foods. The methods described for birds can be used, as well as the use of Peppermint within products such as Ortho Ease or Ortho Sport, which can be applied via Petting. It is likely that large amounts of Peppermint can be consumed safely, however the intense flavor is more likely to limit the amounts that can be mixed into foods.

Cats: There has been opinions that cats and Peppermint oil should not be combined. In practice, I have found this issue to be more of a "how" the Peppermint oil is used, and not a function of Peppermint oil in itself. Peppermint is a strong oil, and with cats I often think of applying oils to them as if I would apply them to my own face, or to the face of my child. I have certainly applied neat Peppermint oil to my own face, and it is quite an intense experience. Even diluted, Peppermint can pack quite a bit of zing to a topical application. With a cat's very opinionated view on the world, an application of Peppermint that would be too intense, is likely to be remembered. Within the Kitty Raindrop Technique, Peppermint is used for some cats even twice a day. The majority of cats absolutely love the Kitty Raindrop Technique, and there is absolutely no issue of the Peppermint being in the solution. However, it is important to remember that there are only 4 drops of Peppermint added to 30 mL (1 ounce) of V-6, making it quite a dilute solution.

The most cat friendly ways to use Peppermint include within the Kitty Raindrop Technique and by addition into Animal Scents Ointment (1 drop per tablespoon). Other uses of Peppermint are best accomplished through the blends and products that contain it, such as Petting a cat with Ortho Ease Massage Oil.

Dogs & Larger: Peppermint can be used in all of the application methods for these animals. The most common methods of use include within the Raindrop Technique, direct application (neat or diluted), addition into Animal Scents Ointment, Shampoo, Massage Oils, adding to wading pools and soaking water, application via Petting (neat or diluted), by water diffusion (usually combined with other oils), addition into foods, addition into drinking water, and by direct oral administration.

For oral use in dogs – 1 drop of Peppermint can be diluted with 10 drops (or more) of V-6. The dilution of Peppermint in this situation is more for the lowering of the intense flavor of the oil, and less as a safety issue. Increased dilution of Peppermint may be necessary for some dogs. 10 drops or more of this diluted solution (basically an entire drop of Peppermint oil) can be given twice a day, for each 20 pounds (9 kg) of body weight. Start with a smaller amount, and gradually increase as needed, as most animals likely do not need that much in actuality.

For horses and others, starting with 1 drop per 100 pounds (45 kg) of body weight, given orally twice a day is a good starting point. Monitor responses and adjust according to individual need. Certainly much larger amounts of Peppermint are administered to these animals orally in certain cases. With colic in horses, 20 drops of Peppermint is administered orally, and 20 drops of Peppermint is applied topically every 20 minutes, often for multiple doses. Please see Colic within the Equine Conditions for more information on this protocol.

Petitgrain (Citrus sinensis)
Petitgrain has not been used extensively as a single oil in animals at this time. Medical properties indicate its use for conditions such as nystagmus and vestibular disease, anxiety, and muscle spasms.

Pine (Pinus sylvestris)

Pine oil is useful in animals for conditions such as lice, fleas, mange and skin parasites, lung infections, arthritis, urinary tract infections, lymphatic stimulation, anxiety, and sinus infections. It may show great value for hormone and cortisone like activity as well as anti-diabetic properties. Pine is found within the blends of Grounding and R.C. Pine oil is not recommended for oral use.

Birds & Exotics: The main use of Pine is through water diffusion (including caging and tenting.) Other appropriate uses of Pine would be through addition of 1 drop to Species Specific Raindrop Technique, addition to Animal Scents Ointment (1 drop per tablespoon), Perch and Hand applications (generally diluted), and Petting (diluted for non-avian species – 1 drop per 10 drops V-6.) For birds and exotics with skin parasites, it is likely that a water diffusion in a tented situation may be sufficient to permeate the skin with the oil. Starting with 1 drop in a diffuser, and with careful monitoring, the amount diffused could gradually be increased in concentration (adding more drops the diffuser.) As the animal tolerates it, 4 drops or more could be water diffused in a tenting situation, for 20 minutes, 2-4 times a day. This technique would be especially useful for skin mites in hedgehogs. However, it is important to recognize that Purification for mites has been used much more commonly and much more aggressively in exotic animals, and it would be a wise first selection.

Cats: Pine is most commonly used in the blends of Grounding and R.C. Other cat friendly methods of the use of Pine include water diffusion, addition of 1 drop to the Kitty Raindrop Technique, Litteroma, and Petting (diluted 1 drop to 10 drops V-6.)

Dogs & Larger: The most common methods of use include within the Raindrop Technique (generally pre-diluted), direct application (diluted), addition into Animal Scents Ointment, Shampoo, Massage Oils, adding to wading pools and soaking water, application via Petting (neat or diluted), or by water or air diffusion.

ESSENTIAL OIL SINGLES

Ravintsara (Cinnamomum camphora)

Ravintsara is highly regarded for antiviral properties in animals, especially for Herpes virus. Ravintsara is also useful for hepatitis, lung infections and pneumonia, and cancer. It is used most commonly in the blend of ImmuPower, and is also found in the blend Raven.

Birds & Exotics: Ravintsara is most commonly used within the blend ImmuPower. Water-based diffusion can be used with both Ravintsara and ImmuPower. More extensive use of Ravintsara is recommended through the use of ImmuPower.

Cats: Ravintsara is also most commonly used within the blend of ImmuPower for cats. Water diffusion, addition of 1-2 drops into Kitty Raindrop Technique, Litteroma, and Petting (diluted) are suggested ways to use Ravintsara as a single oil for cats. However, the use of ImmuPower is recommended and has the most data and guidelines for use.

Dogs & Larger: Ravintsara is also more commonly used within ImmuPower for these species, however Ravintsara has been used as an individual oil in many ways. The most common methods of use of Ravintsara in these animals is by insertion into Raindrop Technique, water or air diffusion, Petting (dilute or neat), and direct topical application (dilute or neat.) Ravintsara is not indicated for oral use in the EODR, however it has been given orally to horses at a rate of 3-7 drops per horse, per day, with no ill effects. Other reference materials refer to the oral use of Ravintsara readily. It is likely that the oral use of Ravintsara is a possibility in all species.

Rose (Rosa damascene)

Rose oil is of the highest vibrational energy reported for essential oils. This makes this oil one of the "Life Force Oils," which we routinely use in our veterinary clinic for animals who are very weak, and who are close to death. When the situation is correct, Rose can elevate an animal's energy and seemingly ability to live, simply by smelling the open bottle. If it truly is the animal's time to pass, then this event is not prevented, however we see a more serene and peaceful transition. Owners and animal friends experience great relief and acceptance of the passing, with the combined use of Rose and Frankincense.

Rose also has properties that suggest it is useful for conditions such as anxiety, hypertension, Herpes infections, skin conditions, and ulcers. Since Rose is also a more expensive oil, it is often used within certain blends and products that contain it. Joy oil is often the first selection as a Rose "replacement", however Rose is also found in Awaken, Egyptian Gold, Envision, Forgiveness, Gathering, Gentle Baby, Harmony, Highest Potential, Humility, SARA, Rose Ointment, Trauma Life, and White Angelica. I can guarantee you, that a bottle of Rose is well worth the investment that you will make in its purchase.

Birds & Exotics: Rose oil is most commonly used within the blends that contain it and through the use of Rose Ointment. Water diffusion of the various blends and of Rose oil itself, is the most common method of use. The indirect diffusion of a human wearing the oils, wafting an open bottle near-by, or placing a drop on a cotton ball or tissue is also used commonly.

Cats: The same statement that was made for birds and exotics also holds true for cats. In some situations, we have applied Rose oil to cats via the Petting technique (either dilute or neat), and 1 drop can certainly be added to the Kitty Raindrop Technique when desired. The vast majority of the use of Rose remains in the use of the blends and products that contain it.

Dogs & Larger: Again, likely only due to the expense of the oil, Rose is not commonly used for these animals. The same previous statements apply to these species as well.

Rosemary (Rosmarinus officinalis CT Cineole)

Rosemary oil has many benefits in the world of animals. It has been used in French hospitals to disinfect the air, and as part of the Thieves blend is used for this purpose in our veterinary hospital. We see vast reduction in transmission of upper respiratory infections and kennel cough when Thieves is diffused on a regular basis in shelters, hospitals, grooming facilities, boarding facilities, or any other location where multiple animals will be in contact. Rosemary as a single oil has been noted to have bug repelling properties, and seems especially good at repelling Asian Beetles and Box Elder Bugs that invade our homes. Through the diffusion of Thieves or Rosemary itself, we have noted continually less of these bugs entering our home and clinic. Rosemary's medical benefits include liver protection, antitumoral, antifungal, antibacterial, and antiparasitic actions as well as the enhancement of mental clarity. Conditions benefiting from

Rosemary would include infectious diseases (especially air borne), liver conditions, lung infections, hair loss, senility, and fungal infections.

There is a cautionary statement in the EODR to not use Rosemary in children under 4 years of age. Rosemary as a single has not been used extensively in animals, and certainly not in very young animals. However, the blend of Thieves has been used extensively, even in day old animals. The use of Rosemary as a single oil, is likely best avoided in animals less than 6 months of age as a precaution, and the use of Thieves is recommended when Rosemary use is desired in young animals.

There is also a caution regarding the use of Rosemary in those with high blood pressure. It may be wise to avoid the use of this oil, with any animal experiencing hypertension. The mild use of Thieves (water diffusion) around cats with hypertension has revealed no ill effects.

Birds & Exotics: The use of Rosemary has mainly been limited through its use within Thieves. Water diffusion (starting with 1 drop, and gradually increasing to 4 drops in a diffuser) is the recommended use for Rosemary as a single. In severe situations, oral use of Rosemary can be considered starting with a toothpick dip added into 1 tablespoon of food. The addition into drinking water is also a likely method of ingestion (1 drop or less per liter.)

Cats: The same comments listed for birds and exotics, applies to cats as well. The most cat friendly methods of the use of Rosemary include the addition of 1 drop into Kitty Raindrop Technique, water diffusion, and Petting (diluted 1 drop in 20 drops of V-6.)

Dogs & Larger: Rosemary can be used in all of the application methods for these animals. The most common methods of use include within the Raindrop Technique (generally pre-diluted), direct application (diluted), addition into Animal Scents Ointment, Shampoo, and Massage Oils, adding to wading pools and soaking water, application via Petting (neat or diluted), by water diffusion, addition into foods, addition into drinking water, and by direct oral administration.

For oral use in dogs – 1 drop of Rosemary can be diluted with 10 drops (or more) of V-6. The dilution of Rosemary in this situation is helpful for lowering of the intense flavor of the oil. Increased dilution of Rosemary may be necessary for some dogs. 1 drop or more of this diluted solution can be given twice a day, for each 20 pounds (9 kg) of body weight. Start with a smaller amount, and gradually increase as needed, as most animals likely do not need that much in actuality.

For horses and others, starting with 1 drop per 500 pounds (225 kg) of body weight, given orally twice a day is a good starting point. Monitor responses and adjust according to individual need.

Sage (Salvia officinalis)

Sage is mainly used in animals within the blends and products that contain it; Awaken, EndoFlex, Envision, FemiGen, Harmony, K&B, Lady Sclareol, Magnify Your Purpose, Mister, and SclarEssence. As a single oil, Sage is indicated for hormonal issues, prostate problems, gall bladder conditions, and liver disease. There is a cautionary statement within the EODR to avoid the use of Sage with epileptics (seizures) and with high blood pressure. It is likely wise to avoid Sage in animals with these conditions.

Birds & Exotics: The use of Sage has mainly been limited to its use within the products and blends that contain it. Water diffusion (starting with 1 drop, and gradually increasing to 4 drops in a diffuser) is the recommended use for Sage as a single. In severe situations, oral use of Sage can be considered starting with a toothpick dip added into 1 tablespoon of food. The addition into drinking water is also a likely method of ingestion (1 drop or less per liter.) It is likely that Sage will be incredibly helpful to ferrets, who are commonly affected with prostatic disease. It is highly likely that Sage can be used with other methods such as Petting (usually diluted), or addition of 1 drop into Species Specific Raindrop Technique. More data is currently known on the use of the products that contain Sage.

Cats: The same comments listed for birds and exotics, applies to cats as well. The most cat friendly methods of the use of Sage include the addition of 1 drop to Kitty Raindrop Technique, water diffusion, and Petting (diluted 1 drop in 20 drops of V-6.)

Dogs & Larger: Sage can be used in all of the application methods for these animals. The most common methods of use include within the Raindrop Technique, direct application (neat or diluted), application via Petting (neat or diluted), by water or air diffusion, addition into foods, addition into drinking water, and by direct oral administration. For prostate disorders, Rectal Instillation can also be considered – please see that chapter for more information.

For oral use in dogs – 1 drop of Sage can be diluted with 10 drops (or more) of V-6. The dilution of Sage in this situation is helpful for lowering the intense flavor of the oil. Increased dilution may be necessary for some dogs. 1 drop or more of this diluted solution can be given twice a day, for each 20 pounds (9 kg) of body weight. Start with a smaller amount, and gradually increase as needed, as most animals likely do not need that much in actuality.

For horses and others, starting with 1 drop per 500 pounds (225 kg) of body weight, given orally twice a day is a good starting point. Monitor responses and adjust according to individual need.

Sandalwood (Santalum album)

Sandalwood is a lovely oil indicated for conditions such as Herpes Virus infections, Papilloma (warts), cancer, and as an immune stimulant. It is used both as a single and is also commonly used within 3 Wise Men, Acceptance, Awaken, Brain Power, Dream Catcher, Forgiveness, Gathering, Harmony, Highest Potential, Inner Child, Inspiration, KidScents Tender Tush, Lady Sclareol, Magnify Your Purpose, Release, Transformation, Trauma Life, and White Angelica. The use of Sandalwood in cancer cases has been powerful emotionally and physically.

Birds & Exotics: Sandalwood can be used within the products and blends mentioned, as well as by water diffusion, addition into Species Specific Raindrop Technique, addition of 1 drop to the Feather Spray Recipe, water misting (1 drop in 4 ounces (120 mL) of distilled water), added to Animal Scents Ointment (1 drop per tablespoon), Petting (generally diluted 1 drop in 5 drops of V-6), direct topical application (diluted 1 drop in 20 drops of V-6), addition to drinking water (1 drop per liter), addition into foods (starting with a toothpick dip in 1 tablespoon of food), Perch and Hand applications (generally diluted), and by indirect diffusion on humans and cotton balls.

Cats: Cats can use Sandalwood in all of the ways mentioned for birds and exotics. The most cat friendly methods of use include addition into Kitty Raindrop Technique, water diffusion, Petting (neat or diluted), Litteroma, and direct application (generally diluted.) Oral administration can be considered, especially in cases of cancer and severe Herpes infection. For oral use in cats, some cats may ingest small amounts within foods. Start with a toothpick dip, and gradually increase the amount. For oral use by capsule, 1 drop of Sandalwood can be diluted with 10 drops of V-6, and 1 or more drops of this solution can be given twice a day. For severe conditions, it is likely that larger amounts given orally will be beneficial. However, since this has not been used widely in cats at this time, using other methods of application is recommended first, along with careful monitoring with a veterinarian.

Dogs & Larger: Sandalwood can be used in all of the application methods for these animals. The most common methods of use include within the Raindrop Technique, direct application (neat or diluted), application via Petting (neat or diluted), by water diffusion, addition into foods, addition into drinking water, and by direct oral administration.

For oral use in dogs – 1 drop of Sandalwood can be diluted with 3 drops (or more) of V-6. 1 drop or more of this diluted solution can be given twice a day, for each 20 pounds (9 kg) of body weight. Start with a smaller amount, and gradually increase as needed, as most animals likely do not need that much in actuality.

For horses and others, starting with 1 drop per 300 pounds (135 kg) of body weight, given orally twice a day is a good starting point. Monitor responses and adjust according to individual need.

Spearmint (Mentha spicata)

Spearmint oil is used in animals for a variety of conditions including increasing metabolism, for obesity, as a mucolytic (breaks up mucus), as a gall bladder stimulant, for liver disorders, and as a digestive aid. Spearmint is commonly used within Citrus Fresh, EndoFlex, GLF, and Thyromin.

Birds & Exotics: Spearmint is commonly used within Citrus Fresh, EndoFlex, and GLF in these animals. Spearmint as a single is most commonly used by addition to drinking water (1 drop per liter), addition to foods (up to 1 drop per tablespoon), or by water diffusion (often mixed with another oil or blend.)

Cats: The same comments for birds and exotics applies to the use of Spearmint with cats. Other cat friendly methods of use include addition into the Kitty Raindrop Technique, Petting (generally diluted), and oral administration. It greatly depends on the cat if they will ingest Spearmint within foods or water. The use of Spearmint is best within Citrus Fresh, which is often accepted in small amounts in drinking water. Starting with a toothpick dip into 1 liter of water, and gradually increasing to 1 drop per liter, is a good method to get cats used to the flavor. For oral use in cats by capsule or direct oral administration, 1 drop of Spearmint can be diluted in 20 drops (or more) of V-6. 1 drop or more of this dilution can be given, twice a day or as needed. Oral use is generally reserved for more severe issues, and is not used commonly for cats.

Dogs & Larger: Spearmint can be used in all of the application methods for these animals. The most common methods of use include within the Raindrop Technique, direct application (neat or diluted), application via Petting (neat or diluted), by water or air diffusion (usually combined with other oils), addition into foods, addition into drinking water, and by direct oral administration.

For oral use in dogs – 1 drop of Spearmint can be diluted with 5 drops (or more) of V-6. The dilution of Spearmint in this situation, lowers the intense flavor of the oil. Increased dilution of Spearmint may be necessary for some dogs. 1 drop or more of this diluted solution can be given twice a day, for each 20 pounds (9 kg) of body weight. Start with a smaller amount, and gradually increase as needed, as most animals likely do not need that much in actuality.

For horses and others, starting with 1 drop per 300 pounds (135 kg) of body weight, given orally twice a day is a good starting point. Monitor responses and adjust according to individual need.

Spikenard (Nardostachys jatamansi)

Spikenard is often referred to as "Jesus' Oil" as it was used to anoint the feet of Jesus before the Last Supper. It has been a precious oil throughout history, even before biblical times, and its health benefits are often powerful. Spikenard is often used for severe conditions such as Tetanus and possible Rabies exposure. Other conditions that benefit from the use of Spikenard include heart arrhythmias, skin conditions, wounds requiring the regeneration of skin, nervous tension, and when stimulation of the immune system is needed. Spikenard is also commonly used within the blends and products of Animal Scents Shampoo, Egyptian Gold, Exodus II, and Humility.

Birds & Exotics: Spikenard is most commonly used by water diffusion, addition of 1 drop to the Feather Spray Recipe, water misting (1 drop per 4 ounces (120 mL) of distilled water), Perch or Hand application (neat or diluted), indirect diffusion, addition into Animal Scents Ointment (1 drop per tablespoon), or for non-avian species by Petting (generally diluted.) Oral use of Spikenard has not been widely used in these species at this time.

Cats: Cat friendly methods of use include water diffusion, addition into Kitty Raindrop Technique, Litteroma, and Petting (neat or diluted.) Oral ingestion of Spikenard will be accomplished through grooming after the Petting technique.

Dogs & Larger: Spikenard can be used in all of the application methods for these animals. The most common methods of use include within the Raindrop Technique, direct application (neat or diluted), application via Petting (neat or diluted), by water or air diffusion, addition into foods, addition into drinking water, and by direct oral administration.

For oral use in dogs - 1 drop of Spikenard can be diluted with 5 drops of V-6. 1 drop or more of this diluted solution can be given twice a day, for each 20 pounds (9 kg) of body weight. Start with a smaller amount, and gradually increase as needed. In severe situations, like Tetanus or Rabies, 1 full drop per 20 pounds of dog, could be considered up to 6 times per day. This is usually reserved for very severe circumstances and symptomatic cases.

For horses and others, starting with 1 drop per 300 pounds (135 kg) of body weight, given orally twice a day is a good starting point. Monitor responses and adjust according to individual need. In cases of Tetanus and suspected Rabies exposure, up to 3 drops, 6 times a day has been given orally to an average sized goat kid (30 pounds, 13.5 kg.) It is likely that this amount does not need to be scaled upwards for use in horses and cattle, and that the dose of 3 drops orally, six times per day, should be used on a "per animal" basis.

Spruce (Picea mariana)

Spruce is a very special oil, rich in spiritual connection and is also indicated for arthritis and bone conditions, sinus and respiratory infections, nerve and back pain, immune stimulation, spasms, inflammation, hormonal concerns, fungal infections, and parasites. It is also used within the blends and products of 3 Wise Men, Abundance, Awaken, Christmas Spirit, Envision, Gathering, Grounding, Harmony, Highest Potential, Hope, Inner Child, Inspiration, Motivation, Present Time, R.C., Relieve It, Sacred Mountain, Surrender, Trauma Life, Valor, and White Angelica. Spruce is helpful to release emotional blocks and is a very balancing and grounding oil. It is helpful in many behavioral conditions.

Birds & Exotics: Spruce can be used in all of the blends listed. Spruce is also used by addition into Species Specific Raindrop Technique, water diffusion (including caging and tenting), addition to water (1 drop to 1 liter), addition to food (starting with a toothpick dip in 1 tablespoon of food), addition of 1 drop to the Feather Spray Recipe, water misting (1 drop added to 4 ounces (120 mL) of distilled water), addition to Animal Scents Ointment or Shampoo, direct topical application (generally diluted 1 drop in 5 drops of V-6), Petting (diluted), addition to soaking water and aquariums (starting with a toothpick dip), Perch applications, and indirect diffusion.

Cats: Cats can utilize Spruce in all of the methods mentioned for birds and exotics. The most cat friendly methods to use Spruce include the addition into Kitty Raindrop Technique, Petting (generally diluted 1 drop per 5 drops V-6), Litteroma, water diffusion, addition to Animal Scents Ointment or Shampoo, and by indirect diffusion (often a drop placed on a cotton ball, and placed inside a cat carrier.) Oral use of Spruce in cats is generally limited to ingestion via grooming after Petting application.

Dogs & Larger: Spruce can be used in all of the application methods for these animals. The most common methods of use include within the Raindrop Technique, direct application (neat or diluted), application via Petting (neat or diluted), by water or air diffusion, addition into Animal Scents Ointment and Shampoo, addition to wading pools and soaking water, addition into Thieves Household Cleaner for bathing or soaking, addition into foods, addition into drinking water, and by direct oral administration.

For oral use in dogs – 1 drop of Spruce can be diluted with 5 drops of V-6. 1 drop or more of this diluted solution can be given twice a day, for each 20 pounds (9 kg) of body weight. Start with a smaller amount, and gradually increase as needed.

For horses and others, starting with 1 drop per 100-200 pounds (45-90 kg) of body weight, given orally twice a day is a good starting point. Monitor responses and adjust according to individual need.

Tangerine (Citrus reticulate)

Tangerine is easily used in all animals and in many routes. Its use is indicated for cases of spasm, tumors and cancer, digestive problems, liver problems, parasites, fluid retention, edema, anxiety, obesity, circulation disorders, and depression.

Tangerine is a photosensitizing oil; avoid applying to skin that will be exposed to sunlight or full spectrum UV light within 24 hours. Caution with full and natural sunlight is more likely needed than with the full spectrum indoor lighting, commonly used for birds and reptiles.

Birds & Exotics: Tangerine oil has been used in many ways: water diffusion (including caging and tenting), added to Species Specific Raindrop Technique, within the Feather Spray Recipe (replacing either Lemon or Orange, drop for drop), added to drinking water (1 or more drops per liter), added to foods (1 or more drops per tablespoon), addition to Animal Scents Ointment, water spritzers (up to 20 drops per 4 ounces), Petting (diluted non-avian), and allowed to be directly ingested when animals chose to lick the oil off of hands and other items.

Cats: Tangerine oil has been used for cats in all of the methods mentioned for birds and exotics. The most cat friendly methods of use include adding to the Kitty Raindrop Technique, water diffusion, Petting (diluted), Litteroma, and direct topical application (usually diluted). Some cats will ingest Tangerine oil in foods or water as described for Birds & Exotics. We have not noted photosensitivity issues for cats who are fully furred, however the recommendation to apply the oil where the sun will not contact the skin (stomach), is a wise recommendation.

Dogs & Larger: Tangerine oil can be used very easily and in all methods of application for these animals. Common methods of use include insertion into Raindrop Technique (often neat), addition into foods, addition into drinking water (1 drop or more per liter for dogs), direct topical application (generally diluted), Petting (diluted or neat), water and air diffusion, and direct oral administration. The amounts and concentrations of Tangerine that can be applied and administered are much higher for these animals, and often 5-10 drops (or more) will be applied topically at a time.

Tangerine oil applied directly to the skin, is usually best diluted (at least 1 drop per 1 drop) in V-6, Coconut Oil, Animal Scents Ointment, Cell-Lite Magic Massage Oil, or another carrier of some sort. Starting with smaller amounts or a more diluted oil, is still recommended as many animals respond to lesser amounts. However, if needed, much larger quantities can be applied safely.

For insertion into Raindrop Technique, Tangerine oil could be applied to the underside of the belly of Goats, Horses, and other Large Animals who may be exposed to the sun. Photosensitivity has not been noted in furred areas, but caution is still a wise idea.

Tansy, Blue (Tanacetum annuum)

Blue Tansy has not been used extensively as a single in animals at this time. It is commonly used in the blends of Acceptance, Australian Blue, Awaken, Dream Catcher, Highest Potential, Juva Flex, JuvaTone, KidScents Tender Tush, Peace & Calming, Release, SARA, and Valor. Medical properties of Blue Tansy indicate its use for inflammation, analgesia, pain control, reduction in itching, hormone-like activity, and as a relaxant.

Birds & Exotics: The use of Blue Tansy has mainly been limited through its use within the products and blends that contain it. Water diffusion (starting with 1 drop, and gradually increasing to 4 drops in a diffuser) is the recommended use for Blue Tansy as a single. It is highly likely that Blue Tansy can be used with other methods such as Petting (usually diluted), addition of 1 drop into the Feather Spray Recipe, addition into Animal Scents Ointment (1 drop per tablespoon), or addition of 1 drop into Species Specific Raindrop Technique. More data is currently known on the use of the products that contain Blue Tansy.

Cats: The same comments listed for birds and exotics, applies to cats as well. The most cat friendly methods of the use of Blue Tansy include the addition to Kitty Raindrop Technique, water diffusion, Petting (diluted), and Litteroma.

Dogs & Larger: Blue Tansy can be used in following methods; within the Raindrop Technique, direct application (neat or diluted), application via Petting (neat or diluted), or by water or air diffusion.

Tansy, Idaho (Tanacetum vulgare)

Idaho Tansy has been used in animals quite extensively. It is well known for its insect repelling action, and also has actions of analgesia and immune stimulation. Although it is listed as an anticoagulant, many people have placed this essential oil onto the wounds of large animals, and have not only found it to stop the bleeding, but at the same time repel flies and other insects from attacking the wound. It is indicated for conditions such as hypertension and arthritis. It is commonly used within ImmuPower, Into the Future, and ParaFree in animals. Idaho Tansy is a common ingredient in many bug repellant recipes.

There is a cautionary statement against using Idaho Tansy while pregnant. It is a wise recommendation to heed this warning for animals as well, however many pregnant horses, cows, goats, and dogs have been exposed to Idaho Tansy within bug repelling recipes, with no ill effects.

Birds & Exotics: Idaho Tansy has mainly been used within ImmuPower and ParaFree. Use of Tansy as a single should begin with 1 drop in water diffusion, and gradually increase to up to 4 drops. It is likely that in non-avian species Idaho Tansy can be added to Species Specific Raindrop Technique and applied via Petting (diluted 1 drop to 20 drops V-6.)

Cats: The same comments made for birds and exotics is true for cats. It is likely that cats will tolerate the use of Idaho Tansy as a single in these cat friendly methods; addition of 1 drop into Kitty Raindrop Technique, Petting (diluted), within bug spray recipes (although cats don't always appreciate being sprayed), and by addition into Animal Scents Ointment (1 drop per tablespoon.)

Dogs & Larger: Idaho Tansy is used most commonly in the following methods of application: within the Raindrop Technique, direct application (neat or diluted), application via Petting (neat or diluted), by water or air diffusion, addition into Animal Scents Ointment and Shampoo, addition into Thieves Household Cleaner for bathing or soaking, and by addition to bug repellant preparations.

Tarragon (Artemisia dracunculus)

Tarragon is used in animals primarily for deworming purposes. Medical properties indicate its use in intestinal disorders, urinary tract infections, for nausea and vomiting, behavioral hormonal issues, and as an antispasmodic. It is found and used within ComforTone, Di-Gize, Essentialzyme, and ICP. Its use as a single is common in the deworming practices of large animals.

There is a cautionary statement in the EODR to avoid the use of Tarragon with epilepsy. Although we have not witnessed any problems with the use of Tarragon containing blends and products with animals known to have seizures, it may be best to avoid the single in these animals when possible.

Birds & Exotics: Tarragon is most commonly used within Di-Gize and Essentialzyme. ComforTone and ICP have been used on a much more limited basis at this time. The use of Tarragon is mainly recommended to be used within these products for these animals. In severe cases of need, certainly Tarragon as a single could be considered. Recommended starting points for its use would include addition into water (starting with a toothpick dip in 1 liter of water), and addition into food (also starting with a toothpick dip into 1 tablespoon of food.) Topical application to non-avian species via Petting (diluted 1 drop in 20 drops of V-6) is also a likely method of application.

Cats: All of the statements for birds and exotics also apply to felines. The most cat friendly methods of the use of Tarragon would include addition into Kitty Raindrop Technique, via Petting (diluted 1 drop in 10 drops of V-6), and by Litteroma.

Dogs & Larger: Tarragon oil can be used in many methods of application for these animals, however its most common use is also within the blend of Di-Gize. Common methods of use include insertion into Raindrop Technique, addition into foods, addition into drinking water (1 drop or more per liter for dogs), direct topical application (diluted or neat), Petting (diluted or neat), and direct oral administration.

For oral use in dogs, 1 drop of Tarragon can be diluted with 5 drops of V-6. 1 drop or more of this diluted solution can be given twice a day, for each 20 pounds (9 kg) of body weight. Start with a smaller amount, and gradually increase as needed.

For horses and others, starting with 1 drop per 200 pounds (45-90 kg) of body weight, given orally twice a day is a good starting point. Monitor responses and adjust according to individual need.

With deworming protocols in horses, 6 drops of Tarragon is given to an average sized horse, in the lip, twice a day for one week. This is generally started on a full moon, and repeated monthly or as needed. Please see Deworming in Equine Conditions for more information.

Thyme (Thymus vulgaris)

Thyme is one of the Raindrop Oils, and has very powerful effects. Medical properties show that Thyme is anti-aging, highly antimicrobial, antifungal, antiviral, and antiparasitic. It is indicated for almost any condition within the Raindrop Technique, and is especially indicated for use as an antibacterial, antioxidant, and immune supportive oil. Thyme is a "hot" oil, and care must be taken to monitor the skin of animals exposed to it, and to also use caution if diffusing.

The repeated use of Thyme, or the use of Thyme that is overly concentrated, can result in hair loss in some animals at the site of application. This occurrence is most common in animals receiving repeated, frequent Raindrop Technique, and the area is almost never irritated and red. Mostly what is seen is a flakey scab, which peels off with the hair. To date, all hair loss has grown back. There may be other oils that contribute to this hair loss phenomena, however Thyme seems to be a prominent component in the event, as often the hair loss is located where a drop of Thyme fell on the skin. In severe cases of illness, we ignore this issue unless it becomes severe, as often the Raindrop Technique application has been more important in the health of the animal, than a beautiful coat. Dilution of the oil is often helpful, but again, frequent application of even diluted oil can result in hair loss.

Thyme is found in Dentarome Ultra, Longevity, Longevity Softgels, Ortho Ease Massage Oil, Ortho Sport Massage Oil, ParaFree, and Rehemogen.

Birds & Exotics: Thyme has mainly been used within the Species Specific Raindrop Techniques and within the products that contain it. In severe situations, addition into foods would begin with 1 toothpick dip of Thyme mixed into 1 tablespoon of food, and would then be gradually increased. This can be used as a powerful antibiotic, antifungal, antiviral, and antiparasitic in resistant cases. Moving towards the oral use of Thyme, is generally reserved for when other methods of use have failed.

Within the Avian Raindrop Technique, Thyme is likely to benefit any condition. However, this technique is not always easy to administer to every bird and is reserved mainly for severe cases and conditions. The use of Thyme within Longevity and ParaFree is also utilized in birds. Water diffusion of this oil could be considered in extremely low amounts (1 drop mixed with another oil or blend), however Longevity is most commonly diffused for birds.

Care must be taken with Rabbits, Guinea Pigs, and Chinchillas as they are considered "hind-gut fermenters." The aggressive use of a powerful antibacterial agent like Thyme, could damage their delicate intestinal flora. Please make sure to see the sections for these animals specifically, for more information on their individual needs and recommendations. Water based diffusion of Thyme is also mainly accomplished through the use of Longevity. Topical applications of Thyme is generally in the form of the Raindrop solution or within the massage oils.

Cats: Thyme is most commonly used within the Kitty Raindrop Technique, ParaFree, Ortho Sport and Ortho Ease Massage Oil, added to Animal Scents Ointment (1 drop or less per tablespoon), or diluted and directly applied to areas of fungal infection (ringworm – 4 drops or more in 30 mL V-6). Please see comments in Birds and Exotics for information on water based diffusion of Thyme.

Dogs & Larger: Thyme can generally be used a bit more aggressively in these animals, than in cats and smaller. The most common methods of application are within the Raindrop Technique, direct application (neat or diluted), addition into Animal Scents Ointment, addition into massage oils and bases, addition into Animal Scents Shampoo, addition into Thieves Household Cleaner (for soaking or bathing Large Animals), addition into foods, and by direct oral administration (generally diluted). In horses, the bottom lip can be "squeezed out" to create a little pocket, and diluted Thyme can be dripped right in. Often, oral Oregano is used as a first choice, as it has been used a more extensively via the oral route, but Thyme is easily an option for stubborn cases. Cattle and other large animals will often ingest diluted Thyme in grain, hay, or feeds. Thyme can be mixed with NingXia Red, Honey, Maple Syrup, Agave, Apple Sauce, or other items and can be delivered orally with a syringe. Thyme is most commonly used orally in cases of severe bacterial, fungal, or parasitic infection.

In dogs, the blend of Longevity or Longevity Softgels, are often used for the oral administration of Thyme. For oral use of Thyme as a single in dogs – 1 drop of Thyme oil can be diluted with 5 drops of V-6. 1 drop or more of this dilution can be given twice a day, for each 20 pounds (9 kg) of body weight. Start with a smaller amount, and gradually increase as needed. Some dogs will lick a more diluted Thyme solution off of your hand, or greatly enjoy the flavor mixed with foods. When mixing into foods, further dilution may be required due to the strong flavor of the Thyme.

On average, approximately ½ drop of Thyme per 20 pounds (9 kg) of dog body weight is given per day. Some dogs may need less, and some dogs may need more, careful monitoring and adjusting for the individual dog is important. For Thyme delivered orally by capsule, generally the desired amount of Thyme is added to the empty capsule (and other oils if indicated), and the capsule is filled the rest of the way with V-6 prior to administration. Special consideration should be made of the gut flora of dogs receiving oral Thyme, and Life 5 should be given after any oral administration of powerful antibacterial essential oils. See the Life 5 description for more information.

For horses and others, starting with 1 drop per 500 pounds (90 kg) of body weight, given orally twice a day is a good starting point. Thyme oil is generally diluted in V-6, NingXia Red, Applesauce, or some other carrier for oral administration. Monitor responses and adjust according to individual need. In cases of severe infections – it is likely that more Thyme can certainly be given. It is more common to use oral Oregano in large animals, so we often rely on this oil as a first choice. Special care should be considered of the gastrointestinal flora, and it is a good idea to follow the use of oral Thyme with probiotics. Life 5 can be used, but often times a specific large animal product is more cost effective.

Tsuga (Tsuga Canadensis)

Tsuga is most commonly used in animals as a blood purifier for detoxification and vaccinosis. It is "related" to the popular Homeopathic remedy Thuja, which is widely used for vaccination detoxification. Medical properties also suggest the use of Tsuga for analgesia, arthritis, respiratory conditions, kidney and urinary infections, skin conditions, and venereal diseases.

Birds & Exotics: Tsuga has not been used extensively in these animals at this time. Water based diffusion would be a recommended starting point, with 1 drop added to a diffuser, and gradually increasing to 4 drops. Although it has not yet been used in these ways, the following methods are likely to be tolerated if Tsuga seems most indicated for a condition that is not responding to more widely used oils: addition of 1 drop into Species Specific Raindrop Technique, addition into drinking water (starting with a toothpick dip into 1 liter of water), addition into foods (starting with a toothpick dip into 1 tablespoon), addition of 1 drop into the Feather Spray Recipe, water misting (1 drop in 4 ounces (120 mL) of distilled water), and by Petting (diluted 1 drop to 5 drops V-6) in non-avian species. It is important to have careful monitoring, in cooperation with a veterinarian, when you use protocols that have not been widely used in your species before. In rabbits, the indication for Tsuga in venereal diseases, such as Syphilis (Vent), seem very probable.

Cats: The same comments stated in birds and exotics also applies to cats, however cats are much more likely to tolerate the following methods quite easily: addition into Kitty Raindrop Technique (starting with 1 drop, and building to 4 drops over time), application via Petting (diluted 1 drop in 5 drops V-6), water diffusion, and Litteroma. The oral consumption of Tsuga will most likely be accomplished through grooming after Petting applications, however in severe cases where Tsuga is considered for oral use, 1 drop of Tsuga would be diluted in 20 drops of V-6. 1 drop or more of this dilution would be given (generally by capsule) twice a day. Careful pre-exposure monitoring with a veterinarian, as well as monitoring of responses, is important. It is important to note that the direct oral use of Tsuga has not been well documented in cats at this time.

Dogs & Larger: Tsuga oil can be used in many methods of application for these animals. Common methods of use include insertion into Raindrop Technique, addition into foods, addition into drinking water (1 drop per liter for dogs), direct topical application (diluted or neat), Petting (diluted or neat), and direct oral administration.

For oral use in dogs – 1 drop of Tsuga can be diluted with 10 drops of V-6. 1 drop or more of this diluted solution can be given twice a day, for each 20 pounds (9 kg) of body weight. Start with a smaller amount, and gradually increase as needed.

For horses and others, starting with 1 drop per 500 pounds (225 kg) of body weight, given orally twice a day is a good starting point. Monitor responses and adjust according to individual need.

Valerian (Valeriana officinalis)

Valerian has been extensively researched for tranquilizer type effects in the medical community. It generally has a very calming effect on the central nervous system. It is well indicated for sleep disturbances and cognitive dysfunction, restlessness, anxiety, and emotional concerns in animals. Mention has been made several times about the herbal preparation of Valerian "building up" within a system, and that caution needed to be taken with the use of Valerian herb. Further research revealed descriptions of the actual need for buildup of the herb to be effective, and no data could be found on actual reports of the herb or essential oil causing issues. The oral use of Valerian has been quite extensively used in humans and animals, and no concern has been noted. Valerian is commonly used within the blend of Trauma Life.

The use of Valerian within several human recipes indicated for pain management has been used in animals.

Birds & Exotics: Valerian has most commonly been used within Trauma Life in these species. The use of Valerian as a single should start with water based diffusion as a general suggestion. Although Valerian has not yet been used extensively in these ways, the following methods are likely to be well tolerated: addition of 1 drop into Species Specific Raindrop Technique, addition into drinking water (starting with a toothpick dip into 1 liter of water), addition into foods (starting with a toothpick dip into 1 tablespoon), addition of 1 drop into the Feather Spray Recipe, Perch and Hand applications, indirect diffusion, and by Petting (diluted 1 drop to 5 drops V-6) in non-avian species. It is important to have careful monitoring, in cooperation with a veterinarian, when you use protocols that have not been widely used in your species before.

Cats: The same comments stated in birds and exotics also applies to cats, however cats are much more likely to tolerate the following methods quite easily: addition into Kitty Raindrop Technique (starting with 1 drop, and building to 4 drops over time), application via Petting (diluted 1 drop in 5 drops V-6), water diffusion, and Litteroma. The oral consumption of Valerian will most likely be accomplished through grooming after Petting applications, however in severe cases where Valerian is considered for oral use, 1 drop of Valerian would be diluted in 20 drops of V-6. 1 drop or more of this dilution would be given (generally by capsule) twice a day. Careful pre-exposure monitoring with a veterinarian, as well as monitoring of responses, is important. It is important to note that the direct oral use of Valerian has not been well documented in cats at this time.

Dogs & Larger: Valerian oil can be used in many methods of application for these animals. Common methods of use include insertion into Raindrop Technique, addition into foods, addition into drinking water (1 drop per liter for dogs), direct topical application (diluted or neat), Petting (diluted or neat), and direct oral administration.

For oral use in dogs – 1 drop of Valerian can be diluted with 10 drops of V-6. 1 drop or more of this diluted solution can be given twice a day, for each 20 pounds (9 kg) of body weight. Start with a smaller amount, and gradually increase as needed.

For horses and others, starting with 1 drop per 500 pounds (225 kg) of body weight, given orally twice a day is a good starting point. Monitor responses and adjust according to individual need.

Vetiver (Vetiveria zizanioides)

Vetiver is well known for anti-inflammatory properties, and is indicated for conditions such as anxiety and behavioral concerns, arthritis, circulatory stimulation, oily skin, and as an antispasmodic. Vetiver is commonly used within Ortho Ease and Ortho Sport Massage Oil, ParaFree, and Thieves Fresh Essence Mouthwash, and is also found in Lady Sclareol (which is less commonly used in animals.)

Given orally, Vetiver has been reported to have wonderful anti-histamine actions, and reduces itching very well.

Birds & Exotics: Vetiver has most commonly been used within ParaFree and the Massage Oils in these species. The use of Vetiver as a single should start with water based diffusion as a general suggestion. Although Vetiver has not yet been used extensively in these ways, the following methods are likely to be well tolerated: addition of 1 drop into Species Specific Raindrop Technique, addition into drinking water (starting with a toothpick dip into 1 liter of water), addition into foods (starting with a toothpick dip into 1 tablespoon), addition of 1 drop into the Feather Spray Recipe, Perch and Hand applications, indirect diffusion, and by Petting (diluted 1 drop to 5 drops V-6) in non-avian species. It is important to have careful monitoring, in cooperation with a veterinarian, when you use protocols that have not been widely used in your species before.

Cats: The same comments stated in birds and exotics also applies to cats, however cats are much more likely to tolerate the following methods quite easily: addition into Kitty Raindrop Technique (starting with 1 drop, and building to 4 drops over time), application via Petting (diluted 1 drop in 5 drops V-6), water diffusion, and Litteroma. The oral consumption of Vetiver will most likely be accomplished through grooming after Petting applications, however in severe cases where Vetiver is considered for oral use, 1 drop of Vetiver would be diluted in 20 drops of V-6. 1 drop or more of this dilution would be given (generally by capsule) twice a day. Careful pre-exposure monitoring with a veterinarian, as well as monitoring of responses, is important. It is important to note that the direct oral use of Vetiver has not been well documented in cats at this time.

Dogs & Larger: Vetiver oil can be used in many methods of application for these animals. Common methods of use include insertion into Raindrop Technique, addition into foods, addition into drinking water (1 drop per liter for dogs), direct topical application (diluted or neat), Petting (diluted or neat), and direct oral administration.

For oral use in dogs – 1 drop of Vetiver can be diluted with 10 drops of V-6. 1 drop or more of this diluted solution can be given twice a day, for each 20 pounds (9 kg) of body weight. Start with a smaller amount, and gradually increase as needed.

For horses and others, starting with 1 drop per 500 pounds (225 kg) of body weight, given orally twice a day is a good starting point. Monitor responses and adjust according to individual need.

In some deworming protocols, Vetiver may be included in higher concentrations as an antispasmodic (decreasing intestinal cramping from the passing of worms.) The majority of oral use of Vetiver is through ParaFree.

Wintergreen (Gaultheria procumbens)

Wintergreen is one of the Raindrop Oils, and certainly carries a bit of controversy with its use within the animal kingdom, and especially in cats. Wintergreen is likely one of the most synthetically created essential oils on the market today, and I believe that this is the primary reason for all of the negative reports and fear-based attitudes towards its use. The use of Young Living Wintergreen is vital for the safe use within animals, to ensure actual plant derived essential oil. When true and pure Wintergreen oil is used, there are literally thousands of cats who have not only been exposed to Wintergreen, but have used it (especially within Kitty Raindrop Technique) on a long term basis. One of our feline patients has been receiving a Kitty Raindrop Technique daily to twice daily for over 2 years! Regular blood monitoring is performed, and not only are there no detrimental effects, we see clear medical benefits and reversal of his neurologic disorder with these applications.

Care must be taken with Wintergreen oil in animals who are bleeding, have a tendency to bleed, or are on any sort of anti-coagulant therapy. The over use of essential oil(s) that have anti-coagulant actions, especially in oral administration, can produce a temporary and dose dependent, increase in bleeding and reduction of clotting. Wintergreen is one of very few essential oils that I feel carries a possibility of being substantially over-dosed when given orally, and could cause significant concern.

There is a cautionary statement in the EODR against the use of Wintergreen in those with epilepsy. Although this precaution is wise to adhere to, in practice many animals who are afflicted with seizures receive Raindrop Techniques (including Wintergreen) on a regular basis, with no ill effects. Wintergreen can be omitted from the Raindrop Technique where there is concern for an animal who has experienced seizures in the past. We have also not witnessed any problems with the use of Wintergreen containing blends and products in animals known to have seizures. It is likely best to avoid the purposeful and aggressive use of Wintergreen as a single in these animals when possible.

Wintergreen is also commonly used within BLM Capsules, Dentarome Toothpaste, Dentarome Ultra Toothpaste, Ortho Ease and Ortho Sport Massage Oils, PanAway, and Raven.

Due to its use within the Raindrop Technique, there is likely not a single condition that wouldn't benefit from its use. However, Wintergreen is especially indicated for conditions such as blood clots, spasms, inflammation, to dilate blood vessels and increase circulation, for analgesia, to reduce blood pressure, arthritis, pain, fatty liver disease, and muscle and nerve pain.

A note on performance and competition animals: Methyl Salicylate, a main constituent of Wintergreen oil, is often contained within the listings of banned substances for horses and other animals entered in competitions such as racing and endurance events. To date, and to my knowledge, there has never been a positive testing result from the use of a truly natural Wintergreen. More studies are being completed to understand the blood levels, metabolism, and clearing of essential oils, however at this time, you may choose to avoid the use of oils such as Peppermint or Wintergreen at least 3 days before an event, or just replace their use with oils that carry no controversy at all, such as Copaiba.

Birds & Exotics: Wintergreen has mainly been used within the Species Specific Raindrop Techniques and within the products that contain it. Within the Avian Raindrop Technique, Wintergreen is likely to benefit any condition, however, this technique is not always easy to administer to every bird and is reserved mainly for severe cases and conditions.

Moving towards the oral use of Wintergreen in these small animals, is generally reserved for when other more commonly used essential oils have failed to yield enough results. Addition into foods would begin with 1 toothpick dip of Wintergreen mixed into 1 tablespoon of food, and would then be gradually increased.

Adding to drinking water can be considered, however for birds or animals that bathe in their water, this may not be a good choice, as it could feel very "cold" and sting the eyes. Wintergreen could also be water diffused, generally added to the diffuser with other oils or blends. Wintergreen is most commonly used within BLM Capsules for oral use in exotics and birds. Wintergreen could also be added to Animal Scents Ointment for topical application to non-feathered areas (1 drop or less to 3 tablespoons.)

With other exotics, the use of Wintergreen within products such as Ortho Ease or Ortho Sport, which can be applied via Petting, is well accepted and tolerated. Perch and Hand applications are also methods of use – and often applying the Species Specific Raindrop Technique lightly to the area is a great idea.

Cats: The use of Wintergreen in cats is likely to remain one of controversy for some time. Those vehemently opposed to its use, are blind to any blood work or massive amounts of data showing the safe use of quality Wintergreen in felines.

In practice, the use of Wintergreen in cats is viewed much like my opinion of Peppermint oil. Wintergreen oil in itself is not "bad," but the quality which is used and "how" it is used is of the utmost importance. Like Peppermint, Wintergreen is a strong oil, and careful consideration must be applied to its application to cats.

Even diluted, Wintergreen as a single oil can pack quite a punch with a topical application. Within the Kitty Raindrop Technique, Wintergreen is used in some cats even twice a day. The majority of cats absolutely love the Kitty Raindrop Technique, and there is absolutely no issue of the Wintergreen being in the solution. However, it is important to remember that there are only 4 drops of Wintergreen added to 30 mL (1 ounce) of V-6, making it quite a dilute solution.

The most cat friendly ways to use Wintergreen include within the Kitty Raindrop Technique, and by addition into Animal Scents Ointment (1 drop per 3 tablespoons). Other uses of Wintergreen is best accomplished through the blends and products that contain it, such as the use of PanAway, or with Petting applications with Ortho Ease or Ortho Sport Massage Oil. Some cats will ingest BLM Capsules mixed into foods, however the flavor of essential oils within the product creates refusal in some cats. See these products for more information on their specific uses in cats.

Dogs & Larger: Wintergreen can be used in all of the application methods for these animals. The most common methods of use include within the Raindrop Technique, direct application (neat or diluted), addition into Animal Scents Ointment, Shampoo, Massage Oils, adding to wading pools and soaking water, application via Petting (neat or diluted), by water diffusion (usually combined with other oils), addition into foods, addition into drinking water, and by direct oral administration.

For oral use in dogs – 1 drop of Wintergreen can be diluted with 20 drops (or more) of V-6. The dilution of Wintergreen in this situation is for the lowering of the intense flavor of the oil, but also as a safety recommendation. Starting with less of this powerful oil initially, then gradually increasing the intake is wise. Start with 2 drops of this diluted solution given twice a day, for each 20 pounds (9 kg) of body weight. Start with a smaller amount, and gradually increase as needed. Many animals respond to small amounts, and so it best to titrate the amount of oil given, to the individual needs of the animal.

For horses and others, starting with 1 drop per 500 pounds (45 kg) of body weight, given orally twice a day is a good starting point. Monitor responses and adjust according to individual need. Certainly much larger amounts of Wintergreen have been administered to these animals orally in certain cases. However, since there are many other anti-inflammatory essential oils to choose from, the aggressive oral use of Wintergreen is unlikely to be necessary.

Ylang Ylang (Cananga odorata)

Ylang Ylang is used in animals for antispasmodic effects, vaso-dilation, antidiabetic effects, antiparasitic properties, to regulate heartbeat, for heart arrhythmias, hypertension, anxiety, depression, hair loss, and intestinal problems. It is often thought of as a "Yin and Yang" oil, balancing male and female or positive and negative energies. Emotionally it combats low self-esteem, increases focus of thoughts, filters out negative energy, and restores confidence and peace. Ylang Ylang is likely an oil that all animals should have exposure to.

Ylang Ylang is commonly found and used within Aroma Life, Australian Blue, Awaken, CardiaCare, Clarity, Dream Catcher, FemiGen, Forgiveness, Gathering, Gentle Baby, Gratitude, Grounding, Harmony, Highest Potential, HRT, Humility, Inner Child, Into the Future, Joy, Lady Sclareol,

Motivation, Peace & Calming, Present Time, Release, Sacred Mountain, SARA, Sensation, and White Angelica.

There is a cautionary statement in the EODR to avoid the use of Ylang Ylang if blood pressure is too low. It may be best to avoid the use of this oil in very debilitated or weak animals, if their blood pressure may be low. Low blood pressures can be subjectively evaluated by feeling the femoral pulse of an animal, located in their groin area. Weak and thready pulses may indicate low blood pressure.

Birds & Exotics: Ylang Ylang has most commonly been used within the blends that contain it for these species. The use of Ylang Ylang as a single should start with water based diffusion as a general suggestion. Although Ylang Ylang has not yet been used extensively in these ways, the following methods are likely to be well tolerated: addition of 1 drop into Species Specific Raindrop Technique, addition into drinking water (starting with a toothpick dip into 1 liter of water), addition into foods (starting with a toothpick dip into 1 tablespoon), addition of 1 drop into the Feather Spray Recipe, Perch and Hand applications, indirect diffusion, and by Petting (diluted 1 drop to 5 drops V-6) in non-avian species. It is important to have careful monitoring, in cooperation with a veterinarian, when you use protocols that have not been widely used in your species before.

Cats: The same comments stated in birds and exotics, also applied to cats, however cats are much more likely to tolerate the following methods quite easily: addition into Kitty Raindrop Technique, application via Petting (diluted or neat), water diffusion, and Litteroma. The oral consumption of Ylang Ylang will most likely be accomplished through grooming after Petting applications, however in severe cases where Ylang Ylang is considered for oral use, 1 drop of Ylang Ylang would be diluted in 10 drops of V-6. 1 drop or more of this dilution would be given (generally by capsule) twice a day. Careful pre-exposure monitoring with a veterinarian, as well as monitoring of responses, is important. It is important to note that the direct oral use of Ylang Ylang has not been well documented in cats at this time.

Dogs & Larger: Ylang Ylang oil can be used in many methods of application for these animals. Common methods of use include insertion into Raindrop Technique, addition into foods, addition into drinking water (1 drop per liter for dogs), direct topical application (diluted or neat), Petting (diluted or neat), and direct oral administration.

For oral use in dogs – 1 drop of Ylang Ylang can be diluted with 10 drops of V-6. 1 drop or more of this diluted solution can be given twice a day, for each 20 pounds (9 kg) of body weight. Start with a smaller amount, and gradually increase as needed.

For horses and others, starting with 1 drop per 500 pounds (225 kg) of body weight, given orally twice a day is a good starting point. Monitor responses and adjust according to individual need.

EMOTIONAL USE OF BLENDS

I decided to separate out certain blends that are mainly used for emotional work with animals, as these oils are typically all applied or used in a similar manner. It is not that these particular blends do not possess medical benefits, certainly they do.

Any of the blends can be used to "obtain" the presence of a particular single oil contained within it. Remember, you can easily cross reference the oils contained within each blend within the EODR. The blends that are used primarily in the ways described in this chapter, will have an "E" located after their name, and their descriptions will contain conditions and situations for their use. You should then refer to this chapter for the suggestions on methods of application.

When selecting an emotional blend, I often find that people who share their lives with an animal, know exactly which oil is indicated for their companion. Quite honestly, I have them read through the list of blend names, and they always come up with the perfect choice. Often, without knowing anything of the properties or oils it contains. There have been many times where I would have selected different oil blends for certain situations for my patients, however an owner had a distinct draw to a certain oil blend. It never fails, that the blend they selected, seemed to be the perfect match for that animal. Now, this is not to say that my selection would not have worked for their pet, but I would say that I am continually impressed by the ability of the owner to "know" their animal, and I respect that ability greatly.

Please read the chapter on Emotional Work with Oils, to make sure you have a full understanding of some of the fundamental philosophies that are recommended. Please recognize, that there is no right or wrong way to do things. These are merely suggestions and recommendations of what has worked well for the majority of animals. Every animal and situation is individual, and respect for that fact is grand.

Use of Emotional Blends: In general, most emotional blends are used by either diffusion or by Petting applications. Some emotional blends can be added to a Species Specific Raindrop Technique, but when emotional work is desired, often an "Emotional Raindrop" is performed. Basically, between 6-8 emotional blends are selected for an animal (sometimes less), and they are applied over the spine in a Raindrop Technique style of application. This has been a phenomenal technique for many animals and situations. There is no right or wrong order in which to apply the emotional oils, let your judgment be your guide. There are some suggestions and case examples within the Emotional Work with Oils chapter as well.

Birds: Most blends will be water diffused, with approximately 1-4 drops within a diffuser. Indirect diffusion is also appropriate, as well as the "human diffuser" and Perch applications.

Exotics: The same comments for birds, applies to exotic animals as well. Exotics are also likely to be able to use Petting applications. Depending on the species, the oil may be diluted or neat, and varying amounts will be left present on the human hands. When in doubt, start with completely absorbed oils (into your hands) and gradually expose the animal to more over time.

Cats: Water diffusion is commonly used, as well as Petting (neat or diluted.) For an Emotional Raindrop Technique, it is best if each individual oil is pre-diluted for each application, instead of mixed all together as they are in the Kitty Raindrop Technique. For example, dilute 1 drop of Trauma Life in 1-2 mL of V-6 (the small sample oil bottles work well for this.) In a separate sample bottle, do the same with Grounding oil blend, and so forth. When you have your assortment of diluted emotional blends, then drip each one up the spine, one at a time, stroking after each oil application.

Dogs & Larger: Water or air diffusion can be utilized, however many times water diffusion is selected for homes where air diffusion is selected for barns. Very often, these animals can have 4 or more drops applied via Petting (neat), have neat Emotional Raindrop Technique (with 4-8 drops applied of each oil), and certainly some even ingest certain emotional blends such as Peace & Calming. If an animal feels drawn to ingesting the essential oil, I let them.

We once had a dog presented to the clinic for being far too hyper and unable to be handled. The dog proceeded to lick up multiple handfuls of Peace & Calming from my hand, ingesting upwards of 20 drops! Once he had his fill, I pet his chest with 3 drops of Peace & Calming on my hand. He then curled up, and went to sleep in a corner of the exam room. Needless to say, the owner went home with a bottle of the essential oil!

The blends that I feel are most commonly used in emotional settings (designated with an E), will have the properties and situations in which they are most beneficial listed. How you use them, and in which situation, is purely up to you. Never forget, often the humans need more emotional oils than the animals do, please treat yourself at the same time!

All blends contain single oils which you may want to use for medical purposes. All of the methods of application discussed previously for the single oils, may be considered for the physical use of the blend. The oral use of the emotional blends, has been less documented, however their use in this manner may be warranted in some situations. A suggestion would be to look up each individual oil contained within the blend you wish to use, and as long as it does not contain a single oil that is contraindicated for oral use your species, you may proceed to use it. Learn about the unique qualities and suggestions that may be listed for the individual oils. Whichever oil has the most conservative recommendations for its use, then choose that oil as a guide for how to use the blend.

As most blends do not truly reveal their exact concentrations of each individual oil, it is often impossible to extrapolate an accurate dose for blends. As a starting point, it is suggested that you start with even smaller amounts orally, than what would be suggested by the single oils. Then gradually increase the use, with careful monitoring of the animal.

PHYSICAL USE OF BLENDS

I wish to express again, that all essential oil blends (and singles for that matter) contain both physical and emotional benefits. However, certain oils tend to be used in a more obvious physical nature. These oils will have a "P" designated behind their name. Oils with the "Physical" representation are often indicated for specific medical concerns or taken orally for medical use.

For most physical blends, the same recommendations for use will apply. However, there are a few blends (such as Di-Gize), which will have more explicit instructions regarding its use. This is generally due to the fact that certain oils are used in much higher quantities orally, or for distinct medical conditions in a specific way. The suggestions in this chapter will apply to the initial use of any of the Physical Blends for each species. Common sense and adjustment to individual needs is always a primary need within every case.

Many of the blends may contain a single oil, which you might want to use for specific medical purposes. A suggestion would be to look up each individual oil contained within the particular blend, and as long as it does not contain a single oil that is contraindicated for use in your species or situation, you may proceed to use it. The single essential oils listed as contained within the blends (in both the EODR and in this book), generally list the most prominent oil ingredient first. So, if Myrrh is listed as the first ingredient (as with Abundance), then Myrrh is generally added to this blend in the largest proportion. This does not necessarily mean that it is the "strongest" oil within the blend, as certainly Cinnamon takes the lead in the mixture.

I'll discuss two blends to fully explain how I look at the use of a blend. With Abundance, a primary ingredient is Myrrh oil. This is generally a mild oil, with a lot of variety of uses for animals. However, Abundance is not an appropriate "source" as a replacement for the general use of Myrrh, due to the similarly high Cinnamon content of the oil. Since Cinnamon, Clove, and Ginger are all contained within Abundance, and would generally be considered the "most aggressive" ingredients, we would respect and use Abundance in a similar way as we would these oils, and not as we would treat Myrrh oil as a single. Since all of the individual essential oils can be consumed, if the oral use of Abundance would be considered, it would be recommended to use the blend in the manner of the single oil that has the most restricted recommendations. This philosophy actually applies to all methods of application, and not just oral use. This means that we would most likely use Abundance, much in the manner and recommendations as for the use of Cinnamon.

Now let's look at Aroma Life. The primary ingredient in this blend is Helichrysum. The other ingredients are generally easily tolerated and well used. Aroma Life would generally be considered an acceptable alternative for Helichrysum oil. Looking up each individual single oil for suggested usage in your species, and adhering to the rule of using the blend to the limits of the most conservative recommendations, is still wise. Aroma Life contains Cypress. For birds and exotics, Cypress oil has not been used extensively in an oral route at this time. Therefore, you would want to use Aroma Life for these animals, in the same manner as Cypress is recommended. For dogs and larger animals, Cypress is used more commonly via the oral route, so Aroma Life could easily be used orally for these animals.

Birds & Exotics: The use of most blends often begins with Water Diffusion. Whether or not a blend is diffused in an open room, small room, via caging, or by tenting widely depends on the main oils found within the blend. Many of the blends can be added to Species Specific Raindrop Technique (generally starting with only 1 drop added), applied via Petting (diluted or neat in non-avian species), applied to Perches, or by indirect diffusion (on a human, cotton ball, or otherwise.) The oral use of blends can generally be considered when all of the single oils are used in oral application. In general, the basic start of using a toothpick dip into 1 liter of water or 1 tablespoon of food is a good recommendation. Some blends may be appropriate to add to the Feather Spray Recipe or to a Water Misting application (generally 1 drop per 4 ounces), but this will largely depend on the individual recommendations for each single ingredient. As with Abundance, many of the ingredients could be appropriate for addition to the Feather Spray Recipe (Orange, Patchouli, Frankincense), however the presence of Cinnamon, Clove, and Ginger basically eliminate the use of this blend in that manner.

Cats: The most cat friendly methods to use Physical Blends in cats include Water Diffusion, addition to the Kitty Raindrop Technique (generally starting with 1 drop, and building to 4 drops), Petting (starting diluted for some blends, and building to neat if needed), Litteroma, and addition into various carriers for topical application. For example, adding several drops of Valor to Animal Scents Ointment for application near a broken bone. Oral use of some blends can be considered, however the most common ingestion for a cat will be via grooming after the Petting application.

Dogs & Larger: The blends can largely be used much more extensively in these species. If a blend is indicated for oral use in humans, then it can generally be consumed for these species quite easily. All of the methods of application can usually be used, including insertion into Raindrop Technique, water and air diffusion, Petting (neat or diluted), direct topical application (diluted or neat), addition into various carriers (Animal Scents Ointment, V-6, Massage Oils), added to pools and soaking water, added to drinking water, added to foods, and by direct oral administration. When oral use is considered, there may be specific recommendations and amounts for certain blends (like Di-Gize), however the following are basic starting points.

For oral use in dogs – 1 drop of a blend (indicated for oral use in humans) can be diluted with 10 drops of V-6. 1 drop or more of this diluted solution can be given twice a day, for each 20 pounds (9 kg) of body weight. Start with a smaller amount, and gradually increase as needed.

For horses and others, starting with 1 drop per 200-300 pounds (90-180 kg) of body weight, given orally twice a day is a good starting point. Monitor responses and adjust according to individual need.

ESSENTIAL OIL BLENDS

For blends that have an "E" designation after their name, please refer to the chapter Emotional Use of Blends for suggestions of their use. For blends that have a "P" designation after their name, please refer to the chapter Physical Use of Blends. For oil blends that have both letters, you may use either set of protocols depending on your main goal of attaining emotional or physical healing.

When recommendations for an oil blend's use may be different from the general suggestions, more information will be listed under that specific blend or within the condition it is indicated for.

Abundance - P
Abundance contains Myrrh, Cinnamon bark, Frankincense, Patchouli, Orange, Clove, Ginger, and Spruce. Abundance can be used on abscesses, cankers, and warts topically (often neat). Abundance may also be useful emotionally for dogs and animals who bolt their food, and never feel that they have "enough."

Acceptance - E
Acceptance contains Neroli, Sandalwood, Blue Tansy, Rosewood, Geranium, Frankincense, and Almond Oil. It is mainly used to impart "Acceptance" into an animal. This may be in situations where the animal has to accept a new housemate, accept a new home, accept a new life, accept the present, or accept being neutered.

Aroma Life - P
Aroma Life contains Helichrysum, Ylang Ylang, Marjoram, Cypress, and Sesame Seed Oil. This oil is especially indicated for conditions such as heart disease, high blood pressure, circulatory problems, and when an alternate source of Helichrysum is desired.

Aroma Siez - P
Aroma Siez contains Basil, Marjoram, Lavender, Peppermint, and Cypress. This oil is especially indicated for muscular conditions, spasms, fatigue, and soreness from injury or training. It is widely used in animals, and can be used easily in oral routes.

Australian Blue – E, P
Australian Blue contains Blue Cypress, Ylang Ylang, Cedarwood, Blue Tansy, and White Fir. It is uplifting while also grounding and stabilizing. Situations of use include anxiety, competition, showing, and obedience. The fact that this emotional blend also carries high antiviral properties, make it a wonderful selection for show and competition animals.

Awaken - E
Awaken contains the blends of Joy, Forgiveness, Present Time, Dream Catcher, and Harmony. It is a wonderfully balancing oil. See the individual oils for more information on their specific benefits.

Believe – E, P
Believe contains Idaho Balsam Fir, Rosewood, and Frankincense. Situations of use include separation anxiety, thunderstorm anxiety, showing and competition, timidness, and just general situations where an animal needs to believe. Medically, this oil is also wonderful for bones, inflammation, and cancer.

Brain Power - P
Brain Power contains Frankincense, Sandalwood, Melissa, Cedarwood, Blue Cypress, Lavender, and Helichrysum. This oil is especially indicated for brain damage, cognitive dysfunction, neurologic disorders in the brain, obsessive behaviors, and where increased production of growth hormone and melatonin are desired (Alopecia X.)

Breathe Again Roll-On - P
Breathe Again contains Eucalyptus staigeriana, Eucalyptus globulus, Eucalyptus radiata, Eucalyptus Blue, Laurus Nobilis, Peppermint, Copaiba, Myrtle, Manuka, Coconut Oil, and Rose Hip Oil. This oil can be used topically (mainly via Petting) and within Neuro Auricular Techniques. It is indicated in any respiratory condition.

Christmas Spirit – E, P

Christmas Spirit contains Orange, Cinnamon Bark, and Spruce. Situations of use include cognitive dysfunction, depression, laziness, and the need for security (such as a pup leaving its family.) Medically, this oil has anticancer and antimicrobial properties.

Citrus Fresh - P

Citrus Fresh contains Orange, Tangerine, Lemon, Mandarin, Grapefruit, and Spearmint Oil. It is well used externally and internally, and is very safe in all forms of species. It is especially indicated for general health and detoxification, immune support, to encourage drinking and adequate hydration (in drinking water), and for cancer situations. Citrus Fresh can generally be used in quite high quantities for ingestion, similar to the single oil recommendations for the various citrus oils. Photosensitivity is a concern with this oil blend.

Clarity - E

Clarity contains Cardamom, Rosemary, Peppermint, Basil, Bergamot, Geranium, Jasmine, Lemon, Palmarosa, Roman Chamomile, Rosewood, and Ylang Ylang. Situations of use include creating a clear mind, amplifying mental alertness, and promoting vitality and energy – such as for showing, hunting, competition, obedience training, tracking, and working.

Common Sense - E

Common Sense contains Frankincense, Ylang Ylang, Ocotea, Ruta, Dorado Azul, and Lime oil. Situations of use include anxiety, increasing brain function, seizures, brain damage, neurologic conditions, and to strengthen learning ability.

Deep Relief Roll-On - P

Deep Relief contains Peppermint, Lemon, Idaho Balsam Fir, Copaiba, Clove, Wintergreen, Helichrysum, Vetiver, Palo Santo, and Coconut Oil. It can be used for any type of pain or discomfort, within the Neuro Auricular Technique, and has been given orally in some situations (although this is not recommended for this blend in the EODR.) Deep Relief is mainly used topically via direct roller application, or by Petting.

Di-Gize -P

Di-Gize contains Tarragon, Ginger, Peppermint, Juniper, Fennel, Lemongrass, Anise, and Patchouli. Di-Gize is likely one of the most commonly used essential oil blends in all forms of animals. It has been used extensively via the oral route, and dosages can become quite high with no ill effects. It is a bit of a "hot" oil, and can be a bit uncomfortable for topical application to cats and smaller. Many cat owners have dripped this oil directly onto their cat's abdomen, rubbed their paws into a puddle of oil, or have dripped it directly into the mouth, much to their cat's disapproval. Such potent methods of use are rarely needed for cats, and they generally respond to much lighter approaches.

Di-Gize is used for parasites, intestinal concerns, diarrhea, vomiting, indigestion, colic, nausea, and motion or car sickness.

Birds & Exotics: The main use of Di-Gize for these species is orally. Water diffusion can also be performed, but the "spicy" nature of the essential oils within it, make it less attractive for this method. Addition to drinking water (1 drop per liter), addition to foods (1 drop per tablespoon), and Petting (non-avian species, diluted 1 drop per 10 drops V-6) are the most common methods of use. Using less quantity within foods may be necessary due to the strong flavor of the oil.

Cats: The most cat friendly methods in which to use Di-Gize includes addition to the Kitty Raindrop Technique, Litteroma, and Petting (diluted 1 drop in 10 drops V-6.) Ingestion of the oil will occur from grooming after Petting applications. Many cats respond to these methods extremely well, and rarely show the need for more aggressive administration.

If oral use is indicated (generally in deworming situations), some cats may eat small amounts of Di-Gize mixed within their foods. Starting with a toothpick dip is recommended, then gradually increasing the amount to allow your cat to get used to the flavor. Giving Di-Gize in a capsule form is usually easier than dripping it directly in the mouth. Dripped into the mouth, cats will foam and froth, and generally wish you would drop off the face of the earth! For deworming purposes, higher levels of Di-Gize are generally required than will be consumed in foods. For oral administration in a capsule, a general starting point is to dilute 10 drops of Di-Gize in 2 mL of V-6 (a sample bottle.) Using this dilution, 5-10 drops (or more) can be placed into a small empty gel capsule, and given orally, twice a day or more frequently. Smaller sized capsules can generally be found at health food stores or through pharmacy supply sources. The 00 sized capsules available through Young Living, are generally too large for oral administration to cats. For deworming purposes, cats have certainly consumed much higher levels of this essential oil, and up to 5 drops per day is not unheard of.

Dogs & Larger: Di-Gize oil can be used in many methods of application for these animals, however it is less commonly diffused. Common methods of use include insertion into Raindrop Technique, addition into foods, addition into drinking water (1 drop or more per liter for dogs), direct topical application (diluted or neat), Petting (diluted or neat), and direct oral administration.

For oral use in dogs – 10 drops of Di-Gize can easily be given per 20 pounds (9kg) of body weight, twice daily or more frequently. Many dogs will respond to less, and it is advised to start with only 1 drop per 20 pounds initially and monitor for response. Start with a smaller amount, and gradually increase as needed. Diluting the Di-Gize is a bit more pleasant for oral administration, and diluting with V-6 drop for drop is suggested, even for capsule administration.

For horses and others, starting with 1 drop per 100 pounds (45 kg) of body weight, given orally twice a day is a good starting point. Monitor responses and adjust and increase according to individual needs. There have been many cases of horses consuming upwards of 200 drops of Di-Gize in a day during severe situations, and the safety of this oil has certainly been demonstrated.

With colic protocols in horses, 20 drops of Di-Gize is given to an average sized horse, in the lip, every 20 minutes. It is also commonly applied topically, and sometimes rectally, at the same time as oral administration is being given. In cases of need, it never concerns me to increase the amounts of Di-Gize that are given.

Dragon Time – E, P
Dragon Time contains Clary Sage, Lavender, Jasmine, Fennel, Marjoram, and Yarrow. Situations for use include hormonal behavioral issues and hormone imbalances such as excessive egg laying, cranky mare syndrome, false pregnancies, and cystic ovaries. This blend is not generally used in animals by the oral route.

Dream Catcher - E

Dream Catcher contains Sandalwood, Blue Tansy, Juniper, Bergamot, Anise, Tangerine, Ylang Ylang, and Black Pepper. Situations of use include cognitive dysfunction and where deep sleep needs to be enhanced.

Egyptian Gold – P

Egyptian Gold contains Hyssop, Frankincense, Spikenard, Myrrh, Cinnamon Bark, Lavender, Rose, Cedarwood, and Idaho Balsam Fir. Situations for its use include abscesses, stimulation of the immune system, stimulation of the respiratory system, and for respiratory infections.

Birds & Exotics: This blend is most commonly used by water diffusion. Caging and tenting methods can be considered.

Cats: The most cat friendly ways to use this blend include the addition of 1 drop to the Kitty Raindrop Technique, water diffusion, Litteroma, Petting (neat or diluted), and by direct topical application (diluted 1 drop in 5 drops V-6 or neat, generally for abscesses.) Oral consumption of this oil is generally accomplished through grooming after Petting application.

Dogs & Larger: See use instructions within Physical Uses of Blends.

EndoFlex – P

EndoFlex contains Spearmint, Sage, Geranium, Myrtle, German Chamomile, Nutmeg, and Sesame Seed Oil. It is indicated for increased metabolism, hormone balancing, Cushing's Disease, insulin resistance, metabolic syndrome, obesity, and diabetes.

En-R-Gee – E, P

En-R-Gee contains Rosemary, Juniper, Lemongrass, Nutmeg, Idaho Balsam Fir, Clove, and Black Pepper. It increases vitality, circulation, and alertness and would be useful in situations such as birthing, hunting, competition, working, tracking or any other activity that requires energy.

Envision - E

Envision contains Sage, Geranium, Orange, Rose, Lavender, and Spruce. It is indicated for situations where animals need to overcome fears and become more independent.

Exodus II - P

Exodus II contains Cassia, Hyssop, Frankincense, Spikenard, Galbanum, Myrrh, Cinnamon Bark, Calamus, and Olive Oil. It is especially indicated for use for abscesses, canker, viral infections, bacterial infections, and immune stimulation. This blend is used carefully with topical use in dogs and smaller, due to the "hot" nature of the oils it contains. Application to abscesses and similar lesions, are often done neat. Oral use of this oil blend is quite common for dogs and larger. Exodus II has anti-coagulant actions due to the Cassia and Cinnamon content, caution should be used for animals who are bleeding, have a tendency to bleed, or are on any sort of anti-coagulant therapy. The over use of essential oil(s) that have anti-coagulant actions, especially in oral administration, can produce a temporary and dose dependent, increase in bleeding and reduction of clotting.

Birds, Exotics, Cats, & Dogs: Refer to Physical Use of Essential Oil Blends for use recommendations.

Horses & Large Animals: Often Exodus II is used orally in these animals in situations of more severe bacterial or viral infection (this may include goats and similar, even though they are smaller than horses). Beginning with the recommendations for Physical Use is a suggested starting point, however occasionally the oral use of Exodus II will increase significantly for certain cases. For oral use in more severe situations, starting with 1 drop per 100-200 pounds (45-90 kg) of body weight, given orally twice a day is a good starting point. Most horses tolerate this oil given neat in the lip very well, and actually seem to enjoy the flavor. Monitor responses and adjust and increase according to individual needs.

Forgiveness - E

Forgiveness contains Rose, Melissa, Helichrysum, Angelica, Frankincense, Sandalwood, Lavender, Bergamot, Geranium, Jasmine, Lemon, Palmarosa, Roman Chamomile, Rosewood, Ylang Ylang, and Sesame seed oil. With all of these great oils, one may only need Forgiveness in their life – medically and emotionally! This blend is used whenever an animal needs to move past a negative event, release hurt feelings, memories, and emotions, and generally forgive and let go. Any situation likely applies, but circumstances may include abuse, neglect, neutering, re-homing, being hit by a car, or being hospitalized or boarded.

Gathering - E

Gathering contains Galbanum, Frankincense, Sandalwood, Rose, Lavender, Cinnamon Bark, Spruce, Ylang Ylang, and Geranium. Situations of use include introduction into a new group of animals (apply to all members), showing and competition, and situations where the animal needs to stay focused and grounded.

Gentle Baby – E, P

Gentle Baby contains Geranium, Rosewood, Lemon, Lavender, Jasmine, Roman Chamomile, Bergamot, Ylang Ylang, Palmarosa, and Rose Oil. This essential oil blend is not generally used for oral administration. Gentle Baby has been incredibly helpful in all sorts of birthing situations. It is indicated for any breeding, pregnancy, lactation, or delivery environments. It is most commonly used by diffusion, however topical Petting of the oil is very common as well. Deliveries in every sort of animal, even birds and reptiles, have been greatly eased and improved by the use of Gentle Baby before, during, and after birthing or egg laying. This blend is also very good for soothing skin conditions as well as aiding in hormonal and emotional balance.

GLF – P

GLF contains Grapefruit, Helichrysum, Celery Seed, Ledum, Hyssop, and Spearmint Oil. The initials GLF stands for "Gall bladder and Liver Flush." This blend is indicated for conditions of the liver or gall bladder. Since all body functions rely heavily on proper liver function, you will see this recommendation in many different situations such as skin lesions, allergies, detoxification, and even cognitive dysfunction.

Birds, Exotics, & Cats: Follow the recommendations for Physical Use of Essential Oil Blends.

Dogs & Larger: Oral use of GLF may increase in amount for certain cases. When larger amounts are called for, it is often suggested to add additional doses to the daily administration (giving the oil four times a day instead of two), instead of purely increasing the number of drops given.

For oral use in dogs – working up to 3 drops of GLF per 20 pounds (9kg) of body weight, twice daily or more, is not out of the question. Many dogs will respond to less, and it is advised to start with lower recommendations initially and monitor for response, often accomplished through blood work evaluation of liver enzymes. Diluting GLF is recommended for oral administration, mixing approximately drop for drop with V-6 is suggested, even for capsule administration.

For horses and others, starting with 1 drop per 100-200 pounds (45-90 kg) of body weight, given orally two to three times a day is a good starting point. Monitor responses and adjust and increase according to individual needs. Certainly larger amounts may be given when monitoring reveals increased need.

Gratitude - E
Gratitude contains Idaho Balsam Fir, Frankincense, Myrrh, Galbanum, Ylang Ylang, and Rosewood. This blend should truly be used more by the humans who are in contact with the animals, than for the animals themselves. We need to appreciate and show gratitude to our animal friends, and in this way we will help them the most.

Grounding - E
Grounding contains Spruce, White Fir, Ylang Ylang, Pine, Cedarwood, Angelica, and Juniper. Situations of use include transportation of animals (especially when their feet leave the ground), trailering and float rides, shipping of animals, airplane flights, car rides, stall confinement, chronically living indoors (felines, exotics, and small dogs living in high rise apartments), and basic anxiety and flighty behavior. Grounding helps an animal feel connected to the earth and Mother Nature again. There has been concern that using Grounding in birds would be contraindicated, but I can assure you, it has no negative connotations to the bird, and is most beneficial. In situations where pet birds are not able to fly free, there is likely other emotional avenues to explore for both bird and owner.

Harmony - E
Harmony contains Geranium, Rosewood, Lavender, Sandalwood, Frankincense, Orange, Lemon, Angelica, Hyssop, Spanish Sage, Jasmine, Roman Chamomile, Bergamot, Ylang Ylang, Palmarosa, Rose, and Spruce. Harmony is especially helpful in introducing new animals to a herd or family. Harmony should be applied to new and old members. Other situations for its use include when an animal dislikes another household member (animal or human), for urination or defecation in the home (after medical causes have been ruled out), and in any situation needing stress

reduction, amplification of well-being, creation of positive attitudes, and the dissipation of feelings of discord.

Highest Potential - E

Highest Potential contains Australian Blue, Gathering, Jasmine, and Ylang Ylang. Situations for use include any form of competition such as showing, dock jumping, barrel racing, dressage, etc...

Hope – E, P

Hope contains Melissa, Spruce, Juniper, Myrrh, and Almond Oil. Hope is very good for emotional issues including depression and anxiety, but is also an excellent source for the very powerful Melissa oil - extending its uses to antiviral, antihistamine, and other conditions where Melissa oil is used.

Humility - E

Humility contains Frankincense, Rose, Rosewood, Ylang Ylang, Geranium, Melissa, Spikenard, Myrrh, Neroli, and Sesame seed oil. Like Gratitude, this blend should be used more by the humans who are in contact with the animals, than for the animals themselves. It is in this way, that we will help them the most.

ImmuPower – P

ImmuPower contains Cistus, Frankincense, Oregano, Idaho Tansy, Cumin, Clove, Hyssop, Ravintsara, and Mountain Savory. This essential oil blend is basically indicated whenever a healthier immune system is needed, which is basically every situation. Even in cancer, the immune system is the responsible party for the elimination of the disorder.

Birds, Exotics, & Cats: Follow the recommendations for use in Use of Physical Blends.

Dogs & Larger: All of the use methods described within the Use of Physical Blends are utilized for ImmuPower, however it can be used in larger amounts orally for severe cases or when needed. When larger amounts are called for, it is often suggested to add additional doses to the daily administration (giving the oil four times a day instead of two), instead of purely increasing the number of drops given.

For oral use in dogs – 1 drop of ImmuPower can be diluted in 3 drops of V-6, and 1 drop (or more) of this dilution can be given per 20 pounds (9kg) of body weight, two or more times per day. Monitor responses and adjust and increase according to individual needs.

For horses and others, starting with 1 drop per 200 pounds (90 kg) of body weight, given orally two to three times a day is a good starting point. Monitor responses and adjust and increase according to individual needs and circumstances.

Inner Child - E
Inner Child contains Orange, Tangerine, Jasmine, Ylang Ylang, Sandalwood, Spruce, Lemongrass, and Neroli. Situations for use include past abuse, abandonment, having a hard time weaning and the leaving the mother, animals who work for a living (such as those who pull plows, wagons, or carriages), older animals who have lost their play drive, and any animal that needs to recapture a bit of play and childhood fun.

Inspiration - E
Inspiration contains Frankincense, Cedarwood, Spruce, Rosewood, Sandalwood, Myrtle, and Mugwort. Situations of use include when connection to Mother Nature, the earth, and inner awareness is needed.

Into the Future - E
Into the Future contains Frankincense, Clary Sage, Jasmine, Juniper, White Fir, Orange, Cedarwood, Ylang Ylang, Idaho Tansy, and White Lotus. Situations for use include anytime an animal or owner seems stuck in an old pattern, or focuses on past issues. Many times, the human needs the use of this blend, more so than the animals, as animals live in the moment. However, our human tendency to continually recount how an animal was abused, rescued, or otherwise had some sort of emotional or physical trauma, actually promotes and secures the continued negative pattern. The brainstem and heart are excellent locations for application.

Joy – E, P

Joy contains Rose, Bergamot, Mandarin, Ylang Ylang, Lemon, Geranium, Jasmine, Palmarosa, Roman Chamomile, and Rosewood. Situations of use include adrenal disorders (Cushing's Disease, Addison's Disease, Ferret Adrenal Tumors), depression and sadness, loss of an animal companion, turmoil in the household, when an animal has to be euthanized (for humans and animals), and for general feelings of grief or sadness. Joy oil resonates at the vibration of the Adrenal Glands, located near the kidney area, which is in the mid-back region on most animals. Right behind where the rib cage ends, on the spinal region, is an excellent location to apply Joy for Adrenal issues. For joyous purposes, application over the heart is often suggested.

Juva Cleanse – P

Juva Cleanse contains Helichrysum, Celery Seed, and Ledum. It is indicated for support, cleansing, detoxification, and repair of the liver. It will benefit any condition involving the liver directly, but also can aid in many other conditions that struggle to heal when the liver is not performing optimally. Oral use of this oil blend is much more likely to be higher than the recommendations within Physical Use of Essential Oil Blends.

Birds, Exotics, & Cats: Follow the recommendations for Physical Use of Essential Oil Blends. However, it is suggested that oral use in birds and exotics can increase to 1 drop per liter of drinking water, or 1 drop per tablespoon of food.

Cats are still most likely to ingest this oil via grooming, however they too can ingest larger volumes (usually via capsule.) It is advised to start with lower recommendations initially and monitor for response, often accomplished through blood work evaluation of liver enzymes. When oral administration is deemed necessary, a general starting point is to dilute 1 drop of Juva Cleanse in 10 drops of V-6. Using this dilution, 1-5 drops (or more) can be placed into a small empty gel capsule, and given orally, twice a day. Cats have also received this solution directly into their mouth, generally provoking the typical cat response of salivation. Smaller sized capsules can generally be found at health food stores or through pharmacy supply sources. The 00 sized capsules available through Young Living, are generally too large for oral administration to cats. For severe situations, cats have certainly consumed much higher levels of this essential oil blend, up to 6 drops per day.

Dogs & Larger: Oral use of Juva Cleanse may increase in amount for certain cases. When larger amounts are called for, it is often suggested to add additional doses to the daily administration (giving the oil four times a day instead of two), instead of purely increasing the number of drops given.

For oral use in dogs – working up to 3 drops of Juva Cleanse per 20 pounds (9kg) of body weight, twice daily or more, is not out of the question. Many dogs will respond to less, and it is advised to start with lower recommendations initially and monitor for response, often accomplished through blood work evaluation of liver enzymes. Diluting Juva Cleanse is suggested for oral administration, mixing approximately drop for drop with V-6 is suggested, even for capsule administration.

For horses and others, starting with 1 drop per 100-200 pounds (45-90 kg) of body weight, given orally two to three times a day is a good starting point. Monitor responses and adjust and increase according to individual needs. Certainly larger amounts may be given when monitoring reveals increased need.

Juva Flex – P
Juva Flex contains Geranium, Rosemary, Roman Chamomile, Fennel, Helichrysum, Blue Tansy, and Sesame Seed Oil. Use this blend as recommended in Use of Physical Blends for conditions such as vaccination detoxification, obesity, liver, kidney, and pancreas conditions, general cleansing, toxin exposure, and lymphatic detoxification. There is likely not many conditions that would not benefit from the use of Juva Flex. This oil blend is not commonly used orally in animals at this time.

Lady Sclareol – E
Lady Sclareol contains Rosewood, Vetiver, Geranium, Idaho Tansy, Orange, Clary Sage, Ylang Ylang, Sandalwood, Spanish Sage, and Jasmine. It is mainly used with hormonal behavioral conditions. This blend is not commonly used by the oral route in animals.

Live with Passion - E

Live with Passion contains Clary Sage, Ginger, Sandalwood, Jasmine, Angelica, Cedarwood, Helichrysum, Patchouli, Neroli, and Melissa. Situations for use include increasing pep, energy, and desire to live and be a part of a home and family. This is beneficial for older animals who have lost their zest for life, do not want to play any longer, or seem sad with a new home situation. It can also ignite a spark for competition animals, and evoke new passion for their work.

Longevity – P

Longevity contains Clove, Thyme, Orange, and Frankincense. This blend is a high powered combination of antioxidants, and is basically indicated whenever you want something to "live longer" or have longevity. It is highly beneficial to many conditions, and it has been noticed that animals ingesting Longevity oil on a daily basis, seem less "appetizing" to biting insects. Longevity is also available in a Softgel form, and both can be used for animals. Each Softgel contains approximately 3 drops of the Longevity oil blend. This blend is considered a "hot" oil, and may not be appropriate for cats and smaller to have applied topically. For larger animals, pre-dilution may be required for topical application.

Birds, Exotics, & Cats: Follow the recommendations for use in Physical Uses of Essential Oil Blends.

Dogs: Follow the recommendations for use in Physical Uses of Essential Oil Blends. For oral use in dogs a general suggestion has been 2-3 drops per day for small sized dogs (up to 20 pounds or 9 kg), 3-5 drops per day for medium dogs (21-50 pounds or 9-23 kg), and 6-7 drops per day as a maximum for dogs over 50 pounds (23 kg). This can be added to foods, placed in a capsule, or given directly in the mouth. Some dogs may prefer this blend to be diluted with V-6 prior to administration.

Horses & Larger: For cows and horses, generally 3-4 drops of Longevity is given twice a day. This can be added to feed, hay, or placed directly into the lip. Goats and smaller sized farm animals can be dosed similarly to dogs initially, and can generally still move towards consuming 3 drops twice a day when necessary.

M-Grain – P

M-Grain contains Marjoram, Lavender, Peppermint, Basil, Roman Chamomile, and Helichrysum. Situations for use include muscular conditions, inflammation, antispasmodic actions, and for any condition that the single oil ingredients are recommended. This blend is highly unappreciated for all of the conditions it can be used for!

Magnify Your Purpose - E

Magnify Your Purpose contains Sandalwood, Nutmeg, Patchouli, Rosewood, Cinnamon Bark, Ginger, and Sage. A word of caution should be placed with the use of this blend with animals. Not for safety or concern for the animal, but for the sheer fact that an animal's "purpose" may not be our own. A show dog who is unhappy being a show dog, may Magnify His Purpose, by leaving the show ring or sitting down! We as humans, often project our feelings and desires onto our animals, without concern of their own wishes. So, although it may be controversial in nature, I will say that there are not many owners willing to accept their own animal's desire for what their purpose should be. However, if you are willing to accept (maybe by using some Acceptance Oil!) your animal's true desires, applying this oil over the heart area can be a beautiful thing.

Melrose – P

Melrose contains Melaleuca alternifolia, Melaleuca quinquenervia (Niaouli), Rosemary, and Clove. Melrose is typically known as a "top down" healing oil, and can quickly seal wounds and aid in the repair of non-healing wounds. It is so efficient in this action, that when continued drainage of a wound is desired, Melrose should be avoided initially, as a direct topical application, in order to circumvent premature closure of the lesion (as with abscesses). Combined with Frankincense, Melrose has been known to accelerate the healing of extremely stubborn wounds almost instantly. Direct neat application is often made to lacerations and wounds of Dogs and Larger animals. In cats and smaller, addition into animal scents ointment is often suggested. Melrose is indicated for ear infections, fungal infections, bacterial infections, and other skin conditions. Use according to the recommendations in Physical Uses of Essential Oil Blends.

Mister – P

Mister contains Yarrow, Sage, Myrtle, Fennel, Lavender, Peppermint, and Sesame Seed Oil. Situations for use include conditions of the prostate and to promote male hormone balance.

Motivation - E

Motivation contains Roman Chamomile, Spruce, Ylang Ylang, and Lavender. Situations of use include anytime an animal needs motivation, and needs to overcome feelings of fear. This may be a dog who previously fell down the stairs, and is reluctant to try them again, or other similar situations. Application to the brainstem area is suggested.

PanAway – P

PanAway contains Helichrysum, Wintergreen, Clove, and Peppermint. Situations for use include reducing pain and inflammation, increasing circulation, and accelerating healing. Conditions that particularly benefit from this blend include laminitis, sprains, bruising, muscle soreness, lacerations, fractures, bone pain and inflammation, joint discomfort, cruciate injuries, and arthritis. Due to the Wintergreen, Clove, and Peppermint content this oil can be considered a little bit "intense" for some applications. Cats and smaller animals may need special considerations and dilutions when PanAway is considered for their use. PanAway has anticoagulant properties, so caution should be used for animals who are bleeding, have a tendency to bleed, or are on any sort of anti-coagulant therapy. The over use of essential oil(s) that have anti-coagulant actions, especially in oral administration, can produce a temporary and dose dependent, increase in bleeding and reduction of clotting. Follow the suggestions for use in the Physical Use of Essential Oil Blends section.

Peace & Calming – E, P

Peace & Calming contains Blue Tansy, Patchouli, Tangerine, Orange, and Ylang Ylang. Situations of use include depression, anxiety, stress, hyperactivity, car rides and transportation, birthing situations, hospital and boarding situations, crating and kenneling animals, training new puppies to crates, and any other situation where general calming is desired. We have seen dogs completely accept being placed in a cage at the hospital, while the diffuser of Peace & Calming was running next to it. The second the diffuser would turn off, the dog would start whining and barking, then as soon as the diffuser was back on, the dog was again peaceful.

Present Time - E

Present Time contains Neroli, Ylang Ylang, Spruce, and Almond Oil. Like Into the Future, Present Time may be more indicated for the human than for the animal. Animals tend to live in the here and now, however, our human influence often drags them back to their past. Anytime movement beyond past experiences or traumas is desired, Present Time is an excellent oil selection.

Purification – P

Purification contains Citronella, Lemongrass, Lavandin, Rosemary, Melaleuca alternifolia, and Myrtle. This blend is excellent at eliminating odors; from skunk smell to doggy odor. Purification can be added to Animal Scents Shampoo or Thieves Household Cleaner for an extra therapeutic and de-skunking bath. Purification diffusion is critical in animal environments for the control of odors, reduction of transmission of disease, and boosting the immune system. Purification is the "go-to" oil for external parasites as well, and has been used in all species of animals for this purpose. Purification is excellent for kennel cough, fungal respiratory infections, ear mites, ear infections, lacerations, abscesses, wounds, insect bites, insect repellant, external parasites, and upper respiratory infections.

Birds & Exotics: Purification has been used in many ways for these animals. Addition into Species Specific Raindrop Technique, water mister (4 drops in 4 ounces (120 mL) of distilled water), direct topical application (neat and diluted), addition to soaking water (1 drop per liter), water diffusion (including caging and tenting), addition into Animal Scents Ointment or Shampoo (1 drop per tablespoon), and via Petting (dilute or neat.) Oral use is not generally used in these species.

Cats: The most cat friendly ways to use Purification is by addition into Kitty Raindrop Technique, water diffusion (including caging and tenting), Petting (neat or diluted), water misting (when tolerated), direct topical application (diluted or neat – especially for ear mites and abscesses), and Litteroma. For Ear Mites, 1 drop of Purification is placed onto a cotton swab, and swabbed inside the infected ear. Care must be taken not to have oil drip directly into the ear canal. See these conditions for more explanation. Oral use in cats is generally limited to ingestion by grooming.

Dogs & Larger: These animals can use Purification in all of the external methods described in Physical Use of Essential Oil Blends. Purification is not commonly used by ingestion, however.

Raven – P

Raven contains Ravintsara, Eucalyptus radiata, Peppermint, Wintergreen, and Lemon. It is indicated for any respiratory condition and is highly antiviral and antiseptic. Follow the use instructions in Physical Use of Essential Oil Blends.

R.C. – P

R.C. contains Eucalyptus globulus, Eucalyptus radiata, Eucalyptus citriodora, Myrtle, Pine, Spruce, Marjoram, Lavender, Cypress, and Peppermint. This blend stands for Respiratory Conditions, and is basically indicated for any sort of respiratory, sinus, lung, or allergy symptom. R.C. has also been known to dissolve bone spurs, and its use in boney conditions such as Spondylosis and Ringbone is suggested. Use as recommended in the Physical Use of Essential Oil Blends, however this blend is not generally used orally in animals.

Release – E, P

Release contains Ylang Ylang, Lavandin, Geranium, Sandalwood, Blue Tansy, and Olive Oil. Situations of use include anytime something is needed to "be let go" physically or emotionally. Situations could include the release of a bladder stone, cancerous tumor, chronic disease, contracted tendon, constipation, difficult labor and delivery, or a purely emotional situation or past event. It opens the subconscious mind to help release any deep-seated traumas, and is generally always part of an emotional clearing. Owners sometimes need a bit of warning when working with this oil and their animal, as they will often release their own baggage as well, benefiting themselves and their animals.

Relieve It – P

Relieve It contains Spruce, Black Pepper, Peppermint, and Hyssop. It is indicated to relieve deep tissue pain, muscle soreness, and inflammation. This oil blend is considered a bit "spicy" and should be significantly diluted when topical use in considered with cats and smaller (1 drop in 20 or more drops of V-6.) Generally for these animals, other essential oils are considered for first use. In dogs and larger, the use of Relieve It can follow the Physical Use recommendations. This oil blend is not commonly used by the oral route in animals.

RutaVaLa and RutaVaLa Roll-On – E, P

RutaVaLa contains Lavender, Valerian, and Ruta. It is beneficial for both emotional and physical needs. Situations of use include anytime calming is desired, for nervousness, anxiety, cognitive dysfunction, restlessness, promoting sleep, compulsive behaviors, but also for situations where physical calming is also needed such as with colic in horses, feather picking in birds, or intestinal cramping. RutaVaLa is also indicated for the repair of nerve damage, and aids in the re-myelination of the nerve sheaths. Application at the brain stem, along the spine, within Neuro Auricular Technique, or at the location needing physical calming (the belly of a horse) is suggested.

Sacred Mountain - E

Sacred Mountain contains Spruce, Idaho Balsam Fir, Cedarwood, and Ylang Ylang. Situations for use include when there is a need to be spiritually uplifted, while at the same time grounded, when a feeling of protection is needed, or when an animal needs to feel strong and empowered in their own life. Many cats love this blend, and it has been a favorite in our veterinary clinic when 1 drop on a cotton ball is placed within a cat's carrier for a car ride.

SARA - E

SARA contains Geranium, Lavender, Rose, Blue Tansy, Orange, Cedarwood, Ylang Ylang, White Lotus, and Almond Oil. SARA stands for Sexual And Ritual Abuse, and although that phrase often makes people uncomfortable, it actually applies to many situations in the animal world. In breeding situations, we select the mate, when the mating occurs, where the mating occurs, and how often the mating occurs. This certainly qualifies as a Sexual and Ritualistic situation for the animal! Other ritualistic forms of emotional stress, may be as simple as a hunting dog who gets so excited every hunting season, that he fails to eat, loses weight, whines, cries, and otherwise experiences high excitement and anxiety repeatedly. Situations for use include past abuse, neglect, any species of breeding animal, puppy mill dogs, show animals, competition animals, hunting dogs, repeated stress due to veterinary visits, repeated surgical procedures (for example multiple "ritualistic" debridement of a wound), and any other event that occurs more than once in an animal's life.

SclarEssence – P
SclarEssence contains Clary Sage, Peppermint, Spanish Sage, and Fennel. This blend is indicated for balancing hormones, hormonal behavioral issues, and hormonal medical conditions (pyometra, false pregnancy, egg laying issues). This blend is often used orally. Use as directed in Physical Use of Essential Oil Blends, however larger amounts of this oil may be consumed when deemed necessary.

Sensation - E
Sensation contains Ylang Ylang, Rosewood, and Jasmine. Situations for use include enhancing romance, balancing hormonal energies, aiding in pair bonding, increasing sexual drive, and encouraging mating.

Slique Essence
Slique Essence blends the essential oils of Grapefruit, Tangerine, Spearmint, Lemon, and Ocotea together with Stevia Leaf Extract. This blend can be used orally for animals in any situation where the use of these oils is indicated. Added to water, the Stevia gives this blend an extra sweet and appetizing taste, and is likely to be helpful for diabetes and obesity. See the individual descriptions and recommendations for the single oils, especially for Ocotea, as well as the Supplements & Products section to read more on Stevia. This blend is only recommended for oral use, in foods or drinking water.

Stress Away Roll-On – E, P
Stress Away Roll-On contains Copaiba, Lime, Cedarwood, Vanilla, Ocotea, Lavender, and Coconut Oil. Situations for use include reduction in stress, improving mental response, lowering hypertension, promoting relaxation, and reducing tension. Anxiety, colic, high blood pressure, transport, muscle spasms and cramping, tightness carried from arthritis and other physical conditions, and many other situations can be benefited from Stress Away. Application near the nasal area (rubbed onto the muzzle of a horse), on the brain stem, or by Neuro Auricular Technique are suggestions.

Surrender - E

Surrender contains Lavender, Roman Chamomile, Angelica, Mountain Savory, Lemon, and Spruce. Situations for use include when an animal needs to surrender aggressive tendencies, has a controlling attitude, resists accepting a pack or herd leader, resists training, is over-protective, tries to control other members of the pack or herd (too much), or generally needs to surrender an attitude or pattern that is not healthy for them. Humans benefit from this oil as well, as we often need to surrender our ideals of what our animal "should be."

The Gift - E

The Gift contains Frankincense, Idaho Balsam Fir, Jasmine, Galbanum, Myrrh, Cistus, and Spikenard. Many animals find this scent quite intriguing. It appears to be quite grounding emotionally, and physically it stimulates the immune system and promotes healing of all forms.

Thieves – P

Thieves contains Clove, Lemon, Cinnamon Bark, Eucalyptus radiata, and Rosemary. Thieves is an incredible mainstay in animal therapies. With antiviral, antifungal, antiseptic, antibacterial, and immune-boosting properties, there are many indications for its use. Thieves is considered a "hot" oil for topical use, so care must be considered when using this route for animals (especially in dogs, cats, and smaller animals.) Thieves is commonly used orally for many needs, primarily as an antibiotic. Thieves is the top recommendation for any human suffering from a cat bite, and the topical and oral use has greatly reduced or eliminated the severe infection that is typical of this injury. Both prevention and treatment of other severe infections, such as MRSA (Methicillin Resistant Staphylococcus aureus), also benefit from the use of Thieves. Thieves is also a very "purging" oil, and is very indicated in abscesses that need to be "pushed out" and for splinters and other types of foreign objects that need to be ejected from the body.

People who groom animals for a living, often get tiny pieces of cut hair embedded into their skin over time. This can create a chronic irritation, fistula, and wound that can become secondarily infected. One groomer had a lesion for over 15 years, and was told she would require a surgery with skin grafts to correct the problem, and that she would never be able to groom again! Her lesion would become secondarily infected on occasion as well, and she was on a chronic cycle of treating the condition medically, as well as worrying about contracting a resistant infection. When I initially applied the Thieves to her wound (fistula) at a grooming convention, the embedded hairs started to immediately discharge from the wound! Then, after 2 months of applying Thieves, the wound had not only resisted infection, but had completely healed over after 15 years! We now routinely use Thieves to eject these tiny hairs from the skin of groomers.

The general diffusion of Thieves is also found to reduce allergy symptoms both in humans and animals. Clove seems to have a wonderful benefit of reducing human responses to airborne allergens, and many people who experience severe symptoms when they enter a household with animals, do not notice the same reaction in households diffusing clove or Thieves regularly. Thieves diffusion also reduces the desire of insects and external parasites to stay in the vicinity of the diffusion. We have noticed drastic decreases in the number of Asian Beetles, Box Elder bugs, and feather mites that would normally invade homes or chicken coops when Thieves is used daily.

Due to the Clove and Cinnamon content of Thieves, caution should be used for animals who are bleeding, have a tendency to bleed, or are on any sort of anti-coagulant therapy. The over use of essential oil(s) that have anti-coagulant actions, especially in oral administration, can produce a temporary and dose dependent, increase in bleeding and reduction of clotting. In general, you can follow the suggestions for the use of Physical Blends, however oral use may reach into larger amounts when needed. After oral administration of powerful antibacterial essential oils (like Thieves), administration of the probiotic Life 5 is suggested. Please read more about this recommendation within the product description for Life 5.

Birds & Exotics: Water diffusion of Thieves is the most common route of administration, and is often performed with caging or tenting (3-4 drops in the diffuser.) Often, 1 drop of Eucalyptus Blue is added to this diffusion batch, as one of my favorite respiratory concoctions. Thieves can be added to foods, but is not often added to drinking water due to the "hot" nature of the oil blend. Indirect diffusion of Thieves is commonly used as well, placing a drop or two on cotton balls or on cage papers. All respiratory conditions will benefit, and Thieves is likely the answer to the horrible fungal condition of Aspergillosis in Raptors and other birds. Thieves has been scientifically researched by Dr. Edward Close, proving the ability to not only kill Aspergillus and other forms of toxic fungi, but to reduce the activity of the spores left behind. In my opinion, any household with birds should be diffusing Thieves on a regular basis.

For oral use, care must be taken in all small animals such as birds and exotics. Since they often enjoy the flavor of Thieves and will eat it readily when mixed into their foods, it is easy to administer too much of the oil and disrupt delicate gastrointestinal flora, or create an anticoagulant effect. We have seen two instances where larger amounts were consumed (over a drop a day in animals weighing 1-2 pounds, less than 1 kg), and bleeding was promoted. At this time, we have not witnessed direct spontaneous bleeding, only the increased tendency for existing sites or diseased tissue to continue or initiate bleeding. However, oral Thieves remains a primary selection for birds in the case of crop infections and when oral antibiotic actions are required. It should be remembered, that when one drop of an essential oil can make a significant shift in health for a 200 pound (90 kg) person, a bird weighing less than a pound may have effects from 1/200th of a drop! We often forget the incredibly small scale of these species of animals, and when it is brought to the forefront of our thoughts, it is actually quite remarkable.

Topical applications of Thieves can be considered in severe situations (such as Ringworm), and mainly would be via addition of 1 drop to a Species Specific Raindrop Technique, direct application (diluted 1 drop in 30 mL of V-6), Petting (dilute or neat), or by addition into shampoo or Animal Scents Ointment (1 drop per tablespoon.) There have been cases of baby bunnies, who when still wet from being born, were handled by hands that had several drops of Thieves completely absorbed into them. This slight residue transferred to the baby bunnies, and great improvements in health and vigor were noted. Oral use in Rabbits, Guinea Pigs, and Chinchillas (hind gut fermenters) should be considered with extra caution as they are much more likely to have their gut flora disrupted by powerful antibacterial actions. See the sections specific to these species for more information.

Cats: Thieves is generally used for cats as described within Physical Use of Blends. All of the comments described for birds & exotics can also be applied to the use in cats. When oral use is considered for more severe cases, administration by capsule is the best route. 1 drop of Thieves can be diluted in 5 drops of V-6, and 1 drop of this dilution can be given twice a day, as a starting point. Smaller "cat friendly" empty gel capsules (number 3 is a nice size) can be obtained through health food stores or pharmacy supply companies. Monitor and adjust amounts given according to response and need.

Dogs & Larger: Again, general use can follow suggestions within Physical Use of Blends. There are so many conditions that benefit from Thieves, that it is difficult to list them all. Any hoof condition in a horse seems to benefit from neat Thieves application, even laminitis. Ringworm, fungal skin infections, bacterial skin infections, and more benefit from additional Thieves added to Animal Scents Shampoo, Thieves Household Cleaner, or Animal Scents Ointment for application. Thieves toothpaste is also used as a wonderful poultice for conditions such as Scratches in horses, and additional drops of Thieves oil can also be added to the toothpaste (or any other oil you desire.) Thieves Fresh Essence Mouthwash is also a wonderful product to use in animals. Please see the descriptions for these products for more information on their use.

Thieves is also contained within the product Inner Defense, which is commonly used in dogs. Oral use of Thieves may increase in amount for certain cases. When larger amounts are called for, it is often suggested to add additional doses to the daily administration (giving the oil four times a day instead of two), instead of purely increasing the number of drops given.

For oral use in dogs – working up to 3 drops of Thieves per 20 pounds (9kg) of body weight, twice daily or more, is not out of the question. Many dogs will respond to less, and it is advised to start with lower recommendations initially and monitor for response. Diluting Thieves is suggested for oral administration, mixing approximately drop for drop with V-6 is suggested, even for capsule administration.

For horses and others, starting with 1 drop per 100-200 pounds (45-90 kg) of body weight, given orally two to three times a day is a good starting point. Monitor responses and adjust and increase according to individual needs. Certainly larger amounts may be given when monitoring reveals increased need.

ESSENTIAL OIL BLENDS

3 Wise Men – P
3 Wise Men contains Sandalwood, Juniper, Frankincense, Myrrh, Spruce, and Almond Oil. It is a wonderful oil to soothe and uplift spirits, and has mainly been used as a wonderful anti-cancer blend, incorporated into many cancer regimens for both spiritual and physical support. 3 Wise Men is also indicated for many viral conditions. Use as directed within the Physical Use of Blends.

Tranquil Roll-On – E, P
Tranquil Roll-On contains Lavender, Cedarwood, Roman Chamomile, and Coconut Oil. As with RutaVaLa, Tranquil can be used anytime calming is desired, for nervousness, anxiety, cognitive dysfunction, promotion of sleep (new puppy), compulsive behaviors, but also for situations where physical calming is also needed such as with colic and choke in horses, intestinal cramping, or muscular stiffness. Application at the brain stem, along the spine, within Neuro Auricular Technique, or at the location needing physical calming (the belly of a horse) is suggested.

Transformation - E
Transformation contains Lemon, Peppermint, Sandalwood, Clary Sage, Frankincense, Idaho Balsam Fir, Rosemary, and Cardamom. Situations for use would include any circumstance where change is desired, whether it is starting a new training program, visiting a new veterinarian, releasing old patterns and memories, learning a new trick, releasing ingrained fears (gun shy, thunderstorm anxiety, noise phobias), or any other time where a transformation from current thoughts is desired. Diffusion is suggested.

Trauma Life - E
Trauma Life contains Valerian, Lavender, Frankincense, Sandalwood, Rose, Helichrysum, Spruce, Geranium, Davana, and Citrus hystrix. Trauma Life is a foundational emotional oil, which should likely be used in every situation. No matter what the issue, some sort of trauma can be associated with it. Whether it is being born, getting neutered or spayed, being hit by a car, potty and crate training, falling off a bed, being abused, losing a race, being afflicted with chronic pain or disease, or having a surgery; it can be guaranteed that Trauma Life will benefit the situation. It is likely that Trauma Life should be included in a regular emotional cleansing program, even for "normal" animals. Making sure to diffuse or apply this oil on a

somewhat regular basis is suggested (for example, every month perform one nightly diffusion.)

Valor and Valor Roll-On – E, P

Valor contains Rosewood, Blue Tansy, Frankincense, Spruce, and Almond Oil. It is indicted whenever bravery, confidence, courage, or self-esteem is needed. It balances and aligns energy, as well as aligns physiology. Valor acts as a primer for the use of other oils as well, and will make all other oil applications more effective. It is often used as the first step (Balancing), in the Raindrop Technique. Uses for Valor include anxiety, stress, fear, competition and showing, but also for physical needs such as the proper alignment of the spine, broken bones, joints, and general physical structure. Valor is often used in the veterinary hospital to aid in setting a bone, applied to the area of broken bones while they heal, and to promote proper conformation of joints and tendons. Valor Roll-On has been applied to the bottom of birds' feet, with phenomenal results and success. It is an oil blend that benefits almost any situation. Valor is not used orally.

White Angelica - E

White Angelica contains Ylang Ylang, Rose, Melissa, Sandalwood, Geranium, Spruce, Myrrh, Hyssop, Bergamot, Rosewood, and Almond Oil. Known as the protector oil, White Angelica is used to protect animals (and people) from others negative energies and thoughts, and promotes a feeling of security. We often don't recognize how much our animal companions are affected by our emotions and beliefs. When a human continually obsesses about a dog's thunderstorm anxiety, a bird mutilating its chest, worries that a horse is going to not load in the trailer, or feels sorry for an animal with a not so pleasant past, we unknowingly project these feelings onto our animals. The energy placed into these negative thoughts, actually encourages more of the unwanted behavior, and a pattern of not being able to release the issue at hand. Diffusing White Angelica or applying over the shoulder area is suggested, sometimes on a daily basis.

SUPPLEMENTS & PRODUCTS

It is important to recognize that the vast majority of supplements and products that are used for humans, can be used in animals. However, just like any dietary change or addition, this should be done slowly to avoid intestinal upset. Some products have been used with more regularity in animals than others. Products that have not had extensive use in animals, may not carry a recommendation for its use. However, it is likely that certain products have indeed been utilized for some animals.

Often times, we do not truly know what the correct dose will be for an animal. Some respond to seemingly tiny amounts, while others require huge amounts. There is certainly individual variation for all of the products, and it is always recommended to start with less than the recommended dose, and gradually build upwards. For example, if one capsule of MultiGreens is recommended for a cat per day, you would begin by opening the capsule and only sprinkling a pinch (a very slight dusting), of the contents into food. You would feed this for 3 or more days, before adjusting the amount upward again. Allowing the body to adjust slowly to the new addition, as well as getting the cat used to the new flavor "hidden" within their meal. You CAN go too fast, but you can never go too slow.

One exception to the "slow" rule, is in critical and emergency cases. Obviously, if a dog has raging diarrhea, we are not going to slowly increase how much Inner Defense is given over the course of 7 days! However, if the cat has been suffering with Herpes symptoms for months or more, we can certainly take a week or two to introduce the MultiGreens.

If there is ever a product that you wish to use, that does not have suggestions listed, you can follow the same rules that I do in the veterinary clinic to evaluate and utilize a new product. First, I may perform a Google search of each ingredient contained within the product along with the species I intend to use it on, just to make sure there has not been any contraindication to its use. Next, I will make sure that a thorough veterinary exam has been performed, and blood work and other laboratory data has been collected. Then, I start with an extremely small amount of the product and gradually increase it every 3-7 days depending on the response of the animal. Laboratory data is recollected at intervals that are determined by the condition and veterinary judgment. Doses are carefully titrated to the exact needs of the body, and if any detrimental laboratory changes, diarrhea, soft stools, inappetance, or any "out of the ordinary" symptoms are detected, the supplement would be immediately stopped.

There are a set of supplements that I basically could recommend for every single animal, and for every single condition. They are part of the fundamental building blocks for good health, and listing them over and over again would become quite repetitive. You can always guarantee, whether they are listed or not in a condition, that NingXia Red, Omega Blue, and Digestive Enzymes are a constant as a recommendation, not only for healing but for health maintenance and prevention. Other items such as Sulfurzyme, Longevity, Life 5, MultiGreens, True Source, and BLM Capsules are not far behind in "constant recommendation."

Digestive Enzymes

An important word about digestive enzymes must be said. EVERY animal needs them! This statement applies to whether an animal is ill or not. Any of the digestive enzymes can be used, and often I will start with what an owner has on hand. There are specific enzymes indicated for certain conditions, and certainly some that are more user friendly for individual species. Again, even if a digestive enzyme is not stated specifically within a condition – the animal will ALWAYS benefit from the addition of at least one enzyme product to every meal. The addition is the same as previously recommended; start with a tiny pinch of the product, and slowly increase over time. Some animals will need more enzymes, and some animals will need less. Tailoring the amount to the individual animal is always recommended, and in general I attempt to get the largest amount that I possibly can into each meal.

Certain enzymes have a very balanced and complete spectrum for the use in animals. Essentialzymes-4, Allerzyme, and MightyZyme (KidScents) are wonderful "general" enzymes to use. Specific qualities and indications for use of the various enzymes will be listed in their individual description. For cats or dogs who will not consume Young Living Digestive Enzymes, I recommend the use of Prozyme Powder in my veterinary practice, which can be found from many animal suppliers.

Xylitol Toxicity

It is important to state that since these supplements are intended for human use, some ingredients may not be suitable for use in animals. Xylitol is one of those ingredients. Although Xylitol is contained in small amounts in many veterinary products, there can be a dose dependent toxicity resulting in hypoglycemia and liver problems. This has mainly been witnessed in dogs, although one cat (who ate an entire dessert tray of Xylitol containing goodies) was included in toxicity reports. At this time, I could find no other references to other animal species having concern. As levels in these products are intended for human use, Xylitol may be contained in certain products, and it is better to avoid their use when possible. Products containing Xylitol levels high enough to cause concern with regular use includes BLM Powder, MegaCal, and Thieves Hard and Soft Lozenges. Dentarome Ultra Toothpaste and KidScents Toothpaste contain Xylitol, however with normal use should not be of concern in any way, especially as Xylitol is found within many oral health products in the veterinary field. However, if your dog chewed up an entire tube of toothpaste and consumed over half of the contents, you may wish to be concerned. Dentarome and Dentarome Plus Toothpastes do not contain Xylitol. Balance Complete and Pure Protein Complete are the other products which also contain Xylitol. There should not be concern with an animal eating a small sprinkling of the product or licking up your left overs, however large amounts should not be given.

AlkaLime

This product is not used extensively in animals at this time. It has been used to correct urine pH in cats and dogs when it has been too acidic. Use must be carefully monitored in cooperation with a veterinarian. The urine pH must maintain an ideal range, and becoming too acidic or too alkaline can cause crystal and stone formation in an animal. If you would like to use the product, starting suggestions would be adding less than 1/8 of a teaspoon per 20 pounds (9 kg) of body weight, to approximately 5 mL of water. This solution can be given by syringe orally, once or twice a day. Maintain the level of administration for at least one week, and checking urine pH with your veterinarian before adjusting doses. This product may be helpful in avoiding grass scald from dogs' urine, however, urine pH in itself is a controversial topic and I personally think people focus too much on it, instead of other factors that affect total health more fully. Urine pH levels fluctuate in animals throughout the day and after a meal, so true and accurate interpretations of most pH levels are imprecise.

Allerzyme

Allerzyme is a well-balanced digestive enzyme complex that works well for most animals, from birds to dogs. It is generally not utilized in animals larger than dogs. Cats may or may not consume this enzyme within their food, due to the essential oil flavors it contains. For all animals, opening up a capsule, and starting with a tiny sprinkling of the enzyme mixed into soft moist foods is the suggested starting point. Gradually increasing the amount, until some is offered with each meal.

Birds & Exotics: Approximately ¼ to ½ of a capsule may be consumed per day (split up between several meals.)

Cats: Approximately 1 capsule per day may be consumed.

Dogs: Approximately 1 capsule or more per meal will be consumed per 20 pounds (9 kg) of body weight.

Horses & Larger: Generally do not use this product.

Animal Scents Ointment

This ointment is by far one of my favorite products. The ingredients include the essential oils of Palmarosa, Geranium, Patchouli, Idaho Balsam Fir, Melaleuca Alternifolia, Myrrh, and Rosewood making it a powerful healing and therapeutic blend. Additional oils can be mixed into this ointment to make it a super-powered custom application. 1 drop or more per tablespoon of ointment is generally added, then mixed in. V-6 can also be added to the ointment, along with additional oils as desired, to create wonderful udder rubs and treatments for larger areas. The ointment is incredibly useful for areas where oil application is difficult, such as the underside of a horse. Animal Scents Ointment speeds the healing of many wounds, however when drying or normal scab production is desired, the ointment may not be the best selection. Conditions such as hotspots or a healing scab, may do better with a less moisturizing application of essential oils.

Animals Scents Ointment is similar to Rose Ointment, and is an economical replacement for it. As discussed in Rose Ointment, Animals Scents Ointment has even been used within eyes for various conditions. Animals Scents Ointment does have a tendency to sting a bit more than Rose Ointment for this application, however it has been quite helpful for several unresponsive cases of eye disease. The ointment should be softened fully by mixing aggressively, prior to placement in the eye.

The ointment is also helpful to repel biting insects from wounds. Areas typically attacked by gnats and biting insects such as the ears and chests of horses or the noses of dogs, are helped greatly by applying Animal Scents Ointment instead of the typical toxic veterinary salves. Additional bug repelling and healing oils (such as Purification) can be added to the ointment to boost these effects.

The ointment is safe if ingested, and often dogs really enjoy doing this. If a dog particularly likes to eat Animal Scents Ointment, then we avoid applying it to locations that we do not want to encourage licking, such as neuter sites and lick granulomas. Animal Scents Ointment can be applied directly to incisions and lacerations, and should usually be used with a sparing touch. Large amounts can be packed into wounds and defects, however the over application of the ointment can cause a wound to become too moist. Common sense should be used to help you decide when a lesion should remain moist or should dry out, and your veterinarian can also help you with this advice. For birds, avoiding applying the ointment to feathered areas is wise, although they can have the ointment applied sparingly to non-feathered areas, wounds, or feet.

Animal Scents Ointment has also been used for help with behavioral and training concerns. Alone or with added selected oils, the ointment was lightly transferred from the hands onto the nose area of horses. The inhalation of these essential oils during the stressful or intense situation, resulted in continued calming effects as well as mental alertness. The ointment is also my "bag balm" of choice as well as my post-milking "teat dip" of sorts. When applied to teats and mammary areas, it is completely safe for ingestion, and is a wonderful route to allow ingestion of essential oils by young animals. Calves, kids, pups, and foals can have great health benefits by suckling on essential oil treated teats.

Animal Scents Shampoo

Animal Scents Shampoo is a wonderful non-toxic product for all animals. It contains the essential oils of Citronella, Lavandin, Lemon, Geranium, and Spikenard making it not only insect repelling but full of health benefits. Additional oils can be added to the shampoo to make a custom therapeutic shampoo, generally starting with 1-2 drops or more per tablespoon. By adding a few drops of Copaiba to the shampoo, you can provide an arthritic dog with anti-inflammatory benefits while you bathe them. The possibilities are truly endless. The shampoo can also be diluted and used as an ear wash or wound flush. Please see more description of creating washes in the section described for Thieves Household Cleaner. Even the Thieves Household Cleaner can be mixed into the Animal Scents Shampoo for a power packed bathing experience. Avoiding toxic shampoos is not only important for the animals, but for the humans who frequently administer the baths. Groomers receive large exposures to toxic chemicals in shampoos and conditioners in their work. Providing non-toxic shampoo options is not only healthier for the animal, but for the human as well.

Balance Complete

This super-food meal replacer can generally be offered in small amounts to most animal species. Due to the content of whey protein (dairy product) and of Xylitol, it may need to be avoided in certain animals. Those who have dairy allergies or are vegetarian in nature should avoid this product. Also, Xylitol in large amounts, has been linked with toxicity effects in dogs, and only very rarely (one case) in cats. A small sprinkling on foods or your animal finishing up your smoothie, is of no concern and has true health benefits.

Bath & Shower Gels

All of the Bath & Shower Gels can be used with animals. Additional oils can be added to them to create a therapeutic wash as desired.

BLM Capsules

BLM stands for Bones, Ligaments, and Muscles. It is very important to state here that the capsule form of BLM should be used for animals. The BLM Powder contains significant enough levels of Xylitol, that it could create an issue for dogs receiving maximal doses. Please see the previous explanation in this chapter for more information. For all animals, opening up a capsule, and starting with a tiny sprinkling of the powder mixed into soft moist foods is the suggested starting point. Gradually increase the amount, over time. BLM is indicated for arthritis, joint discomfort, prevention of joint problems (start as puppies), muscular conditions, cruciate injuries, broken bones, and any condition that affects bones, ligaments, or muscles. BLM Capsules contain a strong Wintergreen flavor which may not be accepted by cats and some dogs.

Each capsule contains approximately ¼ teaspoon of powder. For some people, opening many capsules at once, then measuring out the appropriate amount of powder to give is an easier option. Smaller amounts of powder can be placed into empty gel capsules for administration by "pilling" as well.

Birds & Exotics: BLM Capsules have been extensively used in birds. Other exotic animals may be limited by the flavor of the product and by their species, as to if the product is recommended for use. Start with a very small sprinkling added to soft moist foods, and build up to offering ¼ capsule per day, generally split into several meals.

Cats: For cats who will consume the flavorful powder, build up to ½ of a capsule per day, split into 2-3 doses or meals.

Dogs: For small dogs weighing up to 20 pounds (9 kg) between 1/8 to ¼ of a capsule can be offered 2-3 times a day. For medium dogs 20-50 pounds (9-23 kg) between ¼ to ¾ of a capsule can be offered 2-3 times a day. For large dogs over 50 pounds (23 kg) 1 capsule can be offered 2-3 times a day. For the first 6 weeks of administration or if acutely injured, a loading dose of double or triple the suggested amounts can be given.

Horses & Larger: In general, BLM Capsules are not used in these animals due to cost concerns. However, the product certainly can be used, and it is likely that the powdered product could be used in these species.

BLM Powder

BLM Powder is not recommended for use in animals due to the Xylitol content. BLM Capsules should be used instead.

Blue Agave Nectar

Animals may consume this product with no concerns.

Carbozyme

Carbozyme is not currently available from Young Living. Essentialzymes-4 is an excellent product to replace it with.

CardiaCare

This product is no longer available through Young Living. As a replacement, our veterinary practice recommends Standard Process Cardiac Support available in a feline and canine formulas. Both formulas can be used in all types of animals, including birds and exotics.

Cel-Lite Magic Massage Oil

This massage oil blend contains the essential oils of Cedarwood, Clary Sage, Cypress, Grapefruit, Juniper, and Black Pepper. It is especially helpful in increasing circulation and lymphatic flow, and is helpful in the reduction of lipomas (fatty tumors.) This product can be massaged on location (shaved or haired), have other oils added to it, and is safe if ingested by an animal.

ClaraDerm

ClaraDerm is a soothing spray containing Coconut oil (fractionated), Myrrh, Melaleuca Alternifolia, Lavender, Frankincense, Roman Chamomile, and Helichrysum. It is especially indicated for skin conditions which are dry, itchy, and irritated. It was formulated for use in the "sensitive female areas" for women, and is helpful with yeast infections in these areas. The use of this spray is recommended around irritated vulvar folds of dogs, in cases of vaginitis, around irritated anal glands, on itchy anal areas, in between foot pads, and anywhere secondary infection and irritations may be present. The Coconut oil content in this product makes it less suitable for spraying onto birds, however small amounts could be applied topically (without spraying) to non-feathered areas. Care should be taken in all animals, to make sure that the area being treated is not getting too moist or oily from this preparation. When drying of an area (such as for hot spots) is indicated, ClaraDerm may not be the best selection.

ComforTone

ComforTone is recommended for use in situations of constipation, diarrhea, or other severe digestive concerns. It is generally not used on a regular or long term basis in animals, but can be helpful in correcting digestive issues. If using during diarrhea, ComforTone can sometimes promote the softening of stools, so if no improvement is seen, it is recommended to discontinue administration.

Birds & Exotics: A capsule may be opened and a very small sprinkling of ComforTone added and mixed into a soft moist meal. Generally, not more than a pinch per meal is given, up to three times per day.

Cats: The same directions can be followed as described for birds and exotics, however some cats may consume up to ¼ of a capsule twice a day mixed into soft moist food.

Dogs: Dogs may consume up to ½ capsule or more per meal, per 20 pounds (9 kg) of body weight, 2-3 times a day. Larger amounts may be required for constipation situations.

Horses & Larger: This product is not generally used in these animals.

Copaiba Vanilla Shampoo & Conditioner
These products may be used for animals as well.

CortiStop – Women's
CortiStop – Women's is only used in female animals, and is mainly indicated for Cushing's Disease. For dogs, a dose of 1 capsule per day is given, and then the dog is re-evaluated with a veterinarian in 7-10 days, usually with blood work. The dosage can be increased based on response and needs, however repeat monitoring is recommended to titrate the dosage required. Once a helpful dose has been determined, long term use of the product has been utilized.

Dentarome Toothpastes
See Thieves Dentarome Toothpastes

Detoxzyme
This digestive enzyme is especially indicated for use for detoxification and cleansing, but can also be used to support daily digestion. It is also useful for liver and gall bladder conditions, and when cleansing from parasites is desired. It is generally not utilized in animals larger than dogs. Cats may or may not consume this enzyme within their food, due to the essential oil flavors it contains. For all animals, opening up a capsule, and starting with a tiny sprinkling of the enzyme mixed into soft moist foods is the suggested starting point. Gradually increase the amount, until some is

offered with each meal. For optimal cleansing, Detoxzyme can be given on an empty stomach.

Birds & Exotics: Approximately ¼ to ½ of a capsule may be consumed per day (split up between several meals.)

Cats: Approximately ½ to 1 full capsule per day may be consumed. It is possible to increase to a full capsule per meal in some situations.

Dogs: Approximately 1 capsule (or more) per meal may be consumed per 20 pounds (9 kg) of body weight. Start with smaller amounts, and gradually increase.

Horses & Larger: Generally do not use this product.

Digest + Cleanse

Digest + Cleanse is indicated for conditions such as upset stomachs, gas, digestive disruptions, liver and gall bladder conditions, inflammation of the gastrointestinal tract, and diarrhea. Since liver function often plays a role in skin eruptions and the ability of the skin to heal, skin conditions often benefit from the liver and colon support and cleansing ability of this product.

Birds & Exotics: This product has not been used extensively in these animals at this time, although it is likely to be beneficial.

Cats: This product has not been used extensively in cats at this time. Di-Gize is most commonly used for cats for these purposes.

Dogs: Digest + Cleanse has mainly been used in dogs and in general approximately 1 capsule is given per 30 pounds (14 kg) of body weight per day. The dosage is ideally split up into multiple doses. Capsules can be popped if needed, and smaller amounts given.

Dragon Time Massage Oil

This massage oil blend contains the essential oils of Clary Sage, Fennel, Jasmine, Lavender, Sage, Yarrow, and Ylang Ylang. It is especially helpful in balancing hormones and stabilizing hormonal behaviors. This product can be massaged onto the animal (shaved or haired), have other oils added to it, and is safe if ingested by an animal. For birds, having a residue of the oil on your hands and massaging the feet is a suggestion. Cats and dogs can have light amounts of the massage oil applied via the Petting application when desired.

EndoGize

EndoGize is indicated for use to balance the hormones and endocrine system in both females and males. It has not been used extensively in animals at this time, but may be helpful for dogs and horses in conditions such as Cushing's Disease, hypothyroidism, false pregnancy, pyometra, Alopecia X, Metabolic Syndrome, urinary incontinence, prostate disease, vaginitis, cystic ovaries, obesity, and hormonal behavioral issues. Follow the suggestions outlined at the beginning of this chapter if you choose to use EndoGize for a particular case. It is likely that other species of animals can benefit from this product as well.

Essentialzyme

Essentialzyme is a digestive enzyme that is particularly indicated for use with pancreatitis and pancreatic conditions. It is also particularly helpful in cancer cases, where this specific blend of enzymes appears especially helpful in breaking down and "digesting" the protective barriers created by cancers. It is generally not utilized in animals larger than dogs. Cats may or may not consume this enzyme within their food, due to the essential oil flavors it contains. For all animals, opening up a capsule, and starting with a tiny sprinkling of the enzyme mixed into soft moist foods is the suggested starting point. Gradually increase the amount given, until some is offered with each meal. In cases of cancer, quite high amounts of Essentialzyme have been used.

Birds & Exotics: Approximately ¼ to ½ of a capsule may be consumed per day (split up between several meals.) More may be used in certain cases.

Cats: Approximately ½ to 1 full capsule per day may be consumed. It is possible to increase to a full capsule per meal in some situations.

Dogs: Approximately 1 capsule (or more) per meal may be consumed per 20 pounds (9 kg) of body weight. Start with smaller amounts, and gradually increase.

Horses & Larger: Generally do not use this product.

Essentialzymes-4

Essentialzymes-4 is a relatively new enzyme product, which combines multiple enzyme spectrums into one. This product is the most complete and well-rounded for general use, and is highly recommended. It contains the Lipase enzyme, which is very important in fat digestion and handling, and used to be provided in the product Lipozyme. Due to its recent release (September of 2011), Essentialzymes-4 is relatively new to use for animals. There are two capsules contained within this product, and it is recommended to use a small amount from each capsule during administration. Essentialzymes-4 is being used in dogs, cats, and birds with more and more frequency, and showing wonderful results.

This product is generally not utilized in animals larger than dogs, and large animal products are often substituted. Cats may or may not consume this enzyme within their food, due to the essential oil flavors it contains. For all animals, opening up a capsule, and starting with a tiny sprinkling of the enzyme (some from each capsule) mixed into soft moist foods is the suggested starting point. Gradually increase the amount given, until some is offered with each meal. In some cases, quite high amounts of Essentialzymes-4 have been used.

Birds & Exotics: Approximately 1/8 of each capsule may be consumed per day (split up between several meals.) More may be used in certain cases.

Cats: Approximately ¼ to ½ of each capsule per day may be consumed. It is possible to increase to a full capsule per meal in some situations.

Dogs: Approximately ½ of each capsule per meal may be consumed per 50 pounds (23 kg) of body weight. Start with smaller amounts, and gradually increase.

Horses & Larger: Generally do not use this product.

Estro

Estro is an herbal tincture indicated for helping to balance estrogen levels and regulate hormone imbalances. It has not been used widely in animals at this time, however it may be helpful in dogs, horses, and larger animals for conditions such as pyometra, false pregnancy, cystic ovaries, urinary incontinence, hormonal behavioral issues, Alopecia X, and vaginitis. Follow the suggestions outlined at the beginning of this chapter if you choose to use Estro for a particular case. Tinctures are not typically recommended for use in birds due to the alcohol content contained within them.

FemiGen

FemiGen is indicated for helping to balance estrogen levels and regulate hormone imbalances in females. It has not been used widely in animals at this time, however it may be helpful in dogs, horses, and larger animals for conditions such as pyometra, false pregnancy, cystic ovaries, urinary incontinence, hormonal behavioral issues, Alopecia X, and vaginitis. Follow the suggestions outlined at the beginning of this chapter if you choose to use FemiGen for a particular case.

ICP

ICP is helpful in cases of diarrhea, gas, colon cleansing, constipation, and other intestinal issues. It has mainly been used in dogs, cats, and ferrets at this time. For all animals, a very small sprinkling of the powder is mixed with soft moist foods, and fed 1-3 times a day. Monitor for response and results, and increase or decrease the amount given for each individual animal. For cats and ferrets, gradually increasing to approximately ¼ to ½ of a teaspoon has been used per meal. In dogs ½ to 1 teaspoon per meal has been used. Always start with a very small amount, as many animals do not require the full suggestions. It is likely that this product could be used in horses and other large animals as well. Follow the suggestions outlined at the beginning of this chapter if you choose to use ICP for a particular case.

ImmuPro

ImmuPro is indicated to boost the immune system and contains many anti-cancer super ingredients such as NingXia Wolfberry, Agaricus Mushroom, and Melatonin. ImmuPro is mainly used in cases of cancer in dogs, but is likely to be of benefit in cases of Alopecia X as well. It is likely that birds, exotics, and cats can also benefit from this supplement, however it has not been widely used by these species at this time. Follow the suggestions outlined at the beginning of this chapter if you choose to use ImmuPro in animals other than dogs.

Dogs: Starting with a ¼ tablet per day, gradually increase the amount given. In cases of cancer, doses of up to 6 tablets per day have been given per 50 pounds (23 kg) of body weight (split into 3 or more times per day.)

Inner Defense

Inner Defense is a high powered essential oil combination. It boosts the immune system as well as provides amazing antibacterial, antifungal, and antiviral actions. One capsule contains the equivalent of approximately 2-3 drops of Oregano, 2-3 drops of Thyme, and 2-3 drops of Thieves essential oil blend. Several species of Oregano are included within this formulation, making it a "super-charged" grouping. This product has mainly been used in dogs, although the capsules can be popped and used in large animals as well. Cats are just beginning to use this product, as a veterinarian in Wisconsin has reported amazing results with resistant infections in her patients.

Birds & Exotics: The oral use of the single essential oils of Oregano, Thyme, and/or Thieves are recommended in these species.

Cats: While this is still a rather new therapy for cats, this product is getting good results for a variety of resistant infections, cystitis, and bladder infections. Monitoring of blood work before, during, and after administration is followed closely by the veterinarian who initiated this treatment regimen, and is recommended for all cases. If a cat does not tolerate the Inner Defense administration, then the use of the oils of Oregano, Thyme, and Thieves can be considered together or alone. Within an Inner Defense capsule, there is approximately 1 ½ mL of liquid. The capsule should be popped or emptied with a syringe and needle. For oral administration to cats, 0.1 mL of this liquid is given by mouth, twice a day. In general, this amount is placed within a small empty gel capsule. If the cat tastes this liquid, it is likely to have an extreme dislike of the flavor, resulting in salivation and head shaking. Cats are very unlikely to eat this liquid mixed within food. If you would detect any signs that would be out of the ordinary (poor appetite, soft stools, vomiting, lethargy, etc.), the administration of Inner Defense should be stopped, and blood work rechecked with a veterinarian.

Dogs: Dogs have used Inner Defense on a much wider basis. Although there are still individual dogs who do not seem to tolerate even small doses of Inner Defense, there are others who ingest huge amounts and do just fine. Individual variation seems strong with the use of this product, so start with low doses when possible, and gradually increase according to need. In dogs, one of my favorite uses of Inner Defense is for the acute onset of diarrhea, especially when bacterial in nature. The combination within Inner Defense is actually very similar to a popular veterinary "diarrhea gel" which is sold for use in dogs and cats.

For oral use in dogs, a general starting point is to use 1 capsule or less per day for a dog up to 20 pounds (9 kg), 1-2 capsules per day for a dog 20-50 pounds (9-23 kg), and 1-3 capsules per day for a dog over 50 pounds (23 kg). These amounts should be split into 2-3 doses throughout the day. For diarrhea, one dose may be all that is needed. For repeat use as an antibiotic, giving the Inner Defense along with a meal is recommended. In large dogs (over 50 pounds) with severe infections, even as much as 6 capsules per day have been given.

Large Animals: This product is generally not used in these animals, as the individual oils are more commonly given orally. However, if desired, the capsules could be popped and administered orally.

JuvaPower

JuvaPower is a whole food powder, packed with rich nutrients that nourish and cleanse the liver and intestines. It is extremely tasty, and many animals enjoy it added to foods. Regardless of the animal, start with a tiny sprinkling offered onto a soft moist meal (warmed is nice), and gradually increase the amount according to the animal's desires. In cats and smaller animals, a maximal amount of ½ teaspoon per day is likely. Large dogs over 50 pounds (23 kg), can likely consume up to 1 tablespoon per day during cleansing regimens. Occasional use just for flavoring and health is a wonderful idea. JuvaPower can be made into a broth as well, by adding the desired amount to warmed water. This broth can be used to add additional moisture to any animal meal.

JuvaSpice

JuvaSpice is very similar to JuvaPower, and is intended to be used more as a spice, sprinkled over foods. Any animal can enjoy this flavoring used as a light dusting over foods, just as you would with any other spice mixture used in cooking. It supports the liver in health and cleansing, and regular use in meals is a wonderful idea.

JuvaTone

JuvaTone is a tablet form of herbs, nutrients, and essential oils that nourish and cleanse the liver. Almost every health condition is affected by the health and proper function of the liver, including chronic skin conditions, digestive concerns, anxiety, behavioral issues, cognitive dysfunction, aches and pains, arthritis, and more. All animals can take this product, however since it is in tablet form, certain animals are more likely to consume it. Tablets can be crushed and mixed into foods for easier administration.

Birds & Exotics: Start with a crushed tablet, and offer a tiny sprinkling (less than a pinch) mixed within moist foods. Monitor closely, and gradually increase based on response and need. It is likely that no more than 1/8 to ¼ of a tablet would be consumed per day for these animals.

Cats: Similar directions can be followed as described for birds and exotics, however cats are more likely to consume up to ½ to 1 full tablet per day. This amount should be spread over 2-3 doses throughout the day.

Dogs: Dogs may consume this tablet in foods, pilled, or they may actually chew it. Dogs may consume up to 1 tablet per 20 pounds (9 kg) of body weight, or more per day. Start with a small amount, and gradually increase while monitoring response.

Large Animals: While tablet forms of products are not as commonly used in these animals, this product can be crushed and given within applesauce or other soft foods if desired. For oral administration, approximately 2-4 tablets could be given, 2-4 times a day.

K & B Tincture

K&B is a liquid tincture, and the initials stand for "Kidney & Bladder." Naturally, it is good for all conditions related to the kidney and bladder, including urinary tract infections, bladder stones, urinary crystals, cystitis, kidney failure, kidney disease, kidney infections, FLUTD (Feline Lower Urinary Tract Disorder), fluid retention, and more. As a tincture, there is a distinct taste to this product, that most animals do not enjoy. Dogs are much easier to "convince" to take it, however it is usually just put into the mouth of cats, whether they like it or not. Diluting the product does not always result in improving oral administration, as in general there is just more "bad tasting" liquid to consume instead of a pure dropper full. Mixing into foods or NingXia Red has been successful for many dogs, and for some cats, and is still worth an attempt.

It is important to note, that although dosing of this product is often conveyed as by the "dropper full," in actuality, it is rare to get a full dropper when you suck up the product. It will usually appear to be about ½ of the glass dropper that is supplied with the bottle. This is okay, and the dose termed "dropper full" can simply be whatever is drawn up into the dropper with a normal squeeze of the bulb. The dropper full, when measured, is approximately 1 mL of liquid in actuality.

Birds & Exotics: Ferrets are the main exotic animal to consistently use K&B Tincture, and they can use it as described for cats. Due to the tincture nature of the product, which means that it contains alcohol, it would rarely be recommended for use in birds. Although this product is likely to be helpful for rodents and other exotics, it has not been used commonly at this time.

Cats: Cats have used K&B Tincture quite extensively. Many cats in kidney failure have received 1 dropper of the liquid up to every 3 hours in severe situations. Cats rarely enjoy the administration, and usually salivate. However, since this product has truly saved many cats' lives, it is one of those times when I do not consider being "cat friendly" to be all that important. In general, a few drops to 1 dropper full can be given multiple times throughout the day, depending on the severity and response of the case.

Dogs: For small dogs up to 20 pounds (9 kg) the same dosing can be used as described for cats. For medium dogs 20-50 pounds (9-23 kg) 1-2 droppers of liquid can be given multiple times a day. For large dogs over 50 pounds (23 kg) up to 3 droppers of liquid can be given, three times a day or more.

Large Animals: This product is not commonly used for these animals, but certainly can be. 3 droppers, three times a day is a suggested starting point.

KidScents MightyVites and MightyZyme
Please see listings under MightyVites and MightyZyme.

KidScents Toothpaste
Please see the discussion in Thieves Dentarome Toothpaste.

LavaDerm Cooling Mist
LavaDerm combines the healing benefits of Lavender, Spikenard, and Aloe Vera into a remarkable spray. This spray calms irritated skin and promotes tissue regeneration. It is even misted daily, directly onto birds, much to

their enjoyment. Any animal can utilize this spray for a variety of skin conditions.

Lavender Mint Shampoo & Conditioner
These products can be used for animals as well.

Life 5
Life 5 is a wonderful probiotic product that helps to repopulate the intestinal tract with beneficial bacteria. Even though animal populations of bacteria often differ from humans, great benefits have still been noted with the use of Life 5. This product should be kept refrigerated, however do not throw it away if you accidently leave it out on the counter for a day or two. We have still noted benefits from "less than ideal" Life 5, but with severe situations and cases of need, we make sure that refrigerated and fully potent Life 5 is used. Shipping in the heat of summer can damage the product, so I recommend purchasing several bottles over the winter months (if your region has them), to last you through the hotter season. Some countries do not have access to this product. Life 5 can be given several times a day, mixed with foods, or pilled. In general, you should give this product at least 2 hours away from oral essential oils or antibiotics. Administration at night, right before bed is also helpful.

Long term use of the product is often not necessary for "normal" animals. For routine maintenance, giving Life 5 one week out of every month is a nice suggestion. After oral administration of essential oils (especially powerful antibacterial oils) or antibiotics, giving a course of Life 5 is recommended. This can be done at the same time as the oral essential oils or antibiotics (still respecting the 2 hour rule), however administration of Life 5 should continue for at least 1 week after the oral administration of essential oil or antibiotic has stopped. Longer use is certainly fine when individual cases show the need for it.

Birds & Exotics: Birds, ferrets, rabbits, and others have used this product to help repopulate gastrointestinal flora. Open the capsule and sprinkle a small amount into foods, up to several times a day.

Cats: Cats have routinely used this product after antibiotics, oral essential oils, or with diarrhea and digestive concerns. Open a capsule and mix ¼ to ½ of the contents with some soft moist food. Feed 2-3 times a day or as needed. In cases of diarrhea, often the Life 5 is continued for 1 week or more after symptoms have returned to normal.

Dogs: For general maintenance, ¼ to ½ of a capsule per 20 pounds (9 kg) of body weight can be given per day. For very large dogs, generally no more than a capsule is given at a time. Many times in mild cases or for routine prevention, this dose can be given every 1-3 days instead of daily. In more severe cases of need, a full capsule may be given 2-3 times per day in dogs over 50 pounds (23 kg.)

Horses & Large Animals: Generally do not use this product due to the large amounts needed. Large animal probiotic formulations are often used instead.

Lipozyme

Lipozyme is not currently available from Young Living. The enzyme Lipase is contained within Essentialzymes-4, and several other digestive enzyme products.

Longevity Softgels

Longevity Softgels contain approximately 3 drops of the Longevity essential oil blend, per capsule. This blend is a high powered combination of antioxidants, and is basically indicated whenever you want something to "live longer" or have longevity. It is highly beneficial to many conditions, and it has been noticed that animals ingesting Longevity oil on a daily basis, seem less "appetizing" to biting insects. See Longevity within the Essential Oil Blends for use of Longevity for cats, birds, exotics, and large animals. In general, the Softgels are mainly used for dogs, however the capsules can be popped and the liquid used as recommended for the Longevity oil blend.

Dogs: Dogs up to 20 pounds (9 kg) can consume up to 1 capsule per day. Dogs 21-50 pounds (9-23 kg) can consume 1-2 capsules per day. And dogs over 50 pounds (23 kg) generally consume up to 2 capsules per day.

Master Formula HERS

This product is not routinely used in animals.

Master Formula HIS

This product is not routinely used in animals.

MegaCal
Due to Xylitol content, this product is not recommended for use in animals.

MightyVites
MightyVites is a whole food supplement for children, in a chewable tablet. All animals can ingest this supplement.

Birds & Exotics: Generally consume ¼ to ½ tablet per day. Many small critters enjoy the flavor tablet, and eat it as a treat. Small rodents may consume less, and some animals may consume more.

Cats: Most cats do not enjoy the fruit flavored chews, and other supplements such as MultiGreens or True Source are added to foods for them.

Dogs: Dogs can have approximately 1 tablet per 30 pounds of body weight per day. Many eat this as a treat. Some dogs may need more, some may need less.

Large Animals: Can certainly have this as a treat, but it is rarely used for nutritional benefits.

MightyZyme
MightyZyme is the children's chewable digestive enzyme in the KidScents line of products. This is a well-rounded enzyme complex that is easy to give to most animals. Birds, ferrets, cats, and dogs have consumed this enzyme. Other animals such as rats and mice may use this product, however they are not typically given digestive enzymes.

Birds: Can typically ingest ¼ of a MightyZyme per meal. Birds can just chew a chunk, or have it crushed and added to foods. More can be given if needed.

Ferrets & Cats: ¼ to ½ of a tablet per meal or more.

Dogs: 1-4 tablets per meal. Start with lower amounts and increase as needed. Most dogs chew and eat this tablet as a treat.

Large Animals: Typically do not use this product.

SUPPLEMENTS & PRODUCTS

Mineral Essence

Mineral Essence is a liquid mineral complex combined with honey, royal jelly, and the essential oils of Lemon, Cinnamon, and Peppermint. Minerals are critical to every function in a body, and are especially indicated in conditions of anxiety, behavioral concerns, immune dysfunction, and nerve and brain function. Mineral Essence has a strong flavor, and some animals will require it to be squirted directly into the mouth. Sometimes dilution with water, NingXia Red, or within food is more accepted by an animal.

Due to the Cinnamon content, anticoagulant activities are possible with very high doses. Cats do not usually appreciate the flavor, and perform the typical salivation response, with direct oral administration. Although Mineral Essence has been used in dogs the most, it can be considered for use in other animals. Very small amounts should be started with (1 diluted drop or less in animals smaller than dogs), and the animal should be monitored closely. Amounts given can be increased each week, as the animal demonstrates it is doing well with the supplement. Veterinary monitoring and laboratory testing (complete with electrolytes and minerals) is recommended before, during, and after use of Mineral Essence. A drop or two added to drinking water is also a likely way to use this supplement, starting with 1-2 drops added to a liter of water and gradually increasing the amount is suggested.

Birds & Exotics: Start with 1 drop diluted in 1 ounce (30 mL) of NingXia Red, and give small amounts (1 mL or less) of this solution once or twice a day. 1 or more drops may be added to 1 liter of drinking water as well. Monitor closely with a veterinarian as described, and increase the concentration that is given every week or so. The Mineral Essence can be mixed with water or other foods and given in a similar manner if NingXia Red is not appreciated or available.

Cats: Similar methods can be used as described with birds and exotics. Starting with very small amounts and gradually increasing the concentration given is still recommended, so that the cat will get used to the flavor. However, it would be expected that a cat would typically ingest several drops per day as a therapeutic dose.

Dogs: Mineral Essence can be incredibly helpful for anxiety, pica (eating things you are not supposed to), healing of wounds, neurologic concerns, and immune function. Monitoring with a veterinarian is still recommended as we do not fully know the amounts of minerals that will be required by an individual. Tailoring the amount of Mineral Essence for each specific dog, is the best recommendation. It would not be out of the expected range for a dog to consume 1 dropper of Mineral Essence per 30-50 pounds (14-23 kg) when mineral support is needed. Certainly some dogs may need more, but also some dogs may need much less.

Large Animals: Mineral Essence can be administered directly in the mouth or lip, or added to foods or other liquids for ingestion. 1 dropper per 100-200 pounds (45-90 kg) of body weight for horses and large animals is expected. For smaller goats, pigs, or more "dog-sized" farm animals, dosing can start similarly to what is described for dogs, with 1 dropper per 30-50 pounds (14-23 kg.) The flavor is typically well tolerated by these animals.

MultiGreens

MultiGreens is a wonderful combination of body supporting herbs and essential oils. One essential oil within this product is Melissa, and this product provides an additional way to include this essential oil into a regimen. MultiGreens is beneficial for almost every condition, but is especially indicated for immune support, viral infections, and neurologic support. All forms of animals have consumed this supplement.

Birds & Exotics: Capsules are opened and mixed with foods. In general, up to 1 full capsule can be consumed per day, per animal. Start with a sprinkling added to each meal, and gradually increase as tolerated.

Cats: Cats thrive on this supplement, and it is especially indicated for Feline Leukemia, FIV, FLUTD, FIP, Herpes, chronic respiratory infections, and any viral or immune based concern. Basically, a cat would always benefit from the addition of this supplement! Typically the capsule is opened and mixed with soft moist food. Start with a small amount, and increase as the cat gets used to the flavor. It is not uncommon for a cat to work up to ingesting 1-2 capsules per day with severe cases, however ½ to a full capsule per day is typical.

Dogs: Dogs can likewise ingest large amounts of this supplement. 1 capsule per day for every 10 pounds (5 kg) of body weight is not out of the question, in cases of need. Most dogs start with 1-2 capsules per day, and for routine health and prevention this is a typical dose. Capsules can be opened or given directly.

Large Animals: Can certainly take this product as well. Budget constraints usually dictate how much will be given per day, but 5 or more capsules per day (generally opened and mixed with applesauce, NingXia Red, or other foods and liquids), is a general starting point.

NingXia Red (Juice)

NingXia Red is a whole food drink made from several "super foods" and also contains the essential oils of Orange and Lemon. NingXia Red is very high in antioxidant action, contains many amino acids, vitamins, minerals, supports liver function, blood sugar balance, energy, and generally benefits the immune system and body as a whole.

Grape pomace extract is contained within this product, and fears of grape and raisin toxicity in dogs has prompted questions regarding the use of NingXia Red in animals. I can assure you that massive numbers of dogs, cats, birds, horses, ferrets, and other animals have consumed very large volumes of NingXia Red (both in my veterinary clinic and in the homes of Young Living members), and that there is never a concern for me, even in teeny tiny Chihuahua puppies. We have only ever documented incredible benefits from NingXia Red administration, and if the grape pomace extract could cause any sort of issue, it certainly would have been detected by now.

NingXia Red is good for so many things, it is impossible to list them all. In any condition listing, if NingXia Red is not listed, you can guarantee that the addition of the juice to the regimen will be beneficial. NingXia Red can often be used as a carrier for other supplements and essential oils when internal use is desired, and can even be used externally within various poultices and topical applications. Entire books have been written on the various uses of NingXia Red (*53 Ways to Use NingXia Wolfberry*), and I encourage you to explore this information.

Specific conditions in which NingXia Red is particularly helpful include; soreness due to vaccination, vaccination detoxification, hypoglycemia, failure to thrive, fading kitten syndrome, any liver condition, Diabetes, anxiety, laminitis, inflammation, and allergies. Any animal who appears "near death" will often get 1-3 mL of NingXia Red every 15-60 minutes (less for animals smaller than cats). In numerous situations, this administration has greatly helped in reversing the downward trend in health, and many animals have miraculously "pulled through" from what appeared to be impending death. When situations are this severe, it certainly cannot hurt!

Birds & Exotics: As general maintenance approximately ½ teaspoon can be given per day. Some animals require and crave more, and in general they are allowed to ingest what they desire. However, it is wise to make sure that the amount they are given is gradually increased to avoid diarrhea or problems from a sudden food change. During injury or illness, much higher volumes of NingXia Red are consumed. In life threatening situations, amounts are not increased gradually and occasionally red colored or soft stools are noted. This is of no concern, as the benefits far outweigh the possible stool changes. The juice can be syringed into the mouth, offered mixed into foods, given straight or diluted with water. If NingXia Red is added to drinking water, care must be taken to change it frequently (at least twice a day), as it will start to spoil.

Cats: Some cats love NingXia Red and some cats seem to loath it. It is, of course, their prerogative and they are quite certain you should know about it! Many cats will accept small amounts of NingXia Red added to their drinking water, but it must be made fresh frequently as described in birds and exotics. I find that many cats will eat NingXia Red mixed into some tasty canned food, and there are still a few (like my Sphynx cat Wonka) who will knock over a bottle and drink it straight. For cats who simply refuse to take NingXia Red, and for which syringing it into the mouth is a "traumatic event," there are certainly other supplements that we can use to benefit their health, without the need for Trauma Life afterward. I will often use one or more of MultiGreens, Omega Blue, Sulfurzyme, True Source, and a digestive enzyme to make sure the body is supported fully.

For general maintenance, cats can consume approximately ½ teaspoon per day. During injury or illness 1 tablespoon or more can be given. It is ideal if the amounts are divided up into more frequent doses. So instead of giving 1 full tablespoon all at once, the volume is divided up into 3 or 4 doses throughout the day. The same comments for life threatening situations in birds and exotics, also applies for cats.

Dogs: Dogs are quite easy to give NingXia Red to. It can be added to foods, offered in a bowl (straight or diluted), or syringed into their mouth. For general maintenance small dogs up to 20 pounds (9 kg) can get approximately ¼ ounce (8 mL) per day. Medium dogs 20-50 pounds (9-23 kg) can get ½ ounce (15 mL) per day. Large dogs 50-100 pounds (23-46 kg) can get ¾ ounce (23 mL) per day. Extra-large dogs over 100 pounds (46 kg) can get a full ounce per day.

Senior dogs or dogs with any sort of health complaint can generally receive double maintenance amounts on a long term basis. During injury or illness triple amounts or more are given. Gradually increasing amounts as discussed for other animals, applies for dogs as well.

Horses & Large Animals: NingXia Red can be given straight, added to water, syringed into the mouth, or mixed with various feeds or hay. For general maintenance 1-2 ounces per day can be given. For performance horses and animals, often 3 ounces per day is given. During injury or illness 4 ounces or more can be given. During laminitis episodes in horses, the consumption of 4 ounces or more of NingXia Red per day has greatly reduced the duration of illness and eases pain and inflammation.

Endurance horses have excelled tremendously when the travel packets of NingXia Red (1 ounce each) are given at each check point or rest stop during a race. The packets are just squeezed into their mouth (the rider should take one as well) and they have increased stamina, do not exhibit sore muscles, and recover from the event with amazing speed.

Ningxia Wolfberries (Lycium barbarum)

Ningxia Wolfberries are the small dried red berries, which are often also referred to as Goji Berries in health food stores. Ningxia berries are superior to your typical Goji berry, as they are grown in an ideal, super-fertile region of land, and are of a specific variety that imparts more antioxidant and health benefits. These berries can be ingested by any animal, and soaking them in warm or hot water can make them a bit more digestible to dogs. These berries are an excellent addition to the regular diet of animals such as birds, rodents, rabbits, guinea pigs, and dogs. Start with small amounts, and gradually increase the amount offered. Treat this food as you would any other dried fruit you offer to your animal; if you give too much, too fast, you could cause an intestinal upset.

Omega Blue

Omega Blue is a fish oil source (sardine, anchovy, and mackerel) of omega-3 fatty acids. These fatty acids (EPA, DHA, ALA) are critical in the body, and are just now being discussed by traditional veterinary nutritionists, as to if they should be deemed an "essential nutrient." Of course, holistic veterinarians already recognize how essential these fatty acids truly are, and most protocols will include the addition of these important nutrients. If there is a condition listed that does not contain Omega Blue in the recommendations, you can be assured that it would still be beneficial. In larger animals, Omega Blue is not used, and an appropriate high quality large animal source of omega fatty acids should be selected. Omega Blue is clinically proven and is free from mercury and other toxins.

Omega Blue contains essential oils as well, making it a far superior omega-3 product. Not only do the essential oils themselves have health benefits, but they preserve the fish oil contained within the capsule. Rancid fish oils abound on the animal market, and if you pop one open and smell or taste it, you would be shocked at how many are completely disgusting. There are few omega products on the market today that I will allow my patients to consume. A rancid fish oil is worse than no fish oil at all.

One significant factor to be aware of, is that EPA (one of the omega-3 fatty acids), has been shown in traditional veterinary research to shut off the arthritis feedback cycle. Arthritis feedback is when the body detects inflammation associated with the joints, and actually creates more inflammation and arthritis as an attempt to stabilize the joint. This vicious cycle creates a snowball effect where the arthritis continues to get worse and worse. EPA effectively shuts off this communication, and allows the body to stop laying down more inflammation. This step is critical to allow for full healing by the body.

Birds & Exotics: The capsule can be popped and one drop added to each meal. Start with small amounts and gradually increase according to need and response. Many of these birds and small animals may consume 3-6 drops per day in some conditions. Although many of these species would not typically get their omega-3 fatty acids from a fish source, clinical use has proven it to be one of the most effective sources for these critical fatty acids. Conditions that have not improved on other omega sources (flax, salmon, coconut, hemp, chia) often respond beautifully when Omega Blue is substituted. Clinical response is far more important to me than providing a "nature-typical" source of a nutrient. In our world today, "ideal" sources of nutrients are less and less likely to occur, however more and more health issues are needing correction.

Cats: Some cats will ingest Omega Blue added to foods, and some will not. The capsule is fairly large, so pilling cats is usually not an option. Due to the essential oils within the product, the flavor may "turn off" some cats. Large amounts of Omega Blue can be given, but we are usually more limited by the fact that the cat will refuse to ingest large amounts mixed into their foods. In some situations, cats could easily require 1-2 capsules per day, although ½ capsule would be average on a daily basis. Start with a drop, and gradually increase the amount given every few days. This will avoid intestinal upset, but also get the cat used to the flavor slowly. In some situations, the Omega Blue contents have just been dripped directly into the cat's mouth. This can be done, but is usually met with resistance after a few doses. Since omega fatty acids are so important in cats, and should really be given daily on a continual basis, if they will not easily ingest the Omega Blue, another omega-3 fatty acid product should be supplied. I recommend Standard Process Tuna Omega-3 as an alternative product for the cats in my practice.

Dogs: Dogs can get quite large amounts of Omega Blue and often benefit tremendously from it. Skin conditions, arthritis, inflammation, and basically any condition is indicated for the use of Omega Blue. Dogs can easily consume 1 or more capsule per 20 pounds (9 kg) of body weight per day. Start with small amounts and gradually increase to avoid stomach upset. Capsules can be popped and the liquid added to foods as well. If appetite decreases or stools become soft, this may be an indication of too much Omega Blue being given, but this is a rarity.

Large Animals: Do not often consume this product due to amounts that would need to be ingested. A suitable large animal omega product should be substituted. When Omega Blue is indicated for a condition, it is meant to highlight the importance of omega supplementation for the situation.

Ortho Ease Massage Oil
This massage oil blend contains the essential oils of Eucalyptus Globulus, Eucalyptus Radiata, Juniper, Lemongrass, Marjoram, Peppermint, Thyme, Vetiver, and Wintergreen. It is especially helpful in decreasing inflammation and pain, increasing circulation, reducing discomfort of arthritis, muscle strain, joint inflammation, and also relieves symptoms associated with insect bites, dermatitis, and itching. We have also found

Ortho Ease to have insect repellant properties. It has been used alone, or as a base to add additional oil(s) to, within oil spritzers or by direct application. This product can be massaged, rubbed, sprayed, Pet, or dripped onto location (shaved or haired), and is safe if ingested by an animal. For birds, having a light coating on your hands, and massaging the oil into the feet is suggested.

Ortho Sport Massage Oil

This massage oil blend contains the essential oils of Elemi, Eucalyptus Globulus, Lemongrass, Oregano, Peppermint, Thyme, Vetiver, and Wintergreen. It is especially helpful in decreasing inflammation and pain, increasing circulation, reducing discomfort of arthritis, muscle strain, and joint inflammation. It has a higher phenol content than Ortho Ease, so tends to be a bit more warming in function. We have also found Ortho Sport to have insect repellant properties. It has been used alone, or as a base to add additional oil(s) to, within oil spritzers or by direct application. This product can be massaged, rubbed, sprayed, Pet, or dripped onto location (shaved or haired), and is safe if ingested by an animal. For birds, having a light coating on your hands, and massaging the oil into the feet is suggested.

ParaFree

ParaFree combines the powerful cleansing and antiparasitic essential oils of Cumin, Anise, Fennel, Vetiver, Laurus Nobilis, Nutmeg, Melaleuca Alternifolia, Thyme, Clove, and Idaho Tansy along with Olive Oil Leaf extract and Sesame Seed oil. This product may not be available in countries other than the United States, due to certain restrictions on the Tansy oil it contains. It is a capsule, and is primarily used to kill internal parasites in animals.

When using for a deworming effect, it is often recommended to start your protocol on a full moon. Parasites are more active and accessible it seems, at this time of the moon cycle. Parasites are notoriously difficult to get rid of, and whatever protocol you select, it is imperative that you follow your case with a veterinarian and perform fecal testing to make sure you have adequately eliminated the parasites. There have been many cases of internal parasites that did not respond to traditional dewormers, however responded well to essential oils. Conversely, there have been cases that seem to respond to absolutely nothing but traditional chemical dewormers. Parasites are becoming a bit of a "super bug" and often need pretty heavy tactics to rid the body of them. Careful monitoring is the key, along with rotational therapies and an increase of potency and amounts when necessary.

Parasite Blend: When ParaFree is not available the following recipe can be used:
- Place 40 drops of Di-Gize, 10 drops of Ocotea (see cautionary statements for this oil), 10 drops of Copaiba, and 2 drops of Laurus Nobilis into a 1 ounce (30 mL) glass essential oil bottle.
- Picking 3 oils from the following list, add 5 drops of each to the bottle: Clove, Lemon, Lemongrass, Melaleuca Alternifolia, Mountain Savory, Myrrh, Peppermint, Rosemary, Tarragon, Thyme, and Vetiver. Select the most appropriate oils for your species, and rotate through which oils are selected when repeat use is necessary.
- Fill the bottle the rest of the way with V-6. Rock to mix well, and use 10-20 drops of this solution to replace one ParaFree capsule.

Large Animal Parasite Blend: This is a stronger version of the Parasite Blend, intended for use in larger animals such as horses.
- Place 40 drops of Di-Gize, 10 drops of Ocotea, 10 drops of Copaiba, 10 drops of Longevity, 10 drops of Tarragon, and 2 drops of Laurus Nobilis into a 15 mL glass essential oil bottle.
- Picking 3 oils from the following list, add 5 drops of each to the bottle: Clove, Lemon, Lemongrass, Melaleuca Alternifolia, Mountain Savory, Myrrh, Peppermint, Rosemary, Thyme, and Vetiver. Rotate which oils are selected when repeat use in necessary.
- Fill the bottle the rest of the way with V-6. Rock to mix well. Start by giving 6 drops twice a day in the lip or feed. Start administration on a full moon, and give the mixture for 1-3 weeks, then rest. Increasing up to 20 drops (or more) twice a day may be necessary in certain difficult parasite situations.

Kitty Cocktail Deworming Recipe: This recipe has been used with quite some success in cats, kittens, dogs, and puppies; and it would be appropriate for use in exotic animals as well.
- In ½ ounce (15 mL) of NingXia Red, mix the following ingredients:
- 1 teaspoon of distilled water.
- 1 capsule of ParaFree (pop and squeeze the contents out.)
- 1 capsule of MultiGreens (opened and mixed in.)
- Mix well before use. Refrigerate any unused portions.

- Give 2-3 mL of this solution twice a day to dogs and cats, generally mixed with food. For birds and exotics, start with 1-3 drops of the solution, and gradually increase based on response and need. It is likely that approximately 1 mL would be given per day to a bird or exotic animal. For most animals, starting with a small amount, and gradually increasing the amount given is suggested. Once giving the full suggested amount, the solution would be given for 1 week or more, and stool samples rechecked to determine exact length of use. Veterinary monitoring with blood work and fecal tests is suggested, especially for exotic animals. If stools become soft, or animals experience decreased appetite, the regimen should be reduced in half or stopped.

Birds & Exotics: The use of ParaFree is suggested to be used within the Kitty Cocktail Deworming Recipe. Start with a few drops added to foods or given orally, and gradually increase to approximately 1 mL given per day. Split this amount into several doses if possible. Monitor carefully and recheck laboratory samples with a veterinarian.

Cats: ParaFree can be used as described within the Kitty Cocktail Deworming Recipe. Alternately, ParaFree capsules can be popped and 1-3 drops of the contents can be added to foods or dripped directly into the mouth. Mixing the ParaFree directly into foods or dripping it into the mouth, is usually met with resistance and salivation in most cats. Cats can also use these recommendations, given 2-3 times a week, as Heartworm Prevention. An alternate recommendation for heartworm prevention in cats is listed under Ocotea in the Single Oils chapter.

Dogs: Dogs can use ParaFree in a variety of ways, and are much more likely to eat the capsule or liquid contents mixed into foods. They are also more tolerant of the liquid being placed directly into the mouth, when necessary. Starting points for deworming protocols are 1 capsule of ParaFree per 50 pounds (23 kg) of body weight, twice a day. Again, use veterinary monitoring, start on a full moon, and reduce dosages if soft stools or decrease in appetite occur. Some dogs may require higher doses for deworming to occur.

SUPPLEMENTS & PRODUCTS

Heartworm Prevention Protocol for Dogs: While heartworm has not been "proven" to be prevented by ParaFree, case studies in heartworm positive dogs show tremendous promise in this field. The elimination of microfilaria (baby heartworms) from the blood stream of positive dogs appears to have been demonstrated. More studies are being conducted, but as I refuse to subject a dog to the research type experiments typical of traditional veterinary drugs, evidence based data will happen a little slower. The rescue and rehabilitation of heartworm positive dogs will be a major mission of Crow River Animal Hospital in the future, and will hopefully document for the world the amazing abilities of essential oils. Monitoring heartworm tests every 6 months is suggested when natural protocols are chosen.

- Small dogs up to 20 pounds (9 kg): Give ½ to 1 capsule of ParaFree 2-3 times a week during the entire heartworm season. In many areas of the world, this may be year round.
- Medium dogs 20-50 pounds (9-23 kg): Give 1 capsule of ParaFree 2-3 times a week.
- Large dogs over 50 pounds (23 kg): Give 2-3 capsules per day, split into several doses. Repeat this administration 2-3 times a week.

Large Animals: ParaFree can be popped and used for larger animals, however neat single oils or blends are more commonly used. The Large Animal Parasite Blend is another option for use as well, and the suggestions for its use can be followed in general for any of the antiparasitic remedies.

PD 80/20

PD 80/20 is a supplement that contains Pregnenolone and DHEA which are important in hormone production, mental acuity, cardiovascular health, and immune function. It is used to help maintain a healthy endocrine system, for autoimmune conditions, arthritis, nerve degeneration, and cognitive dysfunction in animals.

Birds & Exotics: This product has not been used in these animals at this time, although in situations of severe need, it can be considered. Careful monitoring before, during, and after administration with a veterinarian is suggested, and giving very small portions of the product is recommended. Combining one small pinch with 1 tablespoon of food, only a very small portion of this mixture would be given daily; likely less than 1/10th of the mixture per day.

Cats: A small pinch from an opened capsule can be given daily in acute conditions. Every other day administration may be possible for maintenance. Careful monitoring with a veterinarian is recommended.

Dogs: For dogs 10 pounds (5 kg) or less, use as directed for cats. For dogs 10-20 pounds (5-9 kg) use ¼ to ½ of a capsule, once per day. Medium dogs 20-50 pounds (9-23 kg) give ½ to ¾ of a capsule, once per day. Large dogs over 50 pounds (23 kg) give up to 1 capsule per day. Daily dosing is recommended for acute conditions, and every other day maintenance dosing may be possible, once the condition is stabilized.

Large Animals: Do not commonly use this product, although they certainly can. Start with 1 capsule per day, and monitor for responses with a veterinarian.

Polyzyme

This enzyme is no longer available from Young Living. Essentialzymes-4 and MightyZyme are among the suggested products to replace Polyzyme.

Power Meal

Power Meal is a powdered vegetarian meal replacement product, that is very high in protein and nutrition. Main ingredients include brown rice protein concentrate and Ningxia wolfberry, however there are many other powerful additions to the formula. It can be supplemented to any animal, and is extremely helpful for cancer patients or animals needing to gain or maintain weight and muscling. It can be mixed with foods or water, and many animals easily ingest the product. Treat this supplement as you would any other food source, start with a small amount, and gradually increase the amount given to avoid intestinal upset. Dogs can easily consume multiple scoops per day in cases of need.

Prenolone + (with DHEA) Body Cream

This cream contains the hormone precursor pregnenolone (derived from soy) and also DHEA (derived from wild yam.) Wild yam products have become popular for use in animals, and various creams have even been being applied regularly to the feet of hormonal birds. This product is likely to benefit hormonal balance of animals, and can be considered for topical application. Starting with a very small amount applied, work with your veterinarian to monitor and adjust according to needs.

Progessence Plus Serum

This product was designed to balance hormone levels in human women. It has not been used widely in animals at this time, but reports are starting to be known of its successful use. The product is mainly being used in horses at this time, and is even including usage in "behaviorally challenged" stallions (male horses who are not castrated.) It is likely that this product will help with all hormonally based issues including pyometra, false pregnancy, cystic ovaries, behavioral concerns, Alopecia X, egg laying concerns, and vaginitis. Starting with a very small amount applied topically, daily to every three days; 1 toothpick dip in small animals and 1 drop in horses or larger is suggested. Work with your veterinarian closely to monitor for response and needs.

Prostate Health

Prostate Health contains Saw Palmetto extract, Pumpkin seed oil, and Geranium, Fennel, Lavender, Myrtle, and Peppermint essential oils in a softgel format. It is indicated for use in males for prostate and urinary related conditions. This product has not been used widely in animals at this time. Follow the suggestions at the beginning of this chapter if you would like to use this product for a particular individual case.

Protec

Protec contains Frankincense, Myrrh, Sage, and Cumin in carrier oils and is designed to be rectally or vaginally instilled for prostate and reproductive tract health. This product is not used commonly in animals, although it could be.

Pure Protein Complete

Pure Protein Complete is a whey based protein powder. It can generally be offered in small amounts to most animal species. Due to the content of whey protein (dairy product) and of Xylitol, it may need to be avoided in certain animals. Those who have dairy allergies or are vegetarian in nature should avoid this product. Also, Xylitol in large amounts, has been linked with toxicity effects in dogs, and only very rarely (one case) in cats. A small sprinkling on foods or your animal finishing up your smoothie, is generally of no concern.

Regenolone Moisturizing Cream

This cream as been used commonly in dogs with arthritis and degenerative joint disease. Topical application daily has been described, shaving the location if needed. It is likely that topical application to all forms of animals would be beneficial for both hormonal concerns as well as inflammation and pain.

Rehemogen

Rehemogen is a liquid herbal tincture used to cleanse, purify, disinfect, and build the blood. It is used most commonly in cats and dogs to detoxify the blood and body, and especially for vaccination detoxification. Due to the alcohol content of a tincture, this product is not recommended for use in birds.

Exotics: Ferrets and rodents are the most likely to utilize this product, although it has not been widely used in these species at this time. Several drops to ¼ of a dropper (0.25 mL) is likely to be given per day. Veterinary monitoring before, during, and after administration is suggested.

Cats: For a cleansing cycle, 1 dropper (approximately 1 mL) can be given per day, for 14 to 28 days. Cats do not always appreciate the alcohol content of the product, and may salivate profusely. There are some herbalists who reduce the alcohol content of tinctures through heating or evaporation, however this product is mainly used straight. Some cats may ingest Rehemogen mixed with foods.

Dogs: For dogs up to 20 pounds (9 kg), 1 dropper (approximately 1 mL), can be given per day for 14-28 days. For medium dogs 20-50 pounds (9-23 kg), 1 dropper can be given per day for approximately 40 days. For large dogs 50-100 pounds (23-45 kg), 1 dropper can be given per day for 55 days (basically an entire bottle of Rehemogen.) For extra-large dogs over 100 pounds (45 kg), 1-2 droppers can be given per day until 1-2 bottles of Rehemogen is given.

Large Animals: 1-2 droppers can be given per day, until a total of 1-2 bottles of Rehemogen are given.

Relaxation Massage Oil

This massage oil blend contains the essential oils of Lavender, Peppermint, Rosewood, Spearmint, Tangerine, and Ylang Ylang. It is especially helpful in decreasing tension and promoting tranquility. Relaxation has been used alone, or as a base to add additional oil(s) to. This product can be massaged, rubbed, sprayed, Pet, or dripped onto location (shaved or haired), and is safe if ingested by an animal. For birds, having a light coating on your hands, and massaging the oil into the feet is suggested.

Rose Ointment

Rose Ointment is similar to Animal Scents Ointment, and can be used in all of the methods recommended in that listing. Rose Ointment has even been placed into the eyes of horses, dogs, and cats with amazing healing results. Placing either Rose or Animal Scents Ointment into an eye, can mildly sting temporarily. Rose Ointment does sting less than Animal Scents, and is the recommended choice for use in eyes. The ointment should be softened fully by aggressive mixing, prior to placement in the eyes. For the most part, Animal Scents Ointment is a more economical choice for use in animals. It is fine if animals ingest this ointment.

Sensation Massage Oil

This massage oil blend contains the essential oils of Jasmine, Rosewood, and Ylang Ylang. It can be used in any situation that calls for the use of these oils. Sensation can be used alone, or as a base to add additional oils to. This product can be massaged, rubbed, sprayed, Pet, or dripped onto location (shaved or haired), and is safe if ingested by an animal. For birds, having a light coating on your hands, and massaging the oil into the feet is suggested.

Sleep Essence

Sleep Essence is a source of Melatonin and may be indicated for conditions that call for its use. Common conditions in animals include Alopecia X and Cognitive Dysfunction in dogs. This product has not been used widely in animals at this time. If you choose to use this product for an individual case, work with your veterinarian, and follow the suggestions at the beginning of this chapter.

Slique Tea

Slique Tea contains caffeine as well as cacao powder and is not appropriate for use in animals.

Stevia Extract

Stevia Extract is not generally being used for medical purposes in animals, however it is safe for them to consume if they were to ingest some in foods or drinks. It is possible that the human benefits of Stevia - including reduction of appetite, improved digestion, inhibition of bacterial growth, and reduction in gum and dental disease - could carry over into the animal kingdom. Human use has also noted that topical application of Stevia has helped to heal acne, seborrhea, dermatitis, cuts, wounds, and reduces scarring.

Sulfurzyme Powder and Capsules

Sulfurzyme is a source of MSM (methylsulfonylmethane) which is a natural anti-inflammatory and vital nutrient for body function. Joined with Ningxia Wolfberry, this product far surpasses any other MSM product on the market, and appears to have much greater bioavailability from the combination. Both the capsule and the powder form can be used in all animals. Sulfurzyme is incredibly helpful in cases of arthritis, all forms of skin conditions, autoimmune diseases, healing of wounds, reduction of scar tissue, and just general cell structure and function. There are not many conditions that are not benefited by Sulfurzyme. Both the opened capsule and powder form can be mixed into foods, and even cats easily ingest it in this way. It is very difficult to give too much of this product, and if you did, you would likely only see softened stools. One capsule of Sulfurzyme contains approximately ¼ teaspoon of the powder.

Birds & Exotics: Start with a small sprinkling into foods, and gradually increase as needed. Approximately ¼ to ½ of a capsule is generally consumed per day. More can certainly be used in cases of need.

Cats: Gradually increase to ¼ to 1 capsule per day. More can be used when needed.

Dogs: Small dogs up to 20 pounds (9 kg) will generally get between 1 capsule once or twice a day, to 1 ½ teaspoons per day. Medium dogs 20-50 pounds (9-23 kg) will generally get between 1 capsule twice a day, to 1 heaping teaspoon per day. Large dogs over 50 pounds (23 kg) will generally get between 2 capsules twice a day, to 1 tablespoon per day. Daily amounts are split into multiple doses throughout the day, and larger amounts can be used if necessary.

Large Animals: Up to 1 heaping tablespoon can be given twice a day in cases of need (especially autoimmune conditions.)

Super B

Super B is a high powered source of B vitamins which are critical for the function, repair, and health of the nervous system, gastrointestinal tract, immune system, and endocrine system. Super B is especially indicated in cases of chronic diarrhea and nerve pain. This is such a potent source of B Vitamins that its use is generally restricted to cats, dogs, and larger animals. Ferrets could use Super B in a similar way to cats, however other exotic animals are recommended to be supplemented with products such as NingXia Red, MultiGreens, True Source, or MightyVites.

Birds & Exotics: Generally do not use this product as it cannot be dosed in small enough amounts. Ferrets can use Super B similarly to cats.

Cats: Super B tablets can be cut into very tiny sections with a scalpel blade. Generally less than 1/8 of a tablet is given per day, and can generally be pilled or mixed with food. If the tablet is pilled, it should be followed with food or water to ensure that it does not "stick" in the esophagus. Super B is best tolerated with food. Work with your veterinarian to decide if higher doses of B Vitamins are indicated.

Dogs: Super B tablets can be cut into sections with a scalpel blade. In general, approximately 1/8 of a tablet is given per 20 pounds (9 kg) of body weight. Super B should be given with a meal. Work with your veterinarian to decide if higher doses of B vitamins are indicated.

Large Animals: Super B tablets can be cut into tiny pieces or crushed, and mixed into NingXia Red, applesauce, or other foods for administration. Approximately ¼ to ½ of a tablet can be given once or twice a day. In some situations, more may be indicated. Work with your veterinarian to decide if higher doses of B Vitamins are indicated.

Super C

Super C is used in animals when a source of Vitamin C is desired. The most common condition in which Super C is used, is for dogs with cancer. An average 50 pound (23 kg) dog with cancer, may get up to 1 tablet, three times per day. You may work with your veterinarian to calculate an appropriate dosage of Vitamin C, and many holistic veterinarians prescribe high doses during times of need. Each tablet contains 650 mg of Vitamin C.

Birds & Exotics: Use Super C Chewable for these animals.

Cats: Approximately ¼ to ½ tablet twice a day can be given as a starting point.

Dogs: Approximately 1 tablet per 50 pounds (23 kg) of body weight can be given two to three times a day.

Large Animals: Work with your veterinarian to determine appropriate Vitamin C doses for your needs. Often large animal products will need to be selected.

Super C Chewable

Super C Chewable is a whole food source of Vitamin C and also contains Orange essential oil. This product can be used in any situation where Vitamin C supplementation is desired, and can be used in any species of animal. Work with your veterinarian to calculate appropriate doses for your needs. Chewable Vitamin C tablets are commonly used for Guinea Pigs, who require a source of Vitamin C from their diet. Guinea Pigs can have ¼ to ½ of a Super C Chewable tablet added to their bottle of drinking water daily. This solution should be made fresh, and changed each day. In cases of cancer, high doses of Vitamin C are often given, and this chewable is perfect for use in ferrets, birds, and for some cats. There is 117 mg of Vitamin C in each chewable tablet.

Birds & Exotics: Start with 1/8 to ¼ of a tablet per day. Work with your veterinarian to determine appropriate doses for your needs.

Cats: Cats could receive 2 tablets twice a day, or more in some circumstances. It may be easiest to use the Super C tablets for cats.

Dogs: It is likely best to use the Super C tablets for dosing Vitamin C in most dogs. A recommended starting point is to give 1 Chewable tablet twice a day, for every 10 pounds (4.5 kg) of body weight.

Large Animals: Super C tablets or large animal products with higher concentrations of Vitamin C are often needed.

Super Cal

Super Cal contains calcium, potassium, magnesium, and zinc in a citrate form, as well as Boron and the essential oils of Marjoram, Wintergreen, Lemongrass, and Myrtle. Each capsule contains 121 mg of calcium, 60 mg of magnesium, 15 mg of zinc, and 30 mg of potassium. Work with your veterinarian to calculate appropriate doses of this supplement for your animal when indicated. Super Cal is a vegetarian product, and may be of benefit to reptiles suffering from Metabolic Bone Disease, for egg-laying birds, and in situations where the supplementation of calcium, potassium, magnesium, and to a lesser extent zinc are indicated.

Tender Tush (KidScents)

Tender Tush is a diaper rash ointment with the phenomenal healing benefits of Sandalwood, Blue Tansy, Rosewood, Roman Chamomile, Lavender, Cistus, and Frankincense essential oils. It can be used topically on all animals, however care must be taken for animals that should not be made "greasy" such as birds and chinchillas. It is recommended not to apply this product in areas that need to dry out (normal scab formation), as the ointment may be too moisturizing.

Thieves Dentarome Toothpaste

All of the toothpastes; Dentarome, Dentarome Plus, Dentarome Ultra, and KidScents can be used for animals. Dentarome Ultra and KidScents contains Xylitol, so please see the discussion on Xylitol Toxicity at the beginning of this chapter. The other toothpastes do not contain Xylitol. The levels of Xylitol contained within the Dentarome Ultra, would require a 50 pound (23 kg) dog to ingest ½ of a tube of toothpaste to acquire toxic levels. Daily use of the toothpaste is of no concern, and Xylitol is included in low amounts in many veterinary oral hygiene products. Some animals show a preference to which toothpaste they enjoy more, so be sure to try them all. Our dogs seem to enjoy the Dentarome Plus Toothpaste over the Ultra.

The Dentarome Toothpastes are also phenomenal when used as a topical poultice. Scratches in horses, hotspots in dogs, and other various wounds, infections, and lesions that require antibacterial, antifungal, and drying actions respond well when the toothpaste is applied. Additional oils can be mixed into the toothpastes as well, for added power and therapeutic benefits.

Thieves Foaming Hand Soap

Thieves Foaming Hand Soap can be used on animals as well. The foam or liquid is simply used as a cleansing agent in place of other shampoos or washes. See more information in Thieves Household Cleaner, for additional ideas on its use. This product is not used orally, although if some is ingested due to regular use, this is okay.

Thieves Fresh Essence Mouthwash

The Thieves Mouthwash is wonderful for oral health. For dogs, cats, ferrets and similar animals who are prone to dental disease, adding a small amount to the drinking water can replace commercial veterinary water additives. Doing this on a regular basis, can help reduce oral bacteria and plaque formation. Start with a very tiny drop added to water, and gradually increase to find the optimal amount to add to the animal's water. Follow similar directions as outlined for adding oils to drinking water, and make sure that a situation is never created where an animal does not want to drink the water.

Thieves Mouthwash can also be directly rubbed and applied onto teeth and gums daily. This can greatly reduce plaque and tartar, and many owners have reported that tartar has fallen off of the teeth with routine application. This can replace the "tartar removing" oral products on the market today, with what I feel is a far superior and safer product.

Thieves Mouthwash can also be ingested and taken orally for gastrointestinal infections and pain. This is generally used in dogs and ferrets, however could be utilized in resistant cases for cats, birds, and other exotics when other items have failed. For dogs 1 teaspoon is a suggested starting point. For ferrets, ¼ teaspoon. In horses and large animals, 1 tablespoon or more could be given. For cats, birds, and other exotics, adding the Mouthwash to the drinking water is the most likely method of use. Starting with a drop added to the water, and gradually increasing based on tolerance and response is suggested. Cats can likely have a direct oral dose of ¼ to ½ teaspoon, which will likely evoke the typical feline salivation response.

Thieves Hard and Soft Lozenges

Thieves Lozenges contain Xylitol and are not recommended for use in animals. If you drop one on the floor, and your dog eats one, this is generally of no concern.

Thieves Household Cleaner

Thieves Household Cleaner should be mandatory for every home or farm, whether they have animals or not! In my veterinary practice, we have documented the resolution of abnormal blood values and chronic conditions, when toxic household cleaners and chemicals were exchanged for Thieves Cleaner. It is amazing how much more health we can bring to our animals when a cleaner that actually has health benefits is used on a regular basis, instead of toxic disinfectants.

Thieves Household Cleaner is used consistently in our veterinary hospital as our disinfectant of choice. Studies are being pursued to document the killing ability for various animal viruses, however these things take time and funding. What can be assured, is that we have witnessed and experienced the powerful disinfecting properties of Thieves Cleaner firsthand for contagious diseases such as Parvo, Strangles, Kennel Cough, Ringworm, Giardia, Upper Respiratory Infections, and various bacterial and viral diarrheas. Every shelter, veterinary clinic, grooming facility, boarding kennel, farm, or animal related environment should be using Thieves Household Cleaner in my opinion.

Thieves Cleaner can be used in garden sprayers, arena sprayers, spray bottles, pressure washers, carpet cleaners, and any other device you may have. Entire farms have been disinfected by using the arena sprayer to treat the grounds and pastures after a Strangles outbreak. Walls, stalls, floors, dirt, tack, laundry, hands, footbaths, shoes, boots, tires, cages, water dishes, troughs, buckets, trailers, trucks, floats, surgical tools, surgical sites, udders, abscesses, wounds, you name it - has been disinfected with Thieves Household Cleaner! Anyone transporting or showing animals should thoroughly disinfect any area where other animals have been, prior to placing your animal in the "clean" stall, cage, wash rack, or similar space.

The concentration in which to use the Thieves Cleaner really relies more on how you plan to use it. I try to make it as strong as possible for my application. So for example, if you are going to add it to an arena sprayer, you will need to make it dilute enough that it does not suds up and create foam that would not allow it to be sprayed. Also, budget may play a role when spraying entire fields, and any amount of Thieves Cleaner sprayed, will still be a benefit over nothing at all. When I use the cleaner topically, as in ear cleaner, I also want it as strong as possible, but not so strong as to leave a soapy residue behind on the skin and in the ear canal. The basic act of just "trying it out" is the best suggestion. Thieves Cleaner has been used straight on skin, even to bathe cats, so the concern is usually not about using it too strong (except when skin irritation is noted.) Largely, proper dilution is attempted so that the cleaner does not have to be rinsed off. So, when I mix up an ear cleaning solution, the goal is not to have to rinse the ear canal again after the cleaning. So, I rub the diluted cleaner onto my hands and allow it to dry there. If it feels comfortable to me, and not weird and tacky, then likely it will be okay to dry inside the ear canal, leaving a beneficial active "slight" residue behind. In situations like anal gland abscesses, I do plan on flushing again after the disinfecting flush is performed. So, a stronger solution can be used initially, followed by a more diluted "rinse" solution.

As mentioned, Thieves Household Cleaner has been routinely used to bathe many animals including cats, ferrets, dogs, and horses. Generally the cleaner is used straight out of the bottle, but pre-dilution is also possible. This is extremely effective for skunk odor, and additional oils such as Purification, can be added to the cleaner prior to the bath for added power. Using the cleaner as a shampoo or wash is extremely effective for odors, yeast skin infections, mange, fleas, lice, Ringworm, Scratches, Rain Rot, and more. The cleaner can be used alone, have additional oils added to it, or be combined with Animal Scents Shampoo. Purposely leaving behind a residue (both with the cleaner or the shampoo) has been very useful for fleas and lice. Even the tiniest baby kitten, covered in fleas, has been bathed up to daily with Thieves Household Cleaner. Fleas quickly are washed off, and start to die when Thieves Cleaner is used as a flea shampoo or dip.

But wait! There are still more wonderful uses for Thieves Household Cleaner! Spray the diluted solution in your yard, bushes, lean-to, or other farm areas to ward off insects, flies, or fleas. You can even spray the solution directly on large animals as an insect repellant. Many animal owners have noted a great reduction in the number of insects in their horse shelters after spraying the area thoroughly with the cleaning solution. Just repeat as necessary. Not only will you be reducing insects and odors, but you will actually be providing disinfecting and immune boosting actions to your animal's environment. A win, win situation.

Not that this is animal related, but it did solidify another use for Thieves Household Cleaner in our veterinary practice. Thieves Cleaner can be used in the holding tanks of motor homes, instead of the nasty toxic chemicals that are recommended for both sewage and drinking water tanks. We were quite resistant to adding a chemical preservative to our potable water in our motor home, so decided to add just a small bit of the Thieves Cleaner instead. We normally don't drink this water much anyway, and use it only for showering and washing dishes. However, my husband ended up acquiring quite a taste for the "Thieves Cleaner water" and started drinking it on a regular basis! We had already had an instance where my son had swallowed a huge mouthful of the fully concentrated Thieves Cleaner, while "pretending" to guzzle a huge jug of it. He actually enjoyed it and asked for more, which prompted my husband to ingest a large mouthful as well – partly to experience it, but partly to make sure there would be no ill effects for our son. Long story short, the word got out that we were drinking Thieves Household Cleaner, and others started to try it as well. Many noted health benefits from it, and also enjoyed the flavor. Not that I am recommending it as a routine therapy, but when contamination of water or contagious diarrhea conditions exist, adding Thieves Household Cleaner to drinking water on a regular basis, could be extremely helpful.

Hendra Virus in Australia is a horrible condition that is largely spread by fruit bats defecating where horses eat and drink. Adding Thieves Household Cleaner and essential oils to the horse troughs could likely help to stop the transmission cycle.

Thieves Cleaner is safe for use around birds and exotics, and can be used to clean cages, aquariums, fish tanks, and ponds safely. Rinsing after cleaning is suggested for super sensitive animals, and care should be taken around Honey Bees, Tarantulas, and other insect-like pets to not adversely repel or harm them with essential oils. Although their environments can be disinfected with the cleaner, it should be thoroughly rinsed and dried, with no odor left behind prior to replacing the insect. Please see the section on Insects within the Exotic Animal section of this book for more recommendations.

It is likely that an entire book could be written on the uses and benefits of Thieves Household Cleaner for animals! Maybe a subject of my next book! With the amazing ability to not only disinfect, but to impart health benefits to animals through a cleaning product, Thieves Household Cleaner plays an important role in maintaining the health of all animals.

Thieves Spray

Thieves Spray is an integral tool in our veterinary practice, thanks to Sara Kenney who formulated an Ear Spray Recipe using this product. The original recipe as well as Sara's adventures in animal aromatherapy can be found in her book *Natural Health Care For Your Four-Legged Friends*. What I have named the "Ear Spray Recipe" has been used to clear up many resistant ear infections in dogs, as well as to treat yeast and bacterial infections of feet and anal regions. This spray is mainly used in dogs, and the use in cats is not suggested, as there are more cat friendly methods that are equally as effective. The use in large animals is certainly appropriate, although it is more likely to be used on skin, rather than in ears. The use of straight Thieves Spray can be considered, but due to the ethanol content, it may sting irritated or broken skin.

Ear Spray Recipe:
- In a 30 mL glass spray bottle, combine the following:
- 7-8 mL of Thieves Spray
- 1 Tablespoon of V-6
- 3 drops of Lemongrass
- 4 drops of Copaiba
- 5 drops of Purification
- Add distilled water to fill the bottle.
- Shake well, and spray into the ear once or twice a day. You are not attempting to fill the ear with the solution, and should only be coating the skin and canal area with the spray.

The Ear Spray Recipe is effective for yeast, bacteria, mites, and inflammation due to the ingredient combination, making it my first selection for any canine ear infection.

Thieves Waterless Hand Purifier

The hand purifier has a higher ethanol content than other Thieves products, and can be used in situations where antibacterial and drying actions are desired. Caution should be used, as the product is likely to sting broken or irritated skin. Occasional use in acute situations, when other items are not available is suggested, such as for hot spots and chin acne.

Thieves Wipes

These can be used on animals or to disinfect animal related areas. There is a possibility of the wipes stinging or irritating delicate or damaged skin areas, so only careful and occasional use is recommended. However, in a pinch, these wipe can be very helpful. Wiping areas such as chin acne, hot spots, ears, or the yeasty infected area between dog foot pads in acute situations can be very helpful when other items are not available.

Thyromin

Thyromin provides nutritional support for thyroid function, however the entire body and endocrine system will benefit from a properly working thyroid gland. Thyromin contains valuable glandular materials, which are drastically missing from animal diets these days. This product has mainly been used in dogs for hypothyroidism at this time, but is likely to benefit many other conditions. It can be used in combination with thyroid medications. Work with your veterinarian to monitor blood levels and responses.

Dogs: Start with ½ of a capsule per 30 pounds (14 kg) of body weight per day. Monitor responses with your veterinarian, which may include blood thyroid levels, approximately every 14-30 days, or based on the discretion of your veterinarian. Increase amounts according to response and need. In humans this product is recommended for use at bedtime, and this guideline can also be followed for dogs, although is not mandatory.

True Source

True Source is a broad spectrum whole food multi-vitamin source. This supplement is appropriate for use in all animals. There are three different colored capsules contained within the package, and each one can be used individually or mixed together when the product is getting added into foods. In general, the capsules are opened and mixed with soft moist foods for administration. Start with a small sprinkling and gradually increase as tolerated

Birds & Exotics: Up to ½ capsule total volume, (if different colored capsules are combined), may be ingested per day. Certainly more can be given in some circumstances, and many animals need much less. Start with a tiny sprinkling and increase as indicated.

Cats: Up to 1 capsule total volume is generally given per day. More may be used when indicated, and some cats need less.

Dogs: In general, 1 capsule total volume, can be consumed per day for every 30 pounds (14 kg) of body weight.

Large Animals: This product is not generally used, however it certainly can be. 2 packages (6 capsules) per day, is the suggested starting point for consumption.

Ultra Young + Oral Spray with DHEA

Ultra Young spray has not been used commonly in animals at this time, however it may be indicated for conditions such as Alopecia X, undescended testicles, and cognitive dysfunction. This product does contain Grape seed/skin extract, which often raises concern for pet owners. Please see the discussion within NingXia Red for more information, however my research has revealed that there has never been a reported case of toxicity in animals from Grape Seed Extract. If you would like to consider using this product for an animal, work closely with your veterinarian to monitor responses and lab work when indicated. Starting with 1 spray of the product into the cheek pocket, once a day after 3 pm is suggested. This product would mainly be considered for use in dogs and horses.

V-6 Enhanced Vegetable Oil Complex

Also just referred to as V-6, this is the plain base oil carrier which contains Almond oil, Coconut oil (fractionated), Grape seed oil, Olive oil, Sesame seed oil, Sunflower seed oil, and Wheat germ oil. It is far superior for use in animals, than a plain vegetable oil or olive oil, as it does not leave as much residue on fur or fabrics. Oil spots that can stain a couch when olive oil is used for animal applications, do not appear to occur with V-6. Certainly, any oil can harm a fabric, however V-6 seems to be the most "user friendly" for fur, feather, and fabric. V-6 is also thin enough that it will spray from a glass spray bottle (as described in Oil Misting.) This oil is completely safe for ingestion by all animals. It is incredibly rare for animals to have allergies to the nut and seed oil ingredients, however if it was noted, the blend should be avoided for that animal.

Yacon Syrup

This syrup is fine for ingestion by animals. It would mainly be consumed in human left overs.

ESSENTIAL OILS: AVIAN

Birds (especially parrots) are a more recent addition into the world of veterinary aromatherapy. Pet birds are extremely sensitive to household toxins, and it is well known by bird owners that even the spray of an air freshener or the burning of a candle can be dangerous to a bird. Since many household fragrances are created with poor grade, adulterated, or synthetic essential oils, it was thought that all essential oils were toxic to birds. This has been found to be untrue. While birds have a distinct way that they should be exposed to essential oils, it is being found that they not only benefit, but thrive, with the addition of essential oils into their lives.

Prior to the use of any essential oil or essential oil based product in a bird, a thorough veterinary examination, by an avian veterinarian, is recommended. It is ideal if blood work (CBC and Chemistry Profile) can be performed prior to any start of natural remedies. Many avian patients initially present with pre-existing blood work abnormalities in my practice. So it is important to be able to document either the improvement of these values, or at least the stability of them while using essential oils. Clinicians have made misinterpretations of abnormal blood values in sick animals, due to the fact that they never obtained "pre-exposure" blood work. If we are using essential oils or other natural remedies for a bird, it is usually because they are already ill. Then if their condition degrades, it becomes a common thought to blame the natural remedy that was given. When in fact, if blood work would be available to compare with, prior to the exposure, we would likely not see any deterioration in the values.

It is an important note, that although some essential oils, products, and supplements may be listed for possible use, that not every recommendation has been used extensively for birds at this time. Read the individual description for a particular product, and if it states that it has not been used commonly in animals, then it most likely has not been used in birds. However, when the use of a product could be considered for difficult cases or life threatening situations, I felt it was important to include as an option to pursue. Certainly, the use of common sense, a very conservative start, and cooperation and testing with an avian veterinarian is advised whenever you may choose to explore the use of a product that does not have much knowledge base behind it. However, in severe situations such as self-mutilation or with conditions that may result in the ultimate death of a bird, great discoveries are often made with natural remedies, that benefit avian medicine as a whole. I felt it was important to share potential avenues with you, however, please understand that some of these treatments would qualify as "breaking new ground," and should be explored with great detail and care.

DIFFUSION:

Diffusion from one of the water-based diffusers is recommended for use in households with birds. Air diffusers can be utilized, however require a farther distance from the bird, or use in a much larger room (such as a barn or large aviary). Almost every essential oil single and blend has been diffused from a water-based diffuser (such as the Aria or Home Diffuser) around birds. In general, start with 3 drops of oil added to the water of the diffuser. Monitor the bird(s) closely for the first 5-10 minutes of diffusion. Increase the amounts and frequency of diffusion gradually, and most homes find that they can diffuse on an almost continual basis - bringing amazing health and benefits to their birds. Please read the chapter on Diffusion for more detailed instructions.

WATER MISTING:

A favorite technique that is being used currently in thousands of birds is the Feather Spray Recipe. This amazing spray was created by Leigh Foster, and had been used on her rescue and wildlife birds prior to its explosion into mainstream bird care. I use this recipe as a fundamental tool for my avian patients. The components of the spray layer so many different properties into a very well-loved application. Benefits for everything from bacterial, viral, and fungal conditions to even immune system support can be found in this spray.

Feather Spray Recipe:

- Place 20 drops of Lavender, 20 drops of Lemon, and 20 drops of Orange essential oils into a 4 ounce (120 mL) glass spray bottle.
- Add distilled water to fill the bottle. Shake well before each application, then mist the bird with the spray up to twice a day. Birds love this spray, and even those who routinely dislike a shower with a traditional spray bottle are attracted to being sprayed in this manner.
- When desired, an additional essential oil or two, may be added to this recipe, for example a drop or two of Frankincense.

- When adding more than just a couple drops to the recipe, you may wish to omit several drops of the base oils in replacement for the new oils. For example, you may add 15 drops of Lemon instead of 20, replacing those drops with 5 drops of Frankincense. This is not always necessary, but if you might add an additional 10 drops or more of essential oil(s) to the recipe, it is wise to attempt to keep the concentration, and thus dilution, of the essential oils to water similar in nature.

Copaiba & Frankincense Spray:
This water misting recipe is wonderful for many things, and can be used whenever these oils are indicated or for general anti-inflammatory or anti-cancer benefits. Frankincense carteri has been used most commonly with birds. This is the basic starting recipe, however variations of it can be made.
- Place 10 drops of Frankincense, and 5 drops of Copaiba essential oils into a 4 ounce (120 mL) glass spray bottle.
- Add distilled water to fill the bottle. Shake well before each application, then mist the bird with the spray up to twice a day.

Copaiba, Frankincense, Helichrysum Spray:
This spray adds the additional healing benefits of Helichrysum.
- Add 5 drops of Helichrysum to the Copaiba & Frankincense Spray recipe, and use as directed.

ADDING ESSENTIAL OILS TO DRINKING WATER:
This is generally done at a rate of 1 drop per liter of water. See the chapter on adding oils to drinking water for more detailed instructions.

ADDING ESSENTIAL OILS TO FOODS:
Please see the chapter Mixing Oils into Food for more detailed instructions.

AVIAN RAINDROP TECHNIQUE:
Birds present a unique situation for Raindrop Technique. Not only do they have feathers instead of fur, but they are also more sensitive to oils and have less data collected on them to date.

In my practice I have reserved the use of Raindrop Technique to birds that have more serious conditions, for which other essential oil protocols have not yielded enough results.

This technique has not been used in thousands of birds like the Feather Spray or diffusion. Likewise it has not been used in hundreds of birds as the Valor Roll-On currently has. I encourage everyone who will use this technique to have tried other methods first, and to also follow and monitor the cases carefully to provide further data and advancement of avian aromatherapy.

Raindrop Technique in birds is likely only to occur in birds that are fairly handle able. Chickens are actually quite easy to give an Avian Raindrop Technique to, and respond beautifully. Certainly, restraint can be used to allow for the application.

For animals cat sized and smaller, the Raindrop Technique is generally going to consist of applying a Raindrop "solution" – in which all of the oils that will be used are mixed into one diluted mixture. Please read the chapter on Raindrop Technique for more details on this technique and its use in animals.

Balancing (optional): Apply Valor Roll-On to the bottom of the feet. This can be directly applied, or be applied by having the bird perch on your hand, which is moistened with oil. Alternately, the Roll-On may be applied to a perch. Perch application should be light and care should be taken to not create too moist of an application.

Avian Raindrop Technique Solution: Start with the less concentrated solution and gradually increase the concentration used as needed or indicated.

- Add 1-2 drops each of Oregano, Thyme, Basil, Cypress, Wintergreen, Marjoram, and Peppermint oils into 30 mL (1 ounce) of V-6.
- If you feel especially cautious with an individual, please start with 1 drop of each Raindrop oil in 60 mL (2 ounces) of V-6. You can always add more later.
- To modify an Avian Raindrop Technique – add 1-2 drops of an additional essential oil to the above recipes. In general, up to 3 additional essential oils can be added.

- Rock the solution to mix thoroughly. Part the feathers, as best you can, over the back. Drip the Avian Raindrop Technique Solution from the tail to neck. Generally 2-3 drops of the solution will be used for most birds. Gently massage the oil into the spine. Vita Flex the spinal area, if possible.
- Monitor skin for any irritation or redness. Repeat use of this technique can result in a dry, flakey skin. This is usually non-irritated, and not painful or inflamed. Likely, it is mostly due to the drying effects of the essential oils. The condition is temporary and resolves when the technique is applied less often or diluted further.

We have used this technique up to daily in parrots and chickens, and most commonly 2-3 times per week. One parrot has been receiving her Avian Raindrop Technique 2-3 times per week, for over a year now. Her blood work has no abnormal changes or variations due to the essential oil use, however we did note that her skin became flakey at times.

Variations in Species:

In my practice, I have worked on parrots worth in excess of $30,000. These are the situations in which we start with REALLY light and conservative methods, and gradually work our way to more aggressive approaches. It is a sound recommendation to use common sense and caution as you progress.

It is important to mention that passerines and psittacines (finches, canaries, parakeets, budgies, parrots, and the like) are often treated with much more of a delicate touch. This may or may not be founded at this time, and we continually are impressed with how they handle essential oil administration when we need to explore new options. However, since they are relatively new to the use of essential oils medically, we will recommend a more cautious advancement for now.

Chickens, Pea Fowl, Turkeys, and other forms of poultry appear far more hardy in their use of essential oils. With these species, I generally do not hesitate to apply an Avian Raindrop Technique, administer essential oils by ingestion, or to use less commonly used oils. These birds are likely to pave the way for more advanced use of essential oils in the avian species.

AVIAN CONDITIONS

ARTHRITIS

(See also BUMBLEFOOT)

Arthritis is a condition of inflammation of the joints. As birds are rarely radiographed or evaluated for arthritis in the traditional sense, one can assume that older birds, or birds with any form of discomfort, may fall into this category of having pain that affects their mobility.

FIRST LINE RECOMMENDATIONS:
WATER MISTING: With a solution of 10 drops of Frankincense and 5 drops of Copaiba in 4 ounces (120 mL) of distilled water. Shake well, and mist directly onto the bird, 1-2 times a day.
INGESTION: Copaiba can be added to foods or drinking water.
SUPPLEMENTS: NingXia Red, Sulfurzyme, BLM Capsules, Omega Blue.

Single Oils:
Balsam Fir (Idaho), Copaiba, Frankincense, Helichrysum, Lavender, Lemon, Marjoram, Myrrh, Nutmeg, Orange, Palo Santo, Peppermint, Pine, Spruce, Tansy (Blue), Vetiver, Wintergreen

Blends:
Aroma Siez, Avian Raindrop Technique, Believe, Feather Spray Recipe, Juva Cleanse, Juva Flex, M-Grain, Stress Away Roll-On, Valor Roll-On

Supplements & Products:
Animal Scents Ointment, BLM Capsules, JuvaTone, MightyZyme, Mineral Essence, NingXia Red, Ningxia Wolfberries, Omega Blue, Ortho Ease Massage Oil, Ortho Sport Massage Oil, Regenolone Moisturizing Cream, Sulfurzyme

ASPERGILLOSIS
(See also RESPIRATORY CONDITIONS)

Aspergillosis is a serious fungal infection that usually affects the lungs and air sacs of the avian species – including parrots, raptors (birds of prey), and more. Symptoms may be varied and include labored breathing, respiratory clicking, tail bobbing, general illness, etc... Aspergillosis is a serious condition that is difficult to treat traditionally, essential oils hold true answers to defeating this condition.

FIRST LINE RECOMMENDATIONS:
WATER DIFFUSION: Thieves via open room, as well as tenting up to multiple times per day.
AVIAN RAINDROP TECHNIQUE: Up to once daily, when indicated and possible.
INGESTION: Thieves or Ocotea.
SUPPLEMENTS: Essentialzymes-4, Life 5, NingXia Red, Omega Blue.

Single Oils:
Copaiba, Eucalyptus Radiata, Geranium, Lavender, Lemon, Lemongrass, Marjoram, Melaleuca Alternifolia, Mountain Savory, Ocotea, Oregano, Palo Santo, Rosemary, Spruce, Thyme

Blends:
Australian Blue, Egyptian Gold, ImmuPower, Longevity, M-Grain, Melrose, Purification, R.C., Thieves

Supplements & Products:
Allerzyme, Detoxzyme, Essentialzymes-4, ImmuPro, MightyZyme, Mineral Essence, MultiGreens, NingXia Red, Ningxia Wolfberries, Omega Blue

BEHAVIORAL CONDITIONS
(See also HORMONAL CONDITIONS)

Any behavioral concern can be assisted by the use of essential oils. The capability of the oils to affect the physical as well as the emotional, is holistically complete. Nutritional supplements are often underestimated in behavioral concerns, and should always be added.

FIRST LINE RECOMMENDATIONS:
WATER DIFFUSION: Rotational diffusion of the emotional blends.
TOPICAL: Feather Spray Recipe
SUPPLEMENTS: MultiGreens, NingXia Red, Omega Blue

Single Oils:
Bergamot, Chamomile (German), Chamomile (Roman), Frankincense, Geranium, Grapefruit, Lavender, Lemon, Marjoram, Melissa, Myrrh, Orange, Palo Santo, Patchouli, Pine, Sage, Spikenard, Spruce, Tangerine, Valerian, Vetiver, Ylang Ylang

Blends:
Acceptance, Believe, Citrus Fresh, Dragon Time, Forgiveness, Harmony, Hope, Joy, Lady Sclareol, M-Grain, Mister, SclarEssence, Stress Away, RutaVaLa, Trauma Life, Valor, White Angelica

Supplements & Products:
Essentialzymes-4, LavaDerm Cooling Mist, MightyZyme, Mineral Essence, MultiGreens, NingXia Red, Ningxia Wolfberries, Omega Blue, Prenolone Plus Body Cream, Relaxation Massage Oil, True Source

BLEEDING

Bleeding of any sort is enough to send a bird owner into a state of panic. It is often described that birds can bleed to death, in a very short amount of time. In practice, this is a little less than accurate. However, it remains important to stop bleeding when it occurs. Veterinary attention is always recommended.

FIRST LINE RECOMMENDATIONS:
TOPICAL: Cistus or Helichrysum
ORAL: Cistus

Single Oils:
Cistus, Geranium, Helichrysum, Lavender

Blends:
Trauma Life

Caution:
Avoidance of oils such as Cinnamon, Clove, Nutmeg, Wintergreen, Abundance, Exodus II, Longevity, Thieves – and other oils that have anticoagulant effects, may be wise.

Supplements & Products:
NingXia Red

BLOOD FEATHER, BROKEN
(See also BLEEDING)

As an avian veterinarian, I rarely recommend the pulling of a blood feather, broken or otherwise. When pulled out, the body will just start the creation of a brand new immature feather, which may be prone to being broken again in the future. When possible, allowing the broken feather to continue its "life cycle," stops the continuation of the problem.

BONES - BROKEN
(See also PAIN MANAGEMENT)

FIRST LINE RECOMMENDATIONS:
See PAIN MANAGEMENT for methods of pain control.
TOPICAL: Valor Roll-On
WATER DIFFUSION: Trauma Life
SUPPLEMENTS: BLM Capsules, NingXia Red, Sulfurzyme

Single Oils:
Balsam Fir (Idaho), Copaiba, Helichrysum, Lavender, Myrrh, Palo Santo, Pine, Spruce

Blends:
Believe, Trauma Life, Valor Roll-On

Supplements & Products:
Animal Scents Ointment, BLM Capsules, NingXia Red, Ningxia Wolfberries, Ortho Ease Massage Oil, Ortho Sport Massage Oil, Sulfurzyme

BORNA VIRUS
(See PROVENTRICULAR DILATATION DISEASE, VIRAL CONDITIONS)

There is still some debate whether Borna Virus is the true cause of Proventricular Dilatation Disease (PDD), or if it simply is a factor in its development. Regardless of the relationship, essential oils support the entire body in many ways. Giving the body tools for complete healing and immune system health will support the correction of the problem on many levels.

BUMBLEFOOT
(See also ARTHRITIS, WOUNDS)

Bumblefoot is an inflammatory condition of the foot, which is often caused by chronic pressure related to perches. Inadequate perch diameter, bearing weight on one leg more than another, poor perch variety, and many other husbandry issues contribute to this condition. Lesions may appear as open wounds, pressure sores, or general swelling and distortion of the foot. This condition is quite common in raptors.

FIRST LINE RECOMMENDATIONS:
TOPICAL: 1 Tablespoon of Animal Scents Ointment with 1-2 drops each of Helichrysum, Idaho Balsam Fir, Copaiba, Melrose, Frankincense mixed into it. Apply sparingly to wound, 1-2 times a day. Do not use if the wound is creating a beneficial dry scab, as these heal better when allowed to remain dry.
WATER MISTING: Place 5 drops Helichrysum, 10 drops Frankincense, 5 drops Copaiba into 4 ounces of distilled water. Shake well, mist directly onto feet 1-2 times a day.
SUPPLEMENTS: NingXia Red, Sulfurzyme, BLM Capsules, Omega Blue.

Single Oils:
Balsam Fir (Idaho), Copaiba, Frankincense, Helichrysum, Lavender, Lemon, Marjoram, Myrrh, Nutmeg, Orange, Oregano, Palo Santo, Patchouli, Spikenard, Spruce, Vetiver, Wintergreen

Blends:
Aroma Siez, Believe, Juva Cleanse, Juva Flex, M-Grain, Melrose, Purification, Thieves

Supplements & Products:
Allerzyme, Animal Scents Ointment, BLM Capsules, ClaraDerm, Detoxzyme, Essentialzymes-4, LavaDerm Cooling Mist, MightyVites, MightyZyme, MultiGreens, NingXia Red, Ningxia Wolfberries, Omega Blue, Ortho Ease Massage Oil, Ortho Sport Massage Oil, Regenolone Moisturizing Cream, Sulfurzyme, True Source

CANCER

Cancer is a difficult condition, which certainly needs to be addressed on many levels. Please see the descriptions in Feline Conditions for an explanation of the holistic approach to cancer. The recommendations made in any of the conditions listings, no matter what the animal species, can be used as described for birds in their individual product description.

FIRST LINE RECOMMENDATIONS:
WATER DIFFUSION: Rotational diffusion of emotional blends. Frankincense diffusion up to 24 hours a day.
TOPICAL: Feather Spray Recipe up to twice a day. Avian Raindrop Technique weekly to daily, or as able.
WATER MISTING: 10-20 drops of Frankincense, and 5 drops of Copaiba in 4 ounces (120 mL) of distilled water. Mist at least twice a day.
INGESTION: Frankincense and Citrus oils in foods and water.
SUPPLEMENTS: Essentialzymes-4, ImmuPro, MultiGreens, NingXia Red, Omega Blue

Single Oils:
Copaiba, Frankincense, Grapefruit, Hyssop, Lavender, Lemon, Orange, Palo Santo, Sandalwood, Tangerine

Blends:
Citrus Fresh, Forgiveness, ImmuPower, Juva Cleanse, Juva Flex, 3 Wise Men

Supplements & Products:
Animal Scents Ointment, Essentialzyme, Essentialzymes-4, ImmuPro, MightyZyme, MultiGreens, NingXia Red, Ningxia Wolfberries, Omega Blue, Power Meal, Super C Chewable, True Source

CHLAMYDIOSIS, CHLAMYDOPHILA PSITTACI
(See PSITTACOSIS)

CROP INFECTION
(See also REGURGITATION)

A crop infection is a serious concern, and requires proper examination and diagnosis by an avian veterinarian. Essential oils provide an amazing tool for the treatment, prevention, and whole body support with this condition.

FIRST LINE RECOMMENDATIONS:
INGESTION: Di-Gize, Thieves
SUPPLEMENTS: Detoxzyme

Single Oils:
Juniper, Laurus Nobilis, Lavender, Lemon, Marjoram, Mountain Savory, Ocotea, Oregano, Patchouli, Peppermint, Spearmint, Spruce, Tarragon, Thyme

Blends:
Citrus Fresh, Di-Gize, ImmuPower, Juva Cleanse, Juva Flex, M-Grain, Purification, Thieves,

Supplements & Products:
Detoxzyme, Life 5, MightyZyme, Power Meal, True Source

CROP STASIS
(See also CROP INFECTION)

Crop stasis is the poor movement of the initial part of a bird's gastrointestinal tract. This can have many causes, and is most common in baby birds who are being hand fed. The root of the problem should always be addressed, however these recommendations can help with motility.

FIRST LINE RECOMMENDATIONS:
INGESTION: Peppermint, Di-Gize

Single Oils:
Marjoram, Mountain Savory, Ocotea, Oregano, Patchouli, Peppermint, Spearmint, Spruce, Tangerine, Tarragon

Blends:
Citrus Fresh, Di-Gize, ImmuPower, Juva Cleanse, Juva Flex, M-Grain, Thieves

Supplements & Products:
Detoxzyme, JuvaPower, JuvaSpice, JuvaTone, Life 5, MightyZyme, Power Meal, True Source

DIARRHEA
(See also GIARDIA)

A thorough work up with a veterinarian is critical to determining the cause for the diarrhea. More specific therapies can be used once the cause is found.

FIRST LINE RECOMMENDATIONS:
INGESTION: Di-Gize

Single Oils:
Laurus Nobilis, Lavender, Lemon, Melissa, Ocotea, Oregano, Peppermint, Tangerine, Tarragon, Thyme

Blends:
Di-Gize, ImmuPower, Purification, Thieves

Supplements & Products:
ComforTone, Detoxzyme, Life 5, MightyZyme, ParaFree, Power Meal, True Source

EGG BINDING
(See also EGG LAYING- EXCESSIVE, HORMONAL CONDITIONS)

Egg binding is the failure to pass an egg from the reproductive tract. Dehydrated, weak, or malnourished birds are much more prone to this disorder. It is often a veterinary emergency, and medical attention should be sought. Hydration and warmth are the most important factors to be addressed in this condition.

FIRST LINE RECOMMENDATIONS:
WATER DIFFUSION: Gentle Baby, Peace & Calming, or Lavender
TOPICAL: Valor Roll-On, Gentle Baby
SUPPLEMENTS: NingXia Red

Single Oils:
Clary Sage, Dorado Azul, Geranium, Hyssop, Lavender, Lemon, Marjoram, Myrrh, Vetiver, Ylang Ylang

Blends:
Aroma Siez, Dragon Time, Gentle Baby, Lady Sclareol, M-Grain, SclarEssence

Supplements & Products:
MightyZyme, NingXia Red, Omega Blue, PD 80/20, Relaxation Massage Oil, Super Cal, True Source

EGG LAYING - EXCESSIVE
(See also HORMONAL CONDITIONS)

Excessive egg laying is described as when a bird lays so many eggs that it becomes detrimental to their health. Attention to light cycles is incredibly important when attempting to have companion birds stop laying.

ANIMAL DESK REFERENCE: AVIAN

FIRST LINE RECOMMENDATIONS:
WATER DIFFUSION: Clary Sage
WATER MISTING: Feather Spray Recipe with 1 drop of Clary Sage added.
SUPPLEMENTS: Support the nutritional needs of egg laying with items such as NingXia Red and MultiGreens.

Single Oils:
Clary Sage, Marjoram, Nutmeg, Orange, Sage, Ylang Ylang

Blends:
Brain Power, Dragon Time, EndoFlex, Lady Sclareol, SclarEssence

Supplements & Products:
Dragon Time Massage Oil, ImmuPro, PD 80/20, Prenolone Plus Body Cream, Progessence Plus Serum, Super Cal, True Source

EGG LAYING – INADEQUATE PRODUCTION
(See also HORMONAL CONDITIONS)

This is most commonly a concern for those who raise laying hens. Making sure there is adequate nutrition, low stress, and proper light cycles.

FIRST LINE RECOMMENDATIONS:
INDIRECT DIFFUSION: Abundance
WATER MISTING: Feather Spray Recipe with 1 drop of Clary Sage added.
SUPPLEMENTS: Support the nutritional needs for proper function of the reproductive system. NingXia Red, Omega Blue, MultiGreens

Single Oils:
Clary Sage

Blends:
Abundance, Dragon Time, EndoFlex, Juva Cleanse, Juva Flex, SclarEssence

Supplements & Products:
Dragon Time Massage Oil, JuvaTone, MightyVites, MightyZyme, MultiGreens, NingXia Red, Ningxia Wolfberries, Omega Blue, PD 80/20, Prenolone Plus Body Cream, Progessence Plus Serum, Super Cal, True Source

FATTY LIVER DISEASE
(See also LIVER DISEASE)

FIRST LINE RECOMMENDATIONS:
INGESTION: Citrus Fresh, Grapefruit
WATER MISTING: Feather Spray Recipe with 1 drop of Juva Cleanse added.
WATER DIFFUSION: German Chamomile, Geranium
SUPPLEMENTS: NingXia Red

Single Oils:
Chamomile (German), Geranium, Goldenrod, Grapefruit, Helichrysum, Juniper, Lavender, Ledum, Lemon, Myrrh, Myrtle, Nutmeg, Orange, Rosemary, Sage, Spearmint, Tangerine, Wintergreen

Blends:
Citrus Fresh, GLF, Juva Cleanse, Juva Flex

Supplements & Products:
Detoxzyme, JuvaPower, JuvaSpice, JuvaTone, MightyZyme, MultiGreens, NingXia Red, Ningxia Wolfberries, Omega Blue, Power Meal, True Source

FEATHER LOSS
(See also FEATHER PICKING)

Feather loss may not always be the same as feather picking. Feather loss may occur when a bird is housed with another bird who plucks the other's feathers. Or, feather loss can also be a result of a medical condition. Loss of feathers from areas that the bird cannot actively reach (the head) is a prime indicator of actual feather loss. A quality medical work up with an avian veterinarian should be sought. Treat specific underlying problems if discovered – such as parasites, bacterial skin infection, or viral infection. Separation from other birds may be helpful in determining the cause. Chickens and poultry are commonly picked and attacked by flock mates.

FIRST LINE RECOMMENDATIONS:
WATER MISTING: LavaDerm or Feather Spray Recipe 1-2 times a day.
INGESTION: Melissa in drinking water.
WATER DIFFUSION: Diffuse listed oils up to 24 hours a day. Follow directions for rotational diffusion of emotional blends.
SUPPLEMENTS: NingXia Red, Omega Blue, MultiGreens, Sulfurzyme.

Single Oils:
Chamomile (Roman), Copaiba, Frankincense, Geranium, Helichrysum, Lavender, Ledum, Lemon, Melissa, Orange, Patchouli, Rosemary, Sandalwood, Tangerine, Ylang Ylang

Blends:
Acceptance, Dragon Time, Forgiveness, GLF, Hope, Juva Cleanse, Juva Flex, LavaDerm Spray, Purification, Thieves, Valor

Supplements & Products:
All forms of feather loss will need nutritional support for the regrowth of feathers – no matter what the cause. Nutritional supplements are a mandatory part of holistic veterinary care.

Allerzyme, ClaraDerm, Essentialzymes-4, JuvaPower, JuvaSpice, JuvaTone, LavaDerm Cooling Mist, Longevity, MightyVites, MightyZyme, MultiGreens, NingXia Red, Ningxia Wolfberries, Omega Blue, Sulfurzyme, True Source

FEATHER PICKING
(See also FEATHER LOSS, HORMONAL CONDITIONS)

Feather picking is an unfortunately common problem amongst companion birds. Causes range from emotional distress to medical conditions such as heart disease. It is important to seek as accurate of a diagnosis as is possible, however even with the most experienced avian veterinarian, often a thorough work up still leaves one clueless. Feather picking is important to differentiate from feather loss. With feather picking, the bird themselves is actually plucking or damaging

AVIAN CONDITIONS

their feathers. This means that areas that the bird cannot reach are still feathered (for example the head). The most successful treatment of feather picking involves discovery and treatment of the underlying condition responsible. For example – if a bacterial infection of the skin initiated the feather plucking – then exposure to anti-bacterial essential oils would be the most beneficial. If heart disease was suspected, then exposure to essential oils that are beneficial to the heart would be indicated.

In all cases, nutritional support is of the utmost importance. This cannot be ignored, and should be ranked very high on the list of things to do.

FIRST LINE RECOMMENDATIONS:
TOPICAL: LavaDerm or Feather Spray Recipe up to 1-2 times a day. Avian Raindrop Technique may be indicated for some cases.
WATER DIFFUSION: Diffusion of Thieves or Purification, with 1 drop of Eucalyptus Blue added, up to 24 hours a day. Rotational diffusion of emotional blends is also recommended.
DRINKING WATER: Melissa
SUPPLEMENTS: NingXia Red, Omega Blue, Sulfurzyme, Essentialzymes-4

Single Oils:
Basil, Chamomile (Roman), Copaiba, Eucalyptus Blue, Frankincense, Geranium, Grapefruit, Helichrysum, Laurus Nobilis, Lavender, Ledum, Lemon, Melissa, Marjoram, Myrrh, Ocotea, Orange, Palo Santo, Patchouli, Rosemary, Spruce, Tangerine, Tansy (Blue), Valerian, Vetiver, Ylang Ylang

Blends:
Acceptance, Believe, Citrus Fresh, Dragon Time, EndoFlex, Forgiveness, GLF, Harmony, Hope, Juva Cleanse, Juva Flex, M-Grain, Present Time, Purification, Thieves, Trauma Life

Supplements & Products:
Dietary supplementation is a must for feather picking. If this portion of care is not met, you will usually be in a trap of continually trying to calm a symptom, while never addressing the body's need for nutrients to repair itself. With all supplements, it is important to start with a small amount and gradually increase the amount given as you determine what your individual bird can

handle, or what they require. Some may need much larger amounts for correction of the dis-ease.

Animal Scents Ointment, ClaraDerm, JuvaPower, JuvaSpice, JuvaTone, LavaDerm Cooling Mist, MightyVites, MightyZyme, MultiGreens, NingXia Red, Ningxia Wolfberries, Omega Blue, ParaFree, Sulfurzyme, True Source.

GASTROINTESTINAL CONDITIONS

(See CROP INFECTION, CROP STASIS, DIARRHEA, REGURGITATION)

GIARDIA

(See also DIARRHEA)

Contamination of drinking water is often the culprit in the spread and continuation of Giardia in bird flocks. Adding essential oils to the water can help disinfect, as well as treat the condition. New research is showing the effectiveness of essential oils such as Clove against Giardia.

FIRST LINE RECOMMENDATIONS:
INGESTION: Di-Gize, Thieves
DRINKING WATER: Purification, Citrus Fresh, or Di-Gize. Thieves Household Cleaner or Fresh Essence Mouthwash may be considered in severe situations or large flocks.
SUPPLEMENTS: Detoxzyme

Single Oils:
Basil, Lavender, Lemon, Melaleuca Alternifolia, Mountain Savory, Nutmeg, Ocotea, Orange, Patchouli, Peppermint, Spearmint, Tangerine, Tarragon, Thyme

Blends:
Citrus Fresh, Di-Gize, ImmuPower, M-Grain, Melrose, Purification, Thieves

Supplements & Products:
Detoxzyme, Life 5, MightyZyme, MultiGreens, NingXia Red, Omega Blue, ParaFree, Thieves Fresh Essence Mouthwash, Thieves Household Cleaner, True Source

GOUT

(See also ARTHRITIS, KIDNEY DISEASE, PAIN MANAGEMENT)

Gout is the accumulation of uric acid deposits within the joints. It is a painful condition, often secondary to kidney disease in birds. The use of oils to encourage drinking of water is strongly recommended, as well as increasing hydration in general.

FIRST LINE RECOMMENDATIONS:
 DRINKING WATER: Citrus Fresh
 INGESTION: Juva Cleanse or GLF
 WATER MISTING: Feather Spray Recipe with 2 drops of Juniper and 2 drops of Copaiba added.
 SUPPLEMENTS: Essentialzymes-4, NingXia Red

Single Oils:
 Copaiba, Juniper, Lemon, Palo Santo, Spruce, Tsuga, Wintergreen

Blends:
 Citrus Fresh, GLF, Hope, Juva Cleanse, Juva Flex

Supplements & Products:
 Animal Scents Ointment, Essentialzymes-4, JuvaPower, JuvaSpice, JuvaTone, MightyZyme, MultiGreens, NingXia Red, Ningxia Wolfberries, Omega Blue, Ortho Ease Massage Oil, Ortho Sport Massage Oil, Regenolone Moisturizing Cream, Sulfurzyme, True Source

HEAD TRAUMA

(See also NEUROLOGIC CONDITIONS)

The most common scenario for this condition is a bird who flies into a window. Often dazed and stunned, they can benefit from essential oils until they are ready to fly away again. The recommendations have been used on countless wild birds to get them up and flying again soon. Providing a warm quiet place to rest is also important.

FIRST LINE RECOMMENDATIONS:

TOPICAL: Place 2 drops of neat Frankincense into the palms of your hand. Allow to absorb almost completely, then cup the bird within your hands. You can allow them to smell it, and also to rub some onto their feet.

TOPICAL: Valor Roll-On applied to the bottoms of the feet also works well.

WATER DIFFUSION: With caging or tenting, diffuse Frankincense, Helichrysum, and Copaiba (3 drops of each) for at least 20 minutes or as needed. Repeat or continue diffusion based on responses.

Single Oils:
Copaiba, Frankincense, Helichrysum, Lavender, Rose

Blends:
Brain Power, Joy, Peace & Calming, Valor

Supplements & Products:
NingXia Red

HEAVY METAL POISONING

FIRST LINE RECOMMENDATIONS:

INGESTION: Helichrysum in food and/or drinking water.
DRINKING WATER: Citrus Fresh, Grapefruit, or Tangerine
TOPICAL: Feather Spray Recipe made with Tangerine instead of Orange oil. Add 3 drops of Helichrysum, and 1 drop of Juniper.
WATER DIFFUSION: GLF, Juva Cleanse, Juva Flex
SUPPLEMENTS: Detoxzyme, MultiGreens, NingXia Red

Single Oils:
Chamomile (Roman), Grapefruit, Helichrysum, Hyssop, Juniper, Lavender, Ledum, Lemon, Nutmeg, Tangerine, Tsuga

Blends:
Brain Power, Citrus Fresh, GLF, Juva Cleanse, Juva Flex, M-Grain

Supplements & Products:
Detoxzyme, JuvaPower, JuvaSpice, JuvaTone, MightyZyme, MultiGreens, NingXia Red, Ningxia Wolfberries, Omega Blue

HORMONAL CONDITIONS
(See also BEHAVIORAL CONDITIONS)

Hormonal conditions can encompass many things, but in birds this most commonly will mean behavioral concerns or sexual and reproductive behaviors. Males may masturbate, females may egg lay, and even feather picking and screaming can be related to hormonal surges. Sometimes these actions are completely normal, however when they become disruptive or unhealthy, the exaggerated responses should be softened.

FIRST LINE RECOMMENDATIONS:
Marjoram is particularly helpful in calming over active sexual activity, particularly masturbation.
WATER MISTING: Feather Spray Recipe with 2 drops of Clary Sage added.
WATER DIFFUSION: Any of the suggested oils.
SUPPLEMENTS: MightyZyme, NingXia Red

Single Oils:
Clary Sage, Dorado Azul, Geranium, Lavender, Marjoram, Melissa, Myrrh, Nutmeg, Orange, Sage, Spikenard, Tansy (Blue), Tarragon, Ylang Ylang

Blends:
Dragon Time, EndoFlex, Forgiveness, Hope, Lady Sclareol, Mister, SclarEssence

Supplements & Products:
Dragon Time Massage Oil, ImmuPro, LavaDerm Cooling Mist, MightyZyme, MultiGreens, NingXia Red, Ningxia Wolfberries, Omega Blue, PD 80/20, Prenolone Plus Body Cream, Progessence Plus Serum, Regenolone Moisturizing Cream, True Source

KIDNEY DISEASE

With Kidney Disease it is important that hydration stays increased. If essential oil use in the drinking water increases water consumption, this is a wonderful bonus. It is important to not add too many new things into a protocol all at once, as if detoxification occurs too quickly for the compromised kidneys to eliminate, an individual could feel more uncomfortable. Go very slowly, adding items gradually in compromised individuals.

FIRST LINE RECOMMENDATIONS:
DRINKING WATER: Citrus Fresh, Lemon, or Grapefruit
INGESTION: Juva Cleanse
TOPICAL: Feather Spray Recipe made with 10 drops of Orange and 10 drops of Grapefruit instead of the entire 20 drops of Orange oil. Add 2 drops of Juniper.
WATER DIFFUSION: Geranium, GLF
SUPPLEMENTS: Detoxzyme, MultiGreens, NingXia Red

Single Oils:
Geranium, Grapefruit, Juniper, Lavender, Ledum, Lemon

Blends:
Citrus Fresh, GLF, Juva Cleanse, Juva Flex

Supplements & Products:
JuvaTone, MightyVites, MightyZyme, MultiGreens, NingXia Red, Ningxia Wolfberries, Omega Blue, True Source

LEAD POISONING
(See HEAVY METAL POISONING)

LIVER DISEASE

FIRST LINE RECOMMENDATIONS:
INGESTION: Helichrysum in food and/or water
DRINKING WATER: Citrus Fresh
WATER DIFFUSION: Any selected oils
TOPICAL: Feather Spray Recipe made with Tangerine instead of Orange oil. Alternately, replace some of the drops of oil in the recipe with 5 drops of Helichrysum or 5 drops of Roman Chamomile.
SUPPLEMENTS: MultiGreens, NingXia Red

Single Oils:
Chamomile (German), Chamomile (Roman), Geranium, Goldenrod, Grapefruit, Helichrysum, Juniper, Lavender, Ledum, Lemon, Myrtle, Nutmeg, Rosemary, Sage, Spearmint, Tangerine

Blends:
Citrus Fresh, GLF, Juva Cleanse, Juva Flex

Supplements & Products:
Detoxzyme, JuvaPower, JuvaSpice, JuvaTone, MightyVites, MightyZyme, MultiGreens, NingXia Red, Ningxia Wolfberries, Omega Blue, True Source

MACAW WASTING DISEASE
(See PROVENTRICULAR DILATATION DISEASE)

MALNUTRITION

The word Malnutrition often makes bird owners feel uncomfortable, or like they have fallen short of caring properly for their bird. However, the vast majority of birds in captivity today suffer from Malnutrition. The simple fact is that we cannot duplicate an adequate diet for them, no matter how hard we try. Eggs are laid and hatched with already-deficient little beings. Malnutrition is labeled when physical or laboratory findings actual confirm that the body is in a state of lack. It is more true that all birds are in this state already, we just don't diagnose it until there are tangible values to detect.

FIRST LINE RECOMMENDATIONS:
DRINKING WATER: Citrus Fresh, Orange, or Tangerine
WATER DIFFUSION: Any selected oil.
SUPPLEMENTS: Essentialzymes-4, MultiGreens, NingXia Red, Omega Blue

Single Oils:
Grapefruit, Helichrysum, Lavender, Ledum, Lemon, Orange, Spearmint, Tangerine, Tarragon

Blends:
Citrus Fresh, Di-Gize, GLF, Juva Cleanse, Juva Flex

Supplements & Products:
Allerzyme, Essentialzymes-4, JuvaPower, JuvaSpice, JuvaTone, Life 5, MightyVites, MightyZyme, Mineral Essence, MultiGreens, NingXia Red, Ningxia Wolfberries, Omega Blue, ParaFree, Power Meal, Super Cal, True Source

MUTILATION, SELF

(See also FEATHER LOSS, FEATHER PICKING, PAIN MANAGEMENT)

Self-mutilation is a disturbing disorder in which a bird bites and chews their own skin to the point of causing damage, sometimes severe in extent. Most commonly this area of mutilation is on the chest area, but can include other locations. Although often linked with emotional concerns, this condition is most certainly grounded in physical conditions. An accurate diagnosis and extensive diagnostic testing is worthwhile. Any concern such as Arthritis, Heart Disease, or Hormonal Conditions should be addressed as they may be a potential cause for the mutilation behavior.

FIRST LINE RECOMMENDATIONS:
Use the basic recommendations for FEATHER PICKING and also slowly incorporate one or all of the following:

WATER MISTING: With 4 drops of Helichrysum, 4 drops of Copaiba, 10 drops of Frankincense, and 4 drops of Myrrh in 4 ounces (120 mL) of distilled water. Shake well, spray mutilated area up to 4 or more times per day.

WATER DIFFUSION: Rotational diffusion of emotional blends. Tented diffusion with Thieves or Purification can be helpful to ease infection and discomfort of the lesion.

INGESTION: Use oils indicated for any medical concerns noted. Also see PAIN MANAGEMENT for methods to control discomfort.

TOPICAL: Mix 1 drop each of Helichrysum, Myrrh, and Frankincense into 1 tablespoon of Animal Scents Ointment. Apply sparingly to wound. Avian Raindrop Technique may be indicated for some cases.

SUPPLEMENTS: BLM Capsules

Single Oils:

Basil, Chamomile (German), Chamomile (Roman), Copaiba, Frankincense, Geranium, Grapefruit, Helichrysum, Laurus Nobilis, Lavender, Ledum, Lemon, Marjoram, Melissa, Myrrh, Nutmeg, Ocotea, Orange, Palmarosa, Palo Santo, Patchouli, Spikenard, Tangerine, Tansy (Blue), Valerian, Vetiver, Wintergreen, Ylang Ylang

Blends:

Citrus Fresh, Di-Gize, Dragon Time, Forgiveness, GLF, Hope, Juva Cleanse, Juva Flex, M-Grain, Peace & Calming, Purification, Thieves, Trauma Life

Supplements & Products:

Animal Scents Ointment, BLM Capsules, ClaraDerm, Detoxzyme, Essentialzymes-4, ImmuPro, JuvaPower, JuvaSpice, JuvaTone, LavaDerm Cooling Mist, Life 5, MightyVites, MightyZyme, Mineral Essence, MultiGreens, NingXia Red, Ningxia Wolfberries, Omega Blue, Ortho Ease Massage Oil, Ortho Sport Massage Oil, ParaFree, PD 80/20, Power Meal, Regenolone Moisturizing Cream, Sulfurzyme, True Source

NEUROLOGIC CONDITIONS

Neurologic conditions can be caused by many different things, heavy metal poisoning, liver disease, viruses, and more. An accurate diagnosis is critical to addressing the foundation of the problem, however these recommendations build and support normal nerve health and regeneration.

FIRST LINE RECOMMENDATIONS:
WATER MISTING: Feather Spray Recipe made with exchanging 6 drops of base oils, with 2 drops Roman Chamomile and 4 drops Helichrysum. Rotationally, also use the Copaiba, Frankincense, and Helichrysum Spray Recipe.
WATER DIFFUSION: Any of the recommended oils.
DRINKING WATER: Melissa
TOPICAL: RutaVaLa or Valor via direct, hand, or perch application to feet.
SUPPLEMENTS: MultiGreens, NingXia Red, Omega Blue

Single Oils:
Chamomile (Roman), Helichrysum, Juniper, Laurus Nobilis, Lavender, Lemon, Marjoram, Melissa, Palo Santo, Spruce

Blends:
Forgiveness, Harmony, Hope, Juva Cleanse, Juva Flex, M-Grain, Peace & Calming, RutaVaLa, Valor Roll-On

Supplements & Products:
Essentialzymes-4, MightyZyme, Mineral Essence, MultiGreens, NingXia Red, Omega Blue, Sulfurzyme, True Source

PAIN MANAGEMENT

Pain management is critical for any bird. Any symptom can be demonstrated as a response to pain, and we should never forget that although an animal cannot communicate that they are painful, pain does exist and is a significant source of stress, immune dysfunction, and delayed healing.

FIRST LINE RECOMMENDATIONS:
INGESTION: Add 1 drop each of Helichrysum, Myrrh, and Copaiba to 1 teaspoon of V-6 or coconut oil. Feed one drop of this mixture, gradually increasing amount and frequency of feeding, based on response.
WATER MISTING: Copaiba, Frankincense, and Helichrysum Recipe.
SUPPLEMENTS: BLM Capsules, Sulfurzyme

Single Oils:
Copaiba, Helichrysum, Lavender, Myrrh, Palo Santo, Peppermint, Spruce, Tansy (Blue), Wintergreen

Blends:
Aroma Siez, M-Grain, Valor

Supplements & Products:
Animal Scents Ointment, BLM Capsules, MightyZyme, NingXia Red, Omega Blue, Ortho Ease Massage Oil, Ortho Sport Massage Oil, Regenolone Moisturizing Cream, Sulfurzyme

PAPILLOMATOSIS

Papilloma was one of the first conditions I treated aggressively with essential oils for a bird. The incredible and significant responses revolutionized the medical use of essential oils for birds. Often times, these cases have been struggling for many years with the wart-like condition, so responses are not expected over night. Immune systems and basic health must be rebuilt to fully address this disorder.

FIRST LINE RECOMMENDATIONS:
WATER MISTING: Alternate between daily to twice daily use of each spray recipe recommended at the beginning of the chapter.
WATER DIFFUSION: Especially Thieves, but any recommended oils.
DRINKING WATER: Melissa essential oil is a must for this condition. Other oils can be used, however it is wise to make sure that ingestion of Melissa oil in particular is achieved.
INGESTION: Rotate ingestion of Melissa, Oregano, and Clove oils mixed into foods.
SUPPLEMENTS: MultiGreens, NingXia Red, Omega Blue, Sulfurzyme, MightyZyme

Single Oils:
Clove, Copaiba, Frankincense, Lavender, Lemon, Melissa, Mountain Savory, Oregano, Palo Santo, Peppermint, Ravintsara, Sandalwood, Thyme

Blends:
Avian Raindrop Technique, Di-Gize, Forgiveness, Hope, ImmuPower, Juva Cleanse, Juva Flex, Longevity, Raven, Thieves, 3 Wise Men

Supplements & Products:
ImmuPro, JuvaTone, MightyZyme, MultiGreens, NingXia Red, Omega Blue, Sulfurzyme, Thieves Fresh Essence Mouthwash, Thieves Household Cleaner, True Source

PARROT FEVER
(See PSITTACOSIS)

PBFD
(See PSITTACINE BEAK AND FEATHER DISEASE)

PDD
(See PROVENTRICULAR DILATATION DISEASE)

PROVENTRICULAR DILATATION DISEASE
(See also NEUROLOGIC CONDITIONS, VIRAL CONDITIONS)

Proventricular Dilatation Disease is thought to be caused by a virus (see Borna Virus), and causes neurologic damage and inflammation. This damage is mainly noted as a disruption in digestion and gastrointestinal function, however other neurologic signs can be seen. This is a devastating disease, and I feel that true hope lies within essential oils for prevention and treatment. Many affected birds are placed on NSAID therapies, and the use of Copaiba can greatly replace these medications. Slow and careful introduction of oils and supplements must be taken, as these birds are often fragile, are malnourished, and have been on prescription medications long term.

Focusing on highly antiviral oils (like Melissa), anti-inflammatory actions, and neurologic repair are important with this condition.

FIRST LINE RECOMMENDATIONS:
>WATER MISTING: Rotational spraying with various recipes. Feather Spray Recipe with 2 drops Roman Chamomile added. Copaiba, Frankincense, and Helichrysum Recipe.
>DRINKING WATER: Melissa
>WATER DIFFUSION: Rotational diffusion of any recommended oils. Up to 24 hours a day, if the bird handles it well.
>INGESTION: Melissa, Helichrysum, Copaiba. Peppermint may help with peristalsis and movement of the gastrointestinal system.
>TOPICAL: Valor Roll-On, RutaVaLa. Avian Raindrop Technique may be indicated in some cases.
>SUPPLEMENTS: Essentialzymes-4, MultiGreens, NingXia Red, Omega Blue. MultiGreens are a source of Melissa oil, and should always be included.

Single Oils:
>Chamomile (Roman), Copaiba, Helichrysum, Hyssop, Laurus Nobilis, Lavender, Lemon, Melissa, Mountain Savory, Patchouli, Peppermint, Ravintsara, Sandalwood, Spearmint, Tarragon, Thyme

Blends:
>Citrus Fresh, Di-Gize, Egyptian Gold, Forgiveness, GLF, Hope, ImmuPower, Juva Cleanse, Juva Flex, Longevity, M-Grain, Raven, RutaVaLa, Thieves, 3 Wise Men

Supplements & Products:
>Allerzyme, Essentialzymes-4, ImmuPro, JuvaPower, JuvaSpice, JuvaTone, Life 5, MightyZyme, Mineral Essence, MultiGreens, NingXia Red, Omega Blue, PD 80/20, Power Meal, Sulfurzyme, True Source

PSITTACINE BEAK AND FEATHER DISEASE
(See also FEATHER LOSS, VIRAL CONDITIONS)

Psittacine Beak and Feather Disease is a viral infection that causes abnormal feather growth, feather loss, and can also affect many other body systems. It is a contagious disease, and continued diffusion of essential oils is likely to reduce transmission and boost immune function in flock situations.

FIRST LINE RECOMMENDATIONS:
Follow the recommendations outlined for VIRAL CONDITIONS and FEATHER LOSS for items that support this disorder.

WATER DIFFUSION: 3-4 drops of Thieves, plus 1-2 drops of Eucalyptus Blue should be diffused on a continual basis as tolerated. Rotating through diffusion of other essential oils for health and environmental decontamination is suggested.
DRINKING WATER: Melissa
WATER MISTING: Feather Spray Recipe with 2 drops Hyssop added.
INGESTION: Melissa, ImmuPower
TOPICAL: Avian Raindrop Technique when possible
SUPPLEMENTS: MultiGreens, NingXia Red, Omega Blue, Sulfurzyme, ImmuPro, MightyZyme

Single Oils:
Eucalyptus Blue, Eucalyptus Globulus, Helichrysum, Hyssop, Lavender, Lemon, Melissa, Mountain Savory, Ravintsara, Rosemary, Sandalwood, Thyme

Blends:
Egyptian Gold, Forgiveness, GLF, Hope, ImmuPower, Juva Cleanse, Juva Flex, Longevity, Raven, Thieves, 3 Wise Men

Supplements & Products:
ImmuPro, JuvaPower, JuvaSpice, JuvaTone, LavaDerm Cooling Mist, MightyZyme, MultiGreens, NingXia Red, Ningxia Wolfberries, Omega Blue, Sulfurzyme, Thieves Household Cleaner, True Source

AVIAN CONDITIONS

PSITTACOSIS

Psittacosis is caused by a bacteria, and is contagious to humans. Traditional therapies include treatment with Doxycycline antibiotics. Prevention is the ideal course, with the use of Thieves Household Cleaner and continual diffusion, critical to boost immune systems and reduce environmental contamination.

FIRST LINE RECOMMENDATIONS:
WATER DIFFUSION: Thieves or Purification in the room, and also via tenting or caging when needed. Rotate through other oils as well.
INGESTION: Thieves
DRINKING WATER: Lemon
TOPICAL: Avian Raindrop Technique may be indicated for some cases.
SUPPLEMENTS: NingXia Red

Single Oils:
Eucalyptus Globulus, Helichrysum, Laurus Nobilis, Lavender, Ledum, Lemon, Mountain Savory, Oregano, Rosemary, Thyme

Blends:
Egyptian Gold, GLF, ImmuPower, Juva Cleanse, Juva Flex, Longevity, Purification, Raven, R.C., Thieves

Supplements & Products:
ImmuPro, JuvaPower, JuvaSpice, JuvaTone, MightyZyme, MultiGreens, NingXia Red, Ningxia Wolfberries, Omega Blue, True Source

REGURGITATION
(See also CROP INFECTION, CROP STASIS, HORMONAL CONDITIONS)

Regurgitation can occur for many reasons, so it is important to have a thorough examination by an avian veterinarian to help determine the cause. If the cause seems hormonal in nature, please see HORMONAL CONDITIONS. Laboratory testing is ideal and can show if kidney, liver, or gastrointestinal systems may be implicated. Once the underlying cause is determined, using recommendations specific to these needs, will aid in healing more thoroughly.

FIRST LINE RECOMMENDATIONS:
DRINKING WATER: Citrus Fresh
INGESTION: Di-Gize, Peppermint
WATER DIFFUSION: Patchouli, Thieves

Single Oils:
Ginger, Juniper, Laurus Nobilis, Lavender, Lemon, Marjoram, Ocotea, Patchouli, Peppermint, Spearmint, Spruce, Tangerine, Tarragon

Blends:
Citrus Fresh, Di-Gize, GLF, ImmuPower, Juva Cleanse, Juva Flex, M-Grain, Purification, Thieves

Supplements & Products:
Allerzyme, Essentialzymes-4, MightyZyme, Life 5, NingXia Red, ParaFree, Power Meal, Thieves Fresh Essence Mouthwash, Thieves Household Cleaner

RESPIRATORY CONDITIONS
(See also ASPERGILLOSIS, SINUS INFECTIONS)

FIRST LINE RECOMMENDATIONS:
WATER DIFFUSION: 3-4 drops of Thieves or Purification with 1 drop of Eucalyptus Blue via caging or tenting. Diffuse for up to 20 minutes, 3 or more times per day, depending on response. Diffusion via open room, can occur 24 hours a day when tolerated, with any oil recommendation.
INGESTION: Thieves when oral antibiotic action is needed.
WATER MISTING: Feather Spray Recipe
SUPPLEMENTS: MultiGreens, NingXia Red

Single Oils:
Copaiba, Cedarwood, Eucalyptus Blue, Eucalyptus Globulus, Eucalyptus Radiata, Hyssop, Laurus Nobilis, Lavender, Lemon, Lemongrass, Marjoram, Melaleuca Alternifolia, Melissa, Myrtle, Oregano, Palo Santo, Pine, Ravintsara, Rosemary, Spruce, Thyme, Tsuga

Blends:
Egyptian Gold, ImmuPower, M-Grain, Melrose, Purification, Raven, R.C., Thieves

Supplements & Products:
MightyZyme, MultiGreens, NingXia Red, Ningxia Wolfberries, Omega Blue, True Source

SCALY FACE MITES

Scaly face mites are common in Budgerigars (Budgies, Common Parakeets), and often cause a grainy overgrowth on the nasal area (cere) and beak. Often the beak is distorted in growth. Infections can be undetected for years, until they become severe enough to warrant a veterinary exam. Mite protection products sold on the avian market, are completely toxic, and generally useless as well. Diffusion of Purification from the acquirement of a bird, would likely avert this problem from festering.

FIRST LINE RECOMMENDATIONS:
TOPICAL: 1 drop of neat Purification is placed on a cotton swab. The swab is carefully applied to the cere (nasal tissue area) and affected beak. Care is taken to avoid contact with the eyes. Monitor responses carefully, however neat application has not been overwhelming to many birds. Repeat the application daily for 7-14 days, depending on how the bird is handling it. Then use direct application every few days to every week, along with other methods of application.
WATER DIFFUSION: Purification via tenting can be performed at least once a day to help permeate the infected tissues with essential oil.
WATER MISTING: Purification can also be used by water misting (4 drops in 4 ounces of distilled water to start), and the bird can be misted once to several times per day. This is a long term problem, and when beak and tissue deformity is present, it can take a long time to repair.
SUPPLEMENTS: Nutritional support is always recommended.

Single Oils:
Citronella, Lavender, Lemon, Palo Santo, Pine

ANIMAL DESK REFERENCE: AVIAN

Blends:
Purification, Thieves

Supplements & Products:
NingXia Red, Ningxia Wolfberries, Omega Blue, Sulfurzyme

SEIZURES

(See also SEIZURES in CANINE CONDITIONS)

FIRST LINE RECOMMENDATIONS:
WATER MISTING: Feather Spray Recipe daily.
WATER DIFFUSION: Water diffusion of Peace & Calming or RutaVaLa is begun, up to 24 hours a day (ideally rotating through many different oils.) Tenting or caging is usually not necessary, but having the diffuser close by the bird is nice.
DRINKING WATER: Melissa or another indicated oils.
TOPICAL: Valor Roll-On applied to the bottom of cooperative bird's feet is helpful as well. RutaVaLa applied to feet via hands or perching is also beneficial.
SUPPLEMENTS: MultiGreens, NingXia Red, and Omega Blue are top recommended supplements.

Single Oils:
Balsam Fir (Idaho), Chamomile (Roman), Frankincense, Helichrysum, Jasmine, Laurus Nobilis, Lavender, Lemon, Melissa

Blends:
Brain Power, Forgiveness, GLF, Hope, Juva Cleanse, Juva Flex, Peace & Calming, RutaVaLa, Stress Away Roll-On, Trauma Life, Valor, Valor Roll-On

CAUTIONS:
These oils have general recommendations to avoid in people with epilepsy. Please see the single oil comments for more information: Basil, Fennel, Hyssop, Sage, Tarragon, Wintergreen.

Supplements & Products:
Essentialzymes-4, JuvaPower, JuvaSpice, JuvaTone, MightyVites, MightyZyme, Mineral Essence, MultiGreens, NingXia Red, Ningxia Wolfberries, Omega Blue, Sulfurzyme, True Source

SINUS INFECTIONS
(See also RESPIRATORY CONDITIONS)

FIRST LINE RECOMMENDATIONS:
WATER DIFFUSION: Thieves or Purification via caging or tenting. Open room diffusion up to 24 hours a day. Caging or tenting for 20 minutes at a time, 3-4 times a day is common.

INGESTION: Thieves when oral antibiotic properties are needed.

SINUS FLUSH: In severe situations, sinus flushes can be prepared with Thieves Household Cleaner. Sinus flushes should only be performed by extremely experienced avian handlers or veterinarians. The person performing the flush will generally have solutions and recipes which they use for the sinus flush. In general, the cleaner is used within the liquid base chosen by the professional. A very dilute solution can be used initially, approximately ½ teaspoon per liter of saline is a starting point. In some cases, following with a weaker Thieves solution (or one with no Thieves Cleaner at all) as an after rinse is recommended.

SUPPLEMENTS: The addition of supplements is always recommended.

Single Oils:
Hyssop, Laurus Nobilis, Lavender, Lemon, Lemongrass, Marjoram, Melaleuca Alternifolia, Melissa, Mountain Savory, Myrtle, Oregano, Pine, Spruce, Thyme

Physical Blends:
Egyptian Gold, Citrus Fresh, ImmuPower, Longevity, Melrose, Purification, Raven, R.C., Thieves

Supplements & Products:
Essentialzymes-4, MightyVites, MightyZyme, MultiGreens, NingXia Red, Ningxia Wolfberries, Omega Blue, Thieves Household Cleaner, True Source

VIRAL CONDITIONS

Any disorder that is affected or caused by a virus, can use these methods to support the body in healing.

FIRST LINE RECOMMENDATIONS:
SUPPLEMENTS: For a bird with a viral condition, I will always make sure that MultiGreens are within the supplements used. The more supplements that I can provide, the better, but MultiGreens remain a number one recommendation.
DRINKING WATER: Melissa drinking water is provided.
WATER MISTING: Feather Spray Recipe is used daily.
WATER DIFFUSION: 3-4 drops of Thieves with 1 drop of Eucalyptus Blue is diffused up to 24 hours a day.
TOPICAL: Avian Raindrop Technique may be indicated for some cases, up to once a day in severe situations.

Single Oils:
Geranium, Helichrysum, Hyssop, Laurus Nobilis, Lavender, Lemon, Melissa, Mountain Savory, Oregano, Peppermint, Ravintsara, Sandalwood, Spikenard, Thyme

Blends:
Citrus Fresh, Egyptian Gold, Forgiveness, GLF, Hope, ImmuPower, Raven, Thieves, 3 Wise Men

Supplements & Products:
MightyVites, MightyZyme, Mineral Essence, MultiGreens, NingXia Red, Ningxia Wolfberries, Omega Blue, Thieves Household Cleaner, True Source

WARTS
(See PAPILLOMATOSIS)

WASTING DISEASE
(See PROVENTRICULAR DILATATION DISEASE)

WOUNDS
(See also BUMBLEFOOT)

FIRST LINE RECOMMENDATIONS:
TOPICAL: 1 drop (or more) of Helichrysum is mixed into 1 tablespoon of Animal Scents Ointment and applied to the area sparingly. Care needs to be taken to not over use the ointment, or to get it onto the feathers.

WATER MISTING: Spraying with the Feather Spray Recipe (even twice a day or more), is also very beneficial. Just the Feather Spray Recipe can be used if it is difficult to handle the bird or to apply ointment. Using sprays containing Helichrysum, or adding several drops to the Feather Spray is also suggested.

INGESTION: If the wound appears infected, Thieves can be used via oral ingestion. If painful wounds are noted, see PAIN MANAGEMENT.

WATER DIFFUSION: Diffusion can also be used to permeate the injured area.

Single Oils:
Geranium, Helichrysum, Lavender, Lemon, Myrrh, Oregano, Palmarosa, Patchouli, Spikenard

Blends:
Melrose, Purification, Thieves

Supplements & Products:
Animal Scents Ointment, BLM Capsules, LavaDerm Cooling Mist, MightyZyme, NingXia Red, Omega Blue, Rose Ointment, Sulfurzyme, Thieves Household Cleaner

ZINC POISONING
(See HEAVY METAL POISONING)

ESSENTIAL OILS: FERRETS

In general, most ferrets are administered essential oils very similarly to cats. In many ways, ferrets are actually easier to give oils orally, topically, and in food. If a similar condition is listed in the Feline Section – using these protocols with a ferret is generally recommended.

As Ferrets are very prone to certain conditions, the use of essential oils and nutrition to aid in the prevention of these disorders is strongly suggested. Waiting until the condition is obvious is not ideal.

FIRST LINE RECOMMENDATIONS:
WATER DIFFUSION: Rotational diffusion of anti-cancer and endocrine supportive oils should be continual. Purification is an excellent choice for odor control.
TOPICAL: Regular Petting applications of various oils is suggested.
SUPPLEMENTS: NingXia Red, MultiGreens, Omega Blue are all helpful in maintaining good health.
BATHING: Animal Scents Shampoo and/or Thieves Household Cleaner can be used for bathing purposes. Adding additional Frankincense or other preventive oils is a convenient way to add health.
LITTEROMA: Just like cats, Ferrets can also benefit from the addition of essential oils to their litter boxes.

Single Oils:
Balsam Fir (Idaho), Frankincense, Orange, Tangerine

Blends:
Citrus Fresh, EndoFlex, Joy, Thieves, Purification, 3 Wise Men

Supplements & Products:
Animal Scents Ointment, Animal Scents Shampoo, MightyZyme, MultiGreens, NingXia Red, Ningxia Wolfberries, Omega Blue, Sulfurzyme, Thieves Household Cleaner, True Source

FERRET – ADRENAL TUMORS

Adrenal disease and tumors are far too common in Ferrets, and almost expected to occur in aged Ferrets. Resulting in hair loss as the most obvious symptom, Ferrets tend to live with this condition on a chronic basis. Household chemicals, food toxins, and preservatives are high on the list of contributing factors. Preventive measures should be followed from kit-hood, for the best scenario of health.

FIRST LINE RECOMMENDATIONS:
  WATER DIFFUSION: Joy, Balsam Fir (Idaho), Frankincense
  PETTING: Joy, Frankincense daily
  INGESTION: Citrus Fresh, Orange, Tangerine, Frankincense
  TOPICAL: Ferret Raindrop Technique
  SUPPLEMENTS: NingXia Red

Single Oils:
  Balsam Fir (Idaho), Frankincense, Helichrysum, Lemon, Orange, Palo Santo, Rosemary, Sandalwood, Tangerine

Blends:
  Citrus Fresh, EndoFlex, GLF, ImmuPower, Juva Cleanse, Juva Flex, 3 Wise Men

Supplements & Products:
  Essentialzyme, ImmuPro, MightyZyme, Mineral Essence, MultiGreens, NingXia Red, Omega Blue, PD 80/20, True Source

FERRET – DIARRHEA, HELICOBACTER PYLORI

Ferrets can exhibit bloody diarrhea and illness with this bacterial condition of the gastrointestinal tract. Antibiotics are generally prescribed, and occasionally veterinary hospitalization is also required. Since there can be significant amounts of blood in the stools, both digested (melena) or fresh, use caution with Thieves and other oils with anticoagulant action. Small amounts of Thieves is very beneficial, however just needs a light touch and careful monitoring. Helichrysum is helpful for intestinal pains and bleeding.

FIRST LINE RECOMMENDATIONS:

WATER DIFFUSION: Thieves, Purification
INGESTION: Di-Gize; Thieves or Oregano
PETTING: Di-Gize, Patchouli, ImmuPower
TOPICAL: Ferret Raindrop Technique with Helichrysum and ImmuPower added.
SUPPLEMENTS: Detoxzyme, ICP, Life 5. Care must be taken to not make the diarrhea worse with the addition of supplements too quickly.

Single Oils:

Helichrysum, Laurus Nobilis, Lemon, Melaleuca Alternifolia, Nutmeg, Oregano, Patchouli, Peppermint, Tangerine, Tarragon, Thyme

Blends:

Citrus Fresh, Di-Gize, GLF, ImmuPower, Juva Cleanse, Juva Flex, Purification, Thieves

Supplements & Products:

ComforTone, Detoxzyme, Digest + Cleanse, ICP, Life 5, MightyZyme, ParaFree, Super B, Thieves Fresh Essence Mouthwash, Thieves Household Cleaner

FERRET - INSULINOMA

An Insulinoma is a pancreas based tumor that is general active and causes excess insulin to be secreted into the body. This can result in severe hypoglycemia episodes. Surgery is often performed to remove the tumors. Ocotea is often used and is helpful in balancing pancreatic function, however careful monitoring should be taken to make sure an individual does not respond to the Ocotea with further blood sugar lowering activity. To date, this has not been witnessed in ferrets.

FIRST LINE RECOMMENDATIONS:

SUPPLEMENTS: NingXia Red given frequently during episodes of hypoglycemia is helpful in maintaining blood sugar levels. Regular administration is suggested as well, not just in critical situations.
INGESTION: Ocotea, Frankincense, Orange
PETTING: Frankincense, Ocotea, EndoFlex, up to twice a day or more depending on the severity of the case.

WATER DIFFUSION: Any of the selected oils.
LITTEROMA: Can also be utilized to layer exposure to beneficial oils.

Single Oils:
Frankincense, Geranium, Grapefruit, Lemon, Ocotea, Orange, Palo Santo, Sandalwood, Tangerine

Blends:
Citrus Fresh, EndoFlex, GLF, ImmuPower, Juva Cleanse, Juva Flex, 3 Wise Men

Supplements & Products:
Essentialzyme, ImmuPro, MightyZyme, MultiGreens, NingXia Red, Omega Blue, True Source

FERRET – LYMPHOMA, LYMPHOSARCOMA

Ferrets are also particularly prone to developing malignant enlargement of the lymph nodes. Juvenile onset of this disorder carries a poorer prognosis. Prevention measures are critical. Supporting health, eliminating household toxins, and providing indicated essential oils and nutritional supplements PRIOR to the disease eruption, is a strong recommendation.

FIRST LINE RECOMMENDATIONS:
WATER DIFFUSION: Diffuse the recommended oils on a regular basis to aid in prevention as well as disease.
PETTING: Frankincense, Sandalwood, Palo Santo
INGESTION: Grapefruit, Lemon, Orange, Citrus Fresh in water or foods
TOPICAL: Ferret Raindrop Technique monthly for prevention, adding various anti-cancer oils. During times of disease, up to daily administration with Frankincense, Orange, and ImmuPower added.
SUPPLEMENTS: Essentialzyme, ImmuPro, MultiGreens, NingXia Red

Single Oils:
Frankincense, Grapefruit, Lemon, Orange, Palo Santo, Sandalwood, Tangerine

Blends:
Citrus Fresh, GLF, ImmuPower, Juva Cleanse, Juva Flex, 3 Wise Men

Supplements & Products:
Essentialzyme, ImmuPro, MightyZyme, MultiGreens, NingXia Red, Omega Blue, Super C, True Source

FERRET – PROSTATIC DISEASE

Male Ferrets can be affected by an enlarged prostate, that can also be infected. This condition often results in discomfort and straining to urinate.

FIRST LINE RECOMMENDATIONS:
TOPICAL: Ferret Raindrop Technique with Copaiba and Sage added.
INGESTION: Thieves
PETTING: Mister
SUPPLEMENTS: NingXia Red, Omega Blue

Single Oils:
Copaiba, Sage, Tarragon, Thyme

Blends:
Mister, Thieves

Supplements & Products:
EndoGize, K&B, MightyZyme, NingXia Red, Omega Blue, PD 80/20, Prostate Health, True Source

FERRET – RAINDROP TECHNIQUE

(See also KITTY RAINDROP TECHNIQUE)

Ferrets receive Raindrop Technique in the same way as Cats. Kitty Raindrop Technique descriptions, techniques, and modifications all apply to use in Ferrets.

FIRST LINE RECOMMENDATIONS:

Mix 4 drops each of Oregano, Thyme, Basil, Cypress, Wintergreen, Marjoram, and Peppermint oils into 30 mL of V-6. Apply 6 or more drops up the spine, and stroke in as described for cats. Balancing prior to the Raindrop Technique can be performed, but is optional. Modifications and additions to the Ferret Raindrop Solution can be made in the same ways, generally adding 4 drops of the desired oil to the recipe. See descriptions for individual oils, Kitty Raindrop Technique, and Raindrop Technique for more instructions.

ESSENTIAL OILS: RABBITS

Most remedies for rabbits will be used with a very gentle approach initially. Starting with water diffusion for every recommended oil is wise. Since rabbits are hind gut fermenters, the use of antibacterial essential oils must be used with caution to avoid killing their natural gut flora. Essential oils that are the most mild are recommended for use first, but it is refreshing to know that in severe cases that are non-responsive to other methods – the use of essential oils is becoming more and more wide spread, and "aggressive" in end stage cases, with good results.

I would recommend starting with rabbits in a few, well documented ways, then advancing to more aggressive administration if these protocols fail you. Reading through all of the conditions, and becoming familiar with Rabbit friendly recommendations, is a wonderful way to incorporate more natural health into your rabbit's life.

RABBITS - BREEDING

Basic disease prevention, stress reduction, healthy immune systems, easy delivery, and a healthy milk supply can all be supported with the use of essential oils.

FIRST LINE RECOMMENDATIONS:
WATER DIFFUSION: Thieves for immune support and disease prevention. Gentle Baby for delivery. Fennel (also contained in Di-Gize) can be used to increase milk production.
DRINKING WATER: Citrus Fresh, Tangerine, Orange can be used to boost immune systems.
PETTING: Even newborn baby bunnies have been handled with Thieves absorbed into the human hands. An extremely small

amount is absorbed through the wet newborns, but significant enough for health benefits.
CLEANING: All cleaning should be done with Thieves Household Cleaner.

Single Oils:
Fennel, Frankincense, Geranium, Lavender, Lemon, Orange, Palo Santo, Rosemary, Tangerine, Tsuga, Ylang Ylang

Blends:
Citrus Fresh, Di-Gize, Gentle Baby, En-R-Gee, Mister, Purification, SclarEssence, Thieves

Supplements & Products:
MightyVites, MultiGreens, Thieves Household Cleaner, True Source

RABBITS - DIARRHEA

Diarrhea can have many causes, and of course dysbiosis, or the disruption of normal intestinal flora must be considered. Probiotics are generally not of the same bacterial culture that is present in the Rabbit digestive tract, however they still appear helpful. Transfaunation (the feeding of morning stools from normal rabbits) remains the best route to repopulate a rabbit's gut. Care must be taken to never use stools from a sick or potentially contagious rabbit. Baby rabbits and rabbits who are housed together, may occasionally eat each other's morning stools, which is a common occurrence in rabbits. Depending on the cause of the diarrhea, recommendations may vary.

FIRST LINE RECOMMENDATIONS:
DRINKING WATER: Citrus Fresh, Lemon, or Di-Gize
PETTING: Di-Gize
WATER DIFFUSION: Thieves, Purification
SUPPLEMENTS: Life 5

Single Oils:
Laurus Nobilis, Lemon, Orange, Peppermint, Tangerine, Tarragon

Blends:
Citrus Fresh, Di-Gize, ImmuPower, Purification, Thieves

Supplements & Products:
Life 5, ParaFree, Thieves Household Cleaner

RABBITS – EXTERNAL PARASITES, MITES

There are many forms of external parasites in Rabbits. The most common include Cheyletiella Mites (walking dandruff), Psoroptes cuniculi (ear mites), and Cuterebra larvae. Cuterebra is contracted through flies, and a grub worm actually develops within the skin. Care must be taken with Cuterebra to not rupture or harm the worm inside the body, as anaphylaxis may result. Prevention with the recommendations is the best suggestion for Cuterebra, with veterinary attention and extraction required for the presence of the actual worm. Topical and area use of essential oils and products are helpful.

FIRST LINE RECOMMENDATIONS:

BATHING: Add 5 drops of Purification to 1 tablespoon of Animal Scents Shampoo and bathe as needed, approximately weekly is suggested.

WATER MISTING: 20 drops of Purification in 4 ounces (120 mL) of distilled water. Shake well and thoroughly mist the rabbit, taking caution near the face and eyes.

PETTING: With neat Purification on your hands, up to twice a day.

TOPICAL: 10 drops of Purification can be diluted in 15 mL of V-6 or in Animal Scents Ointment. This solution can be applied directly, Pet onto locations, or swabbed into the ears. Neat Purification can also be placed on a cotton swab, and swabbed into the ear for ear mites. With ear mites, it is still important to treat the entire body for mites, not only the ears.

WATER DIFFUSION: Regular diffusion of Purification can keep insects to a minimum.

AIR DIFFUSION: For large barns or areas containing rabbits, air diffusion may be called for.

CLEANING: The use of Thieves Household Cleaner for cleaning as well as area control of insects is highly recommended. See the product description for more information.

Single Oils:
   Citronella, Lavender, Palo Santo

Blends:
   Purification, Thieves

Supplements & Products:
   Animal Scents Ointment, Animal Scents Shampoo, LavaDerm Cooling Mist, Thieves Household Cleaner

RABBITS – PASTEURELLOSIS

Infection with Pasteurella multocida bacteria in Rabbits can present in several ways. There can be respiratory infections called "Snuffles," infection that affects the nervous system called "Wry Neck" or torticollis, and there can also be abscesses that form in a variety of locations. Some strains are mild and rabbits will naturally recover, and some strains are more severe and can result in permanent symptoms or even death. Long term antibiotic use is common traditionally. In more severe cases, more aggressive regimens with essential oils can be considered, however it is important to always be mindful of the intestinal flora of the rabbit. For neurologic involvement, oils such as Helichrysum and RutaVaLa are especially indicated.

Starting with diffusion alone initially is recommended. Then gradually adding and layering application methods is suggested. If tented water diffusion does not yield enough results, then moving onto Petting applications is encouraged, and so forth. The main object with Rabbits is to move slowly, and start mildly. However, in life threatening situations, many Rabbits have received quite aggressive treatments with essential oils and have benefited.

FIRST LINE RECOMMENDATIONS:
WATER DIFFUSION: Thieves, ImmuPower, Purification in the open room. Caging or Tenting can be performed with Thieves or Purification as needed.
PETTING: Lemon, Lavender, Laurus Nobilis, Purification
TOPICAL: To abscesses Lavender, Lemon, Purification
RABBIT RAINDROP TECHNIQUE: In serious situations, Raindrop Technique is likely to be indicated. Starting with a "Rabbit Mild" version of the Raindrop is suggested. Combining oils such as Frankincense, Helichrysum, Laurus Nobilis, Lavender,

Lemon, and Purification is a wonderful start. Then moving towards a traditional Rabbit Raindrop if needed is a recommended guideline. Administration up to once a day may be indicated for some cases.

INGESTION: Starting with ingestion of oils such as Lemon is suggested. If use of stronger oral antibiotic oils is deemed necessary, proceed slowly and monitor stools carefully. Placing 1 drop of Lemon in 1 tablespoon of vegetable baby food, and gradually increasing to feeding 1 mL of this mixture two to three times a day is a suggested.

DRINKING WATER: Lemon

SUPPLEMENTS: NingXia Red, MultiGreens, Life 5

CLEANING: Disinfect things well with Thieves Household Cleaner. Abscesses can be flushed and cleaned with this product as well. See the product description for more information.

Single Oils:
Frankincense, Helichrysum, Laurus Nobilis, Lavender, Lemon, Melaleuca Alternifolia, Mountain Savory, Oregano, Thyme

Blends:
Brain Power, Egyptian Gold, GLF, ImmuPower, Juva Cleanse, Juva Flex, Purification, R.C., RutaVaLa, Thieves

Supplements & Products:
Animal Scents Ointment, Animal Scents Shampoo, ImmuPro, Life 5, MightyVites, MultiGreens, Thieves Household Cleaner, True Source

RABBIT – RAINDROP TECHNIQUE

Being hindgut fermenters, Rabbits represent a distinct challenge and require a bit of care when strong antibacterial agents are administered, whether they are natural or chemical in nature. Many Rabbits have tragically been killed when an unknowing veterinarian prescribed a harmful antibiotic for them. As the traditional oils of the Raindrop Technique are very strong in antibacterial actions, we reserve this technique for only very severe situations. With all Rabbits, Guinea Pigs, and Chinchillas starting with the very mildest of oils (ones that you would use on a human baby or on your face) is recommended. Then progressing to stronger or more aggressive oils if needed is suggested. A "Rabbit Mild" Raindrop Technique can be performed, made with various mild oils, and administered in the same way. This technique is often quite helpful.

FIRST LINE RECOMMENDATIONS:

RABBIT MILD RAINDROP TECHNIQUE: Add 1 drop each of Purification, Frankincense, Copaiba, Lavender, Lemon, Helichrysum, Di-Gize, and Tangerine to 30-60 mL (1-2 ounces) of V-6. Apply 3-6 drops of this solution up the back and stroke in as described for Kitty Raindrop Technique. Balancing with Valor beforehand is optional, and performed with 1 drop of Valor completely absorbed into each hand.

RABBIT RAINROP TECHNIQUE – TRADITIONAL: Add 1 drop each of Oregano, Thyme, Basil, Cypress, Wintergreen, Marjoram, and Peppermint to 30-60 mL (1-2 ounces) of V-6. Balancing with Valor beforehand is optional as described previously. Apply 3-6 drops of this solution up the back, from tail to head. Stroke the oils in, and follow with Vita Flex when possible. Starting with the more diluted solution, and then making it stronger if needed, is recommended.

Single Oils:
Chamomile (Roman), Copaiba, Dill, Elemi, Frankincense, Helichrysum, Lavender, Lemon, Myrrh, Orange, Palo Santo, Tangerine

Blends:
Citrus Fresh, Di-Gize, Purification

RABBITS - SNUFFLES

(See PASTEURELLOSIS)

RABBITS - SYPHILIS

Syphilis, also known as Vent, is a sexually transmitted disease caused by Treponema cuniculi. This is a spirochete bacteria similar to that which causes Syphilis in humans. It lives in the bloodstream and can cause lesions, scabs, and weeping sores on the face, mouth, and genitals. Many Rabbits are killed when this diagnosis is made, especially in breeding situations. The disease is difficult to eliminate, even with traditional antibiotics. Hygiene and cleanliness of the environment is very important, and constant diffusion as well as cleaning with Thieves Household Cleaner is a must. The same recommendations and increases in aggressiveness of treatment, that are made for Pasteurellosis, is suggested for Syphilis.

FIRST LINE RECOMMENDATIONS:
Follow the suggestions and recommendations listed for Pasteurellosis. It is likely that Syphilis may require Traditional Rabbit Raindrop Technique as well as oral oils to completely eliminate the disorder.
DIFFUSION: In a Rabbitry, air diffusion may be indicated. Thieves and/or Purification is suggested.
WATER MISTING: Add 10 drops Helichrysum, 10 drops Purification, and 10 drops Lavender to 4 ounces (120 mL) of distilled water. Shake well and mist onto sores, mainly on the genital area. Use caution and common sense if other locations need application.
TOPICAL: Mixing various oils into Animal Scents Ointment for application to wounds is recommended. Start with 1 drop per tablespoon. Multiple oils can be used, and stronger concentrations when indicated.
SUPPLEMENTS: MultiGreens

Single Oils:
Helichrysum, Lavender, Lemon, Mountain Savory, Oregano, Thyme, Tsuga

Blends:
Egyptian Gold, GLF, ImmuPower, Juva Cleanse, Juva Flex, Purification, Thieves

Supplements & Products:
Animal Scents Ointment, Animal Scents Shampoo, MultiGreens, Thieves Household Cleaner, True Source

RABBITS – TUMORS, WARTS, PAPILLOMA

Shope's Papilloma is a viral wart condition that can cause the growth of tumors in Rabbits. The virus is contagious and thought to be spread by insects. Insect control through the use of essential oils (see External Parasites) is helpful. The immune system is important to support to prevent and care for this disorder. Below are recommendations specific to the tumors.

FIRST LINE RECOMMENDATIONS:

DIFFUSION: Reduction of insects by air or water diffusion of Purification. Air diffusion is only recommended for large areas such as Rabbitries.

WATER MISTING: 20 drops of Purification in 4 ounces (120 mL) of distilled water. Shake well and thoroughly mist the rabbit, taking caution near the face and eyes.

PETTING: With neat Purification on your hands, up to twice a day. For reduction of insects.

INSECT CONTROL: See Thieves Household Cleaner for more information on how this cleaner also reduces insects.

TOPICAL: Various essential oils can be applied to warts directly, especially Frankincense. Caution needs to be followed based on the location and ability to apply the oils. Often, neat oils are applied to warts and tumors. One can start with mild and diluted oils (1 drop per 5 drops of V-6), and gradually build up in concentration based on responses. Rabbit Mild or Traditional Rabbit Raindrop Solutions can be applied to tumors and warts directly as well.

RABBIT RAINDROP TECHNIQUE: In severe situations, Raindrop Technique may be indicated. See the description for further instructions.

DRINKING WATER: Melissa

SUPPLEMENTS: NingXia Red, MultiGreens

Single Oils:
Frankincense, Grapefruit, Helichrysum, Lavender, Melissa, Mountain Savory, Orange, Oregano, Palo Santo, Peppermint, Sandalwood, Tangerine

Blends:
Citrus Fresh, Egyptian Gold, Forgiveness, GLF, ImmuPower, Juva Cleanse, Juva Flex, Thieves, 3 Wise Men

Supplements & Products:
Animal Scents Ointment, MultiGreens, NingXia Red, Thieves Household Cleaner, True Source

RABBITS - VENT
(See RABBITS - SYPHILIS)

RABBITS – WRY NECK
(See RABBITS – PASTEURELLOSIS)

ESSENTIAL OILS: EXOTIC ANIMALS

AMPHIBIANS

Amphibians require very light and special techniques when using oils. A fundamental trait of frogs, toads, salamanders, and newts is that they readily absorb things through their skin. Often known as strong indicators of environmental health, the exposure of amphibians to the residues of hand lotions, hand purifiers, cleaners, tap water, and pollutants can be harmful to their health. Aquatic amphibians can be exposed to essential oils much as fish are, starting with a toothpick dip of essential oil added to their water source. Water diffusion of essential oils is often enough to provide systemic absorption of the oil through the skin. Topical administration of oils should involve the complete absorption of the essential oil (neat) into our hands, and then the amphibian can be gently cupped within our hands. Neat oils are recommended for this purpose, as a carrier oil is not compatible with amphibian skin, and is best left off of it. Aquariums and environments can be cleaned with Thieves Household Cleaner, although this should be thoroughly rinsed afterwards for most amphibians. Raindrop Technique is not recommended for these animals.

FIRST LINE RECOMMENDATIONS:
TOPICAL: Place 1 drop of neat Frankincense into the palm of your hand. Rub your hands together until the oil is completely absorbed into your skin. Cup the animal in the palms of your hand. They will absorb the essential oil!
WATER SOAKING: Add 1 toothpick dip of Purification to 1 Liter of water, use as their soaking or swimming water source. Increase concentration only if needed, and based on responses.
WATER MISTING: 1 toothpick dip to 1 drop of essential oil can be placed in 1 Liter of water and the amphibian or the environment can be misted.

WATER DIFFUSION: Place 1-4 drops of essential oil into a water diffuser. Generally, do not diffuse "hot" oils within a room containing an amphibian. Diffusion in an open room setting is generally adequate for these animals.

SUPPLEMENTS: Crickets or mealworms that are fed can be "gut loaded" by feeding them NingXia Red or other supplements.

Single Oils:
Frankincense, Frankincense Sacred, Grapefruit, Helichrysum, Lavender, Lemon, Orange, Palo Santo, Tangerine

Blends:
Citrus Fresh, Purification

Supplements & Products:
Thieves Household Cleaner

CATS LARGE (LIONS, TIGERS, COUGARS...)

Large cats can use essential oils in all of the same methods described for domestic cats. Kitty Raindrop Technique is still utilized for these larger felines, however many more drops can be dispensed. Diffusion may be the most easily administered method, depending on how much the cat can be handled. Air diffusion may be used in large areas such as zoo confinements. For cats who may have a swimming pool or water area, essential oils can be added to the water for absorption. Some large cats may ingest essential oils in food or water. Petting can be used when the technique is possible.

FIRST LINE RECOMMENDATIONS:
DIFFUSION: Water or Air Diffusion is recommended on a consistent basis for health. Rotation through various essential oils and blends are recommended, and especially being considerate of emotional health.

Single Oils:
Bergamot, Frankincense, Geranium, Grapefruit, Helichrysum, Lavender, Orange, Palo Santo, Valerian, Vetiver, Ylang Ylang

Blends:
Citrus Fresh, Hope, Joy, Purification, Thieves

Supplements & Products:
Animal Scents Ointment, MultiGreens, Omega Blue, ParaFree, Sulfurzyme, Thieves Household Cleaner

CHINCHILLAS

See more information about hindgut fermentation and the special care with essential oils within the Rabbit descriptions. Chinchillas contain the most hair follicles per square inch of skin, of any land animal. This means that even diffusion of an essential oil into the air, is likely to achieve systemic levels within their body. Chinchillas should have an especially light touch with the use of oils, and water diffusion is likely all they may need. Many Chinchillas have enjoyed licking essential oils off of their owner's hands, and this is fine if they choose to do so. Oils can also be added to their drinking water. Petting can be utilized in more critical situations, however the oils should be applied to your hands neat, and completely absorbed into your skin prior to handling the Chinchilla. Carrier oils should not be used on Chinchilla fur. Raindrop Technique is not recommended for Chinchillas, however in dire situations, one drop of each Raindrop Oil could be added to a water-based diffuser and diffused in an open room.

FIRST LINE RECOMMENDATIONS:
WATER DIFFUSION: Start with 1 drop of essential oil added to the diffuser. Open room diffusion is suggested, and only very rarely would tenting or caging be used.
DRINKING WATER: Starting with a toothpick dip into 1 Liter of water, gradually increase to 1 drop per Liter. Citrus oils are suggested.

Single Oils:
Frankincense, Grapefruit, Helichrysum, Lavender, Lemon, Orange, Palo Santo, Tangerine

Blends:
Citrus Fresh, Hope, Purification, Thieves

Supplements & Products:
MightyVites, NingXia Red, Ningxia Wolfberries, Thieves Household Cleaner

ELEPHANTS

Elephants can mainly use essential oils in the ways described for large animals. Air Diffusion is a primary recommendation, and rotational diffusion of oils for health and emotional well-being is suggested. Care should be taken with performance elephants, or those who may have emotional concerns, if they will be in contact or near humans after an emotional clearing. We have certainly all heard tales of circus elephants who have become unhappy and subsequently injured a human. Essential oils will certainly help and calm the emotional turmoil that may reside within a particular individual, however just as we may experience anger or sorrow during an emotional release, so may an elephant. Allowing for some "alone time" when performing emotional work and support, is advisable. Raindrop Technique can certainly be performed on elephants. The technique is obviously on a much larger scale, and a creative method is sure to be formed for each individual. Diluting each oil at least 1 drop per 5 drops V-6, for the initial Raindrop Technique is suggested, as it may be quite difficult to deal with skin irritation if it were to occur.

FIRST LINE RECOMMENDATIONS:
AIR DIFFUSION: Rotational diffusion of any essential oil.
SOAKING WATER: Elephants who have a swimming pool or water area to play in, will greatly benefit from the addition of essential oils to the water.
DRINKING WATER: Just as with horses and other large animals, elephants enjoy oils such as Citrus Fresh, Peppermint, or Tangerine added to their water.
CLEANER: Using Thieves Household Cleaner for the environment, but also as an "elephant scrub" and shampoo is wonderful for them.

Single Oils:
Bergamot, Frankincense, Frankincense Sacred, Geranium, Grapefruit, Helichrysum, Lavender, Lemon, Orange, Palo Santo, Tangerine, Valerian, Vetiver, Ylang Ylang

Blends:
Citrus Fresh, Hope, Purification, Thieves

Supplements & Products:
Animal Scents Ointment, Thieves Household Cleaner

EXOTIC ANIMALS

FAIRIES & UNICORNS

My 10 year old daughter Ramie, felt it was quite important to mention that all forms of animals and magical creatures enjoy essential oils. Unicorns can use oils in all of the methods described for horses. However, fairies require an extra special touch. If you find a fairy house, an offering of a drop or two of your favorite oil is very appreciated about 1 foot from the threshold. Fairies also greatly enjoy smelling the mild fragrance wafting from true believers in their midst.

FIRST LINE RECOMMENDATIONS:
Wear your favorite essential oil single or blend, walk through the woods, and regain your inner child.

Single Oils:
Dorado Azul, Patchouli, Wintergreen

Blends:
Awaken, Believe, Christmas Spirit, Dream Catcher, Envision, Gathering, Harmony, Hope, Inner Child, Inspiration, Joy

Supplements & Products:
Unicorns can utilize all of the recommendations for horses. Fairies enjoy Lavender Lemonade, Lavender Tea, and Wolfberry Crisp Bars.

FISH

Adding essential oils to the aquarium or ponds of fish is a wonderful way to expose them to essential oils but to also rid them of fungus, bacteria, viruses, and other health concerns. Glass aquariums should be used, and avoiding plastic components of aquariums, as much as possible, is advised. Many oils have been used with fish, however Peppermint, Lemon, and Purification oils have been used most commonly. I recommend starting with these well used oils, and only moving onto others when needed. Starting with a toothpick dip into the water, and gradually building concentrations is suggested. It is not uncommon for 2-5 drops of oil to be used in a 10 gallon aquarium. With very large areas of water such as ponds, results are often seen with even a few drops added (10-20 per large pond.) Fish are often seen ingesting the droplets of oil from the water's surface, and this is fine if they choose to do so. Essential oils can be added to a separate water supply first, such as 1 drop to 1 Liter of water in an empty and washed NingXia Red bottle. This water can then be used to fill a fish bowl, or to add to the existing water environment. As a broad spectrum blend effective against parasites, bacteria, fungi, and viruses; Purification is often a first choice. Fish have not received a Raindrop Technique, and it is not recommended for them.

FIRST LINE RECOMMENDATIONS:
Add a toothpick dip of Purification to a glass aquarium. Refresh as needed. Some fish receive oils on a weekly and sometimes even daily basis, depending on their need. Gradually increase amounts added to water.

Single Oils:
Frankincense, Grapefruit, Helichrysum, Lavender, Lemon, Orange, Palo Santo, Peppermint, Tangerine

Blends:
Citrus Fresh, Purification

Supplements & Products:
Thieves Household Cleaner

GUINEA PIGS

Please see the description regarding hindgut fermenters in the Rabbit section. Guinea Pigs have a particular need for Vitamin C to be provided through their diet. Please see the product description for Super C Chewable for more information. Water diffusion is always suggested, and most of the ailments that Guinea Pigs confront can be treated in a similar manner to what is recommended for Rabbits. Guinea Pigs are quite commonly affected with Pneumonia, and following the guidelines for Pasteurellosis within Rabbits, is suggested. If Raindrop Technique is considered for a Guinea Pig, it should be provided with the same recommendations as made for Rabbits.

FIRST LINE RECOMMENDATIONS:
SUPPLEMENTS: Add ¼ of a tablet of Super C Chewable to drinking water. NingXia Red is also a great supplement for Guinea Pigs.

WATER DIFFUSION: Generally in an open room, but tenting and caging can be used for respiratory conditions. Any essential oil selection is tolerated in general.

PETTING: Allow the essential oil to be completely absorbed into your hands, and cup and pet the Guinea Pig. This can be repeated as needed, sometimes up to multiple times a day for health conditions. A light residue of essential oil can be left on the hands, when more intense treatment is needed.

DRINKING WATER: Guinea Pigs greatly enjoy Citrus Fresh or other citrus oils in their drinking water. Start with 1 drop per Liter or less, see the chapter on Adding Oils to Drinking Water for more information.

Single Oils:
Frankincense, Grapefruit, Helichrysum, Lavender, Lemon, Orange, Palo Santo, Tangerine

Blends:
Citrus Fresh

Supplements & Products:
Animal Scents Ointment, MightyVites, MultiGreens, NingXia Red, Ningxia Wolfberries, Super C Chewable, Thieves Household Cleaner

HEDGEHOGS

Hedgehogs require a "hands off" sort of application technique most often. Water diffusion and water misting are methods that work very well for these critters. Mites and fungal skin infections are common in hedgehogs, and misting with 4 drops of Purification in 4 ounces (120 mL) of water up to twice a day is suggested. Tumors and cancers are also quite common in hedgehogs, so routine diffusion or misting with Frankincense is also suggested. Dry skin and other skin issues benefit from Omega Blue supplementation. If Raindrop Technique is considered for a severe condition, starting with a similar approach as is recommended for Rabbits is suggested.

FIRST LINE RECOMMENDATIONS:
WATER DIFFUSION: With Purification, Frankincense, Lemon

WATER MISTING: As needed with 4 drops Purification in 4 ounces of water for mites or fungal infections. Mist with Frankincense for tumor related issues.
DRINKING WATER: Orange, Grapefruit or other tasty anti-cancer oils
CLEANING: Clean caging well with Thieves Household Cleaner as many fungal infections are thought to be caused from bedding issues.
SUPPLEMENTS: Omega Blue, NingXia Red, Sulfurzyme

Single Oils:
Frankincense, Grapefruit, Helichrysum, Lavender, Lemon, Orange, Palo Santo, Tangerine

Blends:
Citrus Fresh, Purification, Thieves

Supplements & Products:
ClaraDerm, LavaDerm Cooling Mist, Ningxia Wolfberries, Omega Blue, Thieves Household Cleaner

HIPPOPOTAMUS

Hippos are not always the friendliest of creatures. When treating these animals, we are most often limited to diffusion, misting applications, or by adding essential oils to their swimming water. Due to the large amount of time spent in the water, adding oils to their environment is often the best route of exposure for a hippo. Start with a small amount of the chosen oil, and add it to the water up to once or more per day. The hippopotamus that I treated had a chronic skin condition, for which they would routinely apply a mineral oil based baby oil. This was unfortunately likely adding to the problem. Adding several drops of Lavender essential oil to the water supply, as well as cleaning thoroughly with Thieves Household Cleaner was suggested. Other non-toxic massage oils could also be used in place of the baby oil, and would have had wonderful therapeutic benefits from the essential oils contained within them. Selecting any appropriate oil for the condition at hand is suggested, and then the basic advice is to find an easy method of application for your particular individual. Once you start to look, it is often easy to find multiple routes of exposure that is appropriate for the species you are trying to treat. Depending on the situation and the individual, if Raindrop Technique was desired it is likely that the Kitty Raindrop Technique would be the easiest method to use.

FIRST LINE RECOMMENDATIONS:
SOAKING WATER: Add your chosen essential oil to the water. Start with small amounts and gradually increase. Lavender is a first suggestion.

Single Oils:
Bergamot, Frankincense, Grapefruit, Helichrysum, Lavender, Lemon, Orange, Palo Santo, Tangerine, Valerian, Vetiver

Blends:
Citrus Fresh, Purification

Supplements & Products:
Animal Scents Ointment, LavaDerm Cooling Mist, MultiGreens, Omega Blue, Relaxation Massage Oil, Thieves Household Cleaner

INSECTS, ARACHNIDS, INVERTEBRATES

Care should be taken with insects to not use insecticidal or insect repelling essential oils. Species that are most commonly exposed to essential oils by a human would be Honey Bees, Butterflies, Tarantulas, Ant Farms, Hermit Crabs and other household "pet" critters. Most people may focus on repelling problem insects, however in households where insects may be a part of the family, it is important to respect their needs and health as well. If the species you are considering is from a certain continent or may be exposed to certain foods (such as citrus), then selecting essential oils from the region or from the food category is suggested. So as Hermit Crabs who would naturally eat an orange, would generally tolerate exposure to Orange essential oil very well. Our Hermit Crabs greatly enjoy a misting with the Avian Feather Spray! Honey Bees in Arabian countries, just so happen to frequent the flowers of Frankincense blossoms, so a drop of Frankincense oil on a cotton ball, can be placed inside a hive for immune system benefits. For most of these critters, water or indirect diffusion should be used. When appropriate, many of these species can be offered NingXia Red straight or in their drinking water. And, for those species who consume other insects such as mealworms or crickets, added nutritional benefits can be obtained by "gut-loading" or feeding the food "item" with NingXia Red or other supplements such as MultiGreens. Raindrop Technique or diffusion of the Raindrop Oils is not suggested for these species.

FIRST LINE RECOMMENDATIONS:
WATER DIFFUSION: Should be in an open room environment, and starting with only 1 drop of oil added to the diffuser. Monitor the animal closely for signs of dislike or discomfort. Frankincense and Orange are starting suggestions.
INDIRECT DIFFUSION: Frankincense, Orange
DRINKING WATER: Orange, NingXia Red
SUPPLEMENTS: NingXia Red

Single Oils:
Frankincense, Frankincense Sacred, Helichrysum, Lavender, Lemon, Orange, Tangerine

Blends:
Citrus Fresh

Supplements & Products:
NingXia Red, Ningxia Wolfberries

PRIMATES

Primates can be treated in the same manner as human babies, children, or adults based on their size. The creative portion to administration lies within the ability to handle or work with the individual primate. Use any method which suits your particular needs and ability, even if it is described for a completely different type of animal. Raindrop Technique could be performed similarly to a human, however it is most likely that a Kitty Raindrop Technique or a Dog Raindrop Technique would be performed effectively on a primate.

FIRST LINE RECOMMENDATIONS:
WATER DIFFUSION: Rotate through various oils for physical and emotional health, just as we would for humans.
BATHING: Use Animals Scents Shampoo or the human line of personal care products for primates.
SUPPLEMENTS: NingXia Red, Omega Blue, and any other supplement indicated for use in humans. Adjust dose according to size.

Single Oils:
Frankincense, Orange, Palo Santo

Blends:
Acceptance, Forgiveness, Trauma Life

Supplements & Products:
Animal Scents Ointment, Animal Scents Shampoo, BLM Capsules, MultiGreens, NingXia Red, Ningxia Wolfberries, Omega Blue, Sulfurzyme, Thieves Household Cleaner, True Source

REPTILES

Reptiles such as snakes, lizards, alligators, and crocodiles can greatly benefit from the use of essential oils. Burns from inappropriate heating sources are unfortunately common, and can greatly benefit from Lavender application combined with Animal Scents Ointment or even neat in some situations. Skin mites and ticks can be common, and Purification as a misting application or in soaking water is suggested. Water diffusion is helpful for respiratory infections. Oral flushes, washes, and topical applications for various mouth rot situations are extremely beneficial, and the Thieves Household Cleaner has been effective for even resistant infections.

Metabolic Bone Disease (MBD) is an unfortunately common disorder which is generally caused by poor husbandry practices. Although Young Living supplements can be used for reptiles, careful attention to dosages must be given to avoid excessive supplementation. Working with a reptile veterinarian is important to determine how much and which type of supplement is needed. Essential oils such as Palo Santo can be helpful for MBD, but will not correct the underlying cause of poor nutrition, calcium and phosphorus imbalance, and lack of sunlight and Vitamin D.

Reptiles often require deworming, and fecal tests should be performed at least annually with a veterinarian. Essential oils can be used for deworming, however follow up testing must be performed to ensure elimination. For deworming purposes Di-Gize, Ocotea, Tarragon, or ParaFree can be utilized. 1 drop of the selected oil or blend is diluted into 10 drops of NingXia Red. 1 or more drops of this solution is administered orally, and is often given by an experienced herpetologist by a feeding or gavage tube. Great care must be taken so that a reptile does not aspirate (or inhale) the deworming solutions into their lungs. Inexperienced handlers have done great harm in forcing liquids into the mouths of these animals. Deworming may be achieved by introduction of essential oils into food items. Instilling a drop or two of essential oil inside the mouth cavity of a rodent that will be fed, may provide health benefits for the consuming reptile. Water misting greens and vegetables for herbivorous reptiles is another great way to allow for ingestion of essential oils.

Reptile Raindrop Technique has been performed, and generally a solution of 1 drop each of Oregano, Thyme, Basil, Cypress, Wintergreen, Marjoram, and Peppermint oils are mixed into 30-60 mL of V-6. 3-6 drops of this solution is applied along the spine. Occasionally, scale discoloration has been noted. The technique can be repeated up to once a day.

FIRST LINE RECOMMENDATIONS:
WATER DIFFUSION: Rotate through a variety of essential oils, or choose those indicated for a specific health concern.
WATER MISTING: Add approximately 4 drops per 4 ounces (120 mL) of distilled water and mist the reptile, caging, or food items as needed.
GUT LOADING: Feed the crickets, mealworms, or other food items quality supplements such as NingXia Red, Ningxia Wolfberries, and MultiGreens
SOAKING WATER: Reptiles often soak in their own drinking water or are provided with an opportunity to soak in a larger area of water. Adding essential oils to these water sources is an excellent method of application.

Single Oils:
Frankincense, Frankincense Sacred, Grapefruit, Helichrysum, Lavender, Lemon, Orange, Palo Santo, Tangerine

Blends:
Citrus Fresh, Purification, Thieves

Supplements & Products:
Animal Scents Ointment, ClaraDerm, LavaDerm Cooling Mist, ParaFree, Super Cal, Thieves Household Cleaner, True Source (for herbivorous reptiles)

RODENTS

Rodents can use essential oils in many ways, and are a bit more tolerant of oils than Rabbits or Guinea Pigs. You may use oils in any of the suggestions made for these animals as well as for Ferrets and Cats. Rodent Raindrop Technique is well tolerated, and performed with 1-2 drops of each Raindrop Oil (Oregano, Thyme, Basil, Cypress, Wintergreen, Marjoram, and Peppermint) added to 30-60 mL of V-6. 3 drops of this solution is generally applied and stroked into the spine area. Balancing with Valor can occur beforehand by placing a light coating on the palms of your hands, and gently cupping the rodent within your hands. Alternately, Valor can be placed on two fingers, and in cooperative rodents, the fingers can be placed over the shoulders and rump for the balancing procedure.

Due to the common occurrence of tumors and cancers in rodents, exposure to oils containing antitumoral benefits is highly recommended as a preventive measure. There have been reports of some rodents having difficulty in tolerating diffusion, however doing quite well with licking neat essential oils off of their owner's hands. See the chapter on Diffusion, and adjust for individual needs. Interestingly, these rodents could tolerate ingestion of the essential oils, however diffusion created excessive detoxification for them, likely indicating a health concern or increased need for detoxification within the respiratory system itself. It is likely that the chronic exposure of rodents to various bedding materials, may cause increased respiratory concerns.

FIRST LINE RECOMMENDATIONS:
DRINKING WATER: Citrus Fresh, Orange, Tangerine
WATER DIFFUSION: Frankincense, Orange, Purification
PETTING: Frankincense, 3 Wise Men
SUPPLEMENTS: NingXia Red, Ningxia Wolfberries

Single Oils:
Frankincense, Grapefruit, Helichrysum, Lavender, Lemon, Orange, Palo Santo, Tangerine

Blends:
Citrus Fresh, 3 Wise Men

Supplements & Products:
Animal Scents Ointment, ClaraDerm, ImmuPro, LavaDerm Cooling Mist, MightyVites, MultiGreens, NingXia Red, Ningxia Wolfberries, Omega Blue, ParaFree, Thieves Household Cleaner, True Source

SQUID & OCTOPUS
(See also FAIRIES & UNICORNS)

Yes, you are correct, this heading was added to the book for my 6 year old son Reiker, who is quite the squid and octopus expert! Certainly, these invertebrate animals can benefit from essential oils as well. A toothpick dip or more of oil could be added to their watery environment, just as it would be for fish.

FIRST LINE RECOMMENDATIONS:
Reiker reports that Squid most enjoy Idaho Balsam Fir, while Octopus prefer Blue Spruce.

Single Oils:
Idaho Balsam Fir, Blue Spruce

Blends:
Aroma Siez, Australian Blue, Brain Power, Release

Supplements & Products:
Omega Blue

SUGAR GLIDERS

Sugar Gliders are quite unique little animals, and can greatly benefit from the use of essential oils. They commonly mark areas with their scent glands, but also from their cloaca, which can promote the occurrence of fecal contamination of food, water, and the general environment. Common issues that respond well to essential oil use include Giardia, bacterial diarrhea, skin infections, and parasites. Salmonella and Leptospirosis are two conditions that can actually be shed from healthy Sugar Gliders and given to humans. Good hygiene is the main tool to prevent zoonosis (the spread of disease from animal to human), so cleaning with Thieves Household Cleaner as well as routine water diffusion can help to disinfect the environment and

EXOTIC ANIMALS

reduce risks. Washing your hand with Thieves Foaming Hand Soap or disinfecting with Thieves Waterless Hand Purifier after handling your "Suggie" is a wonderful and non-toxic way to reduce contamination and risk of infection. Bites from Sugar Gliders can become quite infected, and so immediate application of an essential oil (especially Thieves) to any bite wound is recommended. Sugar Gliders eat a variety of foods, and their live prey such as mealworms and crickets can be "gut-loaded" by feeding NingXia Red, Power Meal, and MultiGreens prior to ingestion. Many Sugar Gliders are given yogurt regularly, and you can make your own healthy yogurt by adding 1 capsule of Life 5 to 1 quart of organic (preferably raw) whole milk. Allow to incubate at a warmish temperature (75 degrees Fahrenheit or so) for 24-48 hours, or until the yogurt has been created. Raindrop Technique is not recommended at this time for this species.

FIRST LINE RECOMMENDATIONS:
  WATER DIFFUSION: Purification or Thieves
  DRINKING WATER: Citrus Fresh, citrus oils
  PETTING: Any oil of choice, completely absorbed into your hands.
  SUPPLEMENTS: Make your own Life 5 yogurt for your Sugar Glider. Offer Ningxia Wolfberries and small amounts of NingXia Red (in water or straight.)
  INDIRECT DIFFUSION: Wear essential oils yourself while handling and spending time with your Sugar Glider.
  CLEANING: Use Thieves Household Cleaner as a cage cleaner as well as to wash bedding, toys, and dishes.

Single Oils:
  Frankincense, Grapefruit, Helichrysum, Lavender, Lemon, Orange, Palo Santo, Tangerine

Blends:
  Citrus Fresh

Supplements & Products:
  Life 5, NingXia Red, Ningxia Wolfberries, Thieves Household Cleaner

TORTOISES

Tortoises can use essential oils in all of the manners described for Reptiles. Please see their description for more information. Raindrop Technique is not readily used in this species due to the presence of the shell, however the Reptile Raindrop Solution can be applied to legs, shell, or skin lesions when needed.

FIRST LINE RECOMMENDATIONS:
WATER DIFFUSION: Rotate through a variety of essential oils, or choose those indicated for a specific health concern.
WATER MISTING: Add approximately 4 drops per 4 ounces (120 mL) of distilled water and mist the tortoise, caging, or food items as needed.
SUPPLEMENTS: NingXia Red can be misted onto greens straight or diluted for added nutrition.
CLEANING: Thieves Household Cleaner

Single Oils:
Frankincense, Grapefruit, Helichrysum, Lavender, Lemon, Orange, Palo Santo, Tangerine

Blends:
Citrus Fresh

Supplements & Products:
Animal Scents Ointment, ClaraDerm, LavaDerm Cooling Mist, MultiGreens, NingXia Red, Ningxia Wolfberries, ParaFree, Thieves Household Cleaner, True Source

TURTLES

Turtles should use oils in the same manners as those described for Reptiles and Fish. Please see those descriptions for more information. Raindrop Technique is not readily used in this species due to the presence of the shell as well as their tendency to be in water, however the Reptile Raindrop Solution can be applied to legs, shell, or skin lesions if indicated.

FIRST LINE RECOMMENDATIONS:
SOAKING WATER: Add 1 toothpick dip to several drops of essential oil to aquarium water. Purification is suggested.
WATER DIFFUSION: Purification, Thieves
CLEANING: Thieves Household Cleaner

Single Oils:
Frankincense, Grapefruit, Helichrysum, Lavender, Lemon, Orange, Palo Santo, Tangerine

Blends:
Citrus Fresh

Supplements & Products:
Animal Scents Ointment, LavaDerm Cooling Mist, Omega Blue, ParaFree, Thieves Household Cleaner

ZOO ANIMALS

Depending on the species of Zoo Animal, there are many ways in which to use essential oils. Hopefully, at this point, you have discovered many creative and beneficial ways to incorporate essential oils into the lives of various animals. Zoo animals will greatly benefit from the physical, as well as the emotional, properties of essential oils. Rotational diffusion is likely to be the easiest route of administration. Non-toxic and healthful cleaning with Thieves Household Cleaner is very important. For animals who may participate in petting zoo situations, be sure to provide Thieves Waterless Hand Purifier instead of the typical toxic products on the market. Adding essential oils to foods, drinking water, as well as soaking and swimming water is likely to be very easy for these animals. Water misting applications to the

ANIMAL DESK REFERENCE: EXOTICS

animal and to foods is also well accepted. The possibilities are endless, and the most important factor is that these animals obtain exposure to essential oils. If Raindrop Technique is desired, generally starting with a Kitty Raindrop Technique is suggested.

FIRST LINE RECOMMENDATIONS:
  CLEANING: Thieves Household Cleaner, Thieves Waterless Hand Purifier
  WATER DIFFUSION: Rotate diffusion with any essential oil of choice. Recommendations include Frankincense, Trauma Life, Valor, Orange, Citrus Fresh
  SOAKING WATER: Frankincense, Lavender
  SUPPLEMENTS: NingXia Red

Single Oils:
Frankincense, Grapefruit, Helichrysum, Lavender, Lemon, Orange, Palo Santo, Tangerine, Valerian, Vetiver, Ylang Ylang

Blends:
Citrus Fresh, Hope

Supplements & Products:
Animal Scents Ointment, LavaDerm Cooling Mist, MultiGreens, Ningxia Wolfberries, Omega Blue, ParaFree, Sulfurzyme, Thieves Household Cleaner, True Source

ESSENTIAL OILS: FELINE

Cats present their own unique controversies and requirements to essential oil use. Most cat owners would agree that cats have distinct opinions of the world, and this certainly holds true for aromatherapy. Cats are likely a little proud of the fact that they are indeed, the most contested topic in the world of essential oil use. Human viewpoints of this subject range from the adamant stance that essential oils cannot be used safely for cats, to those who use contraindicated essential oils on a daily basis for their felines.

After hearing all of the cautions and warnings from the veterinary community, I had concerns for my own multi-cat household. Routine blood and urine evaluations calmed the concerns, and no detrimental effects have ever been shown with over 3 years of almost constant diffusion in my home. What I eventually found to be true, was that the veterinarians who were so carefully warning other veterinarians and owners not to use essential oils, had in fact, never used them themselves. The oils that were linked to killing cats and harming animals were also never graded or evaluated by the veterinarians who condemned them.

My current recommendation when considering essential oil use for cats is to choose oils that are used often, have been used in many cats, and to use them with techniques that cats enjoy. Tea Tree Oil, or Melaleuca alternifolia, is another feline controversy which fascinates me. I have directly communicated with people who have sadly exposed their cat to a poor grade Melaleuca oil, resulting in subsequent seizures and death. Conversely, I have also witnessed firsthand a cat receiving 4 drops of Young Living Melaleuca oil orally twice a day, followed with blood work, and showing no ill events. I do not use this example as a recommendation for everyone to use Melaleuca for their cats, as there are many essential oils that can be used in place of this particular oil. It is the best choice to first select an oil which is known to be very safe and well tolerated in cats. However, it is reassuring to note that if I have a particularly resistant medical case, and feel that Melaleuca oil may be useful, that it does have the potential to be used.

Traditional chemical flea and tick preparations are very similar to essential oils in regards to quality, effectiveness, and risk. In the veterinary community, we have seen horrific side effects to the use of over-the-counter, lower cost flea and tick products. The use of better quality products, typically results in a reduction of significantly harmful reactions. Although not completely benign, this is a very different scenario from the reactions of seizuring and drooling cats, neurologic symptoms, dying kittens, or pets who are frantically trying to rub the product off of themselves. Even the most traditional vets can usually relate to this parallel concerning quality variations. Essential oils can vary in quality, much like other veterinary products, and poor quality can equal toxicity.

One factor that is true for cats, is that they are notoriously deficient in the Cytochrome p450 liver metabolism pathway. This particular pathway is utilized for the metabolism and excretion of all sorts of chemicals from their body, including traditional medications. A cat's liver just does not metabolize items in the same manner or efficiency as a large dog or a human. This fact has made cats unique in veterinary medicine, no matter what the substance may be that we are exposing them to. For example, certain traditional Non-Steroidal Anti-Inflammatory (NSAID) drugs can be used in dogs, but if given to a cat, has a high likelihood of causing significant damage to organs and even death.

Medically, I have found that we can actually use many of the contraindicated essential oils in cats, and sometimes quite aggressively. If there are other oil choices for treatment that carry similar benefits and activities, then those should be a first choice. However, when needed and indicated, the use of more aggressive essential oils is completely possible for cats.

Presented in this chapter, are the application methods most commonly used in thousands of cats worldwide. There are many ways to administer oils to cats, but these remain the most cat friendly. It is important to remember that animals are still individuals, and there could be a specific cat that will not respond well to one application method, or may prove more sensitive to use than another feline. Common sense and a tailored approach to each individual is important. Consulting with a veterinarian, and having blood and urine evaluations prior to starting the use of essential oils is a good policy.

Litteroma:

I developed this technique after observing my outdoor cats using pine needles as their "litter box." I began to realize all of the wonderful ways that animals would naturally expose themselves to essential oils in the "wild," and Litteroma was born. Litteroma is possibly one of the easiest methods in which to expose cats to the health benefits of essential oils. It not only replaces the toxic fragrances found in commercial kitty litter, but offers a way to provide preventive and continued health benefits from essential oils on a regular basis.

Start with unscented kitty litter - staying within the same brand that you currently use is often advisable. Add 1-3 drops of your chosen essential oil to 1 cup of baking soda - store this mixture within a glass jar, and allow it to "marinade" and blend overnight, shaking the mixture several times. Later, you may find you can add more essential oil drops to this recipe. Starting with a small portion - sprinkle the baking soda mixture onto your kitty litter. Mix well. Provide a separate litter box that does not contain essential oils, to make sure that your cat does not have an aversion to the essential oil that was selected. Once you are sure your cat is using the litter box with your oil selection and concentration, you can then omit the use of the "plain" litter box.

Selecting and rotating various oils can bring big benefits to your cat. Copaiba can aid with arthritis pains, Di-Gize can aid in intestinal upset, and Frankincense may bring anticancer benefits. The choices are endless, and can provide powerful preventive measures to your feline friends.

Water Diffusion:

Diffusion is usually a method that is well tolerated by all cats, especially from water-based "ultrasonic" diffuser models. Many misconceptions have been placed on what cats "like" or "don't like" - and it appears that these generalizations may have been made based on individual reports, and not from cats as a whole. The dislike of citrus oils may hold true for one cat, but then another cat is found to be attracted the diffusion of Peace & Calming. Allowing a cat to show you their individual preference is a good idea. If a cat can leave the room when you diffuse a certain essential oil, you will quickly find out if they tend to leave the room every time that particular oil is diffused, or if they tend to enter a room every time a certain essential oil is used. Tenting and caging is commonly used for cats with respiratory concerns. See the chapter on Diffusion for more information.

Petting the Cat:

This method is well tolerated by cats, and seems to be far superior to dripping oils directly on the skin. Due to the fact that hair follicles may enhance absorption, spreading the essential oils over a larger area of the cat, may indeed prove more effective. This method involves placing a neat or diluted oil into your hand. Circling your hands together, the essential oils are allowed to absorb to varying degrees into your skin. Once you have the amount of oil on your hands that you desire - which can vary from completely absorbed, to a thin coating - you simply "pet your cat". Even with oils completely absorbed into your hand - if you smell your cat after "petting" - you will find that they smell like essential oils. Adding the fact that cats groom themselves, oral ingestion of the essential oil is likely to occur. See the chapter on Topical Applications for more information.

Oral Administration:

Although not as commonly used for cats, occasionally oils are given directly in the mouth or via capsule. When capsule administration is given, small gelatin capsules can be found for purchase on the internet through various suppliers. There are various sizes of capsules that can be purchased, and size "3" or "4" are often appropriate for use in cats (the higher the number, the smaller the capsule). These capsules can be used to place oils into, small amounts of supplements, or a drop or two from a product such as ParaFree or Inner Defense. When oils are dripped directly into the mouth of a cat, or they are unfortunate enough to bite into a capsule, the cat will often salivate profusely. Some cats shake their heads and paw at their mouths as well. This is usually a short-lived event, but some cats salivate for 15 minutes or more. Occasionally, the salivation seems to lessen as the disease or illness condition improves. In general, the oral route is used after other methods have not yielded enough results, or in critical situations (such as pain or hemorrhage.) Cats will ingest essential oils from the grooming process, after the Petting application has been used. For many cats, this amount of ingestion is adequate to create a therapeutic response.

KITTY RAINDROP TECHNIQUE

This technique was also created by Leigh Foster, and had been used on many of her own rescue cats prior to its mainstream use in the feline world. Although this technique includes oils that are typically contraindicated in cats, veterinarians and cat owners alike, have witnessed amazing health benefits with this technique. Because of its formulation specifically for cats, it is remarkable to watch cats enjoy this application so much. I have documented the safe and even long term use of the Kitty Raindrop Technique (KRDT), in many cats with blood work and veterinary monitoring. One such case study is of a cat named "Cowboy" who has received a KRDT daily to twice a day for over 2 years!

Kitty Raindrop Solution:
Add 4 drops of each Raindrop Technique oil - Oregano, Thyme, Basil, Cypress, Wintergreen, Marjoram, and Peppermint - to a 30mL (1 ounce) glass essential oil bottle. Add V-6 Enhanced Vegetable Oil Complex to fill the remainder of the bottle. Mix by rocking the bottle, and apply approximately 6 drops of the solution up the spine of the cat, from tail to head. Next, gently stroke or feather the essential oil solution up the back of the cat - similarly to a human technique. Amazingly enough, cats often enjoy this backward stroke! If you encounter one that does not, feel free to pet the cat "normally" or omit the strokes all together. When indicated, repeat applying the KRDT solution 3-6 drops at a time along the spine and stroking in. Often I find that it is best to apply no more than 3 applications during a session, although many cats will desire more.

Balancing the cat with Valor (neat or diluted) can be performed prior to the KRDT. The Valor is placed in the palms of your hands, and by rubbing your hands together, allowed to almost completely absorb into your palm. The hands are then placed over the shoulder and rump area, and the balancing procedure is completed much like that described for humans. In some situations, this step is omitted, mainly in cats who are unable to be handled easily.

At the end of the KRDT, I will generally perform Vita Flex up the kitty's back (three times if permitted). Again, this depends on what the cat feels like allowing. But it is a wonderful addition if you can include it.

Modification of the KRDT:

When modification of the KRDT is suggested, this is generally referring to the addition of essential oil(s) to the Kitty Raindrop Solution. In general, 4 drops of the additional oil are added to the existing recipe, unless less is specified for that individual oil. On average, no more than 3 essential oil singles or blends are added to a KRDT solution. If the use of many more oils are desired, I recommend making up several different batches of the KRDT, each one including a different 3 added "modification" oils. This helps to not overwhelm the body with too many things at once. The solution with the added essential oils, is used exactly as the plain KRDT solution would be used.

Frequency of Application:

The chapter How Much, How Often should be referred to for more information. With almost every situation in which a Raindrop Technique is suggested, no matter what species of animal, I will always recommend the same procedure for the initial use of this technique. First, give the animal a Raindrop Technique in a somewhat light and conservative way. So for a cat, 3-6 drops of the KRDT would be applied. Then, you will monitor the cat or animal for signs of improvement or response. If there is no response, then we can administer the KRDT again either more frequently, or with more drops applied. If there was a noticeable response, the length of that response is evaluated, then the Raindrop Technique can be repeated at the length of that time interval.

For example, a cat with arthritis is given a KRDT modified with the addition of 4 drops of Copaiba. The cat enjoyed it, and the owner reported that she felt more comfortable for about 4 days after the application. Even though this cat could get a KRDT every day, giving the application every 3-4 days is a great next step; spacing the timing of the repeat application to the ideal needs of the individual cat.

FELINE CONDITIONS

ABSCESS
(See also PAIN MANAGEMENT)

An abscess is a pus filled pocket of infection, most commonly created from a wound caused by another cat. Cat bites are the most serious in their transmission of bacteria, and cause of serious infections. Cat bites to humans have resulted in infections severe enough to require surgical debridement of the wound. Symptoms of swelling, heat at location, drainage of pus, fever, lethargy, as well as others can develop within hours of the injury and resultant infection. When animals feel poorly, this can be an emergency situation, and often traditional antibiotics are encouraged.

FIRST LINE RECOMMENDATIONS:
Seek Veterinary care when an animal feels poorly or when infection is severe. See also PAIN MANAGEMENT for suggestions regarding discomfort.

TOPICAL: Apply Purification, Thieves, or Lemon neat to the abscess head, up to twice a day. Hot pack the abscess with a very warm, damp wash cloth to help bring the abscess to a "head" or to drain. Once the "head" has opened and drainage is occurring, flush the wound with diluted Thieves Household Cleaner.
KRDT: Apply up to once per day. This solution can also be applied to the abscess directly.
ORAL: Thieves when needed.

Single Oils:
Laurus Nobilis, Lavender, Lemon, Lemongrass, Melaleuca Alternifolia, Mountain Savory, Oregano, Spikenard

Blends:
Egyptian Gold, Purification, Thieves

ANIMAL DESK REFERENCE: FELINE

Supplements & Products:
Animal Scents Ointment, Animal Scents Shampoo, Inner Defense, NingXia Red, Sulfurzyme, Thieves Household Cleaner

ACNE - FELINE
(See also CANINE CONDITIONS – SKIN INFECTIONS)

Feline Acne is often seen as small blackheads on the chin. Commonly, this condition is due to food residues, plastic dishes, food allergies, and exposure to household toxins. Changing the diet, using glass, stainless steel, or ceramic food and water dishes, washing dishes daily, and washing the chin area is helpful.

FIRST LINE RECOMMENDATIONS:
TOPICAL: Wipe chin gently with a very dilute solution of Thieves Household Cleaner, up to once a day.

Single Oils:
Copaiba, Frankincense, Helichrysum, Lavender, Myrrh

Blends:
Melrose, 3 Wise Men

Supplements & Products:
Animal Scents Ointment, ClaraDerm, LavaDerm Cooling Mist, Stevia Extract, Sulfurzyme, Thieves Household Cleaner, Thieves Waterless Hand Purifier, Thieves Wipes

ALLERGIES

Allergies have many different causes, and secondary skin infections can continue the occurrence of symptoms, even after the allergen has been removed. Careful veterinary exams, and accurate diagnosis must be made to effectively treat the allergy complex of symptoms. Diet is often the culprit in cats, and a grain, egg, soy, wheat, corn, and dairy free diet is recommended. Many holistic grain free diets still contain egg products, and we find this to be a common offender in our veterinary practice.

FIRST LINE RECOMMENDATIONS:
KRDT: Up to once a day, with Copaiba added.
WATER DIFFUSION: Thieves
SUPPLEMENTS: Omega Blue, NingXia Red, Sulfurzyme, Allerzyme

Single Oils:
Basil, Copaiba, Frankincense, Geranium, Helichrysum, Lavender, Ledum, Melissa, Ocotea, Pine, Spruce, Tansy (Blue)

Blends:
GLF, Hope, Juva Cleanse, Juva Flex, R.C., Thieves

Supplements & Products:
Animal Scents Ointment, Essentialzymes-4, JuvaPower, JuvaSpice, JuvaTone, LavaDerm Cooling Mist, Life 5, MightyZyme, MultiGreens, NingXia Red, Omega Blue, Sulfurzyme, Thieves Household Cleaner

AORTIC THROMBOEMBOLISM
(See SADDLE THROMBUS)

ANEMIA

Anemia is usually defined as the low count of red blood cells. There are many causes of anemia including iron and nutritional deficiency, renal failure, Feline Leukemia Virus, autoimmune destruction of red blood cells, decreased production of red blood cells by the bone marrow, as well as blood loss due to hemorrhage and bleeding, parasitic infections, intestinal parasites, flea infestation, and more. Anemic cats generally have pale gums or foot pads, are lethargic, and may show signs of dyspnea – or respiratory stress.

FIRST LINE RECOMMENDATIONS:
Ensure accurate diagnosis and work up with your veterinarian. If a diagnosis can be reached, include regimens for those issues (for example: renal disease, intestinal parasites, autoimmune disorders...)

KRDT: Modify by adding oils such as Copaiba, Frankincense, and ImmuPower. Apply up to once a day.

SUPPLEMENTS: NingXia Red, Omega Blue, MultiGreens.

Single Oils:
Frankincense, Copaiba, Helichrysum, Juniper

Blends:
Aroma Life, ImmuPower, Juva Cleanse, Kitty Raindrop Technique

Supplements & Products:
Allerzyme, Detoxzyme, Essentialzymes-4, K&B Tincture, MightyZyme, MultiGreens, NingXia Red, Omega Blue, ParaFree, Power Meal, Rehemogen, Sulfurzyme, True Source

ANOREXIA

Anorexia is often used to describe poor or no eating by an animal. Many times it is accompanied by feelings of nausea or discomfort. There are many reasons for an animal to be anorexic, and an accurate veterinary diagnosis is important. These recommendations generally stimulate appetite and ease digestive concerns and nausea.

FIRST LINE RECOMMENDATIONS:
WATER DIFFUSION: Di-Gize or Lavender
KRDT: Modify by adding Di-Gize, apply up to once a day.
PETTING: As needed with any indicated oil, Patchouli and Di-Gize are recommendations.

Single Oils:
Laurus Nobilis, Lavender, Ledum, Lemon, Patchouli, Tarragon

Blends:
Di-Gize, GLF, Juva Cleanse

Supplements & Products:
JuvaTone, Life 5, MightyZyme, NingXia Red, ParaFree, Power Meal, Super B

ARTHRITIS

(See also CANINE CONDITIONS - ARTHRITIS)

FIRST LINE RECOMMENDATIONS:
KRDT: Modify by adding Copaiba and Frankincense. Apply up to once a day.
PETTING: Copaiba
LITTEROMA: Copaiba

ASTHMA

FIRST LINE RECOMMENDATIONS:
WATER DIFFUSION: Thieves or any of the suggested oils up to 24 hours a day in the home. Tenting or caging can be used when needed.
LITTEROMA: Dorado Azul
PETTING: With any suggested oil as needed.
KRDT: Modify with R.C., Dorado Azul, and Copaiba; apply up to once a day.
SUPPLEMENTS: NingXia Red, Omega Blue, Allerzyme

Single Oils:
Dorado Azul, Eucalyptus Blue, Eucalyptus Globulus, Laurus Nobilis, Lavender, Lemon, Myrtle, Palo Santo, Peppermint, Pine

Blends:
Breathe Again Roll-On, Egyptian Gold, M-Grain, R.C., Thieves

Supplements & Products:
Allerzyme, Detoxzyme, Essentialzymes-4, JuvaTone, Life 5, MightyZyme, MultiGreens, NingXia Red, Omega Blue, ParaFree, PD 80/20, Sulfurzyme, Thieves Household Cleaner

AUTOIMMUNE DISORDERS

FIRST LINE RECOMMENDATIONS:
KRDT: Modify with ImmuPower, Frankincense, and Copaiba; apply up to once a day.
SUPPLEMENTS: NingXia Red, Essentialzymes-4, Omega Blue, Sulfurzyme

ANIMAL DESK REFERENCE: FELINE

Single Oils:
Balsam Fir (Idaho), Eucalyptus Blue, Frankincense, Laurus Nobilis, Ocotea

Blends:
ImmuPower

Supplements & Products:
Essentialzymes-4, Mineral Essence, MultiGreens, NingXia Red, Omega Blue, PD 80/20, Sulfurzyme, Thieves Household Cleaner

BEHAVIORAL CONDITIONS

FIRST LINE RECOMMENDATIONS:
WATER DIFFUSION: Rotational diffusion of emotional blends. Harmony and White Angelica are suggested.
SUPPLEMENTS: Essentialzymes-4, NingXia Red, Omega Blue, MultiGreens
LITTEROMA: Valerian, Roman Chamomile, or Spikenard

Single Oils:
Bergamot, Chamomile (Roman), Geranium, Grapefruit, Lavender, Lemon, Marjoram, Melissa, Orange, Palo Santo, Pine, Rose, Spikenard, Spruce, Tangerine, Valerian, Vetiver, Ylang Ylang

Blends:
Dragon Time, Forgiveness, Harmony, Hope, Joy, Lady Sclareol, Mister, Peace & Calming, SclarEssence, Valor, White Angelica

Supplements & Products:
Essentialzymes-4, MightyZyme, Mineral Essence, MultiGreens, NingXia Red, Omega Blue, Super B

BLADDER INFECTIONS
(See URINARY CONDITIONS)

FELINE CONDITIONS

BLOCKED - URINARY
(See also PAIN MANAGEMENT, URINARY CONDITIONS)

Male cats can commonly suffer from a blocked urethra, which is an emergency situation. The inability to urinate creates a very toxic and dangerous situation, and death can occur. Immediate veterinary attention is required if you suspect your cat has a urinary blockage. These recommendations are to be used to complement veterinary care.

FIRST LINE RECOMMENDATIONS:
PETTING: Vetiver, Lavender
DIFFUSION: By any method, even just letting the cat sniff the bottle. Rose and Frankincense has been used in critical situations to raise the life force, and have been incredibly effective.
SUPPLEMENTS: K&B Tincture

Single Oils:
Copaiba, Juniper, Laurus Nobilis, Lavender, Lemon, Lemongrass, Myrrh, Spruce, Tangerine, Tarragon, Vetiver, Wintergreen, Ylang Ylang

Physical Blends:
Peace & Calming, PanAway, Release, Relieve It

Supplements & Products:
Essentialzymes-4, Inner Defense, K&B Tincture, MightyZyme, Omega Blue, Sulfurzyme

BLOOD CLOT
(See SADDLE THROMBUS)

CANCER

There are many different kinds of cancer, and each type may have a different specific focus for essential oil recommendations. However there is a basic foundation of items that must be met in order for an immune system to function to the fullest, and to give an animal the utmost possibility of clearing cancer. These recommendations apply to all animals, not just cats. However, listed below are cat friendly methods for using essential oils and supplements with cancer.

It is very important in conditions such as cancer, to incorporate as many layers of care as possible. This is one situation, where starting with small amounts of items, but building up to using many and in relatively high amounts (sometimes quickly) is fully warranted.

FIRST LINE RECOMMENDATIONS:

DIET: Every cat with cancer should have their diet fully evaluated and likely changed. Unprocessed and raw whole foods are recommended, but products and recipes available are not always properly balanced or desired by many cats. Work with a holistic veterinarian or nutritionist to determine the best diet option for your cat.

DRINKING WATER: Tap and city water should be avoided at all costs. Spring water is the best recommendation, and even high quality bottled water should be used if needed.

ELIMINATE HOUSEHOLD TOXINS: The use of Thieves Household Cleaner should be a standard recommendation. Scented kitty litter, air fresheners, fabric softeners, household cleaners, human perfumes, lotions, hairsprays, etc… must be eliminated from the home. Microwave ovens should also be completely removed from the household. Electromagnetic fields (cell phones, computers, Wi-Fi) should be evaluated and be lessened or eliminated. This is especially important for the cat that enjoys lying on top of a warm computer!

NINGXIA RED: If your cat is one who likes NingXia Red, or tolerates it easily, gradually build up to giving up to several tablespoons or more per day. Mixing into soft or canned foods, offering plain or diluted, or syringing into the mouth seem to be the best methods of administration for cats. If a cat dislikes the NingXia Red intensely – concentrate on giving other supplements listed, to avoid stress.

OMEGA BLUE: Due to the size of the capsule, this supplement is usually not given to cats in its full form. Capsules can be "popped" and 1-2 drops placed into foods or directly into the cat's mouth. Since the Omega Blue does contain essential oils within the fish oil, this product may be rejected by some cats when they detect these flavors. If this is the case, another high quality fish oil can be used – and definitely should be. I recommend the use of Standard Process Tuna Omega-3 for a cat friendly taste.

DIGESTIVE ENZYMES: Digestive enzymes are incredibly important for health, but especially in cases of cancer. Since cats can be a bit finicky, some may reject the essential oil flavors within some Young Living enzymes. Start with a very small amount, usually sprinkled from an opened capsule, mixed into moist food, generally with each meal. For cats that will not ingest the Young Living enzymes, a product called Prozyme is well tolerated by most felines. I would caution you not to use products that combine probiotics with digestive enzymes. This has become a popular trend, however it would seem that the enzyme would digest and destroy the items combined with it, rendering it less beneficial.

MULTIGREENS: Start by adding a small sprinkling from an opened capsule into a small amount of moist food. Gradually increase until giving up to 1-2 capsules per day or more.

ADDITIONAL SUPPLEMENTS: See the list below for more supplements that can be added. One important recommendation that must be made in cases of cancer, is to also include raw whole food supplements that contain non-vegetarian products and glandulars. Since cats are obligate carnivores, we will not be able to fully fill their nutritional needs with Young Living supplements alone (which are mainly vegetarian in nature) – especially in the case of cancer. I recommend the use of Standard Process supplements as an addition to the use of Young Living products, not necessarily as a replacement. Both bring different qualities to the table. Recommended Standard Process formulas for cats with cancer are: Feline Whole Body Support and Feline Immune System

Support. Adding in other specific formulas is advised if other body systems are showing stress or need support (liver, renal, enteric, etc...).

WATER DIFFUSION: Rotational diffusion of emotional oils is recommended. See also the chapter on Emotional Use of Blends for more information. Diffuse any anti-cancer oils up to 24 hours a day. Rotation through a variety of oils is recommended.

KRDT: Modify the KRDT as described, adding Frankincense, Copaiba, and ImmuPower to the mixture. Apply up to twice a day. Small amounts of the KRDT may be applied directly to some types of tumors.

PETTING: Applying any essential oil you desire in the petting method is very well tolerated by most cats. Apply up to twice a day or more.

INGESTION: Cats will rarely tolerate oral administration of oils for long periods of time. As the resolution of cancer can be a longer term adventure, direct oral administration is often not used. Many cats reject the flavor of essential oils in food or water, however if you are lucky enough to have a cat that will ingest oils in these ways – these routes can be very helpful.

DRINKING WATER: Add one drop of Frankincense or desired oil to 1 liter of spring water.

FOODS: In soft moist favorite foods, dip a toothpick into the essential oil (Frankincense) and mix into the food. Gradually increase the amounts mixed in as tolerated.

Single Oils:

Balsam Fir (Idaho), Copaiba, Frankincense, Grapefruit, Helichrysum, Lemon, Myrrh, Orange, Palo Santo, Sandalwood, Tangerine

Blends:

Acceptance, Believe, Citrus Fresh, Egyptian Gold, Forgiveness, Harmony, Hope, ImmuPower, Juva Cleanse, Kitty Raindrop Technique, Present Time, Release, 3 Wise Men, Trauma Life, White Angelica

Supplements & Products:

Dietary supplementation is a must for cancer. It is important for cats to not be obese, but to also not become thin while on a healthful regimen. With all supplements, it is important to start

FELINE CONDITIONS

with a small amount and gradually increase the amount given as you determine what your individual cat can handle, or what they require.

Allerzyme, Animal Scents Ointment, Essentialzyme, Essentialzymes-4, ImmuPro, MightyZyme, MultiGreens, NingXia Red, Omega Blue, ParaFree, Power Meal, True Source, Sulfurzyme, Super C, Super C Chewable, Thieves Household Cleaner

CARDIOMYOPATHY, HYPERTROPHIC
(See HEART DISEASE)

CAVITY
(See FELINE ODONTOCLASTIC RESORPTIVE LESION)

CERVICAL LINE LESIONS, CERVICAL NECK LESIONS
(See FELINE ODONTOCLASTIC RESORPTIVE LESIONS)

CONJUNCTIVITIS
(See also UPPER RESPIRATORY INFECTIONS)

FIRST LINE RECOMMENDATIONS:
SUPPLEMENTS: MultiGreens, NingXia Red, Omega Blue
WATER DIFFUSION: Tenting or caging with 3-4 drops of Lavender and 1 drop Copaiba.
WATER MISTING: If tolerated (most cats do not appreciate this) – mist the eye area with 4 drops of Lavender, in 4 ounces (120 mL) of distilled water.
TOPICAL: Rose Ointment can be used in the eyes in severe situations.
KRDT: up to once a day.

Single Oils:
Copaiba, Frankincense, Lavender, Melissa

Blends:
Egyptian Gold, Hope, ImmuPower, R.C., Rose Ointment, Thieves

Supplements & Products:
Animal Scents Ointment, MultiGreens, NingXia Red, Omega Blue, Rose Ointment, Sulfurzyme, Thieves Household Cleaner

CRYSTALS - URINARY
(See URINARY CONDITIONS)

CYSTITIS
(See also FLUTD, URINARY CONDITIONS)

DECLAW SURGERY
(See also PAIN MANAGEMENT)

It is unfortunate that many animal caretakers are not informed of the fact that this procedure is mainly unnecessary. There is much information to be found on how to keep cats comfortably in homes without declawing, and I encourage you to seek reputable advice from holistic veterinarians or cat organizations.

Cats who have been declawed, not only have healing to deal with, but emotional and physical traumas as well. Both aspects are important to address. See the chapter on Emotional Use of Blends for more information.

FIRST LINE RECOMMENDATIONS:
PETTING: For discomfort and healing: Place 1 drop each of Helichrysum, Myrrh, and Copaiba into 1 teaspoon of V-6 diluting oil. Mix together, then place 10 drops of this solution into your hand, rub together, and pet onto the leg and foot area. Ideally this is done as close as possible to the completion of surgery. In our veterinary hospital – this is performed prior to bandages being placed onto the feet.
WATER DIFFUSION: During recovery from surgery, or as close as possible, Trauma Life should be diffused for the cat.
ORAL: For severe discomfort: 1 drop of Helichrysum can be given orally, every 1-3 hours or as needed.
KRDT: Modify adding any of the suggested oil(s). Apply up to once per day, especially for anesthesia detoxification.

For Veterinary Professionals, sample protocol: During surgery, Purification is often diffused. Prior to bandaging the feet, the mixture described above is "pet" onto the feet and legs. Upon recovery, Purification (or another chosen oil) with 1 drop of Trauma Life is diffused in the recovery and housing area. If the cat stays for multiple days, additional emotional oils are diffused: Acceptance and Forgiveness are important oils to include. Helichrysum is an important oil for the prevention and treatment of phantom pain syndrome. Oral Helichrysum has been used to help manage pain and can be used with or without other traditional medications.

Single Oils:
Copaiba, Frankincense, Helichrysum, Lavender, Marjoram, Myrrh, Palo Santo

Blends:
3 Wise Men, Acceptance, Aroma Siez, Forgiveness, Kitty Raindrop Technique, M-Grain, Release, Trauma Life

Supplements & Products:
Animal Scents Ointment, BLM Capsules, NingXia Red, Omega Blue, Ortho Ease Massage Oil, Ortho Sport Massage Oil, Sulfurzyme

DENTAL DISEASE
(See also FELINE ODONTOCLASTIC RESORPTIVE LESIONS)

FIRST LINE RECOMMENDATIONS:
DRINKING WATER: Small amounts of Thieves Fresh Essence Mouthwash can be added to drinking water.
ORAL: Brushing teeth with Thieves Dentarome toothpastes is wonderful for cats who allow this.
TOPICAL: Raw Organic Coconut Oil can be rubbed and massaged onto the gum areas. After the cat tolerates this well, tiny amounts of essential oil can be added to the Coconut Oil and gradually increased in concentration.
PETTING: Through grooming cats will ingest various oils off of their fur. This is a great way to get oils into the mouth, however some cats with dental disease do not groom due to pain. Myrrh is suggested.

KRDT: up to once a day.

Single Oils:
Laurus Nobilis, Melaleuca Alternifolia, Myrrh

Blends:
Melrose, Thieves

Supplements & Products:
Essentialzymes-4, BLM Capsules, Inner Defense, MightyZyme, NingXia Red, Omega Blue, Stevia Extract, Sulfurzyme, Thieves Dentarome Toothpaste, Thieves Fresh Essence Mouthwash, True Source

DEWORMING

FIRST LINE RECOMMENDATIONS:
SUPPLEMENTS: See ParaFree for the description of the Kitty Cocktail Deworming protocol.
PETTING: Di-Gize
LITTEROMA: Di-Gize

Single Oils:
Eucalyptus Globulus, Hyssop, Lemon, Lemongrass, Melaleuca Alternifolia, Mountain Savory, Ocotea, Peppermint, Tarragon

Physical Blends:
Di-Gize, ParaFree

Supplements & Products:
Detoxzyme, ParaFree

DIABETES

Diabetes can be difficult to gain control over, and working with a qualified holistic veterinarian is very important to fully address the entire foundation of the cat's health. Dietary changes alone have eliminated Diabetes for some cats, and is incredibly important. See the recommendations within the description for Ocotea, for more information regarding the introduction of essential oils for diabetics. Veterinary cooperation is imperative for animals who are on Insulin.

FIRST LINE RECOMMENDATIONS:
  PETTING: Ocotea
  LITTEROMA: Ocotea
  KRDT: Modified with Ocotea and EndoFlex
  SUPPLEMENTS: NingXia Red, MultiGreens, Essentialzymes-4

Single Oils:
  Geranium, Myrrh, Ocotea, Pine, Ylang Ylang

Blends:
  EndoFlex, Juva Flex, Slique Essence

Supplements & Products:
  Allerzyme, Essentialzymes-4, MightyZyme, MultiGreens, NingXia Red, Omega Blue, Sulfurzyme

DIARRHEA
(See also TRITRICHOMONAS FOETUS)

FIRST LINE RECOMMENDATIONS:
  SUPPLEMENTS: ICP, Life 5
  PETTING: Di-Gize
  ORAL: Di-Gize

Single Oils:
  Lemon, Melaleuca Alternifolia, Melissa, Ocotea, Peppermint, Tarragon, Ylang Ylang

Blends:
Di-Gize, ImmuPower, Melrose, Purification, Thieves

Supplements & Products:
ComforTone, Detoxzyme, Essentialzymes-4, ICP, Inner Defense, Life 5, MightyZyme, MultiGreens, ParaFree, Super B, Thieves Household Cleaner

DISTEMPER - FELINE
(See VIRAL CONDITIONS)

EAR MITES

FIRST LINE RECOMMENDATIONS:
TOPICAL: Place 1-2 drops of Purification onto a cotton tipped applicator. Swab inside the ear up to once a day. See further descriptions within Purification.
PETTING: Purification, up to once a day.
KRDT: Up to once a day or as indicated.

Single Oils:
Citronella, Eucalyptus Polybractea, Lavender, Melaleuca Alternifolia, Palo Santo

Blends:
Melrose, Purification

Supplements & Products:
Animal Scents Ointment, Thieves Household Cleaner

FADING KITTEN SYNDROME

Fading kittens are often cold and/or hypoglycemic. Warming of the kitten is the primary activity that must occur. No oral supplement should be given to a kitten who is too cold to properly digest the nutrient. Hydration, warmth, nutrition, and proper veterinary care are key factors in saving kittens from this condition. The use of life force oils are incredibly beneficial.

FIRST LINE RECOMMENDATIONS:
DIFFUSION: Have the kitten inhale Rose and Frankincense to raise life force energy. Joy can be used when Rose is not available.
PETTING: Frankincense, Joy
SUPPLEMENTS: Give NingXia Red orally as often as needed.

Single Oils:
Frankincense, Helichrysum, Melissa, Orange, Palo Santo, Peppermint, Rose

Blends:
Brain Power, Forgiveness, Hope, Joy

Supplements & Products:
MightyZyme, MultiGreens, NingXia Red, ParaFree, Power Meal

FATTY LIVER DISEASE
(See also LIVER DISEASE)

Fatty Liver Disease is specific to the mobilization of fat into the Liver of sick cats. This is most common in cats who are overweight (even slightly), and who stop eating for one reason or another. Veterinary care and diagnostics are very important. Addressing any other underlying cause (such as Kidney Disease) is important.

FIRST LINE RECOMMENDATIONS:
SUPPLEMENTS: Super B, Detoxzyme, MightyZyme, NingXia Red
PETTING: German Chamomile, Geranium, Helichrysum
ORAL: Helichrysum when indicated, and for severe Liver Failure.

Single Oils:
Chamomile (German), Geranium, Goldenrod, Grapefruit, Helichrysum, Juniper, Ledum, Lemon, Myrrh, Myrtle, Nutmeg, Rosemary, Spearmint, Tangerine, Wintergreen

Blends:
Citrus Fresh, Di-Gize, GLF, Juva Cleanse, Juva Flex

Supplements & Products:
Detoxzyme, Essentialzyme, JuvaPower, JuvaSpice, JuvaTone, MightyZyme, MultiGreens, NingXia Red, Omega Blue, Super B

FELINE LEUKEMIA
(See VIRAL CONDITIONS)

FELV
(See VIRAL CONDITIONS)

FELINE IMMUNODEFICIENCY VIRUS
(See VIRAL CONDITIONS)

FELINE INFECTIOUS PERITONITIS
(See also VIRAL CONDITIONS)

Feline Infectious Peritonitis (FIP) is a very severe condition which is caused by the mutation of the Corona Virus in cats. Prevention and good health is the best stance for this disease, as once symptoms have fully developed, reversal is very difficult. This is one disease in which extremely aggressive protocols are needed, and the prognosis is generally poor. Regular use of KRDT, nutritional supplements, and diffusion to support general health and immune function is recommended for every feline.

FIRST LINE RECOMMENDATIONS:
KRDT: Modified with Hyssop, Sandalwood, and 2 drops Melissa; applied up to twice a day.
SUPPLEMENTS: MultiGreens, NingXia Red, Omega Blue, Essentialzymes-4
LITTEROMA: Hope, Purification, Raven
PETTING: up to twice a day with any suggested oil.
WATER DIFFUSION: Any essential oil suggested, or for prevention purposes routine rotation of any essential oil.

Single Oils:
Frankincense (Carteri & Sacred), Helichrysum, Hyssop, Laurus Nobilis, Melissa, Mountain Savory, Ravintsara, Sandalwood, Thyme

Blends:
Egyptian Gold, Forgiveness, Hope, ImmuPower, Longevity, Raven, Thieves, 3 Wise Men

Supplements & Products:
Essentialzymes-4, MightyZyme, Mineral Essence, MultiGreens, NingXia Red, Omega Blue, Thieves Household Cleaner, True Source

FELINE LOWER URINARY TRACT DISEASE
(See FLUTD – FELINE LOWER URINARY TRACT DISEASE)

FELINE ODONTOCLASTIC RESORPTIVE LESION
(See also DENTAL DISEASE, PAIN MANAGEMENT)

Feline Odontoclastic Resorptive Lesions, also known as FORL's, are often described as a cavity in the tooth of a cat. They are different from human cavities, and are not caused by decay and bacteria as with human teeth. There is much controversy regarding this disorder, and no agreement has been made regarding causes or consistent treatments. Holistically, one can be sure that eliminating toxins, detoxifying the body, and providing foundational tools of health (essential oils and supplements) are key for prevention and treatment. Currently, affected teeth are best extracted from the mouth, as they are often painful and continue to worsen despite our best attempts. Prevention of additional teeth succumbing to the disorder is a primary focus, as well as decreasing pain and inflammation associated with the condition.

FIRST LINE RECOMMENDATIONS:
KRDT: up to once a day
PETTING: Myrrh, Helichrysum
TOPICAL: Coconut Oil – see Dental Disease for further information.
DRINKING WATER: Thieves Fresh Essence Mouthwash

Single Oils:
Helichrysum, Laurus Nobilis, Myrrh, Wintergreen

Blends:
Juva Cleanse, Juva Flex, PanAway, Thieves

Supplements & Products:
Essentialzymes-4, JuvaTone, MightyZyme, Mineral Essence, MultiGreens, NingXia Red, Omega Blue, PD 80/20, Stevia Extract, Sulfurzyme, Thieves Dentarome Toothpaste, Thieves Fresh Essence Mouthwash

FEVER OF UNKNOWN ORIGIN
(See also PAIN MANAGEMENT)

As the name suggests, this condition is a fever in a cat, for which the cause cannot be determined. In this situation, an approach of providing tools against every cause of a fever is recommended. Kitty Raindrop Technique is ideal for this need. It is important to address pain if that may also be a contributing factor.

FIRST LINE RECOMMENDATIONS:
KRDT: Applied up to twice a day.
WATER DIFFUSION: Thieves, Purification
SUPPLEMENTS: NingXia Red

Single Oils:
Copaiba, Helichrysum, Lavender, Lemon, Melissa, Myrrh, Palo Santo, Peppermint, Ravintsara, Thyme

Blends:
Egyptian Gold, Hope, ImmuPower, Raven, Purification, Thieves

Supplements & Products:
Inner Defense, Mineral Essence, MultiGreens, NingXia Red

FIP
(See FELINE INFECTIOUS PERITONITIS, VIRAL CONDITIONS)

FIV
(See VIRAL CONDITIONS)

FLEAS

Fleas are one of the most difficult parasites to eliminate. Often many multiple layers of prevention are needed. All animals in the household must be treated for fleas, not just one or two.

FIRST LINE RECOMMENDATIONS:
DIFFUSION: See the description for Pepper (Black), for directions for a household Flea Bomb Recipe.
KRDT: Modified with Palo Santo and Purification, apply up to once a day. Fleas particularly dislike the KRDT solution, and it is helpful to apply this solution to locations where the fleas are the worst (rear end.)
PETTING: Purification, KRDT
LITTEROMA: Purification
TOPICAL: Bathe with Thieves Household Cleaner
CLEANING: Cleaning, laundering, and spraying with Thieves Household Cleaner indoors and out is suggested.
SUPPLEMENTS: Healthier cats are less attractive to fleas and other insects. NingXia Red, Omega Blue, MultiGreens

Single Oils:
Citronella, Eucalyptus Polybractea, Lavender, Melissa, Orange, Palo Santo, Pine, Spruce, Tansy (Idaho)

Blends:
ImmuPower, Purification, Thieves

Supplements & Products:
Animals need to be as healthy as possible to avoid infestations with fleas. A layered approach to providing supplements is recommended.

Animal Scents Ointment, ClaraDerm, Essentialzymes-4, JuvaTone, LavaDerm Cooling Mist, MightyZyme, Mineral Essence, MultiGreens, NingXia Red, Omega Blue, Ortho Ease Massage Oil, Ortho Sport Massage Oil, ParaFree, Thieves Household Cleaner, True Source

FLUTD – FELINE LOWER URINARY TRACT DISEASE
(See also PAIN MANAGEMENT, URINARY CONDITIONS)

FLUTD is a poorly understood condition that could have underlying viral and stress related causes. Cats experience periods of bladder inflammation (cystitis), and often strain and pass bloody urine during an episode. Good hydration and the feeding of foods with additional moisture (canned, raw, or otherwise) is helpful for the condition. Often courses of antibiotics are prescribed, but are not truly indicated as there is usually no bacterial infection present. Given time, the cat will generally get over the episode on their own, but may flare up again at a later date. A holistic approach to this disorder is mandatory for correction.

FIRST LINE RECOMMENDATIONS:
PETTING: Copaiba
INGESTION: Copaiba in drinking water or foods if possible
LITTEROMA: Copaiba, Elemi, Helichrysum
KRDT: Modified with Copaiba, Lavender, Valerian; applied up to once per day.
WATER DIFFUSION: oils for stress relief as well as antiviral oils may be indicated. Rotational diffusion of many oils is suggested.
SUPPLEMENTS: NingXia Red, Omega Blue, Sulfurzyme, K&B Tincture

Single Oils:
Elemi, Eucalyptus Polybractea, Goldenrod, Helichrysum, Juniper, Laurus Nobilis, Lavender, Lemon, Melissa, Mountain Savory, Myrrh, Oregano, Pine, Spruce, Tansy (Blue), Thyme, Valerian, Vetiver, Wintergreen, Ylang Ylang

Blends:
Hope, ImmuPower, Juva Cleanse, Juva Flex, PanAway, Raven, Relieve It, Thieves

Supplements & Products:
Essentialzymes-4, ImmuPro, Inner Defense, K&B Tincture, MightyZyme, Mineral Essence, MultiGreens, NingXia Red, Omega Blue, Ortho Ease Massage Oil, Ortho Sport Massage Oil, PD 80/20, Sulfurzyme, True Source

FORL
(See FELINE ODONTOCLASTIC RESORPTIVE LESION)

FUO
(See FEVER OF UNKNOWN ORIGIN)

GASTROINTESTINAL CONDITIONS
(See INFLAMMATORY BOWEL DISEASE)

GINGIVITIS
(See also DENTAL DISEASE, FELINE ODONTOCLASTIC RESORPTIVE LESIONS, STOMATITIS)

HAIRBALLS

Hairballs are not a normal occurrence in cats. As much as we have been lead to believe that this is an expected event, I have found that dietary changes, detoxification, and removal of household chemicals and toxins often eliminate the expulsion of hairballs. There may still be an occasional episode, but these should be few and far between, and mainly limited to very long haired cats.

FIRST LINE RECOMMENDATIONS:
DIET: Grain free or raw. Eliminate egg, corn, soy, wheat, and dairy. Some protein sources may need to be eliminated.
SUPPLEMENTS: Essentialzymes-4, MightyZyme, Allerzyme
LITTEROMA: Di-Gize
PETTING: Di-Gize

Single Oils:
Juniper, Lavender, Marjoram, Patchouli, Tarragon

Blends:
Di-Gize, Juva Cleanse, M-Grain

Supplements & Products:
Allerzyme, ComforTone, Detoxzyme, Essentialzymes-4, ICP, Life 5, MightyZyme, ParaFree

HCM – HYPERTROPHIC CARDIOMYOPATHY
(See HEART CONDITIONS)

HEART CONDITIONS

FIRST LINE RECOMMENDATIONS:
PETTING: Aroma Life up to once a day or as needed.
LITTEROMA: Aroma Life, Helichrysum
SUPPLEMENTS: Standard Process Feline Cardiac Support, NingXia Red, Omega Blue, Super B

Single Oils:
Goldenrod, Helichrysum, Ledum, Marjoram, Nutmeg, Ocotea, Orange, Patchouli, Spikenard, Wintergreen, Ylang Ylang

Blends:
Aroma Life, Juva Cleanse, Longevity, PanAway

Supplements & Products:
CardiaCare, Essentialzymes-4, MightyZyme, NingXia Red, Omega Blue, PD 80/20, Super B

HEART MURMUR
(See HEART CONDITIONS)

HERPES VIRUS
(See also VIRAL CONDITIONS)

FIRST LINE RECOMMENDATIONS:
SUPPLEMENTS: MultiGreens, NingXia Red, Omega Blue
KRDT: Modified with Mountain Savory in place of Oregano, and with 1-2 drops of Melissa, 4 drops of Hyssop, and 4 drops of Ravintsara added. Apply up to once a day.
PETTING: Hope, Geranium, Elemi
LITTEROMA: Raven, 3 Wise Men
WATER DIFFUSION: Hope, Raven, Eucalyptus Polybractea
TOPICAL: In severe situations Rose Ointment has been used in the eyes.

Single Oils:
Elemi, Eucalyptus Polybractea, Geranium, Helichrysum, Marjoram, Melaleuca Ericifolia, Melissa, Mountain Savory, Peppermint, Ravintsara, Rose, Sandalwood, Thyme

Blends:
Forgiveness, Hope, ImmuPower, Raven, Thieves, 3 Wise Men

Supplements & Products:
Essentialzymes-4, MightyZyme, Mineral Essence, MultiGreens, NingXia Red, Omega Blue, Thieves Household Cleaner

HIT BY CAR
(See also PAIN MANAGEMENT)

FIRST LINE RECOMMENDATIONS:
WATER DIFFUSION: For lung trauma Tent or Cage Diffuse with the following recipe: 3 drops Helichrysum, 2 drops Frankincense, 1 drop Cedarwood, 1 drop Copaiba.
ORAL: Helichrysum – see PAIN MANAGEMENT
PETTING: Lavender, Helichrysum, Myrrh
TOPICAL: Animal Scents Ointment to wounds as indicated.

Single Oils:
Cedarwood, Copaiba, Frankincense, Helichrysum, Lavender, Marjoram, Myrrh, Palo Santo

Blends:
Brain Power

Supplements & Products:
Animal Scents Ointment, ClaraDerm, LavaDerm Cooling Mist, Ortho Ease Massage Oil, Ortho Sport Massage Oil, NingXia Red, Sulfurzyme

HORNER'S SYNDROME

(See also NEUROLOGIC CONDITIONS)

FIRST LINE RECOMMENDATIONS:
KRDT: Modified with Helichrysum, Roman Chamomile, and RutaVaLa.
PETTING: Roman Chamomile, Helichrysum
LITTEROMA: Laurus Nobilis
SUPPLEMENTS: NingXia Red, Omega Blue

Single Oils:
Chamomile (Roman), Elemi, Helichrysum, Juniper, Laurus Nobilis

Blends:
Brain Power, RutaVaLa

Supplements & Products:
MightyZyme, MultiGreens, NingXia Red, Omega Blue, Sulfurzyme, Super B

HYPERESTHESIA

(See also ARTHRITIS, NEUROLOGIC CONDITIONS, PAIN MANAGEMENT)

Hyperesthesia is the over-sensitivity of a cat to touch. This is generally associated with pain, however it can be hard to determine the exact cause. Supporting multiple levels of nutrition, detoxification, and pain control is suggested. See the other condition listings for further recommendations.

FIRST LINE RECOMMENDATIONS:
KRDT: Modified with Helichrysum, Copaiba, and Frankincense. Apply as needed.
SUPPLEMENTS: Sulfurzyme, BLM Capsules, MightyZyme

Single Oils:
Copaiba, Helichrysum, Wintergreen, Ylang Ylang

Blends:
Aroma Life, Aroma Siez, Juva Cleanse, Juva Flex, M-Grain, PanAway, Relieve It

Supplements & Products:
BLM Capsules, MightyZyme, MultiGreens, NingXia Red, Omega Blue, Ortho Ease Massage Oil, Ortho Sport Massage Oil, PD 80/20, Sulfurzyme, Super B

HYPERTENSION
(See also KIDNEY DISEASE)

FIRST LINE RECOMMENDATIONS:
PETTING: Aroma Life up to daily or more.
LITTEROMA: Aroma Life, Ylang Ylang, Lavender
SUPPLEMENTS: NingXia Red, Omega Blue

Single Oils:
Goldenrod, Helichrysum, Lavender, Lemon, Marjoram, Melaleuca Alternifolia, Melissa, Nutmeg, Ocotea, Orange, Patchouli, Rose, Tansy (Idaho), Wintergreen, Ylang Ylang

Blends:
Aroma Life, Gentle Baby, Hope, Juva Cleanse, Juva Flex, M-Grain, Stress Away

Supplements & Products:
Essentialzymes-4, MightyZyme, MultiGreens, NingXia Red, Omega Blue, Super B

HYPERTHYROIDISM

FIRST LINE RECOMMENDATIONS:
LITTEROMA: Myrrh, EndoFlex
PETTING: Myrrh, EndoFlex, Juva Cleanse
SUPPLEMENTS: Standard Process Feline Hepatic Support, NingXia Red, Omega Blue, Sulfurzyme

Single Oils:
Myrrh

Blends:
EndoFlex, GLF, Juva Cleanse, Juva Flex

Supplements & Products:
Essentialzymes-4, JuvaTone, MightyZyme, NingXia Red, Omega Blue, PD 80/20, Sulfurzyme, Thieves Household Cleaner

HYPERTROPHIC CARDIOMYOPATHY
(See HEART CONDITIONS)

IBD
(See INFLAMMATORY BOWEL DISEASE)

INNAPROPRIATE ELIMINATION
(See also BEHAVIORAL CONDITIONS, FLUTD, KIDNEY DISEASE, URINARY CONDITIONS)

Cats may urinate or defecate outside of their litter box for a number of reasons. It is important to have a thorough evaluation with a veterinarian to rule out medical causes. Common things that are helpful include getting a brand new litter box, changing styles of litter boxes, adding additional litter boxes, changing locations of litter boxes, and making sure that other animals are not ambushing the elimination event. Most commonly there is some sort of underlying issue that can be found. Even though we may desire to have the litter box "out of sight" within our basement, our cat with arthritis may have a hard time getting to that location. Or, a cat just may decide they do not like our chosen bathroom location, so they will create their own. Daily cleaning of the litter box (or more) is mandatory, as well as providing one litter box for each cat in the household, plus one additional litter box for good measure.

FIRST LINE RECOMMENDATIONS:
WATER DIFFUSION: Acceptance, Harmony
CLEANING: Thieves Household Cleaner with additional Purification for odor elimination

WATER MISTING: Odor Eliminating Recipe to be sprayed on household areas (not on the cat). 27 drops Purification, 13 drops Lemongrass, 7 drops Orange, 7 drops Peppermint into 4 ounces (120 mL) of distilled water. Shake well and mist areas of concern. Test an area of carpet or fabric prior to treatment with the solution.

Single Oils:
Valerian, Vetiver, Ylang Ylang

Blends:
Acceptance, Di-Gize, Dragon Time, Harmony, Hope, Lady Sclareol, Mister, Purification, SclarEssence

Supplements & Products:
Life 5, MightyZyme, NingXia Red, Omega Blue, ParaFree, Thieves Household Cleaner

INFLAMMATORY BOWEL DISEASE
(See also DIARRHEA)

FIRST LINE RECOMMENDATIONS:
KRDT: Modified with Copaiba, Di-Gize, and Helichrysum; apply up to once a day or as needed.
INGESTION: Copaiba in foods if possible, and needed. In severe situations or where bacterial infection is present, oral capsules of Thieves may be indicated.
SUPPLEMENTS: Detoxzyme, MightyZyme

Single Oils:
Copaiba, Helichrysum, Lemon, Myrrh, Nutmeg, Ocotea, Pine, Spruce, Tarragon, Ylang Ylang

Blends:
Di-Gize, GLF, Juva Cleanse, Thieves

Supplements & Products:
ComforTone, Detoxzyme, Essentialzymes-4, ICP, Life 5, MightyZyme, NingXia Red, Omega Blue, ParaFree, PD 80/20, Sulfurzyme, Super B, Thieves Fresh Essence Mouthwash

KIDNEY DISEASE

FIRST LINE RECOMMENDATIONS:
SUPPLEMENTS: K&B Tincture, MultiGreens
PETTING: Juniper, Grapefruit
LITTEROMA: Helichrysum, GLF, Juva Cleanse

Single Oils:
Grapefruit, Helichrysum, Juniper, Marjoram, Tsuga

Blends:
Citrus Fresh, GLF, Juva Cleanse

Supplements & Products:
K&B Tincture, MightyZyme, MultiGreens, NingXia Red, Omega Blue, Sulfurzyme, Thieves Household Cleaner

LIMPING KITTEN SYNDROME
(See also PAIN MANAGEMENT, VACCINATION DETOXIFICATION)

FIRST LINE RECOMMENDATIONS:
ORAL: Follow suggestions in Pain Management if needed.
KRDT: Modified with Tsuga, Myrrh, and Copaiba; applied up to twice a day or as indicated.
SUPPLEMENTS: NingXia Red, BLM Capsules, Sulfurzyme
PETTING: Ortho Ease or Ortho Sport Massage Oil, Aroma Siez

Single Oils:
Copaiba, Frankincense, Helichrysum, Lavender, Marjoram, Melissa, Mountain Savory, Myrrh, Palo Santo, Pine, Spikenard, Spruce, Tansy (Blue), Thyme, Tsuga, Wintergreen

Blends:
Aroma Siez, GLF, Hope, ImmuPower, Juva Cleanse, Juva Flex, M-Grain, PanAway, Relieve It, Thieves

Supplements & Products:
BLM Capsules, JuvaPower, JuvaSpice, JuvaTone, K&B Tincture, MightyZyme, MultiGreens, NingXia Red, Omega Blue, Ortho Ease Massage Oil, Ortho Sport Massage Oil, PD 80/20, Sulfurzyme, Thieves Household Cleaner

LIVER DISEASE

FIRST LINE RECOMMENDATIONS:
SUPPLEMENTS: Super B, Detoxzyme, MightyZyme, NingXia Red
PETTING: Helichrysum, Ledum, GLF
ORAL: Helichrysum when indicated, and for severe Liver Failure.
LITTEROMA: GLF, Juva Cleanse, Juva Flex
KRDT: Modified with Ledum, Helichrysum, and Grapefruit.

Single Oils:
Geranium, Goldenrod, Grapefruit, Helichrysum, Juniper, Ledum, Myrrh, Myrtle, Nutmeg, Rosemary, Sage, Spearmint, Tangerine

Blends:
Citrus Fresh, GLF, Juva Cleanse, Juva Flex

Supplements & Products:
Detoxzyme, JuvaPower, JuvaSpice, JuvaTone, MightyZyme, MultiGreens, NingXia Red, Omega Blue, Super B, Thieves Household Cleaner

LYMPHOCYTIC PLASMACYTIC STOMATITIS/GINGIVITIS
(See STOMATITIS)

NEUROLOGIC CONDITIONS

FIRST LINE RECOMMENDATIONS:
ADVANCED TECHNIQUES: Neuro Auricular Techniques can be applied with oils such as with RutaVaLa, Valor, Helichrysum, Copaiba, Roman Chamomile, and Laurus Nobilis.
PETTING: With any selected oil.
KRDT: Modified with Helichrysum, Roman Chamomile, and RutaVaLa.
LITTEROMA: Laurus Nobilis, Roman Chamomile

SUPPLEMENTS: NingXia Red, Omega Blue, MultiGreens

Single Oils:
Chamomile (Roman), Frankincense, Helichrysum, Juniper, Laurus Nobilis, Marjoram, Palo Santo

Blends:
Brain Power, Juva Cleanse, Juva Flex, M-Grain, RutaVaLa, Valor

Supplements & Products:
MightyZyme, Mineral Essence, MultiGreens, NingXia Red, Omega Blue, PD 80/20, Sulfurzyme, Super B

PAIN MANAGEMENT

Pain is an important item to address. The presence of pain is not only uncomfortable for an animal, but it will actually suppress the immune system and inhibit healing. All of the recommendations can be used alongside of traditional medications when they are being used. Careful monitoring and care with a veterinarian is recommended to make sure that adequate control of pain is always met.

FIRST LINE RECOMMENDATIONS:
ORAL: 1 drop of Helichrysum dripped into the mouth, up to every 20 minutes or as needed. For more severe or unresponsive pain; Myrrh and Copaiba are often diluted (1 drop per 10 drops of V-6) and 1 drop or more of these solutions are added to 1 drop of Helichrysum. This is generally given by capsule. Administration of any oil directly into the mouth, usually results in salivation.
KRDT: Modified by adding Copaiba, Myrrh, Helichrysum.
PETTING: Copaiba, Helichrysum, Myrrh
LITTEROMA: Copaiba, Lavender
SUPPLEMENTS: Sulfurzyme

Single Oils:
Copaiba, Helichrysum, Lavender, Marjoram, Myrrh, Palo Santo, Tansy (Blue), Wintergreen

Blends:
M-Grain, PanAway, Relieve It

Supplements & Products:
BLM Capsules, NingXia Red, Omega Blue, Ortho Ease Massage Oil, Ortho Sport Massage Oil, Sulfurzyme

PANCREATITIS

FIRST LINE RECOMMENDATIONS:
PETTING: Copaiba, Di-Gize
KRDT: Modified with Copaiba, Ocotea, and Di-Gize; applied up to once a day as needed.
SUPPLEMENTS: When tolerated; Detoxzyme, MightyZyme

Single Oils:
Copaiba, Geranium, Helichrysum, Lemon, Ocotea, Patchouli, Peppermint, Spearmint, Pine, Spruce, Tarragon, Wintergreen

Blends:
Citrus Fresh, Di-Gize, GLF, Juva Cleanse, Juva Flex, M-Grain, PanAway

Supplements & Products:
Detoxzyme, Essentialzyme, Essentialzymes-4, ICP, Life 5, MightyZyme, NingXia Red, Omega Blue, Sulfurzyme, Super B

PARASITES - INTERNAL
(See DEWORMING)

PARVO VIRUS - FELINE
(See VIRAL CONDITIONS)

PILLOW PAW
(See AUTOIMMUNE CONDITIONS)

PLASMA CELL PODODERMATITIS
(See AUTOIMMUNE CONDITIONS)

PREGNANCY & DELIVERY

We have had many litters of kittens delivered in our home, and most of them directly next to a water-based diffuser. Although I was very cautious at first, and attempted to not have my Queen near essential oils, she in fact, decided to set up her "nest" right where a diffuser of Peace & Calming consistently ran. We trusted her instincts, and have never regretted her decision to create what we term "oil babies." The continual diffusion of any essential oil selection, created wonderfully healthy kittens and reduced any goopy eyes we may have seen in previous litters.

Prior to birthing, Gentle Baby is diffused almost daily. During birthing, Frankincense and Gentle Baby are top favorites, generally diffused, but can also be applied to the Queen via Petting. After delivery, each of our kittens is anointed with Frankincense, both in a Petting Technique (almost completely absorbed into our hands), as well as applied neat and directly to their umbilical cord. Myrrh can also be applied neat to the umbilical cord after delivery. We have applied oils to kittens who were still wet from delivery, and as rescue kittens, we saw significant improvements in health and vitality for those kittens who received oils.

If there are signs of extreme stress or dystocia (difficulty delivering), Petting or Diffusing Lavender has a soothing effect. We generally do not use Lavender extensively during normal delivery, as it is quite relaxing. NingXia Red can be used to keep up energy and stamina during birth for cats who take it easily. Petting with Myrrh, Gentle Baby, and/or Frankincense is also suggested while in the process of seeking medical attention for dystocia.

FIRST LINE RECOMMENDATIONS:
 WATER DIFFUSION: Frankincense, Gentle Baby
 LITTEROMA: Myrrh, Gentle Baby
 SUPPLEMENTS: NingXia Red, Omega Blue, Essentialzymes-4, MultiGreens
 PETTING: Gentle Baby, Frankincense

Single Oils:
 Chamomile (Roman), Frankincense, Lavender, Myrrh, Palo Santo

Blends:
Gentle Baby, M-Grain

Supplements & Products:
Essentialzymes-4, MultiGreens, NingXia Red, Omega Blue, ParaFree, Sulfurzyme, Thieves Household Cleaner

QUEENING
(See PREGNANCY & DELIVERY)

RESORPTIVE LESIONS
(See FELINE ODONTOCLASTIC RESORPTIVE LESIONS)

RESPIRATORY CONDITIONS
(See ASTHMA, UPPER RESPIRATORY INFECTION)

RINGWORM

Ringworm is a fungal condition of the skin that is contagious to humans. Some Ringworm infections can be quite resistant to treatment, and rotation of different essential oils is suggested, especially if very little results are noted after a week of application. Making "super-charged" Kitty Raindrop Technique Solutions, each with a different combination of antifungal additions, is a great way to treat not only the cat but the lesions themselves. Good health is critical in clearing the infection, and supplements should always be provided.

FIRST LINE RECOMMENDATIONS:
KRDT: Modified by adding Lavender, Ocotea, Melaleuca Alternifolia, and Thieves. Apply at least weekly, and often daily. Application to the site of Ringworm is suggested up to multiple times a day, when located in a position that can be treated topically.
TOPICAL: Lavender neat to the lesion, at least once a day.
WATER DIFFUSION: Aid in disinfecting the environment by continually diffusing antifungal essential oils. Cats can be tented with Lavender or Thieves to permeate the fur as well, this is

especially helpful for extensive lesions on the face which are hard to access.
PETTING: With Lavender, Geranium, Ocotea, Ortho Ease Massage Oil, or KRDT Solution at least once a day.
BATHING: Bathing in Thieves Household Cleaner at least weekly is suggested.
CLEANING: Clean all areas frequently and thoroughly with Thieves Household Cleaner. Disinfect hands immediately after handling with Thieves Waterless Purifier.

Single Oils:
Eucalyptus Radiata, Geranium, Lavender, Lemongrass, Marjoram, Melaleuca Alternifolia, Melaleuca Ericifolia, Mountain Savory, Myrrh, Ocotea, Oregano, Palo Santo, Thyme

Blends:
Australian Blue, Melrose, Purification, R.C., Thieves

Supplements & Products:
Animal Scents Ointment, NingXia Red, Omega Blue, Ortho Ease Massage Oil, Ortho Sport Massage Oil, Thieves Household Cleaner

ROUNDWORM
(See DEWORMING)

SADDLE THROMBUS

See also PAIN MANAGEMENT for suggestions on how to deal with this painful condition. A Saddle Thrombus is a blood clot, which is generally located in the pelvic area of a cat, and can result in paralysis and pain of one or both back legs. Other areas of the body can also be affected. This disorder generally carries a very poor prognosis traditionally, and aggressive holistic treatments are necessary. This is one condition where "cat friendly" methods are disregarded, and many application techniques are layered together.

FIRST LINE RECOMMENDATIONS:
ORAL: Cistus, Helichrysum – for the blood clot. Starting with 1 drop given multiple times a day, increasing amounts given can occur quite aggressively when needed. It is important to closely

work with a veterinarian who can help determine if beneficial effects are being noted (return of pulses.)

ORAL: If anticoagulant actions are desired, generally Thieves will be used via capsule administration. Up to 5 drops twice a day (or to effect) may be given, as we are trying to achieve anticoagulant activity. This is reserved for critical cases, however most of these cases qualify.

TOPICAL: Cistus, Helichrysum neat to the site of the clot

KRDT: Modified by adding Cypress, Cistus, Helichrysum, and Copaiba; applied up to twice a day as indicated.

SUPPLEMENTS: High doses of Omega Blue is suggested. Up to 3 or 4 capsules per day for critical situations. High doses of digestive enzymes are also suggested, as they are needed to break down the blood clot that is present. Up to 3 or 4 capsules or tablets per day is suggested. MightyZyme is recommended.

Single Oils:
Cistus, Cypress, Geranium, Helichrysum, Hyssop, Laurus Nobilis, Lavender, Marjoram, Nutmeg, Orange, Wintergreen

Blends:
Aroma Life, Juva Cleanse, Juva Flex, Longevity, M-Grain, PanAway

Supplements & Products:
Essentialzymes-4, MightyZyme, NingXia Red, Omega Blue

SARCOMA – VACCINE INDUCED
(See also CANCER)

As this form of cancer is caused from vaccination, both following the recommendations for Cancer as well as for Vaccination Detoxification is important. These tumors tend to be very aggressive, and unfortunately surgical removal tends to result in a more aggressive and faster regrowth. Some specific recommendations are made specifically for this tumor, due to its particularly aggressive nature.

FIRST LINE RECOMMENDATIONS:
KRDT: Modify by adding Sandalwood, Frankincense, and Hyssop. Apply up to twice a day, and onto the tumor site as well.

TOPICAL: An antitumoral "Raindrop Solution" can be created with 7-10 of the suggested singles or blends. Add 4 drops of each to 30 mL of V-6, alternate this solution with the KRDT and apply in a similar fashion, as well as to the tumor.

Single Oils:
Balsam Fir (Idaho), Frankincense, Grapefruit, Helichrysum, Hyssop, Lemon, Melissa, Orange, Palo Santo, Ravintsara, Sandalwood, Tangerine

Blends:
Citrus Fresh, Hope, ImmuPower, 3 Wise Men

Supplements & Products:
Essentialzyme, Essentialzymes-4, ImmuPro, MightyZyme, Mineral Essence, MultiGreens, NingXia Red, Omega Blue

SEIZURES

(See also NEUROLOGIC CONDITIONS, and SEIZURES in CANINE CONDITIONS)

For Cats, also follow the recommendations made for Seizures in Canine Conditions, using them in the cat suggested ways. For some cats, performing a Vaccination Detoxification or addressing other forms of illness may be necessary. All recommendations can be used with other medications. Cats are not as commonly affected with Epilepsy, so other causes of seizures such as trauma, toxins, viral infections, or other medical concerns should be fully investigated with a veterinarian.

FIRST LINE RECOMMENDATIONS:
SUPPLEMENTS: NingXia Red, Omega Blue, Detoxzyme, MightyZyme, MultiGreens
KRDT: Modified with Idaho Balsam Fir, Frankincense, and Copaiba.
WATER DIFFUSION: Frankincense, Idaho Balsam Fir, Jasmine
LITTEROMA: Valerian, Roman Chamomile, Lavender
PETTING: Lavender, Valerian, RutaVaLa

ORAL: During a prolonged seizure, 1 drop of Lavender, Roman Chamomile, or Valerian can be dripped into the cheek area of the mouth. This is generally only utilized in critical situations, as the cat may foam at the mouth, and this is not ideal during a seizure.

SQUAMOUS CELL CARCINOMA

(See also CANCER)

Squamous Cell Carcinoma is unfortunately common, aggressive, and very difficult to treat. It is common within the mouth of cats, and is often not found until it is in the later stages. Very aggressive and layered approaches must be taken with this form of cancer. Incorporating many holistic methods and modalities (such as Acupuncture or Herbals) is encouraged.

FIRST LINE RECOMMENDATIONS:

Follow all of the suggestions within CANCER. Utilizing every supplement and lifestyle change, as well as multiple application methods of essential oils, is strongly recommended.

INGESTION: For this cancer, oral use of essential oils within capsules may be necessary. Start with 1 drop, and gradually increase the amounts given based on responses. There has been no maximum amount determined, and it has purely been based on what the budget will allow and what the cat will tolerate.

ORAL: Dripping oils directly into the mouth may be helpful to coat oral tumors. Helichrysum and Frankincense are suggested.

Single Oils:
Copaiba, Frankincense, Grapefruit, Helichrysum, Lemon, Melissa, Orange, Palo Santo, Sandalwood, Tangerine

Blends:
3 Wise Men, Citrus Fresh, ImmuPower, Thieves

Supplements & Products:
Essentialzyme, Essentialzymes-4, ImmuPro, MightyZyme, MultiGreens, NingXia Red, Omega Blue

STOMATITIS

(See also FELINE ODONTOCLASTIC RESORPTIVE LESIONS)

Stomatitis is a particularly horrible inflammation of the mouth, which is usually also complicated by bacterial infection. Treatment with traditional antibiotics is often helpful, however never addresses the underlying cause or healing needed by the cat. Change in diet and the addition of nutritional supplements are very important. Some cats will not groom properly due to this painful condition, however if they do, residual essential oils applied via Petting are very beneficial to the mouth. Also see the Pain Management recommendations for suggestions.

FIRST LINE RECOMMENDATIONS:
KRDT: Modified with Copaiba, Myrrh, and Laurus Nobilis; apply up to once a day or as needed.
PETTING: Copaiba, Laurus Nobilis, or Myrrh
ORAL: Raw Organic Coconut oil can be fed or rubbed into the mouth. Small amounts of essential oils can be slowly added if the cat will accept them.
DRINKING WATER: Thieves Fresh Essence Mouthwash
SUPPLEMENTS: NingXia Red, Omega Blue, Sulfurzyme, MultiGreens, MightyZyme

Single Oils:
Copaiba, Helichrysum, Laurus Nobilis, Lemon, Melaleuca Alternifolia, Melissa, Myrrh, Spruce, Thyme

Blends:
Juva Cleanse, Juva Flex, Melrose, Thieves

Supplements & Products:
Essentialzymes-4, Inner Defense, MightyZyme, Mineral Essence, MultiGreens, NingXia Red, Omega Blue, PD 80/20, Power Meal, Stevia Extract, Sulfurzyme, Thieves Dentarome Toothpaste, Thieves Fresh Essence Mouthwash, True Source

TAPEWORM
(See DEWORMING)

FELINE CONDITIONS

THROMBOCYTOPENIA
(See AUTOIMMUNE CONDITIONS)

TOOTH LESIONS
(See FELINE ODONTOCLASTIC RESORPTIVE LESIONS)

TOXOPLASMOSIS

FIRST LINE RECOMMENDATIONS:
WATER DIFFUSION: Thieves
KRDT: Modified by adding Hyssop, Patchouli, and ImmuPower.
ORAL: Inner Defense, or Thieves, Oregano, and Thyme. See descriptions for more information.
PETTING: Juva Cleanse
LITTEROMA: Juniper, Hyssop

Single Oils:
Hyssop, Juniper, Lemon, Mountain Savory, Oregano, Patchouli, Tarragon, Thyme

Blends:
Di-Gize, ImmuPower, Juva Cleanse, Thieves

Supplements & Products:
Essentialzymes-4, Inner Defense, MightyZyme, Mineral Essence, MultiGreens, NingXia Red, Omega Blue, ParaFree, Thieves Fresh Essence Mouthwash, Thieves Household Cleaner, True Source

TRITRICHOMONAS FOETUS
(See also DIARRHEA)

Tritrichomonas is a flagellated protozoan parasite which can create severe and long term diarrhea in cats. The disease is hard to diagnose, and often is overlooked.

FIRST LINE RECOMMENDATIONS:
SUPPLEMENTS: ICP, Inner Defense, Life 5
KRDT: Modified with ImmuPower, Di-Gize, and Ocotea.
LITTEROMA: Purification
DRINKING WATER: Thieves Fresh Essence Mouthwash

Single Oils:
Lemon, Melaleuca Alternifolia, Mountain Savory, Ocotea, Oregano, Tarragon, Thyme, Vetiver, Ylang Ylang

Blends:
Di-Gize, Egyptian Gold, ImmuPower, Juva Cleanse, Juva Flex, Melrose, Purification, Thieves

Supplements & Products:
ComforTone, Detoxzyme, Essentialzymes-4, ICP, Inner Defense, Life 5, MightyZyme, Mineral Essence, MultiGreens, ParaFree, Super B, Thieves Fresh Essence Mouthwash, Thieves Household Cleaner, True Source

UPPER RESPIRATORY INFECTION

Upper Respiratory Infections are often chronic in nature, and can seem to never go away. This is always due to nutritional deficiency, as once a cat receives the nourishment they are lacking, the infections go away and stay away. The nutritional deficiency is not always about what diet is being fed currently. It is my opinion that many felines are born in a deficient state, not only in nutrition but in digestive enzymes. No matter which diet you select, you will need to supplement your cat with additional items to make up for lost time. Since generations of cats have been born and raised on deficient, processed diets – their shorter generation cycle reveals their chronic deficiency in the form of disease.

FIRST LINE RECOMMENDATIONS:
WATER DIFFUSION: Via caging or tenting, with 3-4 drops of Thieves or Purification, and 1 drop of Eucalyptus Blue. Diffuse for 20 minutes, 3-4 times a day.
SUPPLEMENTS: MultiGreens, NingXia Red
PETTING: With any suggested oil.
KRDT: Modified with ImmuPower, R.C., Copaiba.

Single Oils:
Copaiba, Eucalyptus Blue, Eucalyptus Globulus, Eucalyptus Radiata, Hyssop, Laurus Nobilis, Lavender, Lemon, Lemongrass, Marjoram, Melaleuca Alternifolia, Melissa, Mountain Savory, Myrtle, Oregano, Palo Santo, Pine, Ravintsara, Rosemary, Spruce, Thyme, Tsuga

Blends:
Breathe Again Roll-On, Egyptian Gold, Hope, ImmuPower, M-Grain, Melrose, Purification, Raven, R.C., Thieves

Supplements & Products:
Essentialzymes-4, Inner Defense, MightyZyme, Mineral Essence, MultiGreens, NingXia Red, Omega Blue, Thieves Household Cleaner, True Source

URI – UPPER RESPIRATORY INFECTION
(See UPPER RESPIRATORY INFECTION)

URINARY CONDITIONS

FIRST LINE RECOMMENDATIONS:
SUPPLEMENTS: K&B Tincture
PETTING: Laurus Nobilis, Juniper, Geranium
ORAL: Thieves and Oregano combined into a capsule. See Inner Defense for more information on its use in bladder infections.
KRDT: Modified by adding R.C., Copaiba, and Juniper. This solution may also be applied over the bladder area in a Petting fashion.

Single Oils:
Eucalyptus Polybractea, Geranium, Goldenrod, Grapefruit, Juniper, Laurus Nobilis, Ledum, Lemon, Lemongrass, Pine, Spruce, Tarragon, Tsuga, Vetiver

Blends:
Thieves

Supplements & Products:
Essentialzymes-4, Inner Defense, K&B Tincture, MightyZyme, NingXia Red, Omega Blue, Sulfurzyme

ANIMAL DESK REFERENCE: FELINE

URINATING IN THE HOUSE
(See also FLUTD, INAPPROPRIATE ELIMINATION, URINARY CONDITIONS)

UTI – URINARY TRACT INFECTION
(See URINARY CONDITIONS)

VACCINATION DETOXIFICATION

Vaccinations can cause many health concerns and have even been linked with the formation of cancerous tumors (Sarcomas.) It is likely that any animal can benefit from the described cleansing cycle, whether they have been vaccinated or not. Even asymptomatic animals will benefit from detoxification from past vaccinations. In animals experiencing symptoms such as thyroid imbalance, allergies, asthma, autoimmune disorders, or other chronic illnesses; detoxification from previous vaccines becomes much more critical for healing to occur.

FIRST LINE RECOMMENDATIONS:
KRDT: Modified by adding Tsuga, Juva Cleanse, and Helichrysum. Apply once a week for 3 months. Apply more frequently if symptoms require it.
SUPPLEMENTS: Rehemogen, Omega Blue, NingXia Red, Detoxzyme
PETTING: Juva Cleanse
LITTEROMA: German Chamomile, Roman Chamomile, Juva Cleanse

Single Oils:
Chamomile (German), Chamomile (Roman), Geranium, Grapefruit, Helichrysum, Hyssop, Juniper, Ledum, Lemon, Mountain Savory, Tsuga

Blends:
Brain Power, Citrus Fresh, GLF, Juva Cleanse, Juva Flex

Supplements & Products:
Detoxzyme, Essentialzymes-4, JuvaPower, JuvaSpice, JuvaTone, K&B Tincture, MightyZyme, MultiGreens, NingXia Red, Omega Blue, Rehemogen, Sulfurzyme, True Source

VACCINOSIS
(See VACCINATION DETOXIFICATION)

VIRAL CONDITIONS

There are many viral conditions in cats, and thankfully, all of the antiviral essential oils will benefit each condition. There are specific oils that may target Herpes Virus more so than another virus, but thankfully, when providing the body with multiple tools for healing, many benefits are seen. Even when only diffusion of essential oils is provided, we have seen a great reduction in viral infections and transmission of disease where multiple cats are exposed to each other.

FIRST LINE RECOMMENDATIONS:
SUPPLEMENTS: MultiGreens, NingXia Red, Omega Blue
KRDT: Modified with 1-2 drops of Melissa, 4 drops of Hyssop, and 4 drops of ImmuPower. Apply up to once a day.
PETTING: Hope, ImmuPower
LITTEROMA: Raven, 3 Wise Men
WATER DIFFUSION: Hope, Raven, Egyptian Gold on an open room basis, up to 24 hours a day. Tenting and Caging can also be performed, as described in Upper Respiratory Infections.

Single Oils:
Frankincense, Geranium, Helichrysum, Hyssop, Laurus Nobilis, Lemon, Melissa, Mountain Savory, Ravintsara, Sandalwood, Thyme

Blends:
Egyptian Gold, Forgiveness, Hope, ImmuPower, Kitty Raindrop Technique, Raven, Thieves, 3 Wise Men

Supplements & Products:
Essentialzymes-4, ImmuPro, MightyZyme, Mineral Essence, MultiGreens, NingXia Red, Omega Blue, Thieves Household Cleaner

VOMITING

(See also HAIRBALLS, PANCREATITIS)

Vomiting can have many causes, and it is important that they be thoroughly explored by a veterinarian. Once you have determined the cause of the vomiting, more exact remedies can be provided.

FIRST LINE RECOMMENDATIONS:
  PETTING: Di-Gize
  LITTEROMA: Di-Gize
  KRDT: Modify by adding Di-Gize.

Single Oils:
  Juniper, Lavender, Ledum, Lemon, Patchouli, Peppermint, Spearmint, Tarragon

Blends:
  Citrus Fresh, Di-Gize, GLF, Juva Cleanse, Thieves

Supplements & Products:
  Detoxzyme, Life 5, MightyZyme, ParaFree, Thieves Household Cleaner

CANINE RAINDROP TECHNIQUE

Raindrop Technique is one of the most powerful and helpful, broad spectrum application of oils. When in doubt, I will reach for a Raindrop Technique as a first line application for my patients. It is highly beneficial in many areas, due to the high number and variety of oils being applied. Basically, there may be a benefit for almost every condition within the Raindrop Technique.

For dogs – Raindrop application is fairly straight forward. The following will be generic guidelines, but the individual dog must always be considered when doing the application. Varying the amount of drops applied, based on the size of the dog is generally followed. For small dogs less than 20 pounds (9 kg), often only 2-3 drops each of undiluted Raindrop oil is used. For medium dogs 20-50 pounds (9-23 kg) 3-5 drops of each oil can be used. For large dogs over 50 pounds (23 kg), 6-8 drops of each oil can generally be applied. With any of the oils, do not worry if a few more drops are applied than you planned on, generally this is nothing to be concerned about. It is also common that drops may fall on the side of the dog, and not on the spinal area. This is a common occurrence as some dogs may lay down or move around. It is usually of no concern, but just monitor the area to make sure that additional V-6 is applied if needed.

The technique of applying a Raindrop is basically always the same. However, it is a pleasure to know, that you really can't do it wrong. As long as the fundamentals are in place, many variations of the technique are perfectly acceptable. For me, this is extremely helpful – as my dog patients often decide on how, when, where – and for how long - a Raindrop application will last. Some dogs are quite content to sit for hours being stroked and massaged, and love every minute of it. With other dogs, I am working on a moving target, and I am lucky if I get to stroke the dogs back at all.

If you are new to essential oils and the Raindrop Technique, or have a particularly sensitive or small dog, it is probably best to start out with pre-diluted oils for your first few applications; until you develop a comfort level with using essential oils. It would be perfectly fine to dilute the oils 50:50 or more, with V-6 prior to dripping on your dog's back. When I use the Raindrop Technique for a medical concern – I often choose to apply the oils neat (or undiluted.)

Here is the basic sequence that I follow when applying a Raindrop to a dog. This sequence will outline the neat, or undiluted, version that I use. If you use pre-diluted essential oils, you may not need to use the additional step of applying V-6. Remember, there are basic steps that are always followed – however, there is no right or wrong way to do it. If someone likes to apply one oil prior to another, this is fine. This is only my version that I have used in our animal hospital regularly. Do not fret if you have a different version, or learn another technique. I have found many versions of the Raindrop Technique presented for animals – they are all right, and they are all good. Please pick one that feels good to you.

These are the basic steps that are generally performed. The dog can be sitting, lying down, or standing. Whatever is comfortable for the dog and the human.

- Balance with Valor (optional). Apply between 1-3 drops of Valor to each hand. Place one hand over the shoulders and one over the rump area. You do not need to rub the oils in or rub your hands together. Just place your hands with the puddle of oils in your palm, directly onto the dog.
- With Oregano, drip the selected number of drops up the spine, from the tail to the base of the head. Hold the bottle about 3-6 inches above the back. Space the drops evenly if possible. Oregano is a "hot" oil, and can be very uncomfortable if gotten into the eyes or in contact with other sensitive areas. Be very aware of where this oil is applied.
- After each application of a Raindrop oil, you will stroke the oils into the spinal area with the back of your finger nails. Just drag your fingers up the center of the spine, in alternating 3 inch strokes. You will be brushing the fur backwards, towards the head. Do one hand, and then the other. Repeat this stroking, going from tail to head, three full times when possible. Basically, you are doing the same type of feather strokes that you would use in a human application.
- If the dog and time allows, I may add 6 inch strokes, 9 inch strokes, 12 inch strokes, side strokes, and even "angel wing" strokes into each application of an oil. Many times, multiple strokes are not possible as the dog is moving or we do not have enough time in our busy practice to sit and stroke each dog for 45 minutes. This is okay – do what is allowed.

- Next, Thyme will be applied in the same fashion as Oregano. Drip it on, and stroke it in. If possible, I try to stagger the location of the drops so that the Thyme is not landing in the exact location as the Oregano did. It is best if the skin does not receive each drop of essential oil in exactly the same location.
- After the Oregano and Thyme are applied and stroked in, V-6 is then applied along the spine. This step may not be necessary if you are using pre-diluted oils. Enough V-6 is applied to make a slightly greasy strip up the back. This oil is not applied in small drops, but rather in a streaky squirt of oil all the way up the spine. Massage this oil into the area, either with feather strokes or a basic massage. This acts to dilute the first two "hot" oils, and causes them to be absorbed a little slower. It will also tend to calm any skin "heat" that may be produced. Monitor the pet for discomfort or pinkness to the skin. Apply more V-6 as needed and dictated by the pet. Never wash your pet with water if the oils become uncomfortable. Dilute the area with more V-6 oil, as water will cause the spread the oils farther and drive them into more delicate tissues.
- After the V-6 is massaged in, the rest of the Raindrop oils (Basil, Cypress, Wintergreen, Marjoram, and Peppermint), can be applied in the same fashion as the Oregano and Thyme. Follow the modification guidelines for inserting or interchanging essential oils within the Raindrop Technique. If insertion of oils is desired, this is generally done between Wintergreen and Marjoram.
- Peppermint is applied last, as a driving oil. As Peppermint is a very "cool" oil, this amount may be reduced or omitted in cold weather or for small or sensitive dogs.
- Vita Flex is performed last, with your thumbs or your fingers – from the base of the tail to the top of the head. Repeat three times if possible.
- For a basic application of therapeutic oils you are now done! There are Raindrop Techniques for animals that also apply oils to the feet, or follow the spinal application with a wet, warm towel. Again, if you and your pet are so inclined, these can be great additions to the complete Raindrop experience.

CANINE CONDITIONS

ABSCESS

An abscess is a pus filled pocket generally located under the skin, however can be located anywhere within the body. Most abscesses contain bacteria of various sorts, although there are conditions in which sterile abscesses form. Abscesses can erupt very quickly and result in severe systemic illness including fever, lethargy, inappetance, and more.

FIRST RECOMMENDATIONS:

TOPICAL: Apply Thieves neat to the abscess head, up to twice a day or more. If the abscess is open and draining, diluted Thieves Household Cleaner can be used to clean and flush the abscess. Additional drops of essential oils may be added to the soap concentrate prior to diluting, for added strength.

SUPPLEMENTS: Give Inner Defense capsules orally as an antibiotic. Give NingXia Red and other supplements for support and healing.

RAINDROP TECHNIQUE: Can be administered for general immune support and anti-bacterial actions. Each Raindrop Oil can also be applied to very large abscesses during administration.

ORAL: 1 drop each of Thieves, Oregano, and Thyme per 25 pounds of dog can be given once or twice a day for antibacterial action. Do not use this option if Inner Defense is selected to be given. See also Pain Management for suggestions if indicated.

Single Oils:

Copaiba, Laurus Nobilis, Lavender, Lemongrass, Melaleuca Alternifolia, Mountain Savory, Oregano, Spikenard, Thyme

Blends:
Abundance, Egyptian Gold, Exodus II, Longevity, Purification, Thieves

Supplements & Products:
If oral antibiotics or essential oils have been given, rebuilding gut flora with Life 5 is recommended.

Animal Scents Ointment, Inner Defense, Life 5, Longevity, NingXia Red, Omega Blue, Sulfurzyme, Thieves Household Cleaner

ACNE
(See also ALLERGIES, HOT SPOTS, SKIN INFECTIONS, and FELINE CONDITIONS - ACNE)

ADDISON'S DISEASE
(aka HYPOADRENOCORTICISM, ADRENAL INSUFFICIENCY)

Addison's Disease is the under-activity of the adrenal gland, resulting in low levels of critical hormones. Symptoms include weakness and generalized, "crashing" due to electrolyte disorders. In critical situations, veterinary care is almost certainly needed – with IV electrolyte replacement via fluids. Steroid medications are also given in attempts to normalize the critical patient.

FIRST RECOMMENDATIONS:
SUPPLEMENTS: NingXia Red, Mineral Essence, Essentialzymes-4
RAINDROP TECHNIQUE: Modified by inserting Nutmeg, EndoFlex, and Frankincense inserted.
PETTING: EndoFlex

Single Oils:
Chamomile (German), Clove, Copaiba, Frankincense, Nutmeg, Pine, Spikenard, Spruce

Blends:
EndoFlex, Joy, Juva Cleanse, Longevity

Supplements & Products:

Detoxzyme, Essentialzyme, Essentialzymes-4, ImmuPro, Longevity Softgels, MightyZyme, Mineral Essence, MultiGreens, NingXia Red, Ningxia Wolfberries, Omega Blue, Sulfurzyme, True Source

ALLERGIES

(See also SKIN INFECTIONS)

Allergies are a complex problem, however many fundamental basics of holistic health will benefit the condition. There are definite, multi-factorial issues involved with allergies – and often a multi-layer approach is needed. Secondary skin infections must be detected and treated, or symptoms will continue to be seen, even if the allergies are improved. Diet is important to address, as well as liver health and cleansing.

FIRST LINE RECOMMENDATIONS:

RAINDROP TECHNIQUE: Up to once a day, as needed for comfort. Often the Raindrop Technique is used in place of steroids.
ORAL: Basil, Ocotea
SUPPLEMENTS: Essentialzymes-4, Allerzyme, Omega Blue, Sulfurzyme
CLEANING & BATHING: Thieves Household Cleaner
DIFFUSION: Thieves

Single Oils:

Basil, Clove, Lavender, Ledum, Melissa, Ocotea, Pine, Spruce, Tansy (Blue)

Blends:

GLF, Hope, ImmuPower, Juva Cleanse, Juva Flex, Longevity, R.C., Thieves

Supplements & Products:

Dietary supplementation in allergy conditions may be more important than anything else. Although the body can feel better from an application of essential oils, the body needs true resources in order to heal completely.

Allerzyme, Animal Scents Ointment, ClaraDerm, Detoxzyme, Digest + Cleanse, Essentialzymes-4, JuvaPower, JuvaSpice, JuvaTone, LavaDerm Cooling Mist, Life 5, Longevity Softgels, MightyZyme, MultiGreens, NingXia Red, Ningxia Wolfberries, Omega Blue, Sulfurzyme, Thieves Household Cleaner, True Source

ALOPECIA X

Alopecia X is a condition, mainly of hair loss, that is currently poorly understood. A direct cause or treatment has not been discovered. Melatonin has been recommended from many references as being a treatment option, but with variable results. The best answer for this condition is a complete holistic approach, to give the body the tools it needs to correct the "undiscovered" problems at hand.

FIRST LINE RECOMMENDATIONS:
SUPPLEMENTS: ImmuPro, Sleep Essence – for Melatonin sources. Ultra Young + Oral Spray with DHEA. For basic holistic health: NingXia Red, Essentialzymes-4, Sulfurzyme, Omega Blue.
PETTING: As desired with suggested oils.
RAINDROP TECHNIQUE: Monthly for general health, adjust as indicated.
DIFFUSION: With any suggested oil.

Single Oils:
Sandalwood, Ylang Ylang

Blends:
3 Wise Men, Brain Power, Dragon Time, EndoFlex, Juva Cleanse, Juva Flex, Longevity, SclarEssence, 3 Wise Men

Supplements & Products:
Animal Scents Ointment, Digest + Cleanse, EndoGize, Essentialzymes-4, Estro, FemiGen, ImmuPro, JuvaPower, JuvaSpice, JuvaTone, Longevity Softgels, MightyZyme, Omega Blue, PD 80/20, Sleep Essence, Sulfurzyme, True Source, Ultra Young + Oral Spray with DHEA.

AMYLOIDOSIS
(See also COGNITIVE DYSFUNCTION, KIDNEY DISEASE)

Amyloidosis occurs when abnormal proteins are deposited within various body tissues. This can happen in other animals, such as cats and horses, and some breeds are more prone to this disease than others, and display hereditary and genetic tendencies. It is commonly found in the spleen and kidneys however the liver, brain, and other body tissues can be affected. Amyloid in the brain is a major factor in Cognitive Dysfunction of senior dogs, as well as Alzheimer's in humans. Inflammation appears to play a primary role in stimulating the deposition of this material, and providing holistic tools that are anti-inflammatory, should be an integral part to prevention and treatment. Enzymes are incredibly important to be supplemented, as the only way to break down these deposits, is with the enzymes within the body. High doses of enzymes, especially containing Protease, should be provided.

FIRST LINE RECOMMENDATIONS:
SUPPLEMENTS: Essentialzymes-4, Detoxzyme, Omega Blue, NingXia Red, Longevity Softgels
ORAL: Longevity, Copaiba
RAINDROP TECHNIQUE: At least monthly, or as indicated.
PETTING: With any oil suggested.
DRINKING WATER: Citrus Fresh

Single Oils:
Copaiba, Frankincense, Grapefruit, Juniper, Ledum

Blends:
Citrus Fresh, GLF, Juva Cleanse, Juva Flex, Longevity

Supplements & Products:
Allerzyme, Detoxzyme, Digest + Cleanse, Essentialzymes-4, JuvaTone, K&B Tincture, Longevity Softgels, MightyZyme, NingXia Red, Omega Blue, Sulfurzyme, True Source

ANAL GLANDS
(See also ABSCESS)

The need for routine Anal Gland expression is not normal. Often the act of expression actually causes inflammation and can drive bacteria into the gland, resulting in bacterial infection and possibly the formation of an abscess. Abnormal stools, either too soft or too hard, can cause the glands to not express adequately upon defecation. Addressing the diet, providing tools for health, and addressing other conditions such as allergies or skin infections is important.

FIRST LINE RECOMMENDATIONS:
RAINDROP TECHNIQUE: At least monthly, or as indicated.
WATER MISTING: Place 20 drops of Lavender, 10 drops of Copaiba, and 10 drops of Melaleuca Alternifolia in 4 ounces (120 mL) of distilled water and mist the anal area twice a day or as needed.
TOPICAL: Animal Scents Ointment, LavaDerm Cooling Mist
SUPPLEMENTS: Essentialzymes-4, Omega Blue, Sulfurzyme

Single Oils:
Helichrysum, Laurus Nobilis, Lavender, Lemon, Melaleuca Alternifolia, Mountain Savory, Oregano

Blends:
Melrose, Purification, Thieves

Supplements & Products:
Animal Scents Ointment, ClaraDerm, Essentialzymes-4, ICP, Inner Defense, LavaDerm Cooling Mist, Life 5, MightyZyme, Omega Blue, Sulfurzyme, Thieves Household Cleaner

ANAPLASMA
(See TICK BORNE DISEASE)

ANESTHESIA DETOXIFICATION
(See EQUINE CONDITIONS)

ANOREXIA

Anorexia is often used to describe poor or no eating by an animal. Many times it is accompanied by feelings of nausea or discomfort. There are many reasons for an animal to be anorexic, and an accurate veterinary diagnosis is important. These recommendations generally stimulate appetite and ease digestive concerns and nausea.

FIRST LINE RECOMMENDATIONS:
    PETTING: Di-Gize, Peppermint, or Patchouli
    ORAL: Ginger or Di-Gize for extreme nausea.
    DIFFUSION: Di-Gize

Single Oils:
    Ginger, Juniper, Laurus Nobilis, Lavender, Patchouli, Peppermint, Tarragon

Blends:
    Di-Gize, GLF, Juva Cleanse, Juva Flex

Supplements & Products:
    Detoxzyme, Digest + Cleanse, Life 5, MightyZyme, ParaFree, Power Meal

ANTIHISTAMINE-LIKE ACTIONS
   (See also STEROIDS - REPLACMENT)

Some essential oils can be used for their antihistamine type of actions. These suggestions can be used when an antihistamine would be called for.

FIRST LINE RECOMMENDATIONS:
    RAINDROP TECHNIQUE: As indicated for comfort.
    PETTING: Basil or Spruce
    ORAL: Melissa, Basil, Ocotea, or Vetiver

Single Oils:
    Basil, Lavender, Melissa, Ocotea, Pine, Spruce, Tansy (Blue), Vetiver

Blends:
   Hope, Thieves

Supplements & Products:
   Allerzyme, MultiGreens, Omega Blue, Sulfurzyme

ANXIETY
(See also BEHAVIORAL CONDITIONS)

Anxiety can be helped specifically through the supplementation of minerals and enzymes. Pack leadership and good training is the foundation of correction of all anxiety issues, but addressing physical needs are important as well.

FIRST LINE RECOMMENDATIONS:
   SUPPLEMENTS: Essentialzymes-4, MightyZyme, Mineral Essence
   DIFFUSION: Of any selected oil. See also the chapters Emotional Work with Oils and Emotional Use of Blends.
   PETTING: Valor, Believe

Single Oils:
   Frankincense, Grapefruit, Lavender, Lemon, Melissa, Ocotea, Orange, Petitgrain, Pine, Rose, Tangerine, Valerian, Vetiver, Ylang Ylang

Blends:
   Acceptance, Australian Blue, Believe, Christmas Spirit, Envision, Forgiveness, GLF, Hope, Juva Cleanse, Juva Flex, RutaVaLa, 3 Wise Men, Valor

Supplements & Products:
   Detoxzyme, Essentialzymes-4, JuvaTone, Life 5, Longevity Softgels, MightyVites, MightyZyme, Mineral Essence, MultiGreens, Omega Blue, ParaFree, Relaxation Massage Oil, Super B, True Source

ARTHRITIS

(See also PAIN MANAGEMENT)

This regimen has been used successfully in our veterinary practice to eliminate and replace the use of traditional NSAIDs.

FIRST LINE RECOMMENDATIONS:
ORAL: Copaiba
SUPPLEMENTS: NingXia Red, Essentialzymes-4, Omega Blue, BLM Capsules, Sulfurzyme
PETTING: Copaiba or other selected oils.

Single Oils:
Balsam Fir (Idaho), Copaiba, Frankincense, Helichrysum, Lavender, Lemongrass, Marjoram, Myrrh, Nutmeg, Palo Santo, Peppermint, Pine, Spruce, Tansy (Blue), Tansy (Idaho), Vetiver, Wintergreen

Blends:
Aroma Siez, Deep Relief Roll-On, GLF, Juva Cleanse, Juva Flex, Longevity, M-Grain, PanAway, Relieve It

Supplements & Products:
Animal Scents Ointment, BLM Capsules, Detoxzyme, Essentialzymes-4, JuvaPower, JuvaSpice, JuvaTone, Life 5, Longevity Softgels, MightyZyme, NingXia Red, Ningxia Wolfberries, Omega Blue, Ortho Ease Massage Oil, Ortho Sport Massage Oil, PD 80/20, Sulfurzyme, Regenolone Moisturizing Cream, True Source

ASCITES

(See also LIVER DISEASE)

Ascites is an accumulation of fluid within the abdomen, most commonly related to advanced liver or heart disease. Providing additional support to any body system that is involved, is recommended.

FIRST LINE RECOMMENDATIONS:
SUPPLEMENTS: NingXia Red, JuvaTone, K&B Tincture
ORAL: Grapefruit, Ledum, Helichrysum
PETTING: Any selected oil.

Single Oils:
Goldenrod, Grapefruit, Helichrysum, Juniper, Ledum, Lemon, Lemongrass, Marjoram, Melaleuca Alternifolia, Tangerine

Blends:
Aroma Life, GLF, Juva Cleanse, Juva Flex

Supplements & Products:
Detoxzyme, Digest + Cleanse, JuvaPower, JuvaSpice, JuvaTone, K&B Tincture, Longevity Softgels, MightyZyme, Omega Blue, True Source

ASPIRATION PNEUMONIA
(See COUGH, MEGAESOPHAGUS, RESPIRATORY INFECTIONS)

ATOPY
(See ALLERGIES)

AURAL HEMATOMA

An Aural Hematoma is a blood filled pocket on the ear flap of a dog. This can occur in cats and other animals as well, but is most commonly seen in canines. Often, there is an ear infection (see Ear Infections) that causes repeated shaking of the head and trauma to the ear. The cartilage of the ear separates, and is filled with blood. Other direct trauma to the ear can cause this condition as well. It is very important that any ear infections or other conditions are corrected for this problem to heal. Many veterinarian recommend surgical drainage of the ear, and some are even injecting them with steroids. Ears can become scarred and misshapen if the disorder is allowed to become chronic. If response is not noted to the following suggestions in approximately 2 weeks, veterinary treatment may be necessary.

FIRST LINE RECOMMENDATIONS:
TOPICAL: Helichrysum, Cistus, Cypress onto hematoma 2-3 times a day. Generally neat if tolerated. Effects can be amplified by applying Copaiba followed by Peppermint, after application of other oils.
SUPPLEMENTS: BLM Capsules, Sulfurzyme

Single Oils:
Cistus, Copaiba, Cypress, Geranium, Helichrysum, Lavender

Blends:
Aroma Life

Supplements & Products:
Animal Scents Ointment, BLM Capsules, Essentialzymes-4, MightyZyme, Sulfurzyme

AUTOIMMUNE CONDITIONS

FIRST LINE RECOMMENDATIONS:
SUPPLEMENTS: Sulfurzyme, NingXia Red, Omega Blue
RAINDROP TECHNIQUE: Modified by inserting ImmuPower, Frankincense, and Idaho Balsam Fir.
PETTING: ImmuPower

Single Oils:
Balsam Fir (Idaho), Copaiba, Frankincense, Helichrysum, Longevity, Tsuga

Blends:
ImmuPower

Supplements & Products:
Essentialzymes-4, Life 5, Longevity Softgels, MightyZyme, MultiGreens, NingXia Red, Ningxia Wolfberries, Omega Blue, PD 80/20, Sulfurzyme

BEHAVIORAL CONDITIONS
(See also ANXIETY)

FIRST LINE RECOMMENDATIONS:
PETTING: Valor, Believe
DIFFUSION: Peace & Calming
SUPPLEMENTS: MightyZyme, Mineral Essence, Omega Blue
RAINDROP TECHNIQUE – EMOTIONAL: See chapter on Emotional Use of Blends.

Single Oils:
Bergamot, Cedarwood, Chamomile (German), Chamomile (Roman), Geranium, Grapefruit, Lavender, Lemon, Marjoram, Melissa, Palo Santo, Patchouli, Pine, Rose, Rosemary, Spikenard, Spruce, Tangerine, Valerian, Vetiver, Ylang Ylang

Blends:
Believe, Brain Power, Dragon Time, EndoFlex, Forgiveness, Hope, Inner Child, Mister, Peace & Calming, RutaVaLa, SclarEssence, Tranquil Roll-On, Valor

Supplements & Products:
Essentialzymes-4, MightyZyme, Mineral Essence, MultiGreens, NingXia Red, Omega Blue, Relaxation Massage Oil, Super B

BELL'S PALSY
(See also NEUROLOGIC CONDITIONS)

FIRST LINE RECOMMENDATIONS:
PETTING: Helichrysum, especially near face.
ADVANCED TECHNIQUES: Neuro Auricular Technique, see chapter on Advanced Techniques.
SUPPLEMENTS: Super B, NingXia Red, Omega Blue

Single Oils:
Elemi, Helichrysum, Juniper, Laurus Nobilis

Blends:
Forgiveness, RutaVaLa

ANIMAL DESK REFERENCE: CANINE

Supplements & Products:
Essentialzymes-4, Longevity Softgels, MightyZyme, MultiGreens, Omega Blue, PD 80/20, Sulfurzyme, Super B

BENIGN PROSTATIC HYPERTROPHY (BPH)
(See PROSTATE CONDITIONS)

BENIGN TUMOR

FIRST LINE RECOMMENDATIONS:
TOPICAL: Apply neat Frankincense, Copaiba, and Peppermint to the tumor, generally in that order, up to twice a day based on response and tolerance.

Single Oils:
Frankincense, Grapefruit, Lavender, Lemon, Orange, Palo Santo, Sandalwood, Tangerine

Blends:
Citrus Fresh, Forgiveness, GLF, ImmuPower, 3 Wise Men

Supplements & Products:
Animal Scents Ointment, Essentialzyme, Longevity Softgels, MightyZyme, NingXia Red, Omega Blue

BILIOUS VOMITING

Bilious Vomiting is when a dog vomits due to having an empty stomach. There can be medical reasons behind this event, however it seems to be closely associated with an empty stomach or a delayed meal. Sometimes this issue has been eliminated by simply providing the dog with a late night snack. Providing holistic tools for normal digestive function is likely a better answer.

FIRST LINE RECOMMENDATIONS:
SUPPLEMENTS: MightyZyme
PETTING: Di-Gize
DRINKING WATER: Peppermint, Citrus Fresh

Single Oils:
Helichrysum, Juniper, Laurus Nobilis, Lemon, Marjoram, Melissa, Patchouli, Peppermint, Spearmint, Tangerine, Tarragon, Valerian

Blends:
Citrus Fresh, Di-Gize, GLF, Juva Cleanse, Juva Flex, M-Grain

Supplements & Products:
Detoxzyme, Digest + Cleanse, Essentialzymes-4, JuvaPower, JuvaSpice, JuvaTone, Life 5, MightyZyme, ParaFree, Power Meal, True Source

BLADDER INFECTION

FIRST LINE RECOMMENDATIONS:
SUPPLEMENT: Inner Defense, K&B Tincture

Single Oils:
Goldenrod, Grapefruit, Juniper, Laurus Nobilis, Ledum, Lemon, Lemongrass, Mountain Savory, Oregano, Pine, Tarragon, Thyme, Tsuga

Blends:
ImmuPower, Thieves

Supplements & Products:
Essentialzymes-4, Inner Defense, K&B Tincture, Longevity Softgels, MightyZyme, Omega Blue

BLADDER STONES
(See also BLADDER INFECTION, PAIN MANAGEMENT)

Bladder Stones should be evaluated by a veterinarian for type and cause. Some stones may require surgical removal. Dietary adjustments are important, and increased moisture intake through the diet as well as through drinking is recommended.

FIRST LINE RECOMMENDATIONS:
DRINKING WATER: Citrus Fresh
PETTING: Relieve It over the bladder area.
SUPPLEMENTS: K&B Tincture

Single Oils:
Goldenrod, Grapefruit, Juniper, Laurus Nobilis, Lavender, Ledum, Lemon, Myrrh, Spruce, Tsuga, Vetiver, Wintergreen

Blends:
Citrus Fresh, Deep Relief Roll-On, PanAway, Relieve It

Supplements & Products:
Essentialzymes-4, Inner Defense, K&B Tincture, Longevity Softgels, MightyZyme

BLASTOMYCOSIS
(See also RESPIRATORY INFECTION)

Blastomycosis is a severe fungal infection primarily of the lungs, but which can affect skin, eyes, and other tissues.

FIRST LINE RECOMMENDATIONS:
DIFFUSION: Thieves via tenting and caging, 3 or more times a day. Diffusion of any oil within an open room is suggested 24 hours a day.
ORAL: Inner Defense
SUPPLEMENTS: Longevity, Essentialzymes-4
RAINDROP TECHNIQUE: Modified by inserting R.C., Egyptian Gold, and ImmuPower. Apply up to once a day or as indicated.

Single Oils:
Laurus Nobilis, Lavender, Lemongrass, Marjoram, Melaleuca Alternifolia, Melaleuca Ericifolia, Mountain Savory, Ocotea, Oregano, Palo Santo, Peppermint, Rosemary, Spruce, Thyme

Blends:
Breathe Again Roll-On, Egyptian Gold, ImmuPower, M-Grain, Melrose, Purification, Raven, R.C., Thieves

Supplements & Products:
　　Detoxzyme, Essentialzymes-4, ImmuPro, Longevity Softgels, MightyZyme

BLOAT
　　(See GASTRODILITATION VOLVULUS)

BONE - BROKEN
　　(See also PAIN MANAGEMENT)

These oils will aid in healing time, inflammation, and alignment of the bone.

FIRST LINE RECOMMENDATIONS:
　　PETTING: Valor, Idaho Balsam Fir, Helichrysum near the fracture area as often as tolerated, generally 2-3 times a day for the first week, then less often later.
　　SUPPLEMENTS: BLM Capsules, Sulfurzyme

Single Oils:
　　Balsam Fir (Idaho), Copaiba, Helichrysum, Myrrh, Palo Santo, Pine, Spruce, Wintergreen

Blends:
　　Believe, Deep Relief Roll-On, PanAway, Relieve It

Supplements & Products:
　　Animal Scents Ointment, BLM Capsules, Omega Blue, Ortho Ease Massage Oil, Ortho Sport Massage Oil, Sulfurzyme

BONE - CANCER
　　(See CANCER - BONE)

BONE CONDITIONS

These suggestions support bone health in general. Any condition affecting a bone will benefit with these oils.

FIRST LINE RECOMMENDATIONS:
   PETTING: Any of the suggested oils.
   RAINDROP TECHNIQUE: With Idaho Balsam Fir, Palo Santo, and Copaiba inserted.
   SUPPLEMENTS: BLM Capsules

Single Oils:
   Balsam Fir (Idaho), Palo Santo, Pine, Spruce

Blends:
   Believe, Deep Relief Roll-On, PanAway, Relieve It

Supplements & Products:
   Animal Scents Ointment, BLM Capsules, Longevity Softgels, Omega Blue, Ortho Ease Massage Oil, Ortho Sport Massage Oil, Sulfurzyme

BRUCELLA CANIS

Brucella Canis, also called Brucellosis, causes abortions and reproductive concerns in breeding dogs. It is transmitted through ingestion of contaminated materials and sexual contact. Many dogs who contract this disease are sterilized or euthanized. Careful monitoring with a veterinarian is important if you attempt to clear the infection in an intact dog, as it is very difficult. Sterilization is recommended for many cases, where the spread of the disease is hard to prevent.

FIRST LINE RECOMMENDATIONS:
   RAINDROP TECHNIQUE: Modify by inserting Tsuga, Melaleuca Alternifolia, and ImmuPower. Rotation of the insertion of other recommended oils is suggested. Up to daily administration may be necessary in some cases.
   ORAL: Longevity
   SUPPLEMENTS: Inner Defense

Single Oils:
  Lemon, Melaleuca Alternifolia, Mountain Savory, Oregano, Thyme, Tsuga

Blends:
  Exodus II, ImmuPower, Longevity, Melrose, Thieves

Supplements & Products:
  Essentialzymes-4, ImmuPro, Inner Defense, Longevity Softgels, MightyZyme, MultiGreens

CALLUS

Elbows and pads of dogs sometimes produce excess skin, become bald or damages, or over grow with keratin or "corns." Some conditions are quite a normal occurrence for some dogs, however pressure sores and wounds may need veterinary attention. General skin care as well as liver and colon cleansing and support, will aid in the health and resilience of the skin.

FIRST LINE RECOMMENDATIONS:
  SUPPLEMENTS: Omega Blue, Sulfurzyme, MightyZyme
  TOPICAL: Animal Scents Ointment with additional oils mixed in.

Single Oils:
  Geranium, Helichrysum, Myrrh, Rose

Blends:
  GLF

Supplements & Products:
  Animal Scents Ointment, ClaraDerm, Essentialzymes-4, MightyZyme, Omega Blue, Rose Ointment, Sulfurzyme

CANCER

(See also MAST CELL TUMOR, CANCER in FELINE CONDITIONS)

There are many different kinds of cancer, and each type may have a different specific focus for essential oil recommendations. If certain oils are more indicated for specific types of Cancer, they are listed. However there is a basic foundation of items that must be met in order for an immune system to function to the fullest, and to give an animal the utmost possibility of clearing cancer. These recommendations apply to all animals. Please see the Feline Cancer section for further descriptions.

It is very important in conditions such as cancer, to incorporate as many layers of care as possible. This is one situation, where starting with small amounts of items, and building up to using many items, in relatively high amounts (sometimes quickly) is fully warranted.

FIRST LINE RECOMMENDATIONS:
DIET: See Feline comments.
WATER: See Feline comments.
ELIMINATE HOUSEHOLD TOXINS: See Feline comments.
SUPPLEMENTS: See Feline comments for more descriptions. NingXia Red, Omega Blue, Super C, ImmuPro, MultiGreens, and Longevity Softgels (if not using the oil blend) are highly recommended for dogs with cancer.
DIGESTIVE ENZYMES: Digestive enzymes are incredibly important for health, but especially in cases of cancer. Essentialzyme should always be included, and the use of additional enzymes such as Detoxzyme, MightyZyme, and Essentialzymes-4 is often incorporated.
ADDITIONAL SUPPLEMENTS: See Feline comments.
WATER DIFFUSION: Rotational diffusion of emotional oils is recommended. See also the chapter on Emotional Use of Blends for more information. Diffuse any anti-cancer oils up to 24 hours a day. Rotation through a variety of oils is recommended.
RAINDROP TECHNIQUE: Modify by inserting Frankincense, Copaiba, and ImmuPower to the mixture. Apply up to once a day, and at least weekly. Each time a Raindrop is given, you can rotate through which recommended oils are inserted. I strongly recommend a weekly Raindrop Technique for the owner as well.

CANINE CONDITIONS

RAINDROP TECHNIQUE – EMOTIONAL: It is very important to address emotional cleansing with Cancer. See Emotional Work with Oils and Emotional Use of Blends. I strongly recommend emotional work and cleansing for the owner as well.

PETTING: Applying any essential oil you desire up to twice a day or more.

ORAL: Frankincense and Longevity. Frankincense is commonly given orally in quite high doses for cancer. Usually, limits on the amount of Frankincense given, are placed due to budget constraints, and not due to giving "too much." Dogs have consumed extremely high amounts of Frankincense (60 or more drops per day) with no ill effects. Both oils have been given long term. Frankincense is generally given by capsule.

DRINKING WATER: Frankincense, Citrus Fresh, Orange, Tangerine, or other desired oil.

FOODS: Many dogs will ingest essential oils mixed into their foods.

Single Oils:
Balsam Fir (Idaho), Copaiba, Frankincense, Grapefruit, Lemon, Orange, Palo Santo, Sandalwood, Tangerine

Blends:
Acceptance, Believe, Citrus Fresh, Forgiveness, Hope, ImmuPower, Longevity, Present Time, Release, 3 Wise Men, Trauma Life, Valor, White Angelica

Supplements & Products:
Dietary supplementation is a must for cancer. It is important for dogs to not be obese, but to also not become thin while on a regimen. With all supplements, it is important to start with a small amount and gradually increase the amount given as you determine what your individual dog can handle, or what they require.

Animal Scents Ointment, Essentialzyme, Essentialzymes-4, ImmuPro, Longevity Softgels, MightyZyme, MultiGreens, NingXia Red, Ningxia Wolfberries, Omega Blue, ParaFree, Power Meal, Super C, Thieves Household Cleaner

CANCER - BONE

Bone Cancer can benefit from additional support to the bones themselves. Orange oil has also been commonly incorporated into many bone cancer regimens, being added to the Raindrop Technique, added to drinking water, or given by capsule.

FIRST LINE RECOMMENDATIONS:
Also incorporate oil suggestions from BONE CONDITIONS.

CANCER - LIVER
(See also LIVER DISEASE)

Liver Cancer can benefit from additional support to the liver. Please read recommendations for Liver Disease, and incorporate items such as Geranium, Ledum, JuvaPower, Helichrysum, and other liver supporting products.

Additional Single Oils:
Geranium, Helichrysum, Juniper, Ledum, Sage

Additional Blends:
GLF, Juva Cleanse, Juva Flex

Additional Supplements & Products:
JuvaPower, JuvaSpice, JuvaTone

CANCER - LUNG

Palo Santo is especially indicated in cases of Lung Cancer. Adding additional support for lung conditions such as coughs and infections is suggested. Tenting with direct diffusion (Palo Santo, Frankincense) into the airways is recommended with lung cancer. Do as often, and intensely as the animal will tolerate. This may include air diffusion.

Additional Blends:
Breathe Again Roll-On, R.C.

CANCER – LYMPHOSARCOMA, LYMPHOMA

Follow the basic recommendations for Cancer. Incorporating items that are beneficial for the Lymphatic System is helpful such as Aroma Life and Cel-Lite Magic Massage Oil.

Additional Single Oils:
Cypress

Additional Blends:
Aroma Life, Juva Flex

Additional Supplements & Products:
Cel-Lite Magic Massage Oil

CANCER - MAMMARY

Follow the basic recommendations for cancer. Mammary Cancer can specifically benefit from using oils such as Frankincense, Sandalwood, Myrtle, and Tsuga.

CANCER - SPLEEN
(See also HEMORRHAGE – INTERNAL)

Follow the basic recommendations for cancer. If bleeding and hemorrhage are present, the use of Helichrysum and Cistus are recommended for. See Hemorrhage, Internal for more information.

Additional Single Oils:
Cistus, Helichrysum

CANINE INFLUENZA
(See VIRAL CONDITIONS)

CARDIOMYOPATHY

(See also HEART DISEASE)

FIRST LINE RECOMMENDATIONS:
Use the recommendations within Heart Disease, but also add selected oils and supplements which are helpful for muscular conditions – such as Marjoram and Lavender.

Single Oils:
Helichrysum, Lavender, Marjoram, Nutmeg, Ocotea, Spikenard, Wintergreen, Ylang Ylang

Blends:
Aroma Life, Longevity

Supplements & Products:
BLM Capsules, CardiaCare, Essentialzymes-4, Longevity Softgels, MightyZyme, NingXia Red, Ningxia Wolfberries, Omega Blue, PD 80/20, Super B

CATARACTS

(See also LENTICULAR SCLEROSIS, EYE CONDITIONS, DIABETES)

The word "cataract" is often misused by owners and occasionally by veterinarians to describe a general cloudy appearance in the eye. It is important not to confuse Lenticular Sclerosis (the clouding of the lens of the eye) with a true cataract, as they are separate conditions. With a true cataract, many dogs will not be visual from the affected eye. Diabetes is a common cause of true cataracts, and once they are formed, it is a difficult condition to reverse. It is very important to obtain an accurate diagnosis, possibly from a veterinary ophthalmologist, and to address the underlying cause of the cataract formation. Prevention of the cataract is the ideal situation.

FIRST LINE RECOMMENDATIONS:
Use recommendations within Lenticular Sclerosis and Eye Conditions.
SUPPLEMENTS: NingXia Red in very large amounts. Omega Blue

Single Oils:
Frankincense, Helichrysum

Blends:
GLF, Juva Cleanse, Longevity

Supplements & Products:
Detoxzyme, Essentialzymes-4, JuvaPower, JuvaSpice, JuvaTone, Longevity Softgels, MightyZyme, MultiGreens, NingXia Red, Ningxia Wolfberries, Omega Blue, Sulfurzyme, True Source

COGNITIVE DYSFUNCTION

Cognitive dysfunction in dogs is becoming more and more common. Possibly due to the older ages that dogs are reaching these days, but more likely to be a result of chronic deficiencies, poor diets, and toxin exposures. A dog with cognitive dysfunction may forget to go outside to go to the bathroom, may forget that they were just outside and ask to go out again, bark at nothing, whine for no reason, stare off into space, exhibit behavioral changes, and more. Nutritional support is mandatory in this condition, along with essential oils to support the brain. A buildup of plaques within the brain may be the cause of this disorder, and digestive enzyme supplementation is greatly important to support the body's ability to "digest away" these deposits. See also Amyloidosis.

FIRST LINE RECOMMENDATIONS:
SUPPLEMENTS: Longevity Softgels, Omega Blue, NingXia Red, MightyZyme, Essentialzyme 4, Allerzyme.
WATER DIFFUSION: 3 or more drops of Frankincense. Diffuse up to 24 hours a day or as comfortable for the animal and their humans.
PETTING: Frankincense, Brain Power
RAINDROP TECHNIQUE: Modify with insertion of Brain Power, Frankincense, and Copaiba. Apply as indicated by the response of the animal – approximately every 1-7 days.
NEURO AURICULAR TECHNIQUE: Especially with RutaVaLa Roll-On – along the head and spine as described for the technique.

ANIMAL DESK REFERENCE: CANINE

Single Oils:
Cedarwood, Chamomile (German), Chamomile (Roman), Copaiba, Elemi, Frankincense (Carteri), Frankincense (Sacred), Grapefruit, Helichrysum, Juniper, Laurus Nobilis, Lavender, Lemon, Melissa, Orange, Peppermint, Pine, Rose, Rosemary, Spikenard, Valerian, Vetiver, Ylang Ylang

Blends:
Awaken, Believe, Brain Power, Christmas Spirit, Citrus Fresh, Clarity, Common Sense, Dream Catcher, Forgiveness, Gathering, GLF, Grounding, Harmony, Hope, Juva Cleanse, Juva Flex, Longevity, Peace & Calming, RutaVaLa, 3 Wise Men Transformation, Trauma Life, Valor, White Angelica

Supplements & Products:
Dietary supplementation and the use of digestive enzymes are imperative in this condition. Introduce gradually, and generally continue long term.

Allerzyme, Detoxzyme, Essentialzymes-4, ImmuPro, JuvaPower, JuvaSpice, JuvaTone, Life 5, Longevity Softgels, MightyVites, MightyZyme, Mineral Essence, MultiGreens, NingXia Red, Ningxia Wolfberries, Omega Blue, ParaFree, PD 80/20, Rehemogen, Relaxation Massage Oil, Sleep Essence, Super B, Thieves Household Cleaner, True Source, Ultra Young + Oral Spray with DHEA.

COLLAPSING TRACHEA
(See also COUGH)

A collapsing trachea is a frustrating condition in veterinary medicine. The wind pipe literally collapses upon itself during expiration, inspiration, or both – and causes irritation and reduction in air flow during respiration. There is little that can be done for the condition traditionally, and many attempts have been made to improve the situation with various forms of surgery – which are largely difficult, expensive, and not that helpful. Supporting the correction of inflammation, helping the animal to oxygenate, and nutritionally supporting the structural integrity of the trachea and surrounding tissues is important for improvement of the condition. Although we see improvement in this condition with holistic remedies – lifelong support is often needed and recommended.

FIRST LINE RECOMMENDATIONS:
ORAL: Copaiba
WATER DIFFUSION: Diffuse up to 24 hours a day – 3 drops of Thieves, 2 drops Copaiba, 2 drops Frankincense. Open rooms, small closed rooms, caging, and tenting may be utilized for additional comfort and support.
RAINDROP TECHNIQUE: Modify by inserting Copaiba, Palo Santo, and Idaho Balsam Fir. Apply up to once per day, or as indicated based on response.
SUPPLEMENTS: BLM Capsules, Sulfurzyme, NingXia Red, Omega Blue.

Single Oils:
Balsam Fir (Idaho), Cedarwood, Copaiba, Frankincense, Helichrysum, Laurus Nobilis, Lavender, Lemongrass, Marjoram, Palo Santo, Pine, Vetiver, Wintergreen

Blends:
Aroma Life, Aroma Siez, Breathe Again Roll-On, Purification, R.C., Thieves

Supplements & Products:
BLM Capsules and Sulfurzyme are very important in supporting the structural integrity of the trachea, and should always be included.

Allerzyme, BLM Capsules, Essentialzymes-4, Longevity Softgels, MightyZyme, NingXia Red, Omega Blue, ParaFree, Relaxation Massage Oil, Sulfurzyme, True Source

CONSTIPATION

Constipation is most commonly related to dehydration and improper food choices. Having a quality veterinary exam to look for issues that may contribute to this condition is important. Prostatic disease can often be confused for constipation.

FIRST LINE RECOMMENDATIONS:
Evaluate the dog's diet. Consult with a holistic veterinarian or nutritionist. Add water to every meal, to increase hydration.

SUPPLEMENTS: Add ComforTone or ICP to every meal. Start slowly, and gradually increase the amounts given. Monitor stools closely for positive changes in stool form. If stools become harder or dryer – discontinue the selected supplement and try a different supplement.
PETTING: Di-Gize
ORAL: Di-Gize

Single Oils:
Basil, Fennel, Ginger, Juniper, Lavender, Lemon, Marjoram, Peppermint, Spearmint, Tarragon, Vetiver, Wintergreen

Blends:
Aroma Siez, Citrus Fresh, Deep Relief Roll-On, DiGize, GLF, Juva Cleanse, Juva Flex, M-Grain, PanAway, Peace & Calming

Supplements & Products:
Some supplements are beneficial in creating softer stools. There appears to be individual variation between animals, as to if their stools get softer with the addition of more supplements. Starting with one supplement and gradually increasing the amounts given is recommended – while monitoring stool consistency. If stools become harder with a particular supplement – discontinue it or decrease the amount given.

Allerzyme, ComforTone, Detoxzyme, Digest + Cleanse, Essentialzymes-4, ICP, JuvaPower, JuvaSpice, JuvaTone, Life 5, MightyZyme, NingXia Red, Ningxia Wolfberries, Omega Blue, ParaFree, Power Meal, Relaxation Massage Oil, Sulfurzyme, True Source

COPROPHAGIA

Coprophagia is the eating of stool, mainly by dogs but other animals are occasionally witnessed in this activity. For the most part, deficiency in vitamins, minerals, and digestive enzymes are a large component of this occurrence.

FIRST LINE RECOMMENDATIONS:
SUPPLEMENTS: Essentialzymes-4, Mineral Essence, MultiGreens, NingXia Red

Single Oils:
Juniper, Spearmint, Tarragon, Vetiver

Blends:
Abundance, Citrus Fresh, Di-Gize, GLF, Juva Cleanse, Juva Flex

Supplements & Products:
Allerzyme, ComforTone, Detoxzyme, Digest + Cleanse, Essentialzymes-4, ICP, Inner Defense, JuvaTone, Life 5, MightyVites, MightyZyme, Mineral Essence, MultiGreens, NingXia Red, Ningxia Wolfberries, ParaFree, Power Meal, Super B, True Source

CORNEA – ABRASION, LACERATION, ULCER, EDEMA

(See also EYE CONDITIONS)

Damage to the Cornea is painful and can be a very dangerous situation. Veterinary attention is always recommended. Purification and Thieves are recommended for infected corneal conditions, and exposure via Water Diffusion would be recommended routes.

FIRST LINE RECOMMENDATIONS:
TOPICAL: Rose Ointment
WATER MISTING: See Essential Oils & Eyes for misting recipes for the eyes. Lavender or Therapeutic Eye Spritzers are recommended, 2-3 times a day or as needed for comfort and healing.

WATER DIFFUSION: Frankincense, Helichrysum, and Copaiba via tenting or caging. 20 minutes, 3 times a day or as needed and tolerated for healing and comfort. The mist will contact the surface of the cornea from this application.

Single Oils:
Frankincense, Helichrysum, Lavender

Blends:
Purification, Thieves

Supplements & Products:
Animal Scents Ointment, NingXia Red, Ningxia Wolfberries, Rose Ointment, Sulfurzyme

CORNS

(See CALLUS)

COUGH

(See BLASTOMYCOSIS, COLLAPSING TRACHEA, KENNEL COUGH, RESPIRATORY INFECTIONS)

Accurate diagnosis is important to determine the cause of a cough.

FIRST LINE RECOMMENDATIONS:
WATER DIFFUSION: 3 drops Thieves, 1 drop Eucalyptus Blue via caging. Repeat as needed based on response, usually 20 minutes, 3 times a day.

Single Oils:
Hyssop, Laurus Nobilis, Lavender, Lemon, Lemongrass, Marjoram, Myrtle, Palo Santo, Peppermint, Pine, Rosemary, Spruce, Tsuga

Blends:
Aroma Siez, Breathe Again Roll-On, Egyptian Gold, Exodus II, M-Grain, Purification, Raven, R.C., Thieves

Supplements & Products:
Essentialzymes-4, Inner Defense, ParaFree

CRUCIATE LIGAMENT INJURY
(See also PAIN MANAGEMENT)

A Cruciate injury can generally be categorized into two different types; partial tears and total tears. With a partial tear of the ligament, often natural protocols can result in great healing and pain control. Full tears may still require a surgical correction. Accurate diagnosis is very important. In general, I will allow up to 3 months of natural remedies and treatments before deciding if surgery will be a necessary course of action. For very severe total tears, or for knee injuries with significant cartilage damage, sometimes surgery is best performed right away. Many people who fail at healing this condition, have not used adequate amounts of supplements or oils. Restriction or budgeting of supplements, is greatly discouraged if you would like the best results.

FIRST LINE RECOMMENDATIONS:
SUPPLEMENTS: BLM Capsules, Sulfurzyme, Omega Blue, NingXia Red. All of these supplements should be given.
ORAL: Copaiba
PETTING: Daily to 3 times a day to knee. With any of the recommended oils, or with oils added to Ortho Ease or Ortho Sport Massage Oil.

Single Oils:
Balsam Fir (Idaho), Copaiba, Frankincense, Helichrysum, Lavender, Lemongrass, Marjoram, Palo Santo, Peppermint, Pine, Spruce, Tansy (Blue), Wintergreen

Blends:
Aroma Siez, Deep Relief Roll-On, M-Grain, PanAway, Relieve It

Supplements & Products:
Animal Scents Ointment, BLM Capsules, Essentialzymes-4, Longevity Softgels, Omega Blue, Ortho Ease Massage Oil, Ortho Sport Massage Oil, PD 80/20, Regenolone Moisturizing Cream, Sulfurzyme

CRYPTORCHID
(See TESTICLE - UNDESCENDED)

CUSHING'S DISEASE

FIRST LINE RECOMMENDATIONS:
ORAL: Frankincense, Fennel, and Clary Sage in the morning. Idaho Balsam Fir and Copaiba at night.
SUPPLEMENTS: Female dogs may use CortiStop Women's.

Single Oils:
Clary Sage, Fennel, Frankincense, Helichrysum, Juniper, Ledum, Myrrh

Blends:
EndoFlex, GLF, Juva Cleanse, Longevity

Supplements & Products:
CortiStop Women's (Females only), EndoGize, JuvaTone, Longevity Softgels, MightyZyme, NingXia Red, Ningxia Wolfberries, Omega Blue, PD 80/20, Sulfurzyme

CUTS
(See LACERATIONS)

DEMODEX
(See also SKIN INFECTIONS)

Demodex is a mite that lives and reproduces in the hair follicle. It is not contagious, and is largely related to a poor immune system. If secondary skin infections are present, it is very important that they are treated as well. Often secondary infections are overlooked while treating this condition.

FIRST LINE RECOMMENDATIONS:
SUPPLEMENTS: Omega Blue, NingXia Red, Sulfurzyme, ImmuPro, MightyZyme
TOPICAL: Animal Scents Ointment with Purification mixed in. Apply to severely affected areas.
RAINDROP TECHNIQUE: If the skin will tolerate it, generally weekly application with the insertion of ImmuPower, Purification, and Pine.
BATHING: In Animal Scents Shampoo or Thieves Household Cleaner with additional Purification added.

Single Oils:
Citronella, Geranium, Helichrysum, Lavender, Pine, Tansy (Idaho)

Blends:
ImmuPower, Juva Cleanse, Juva Flex, Longevity, Purification

Supplements & Products:
Animal Scents Ointment, ClaraDerm, Essentialzymes-4, ImmuPro, JuvaPower, JuvaSpice, JuvaTone, LavaDerm Cooling Mist, Longevity Softgels, MightyZyme, Mineral Essence, MultiGreens, Omega Blue, ParaFree, Sulfurzyme, Thieves Household Cleaner

DENTAL DISEASE

FIRST LINE RECOMMENDATIONS:
DRINKING WATER: Thieves Fresh Essence Mouthwash
ORAL: Brushing teeth with Thieves Dentarome toothpastes or wiping Thieves Fresh Essence Mouthwash onto the teeth daily.
TOPICAL: Thieves can be rubbed onto an area of need directly.

Single Oils:
Clove, Helichrysum, Laurus Nobilis, Melaleuca Alternifolia, Myrrh, Wintergreen

Blends:
Abundance, Exodus II, Longevity, Melrose, Thieves

Supplements & Products:
BLM Capsules, Essentialzymes-4, Inner Defense, Longevity Softgels, MightyZyme, Mineral Essence, Omega Blue, Stevia Extract, Sulfurzyme, Thieves Dentarome Toothpaste, Thieves Fresh Essence Mouthwash, True Source

DETOXIFICATION

(See VACCINOSIS)

Detoxification from any situation will be similar to the detoxification described within the issue of Vaccinosis.

ANIMAL DESK REFERENCE: CANINE

DEWORMING

FIRST LINE RECOMMENDATIONS:
SUPPLEMENTS: ParaFree
ORAL: Di-Gize

Single Oils:
Hyssop, Lemon, Lemongrass, Melaleuca Alternifolia, Mountain Savory, Nutmeg, Ocotea, Peppermint, Tarragon, Thyme

Blends:
Di-Gize

Supplements & Products:
ComforTone, Detoxzyme, Digest + Cleanse, Life 5, MightyZyme, ParaFree

DIABETES MELLITUS

FIRST LINE RECOMMENDATIONS:
ORAL: Ocotea – please see additional descriptions and cautions for treating and using this oil in dogs with Diabetes or who receive Insulin.
SUPPLEMENTS: NingXia Red, MultiGreens, Essentialzymes-4

Single Oils:
Coriander, Dill, Fennel, Geranium, Myrrh, Ocotea, Pine, Ylang Ylang

Blends:
EndoFlex, Juva Cleanse, Juva Flex, Longevity, Slique Essence

Supplements & Products:
Essentialzymes-4, Longevity Softgels, MightyZyme, MultiGreens, NingXia Red, Ningxia Wolfberries, Omega Blue

DIARRHEA
(See also INFLAMMATORY BOWEL DISEASE)

In conditions of diarrhea, a fast is often the recommended starting point. Please consult with a veterinarian, however offering no food (water is generally okay if no vomiting is present) for approximately 24 hours is the best start to ending a cycle of diarrhea. If a dog is lethargic, vomiting, or acting abnormal in any other way, a veterinary exam is suggested immediately. When food is re-introduced after the fast, very small amounts of a bland diet should be given every 1-3 hours. Any food, meals, or supplements that are introduced too quickly to a dog suffering from diarrhea, will only encourage the condition.

FIRST LINE RECOMMENDATIONS:
SUPPLEMENTS: Inner Defense, Life 5
ORAL: Di-Gize
PETTING: Di-Gize

Single Oils:
Lemon, Lemongrass, Mountain Savory, Ocotea, Oregano, Peppermint, Spearmint, Tarragon, Vetiver

Blends:
Citrus Fresh, Di-Gize, Exodus II, Longevity, Purification, Thieves

Supplements & Products:
ComforTone, Detoxzyme, Digest + Cleanse, Essentialzymes-4, ICP, Inner Defense, Life 5, Longevity Softgels, MightyZyme, ParaFree, Super B, Thieves Fresh Essence Mouthwash, Thieves Household Cleaner

DRY EYE
(See also AUTOIMMUNE CONDITIONS, EYE CONDITIONS)

Dry Eye is a condition where not enough tears are produced by the tear glands. This often is related to an autoimmune process within the body. Hydration is of major importance, and adding additional water to every meal the dog eats is suggested. No dry kibble should be fed, without it being completely soaked in water.

ANIMAL DESK REFERENCE: CANINE

FIRST LINE RECOMMENDATIONS:
See recommendations for Autoimmune Conditions, Cornea, and Eye Conditions.
WATER MISTING: Lavender Eye Spritzer as needed for comfort. See Essential Oils & Eyes for more information.
TOPICAL: Rose Ointment

Single Oils:
Helichrysum, Lavender

Blends:
Juva Cleanse

Supplements & Products:
Animal Scents Ointment, JuvaTone, Longevity Softgels, Omega Blue, PD 80/20, Rose Ointment, Sulfurzyme

DYSTOCIA
(See PREGNANCY & DELIVERY)

EAR INFECTIONS
(See also ALLERGIES)

FIRST LINE RECOMMENDATIONS:
Ear Spray Recipe:
- In a 30 mL glass spray bottle, combine the following:
- 7-8 mL of Thieves Spray
- 1 Tablespoon of V6
- 3 drops of Lemongrass
- 4 drops of Copaiba
- 5 drops of Purification
- Add distilled water to fill the bottle.
- Shake well, and spray into the ear once or twice a day. You are not attempting to fill the ear with the solution, and should be coating the skin and canal area with the spray.

Single Oils:
Copaiba, Geranium, Helichrysum, Lavender, Lemongrass, Melaleuca Alternifolia, Ocotea

Blends:
Melrose, Purification, Thieves

Supplements & Products:
Animal Scents Ointment, ClaraDerm, Digest + Cleanse, Essentialzymes-4, Inner Defense, LavaDerm Cooling Mist, Life 5, Longevity Softgels, Omega Blue, Sulfurzyme, Thieves Household Cleaner, Thieves Spray, Thieves Wipes

EMOTIONAL CLEANSING

Emotional Cleansing is very important for almost every aspect of healing, and especially in cases of cancer. Rotational use of various essential oil blends is incredibly helpful. See the chapters Emotional Work with Oils and Emotional Use of Blends for more information.

FIRST LINE RECOMMENDATIONS:
PETTING: Trauma Life, Forgiveness, Acceptance, Release, White Angelica, Palo Santo
WATER DIFFUSION: Rotational diffusion of any oil selection.
RAINDROP TECHNIQUE: Traditional Raindrop Technique is beneficial for emotional cleansing. Use as often as dictated by the case and the individual animal.
EMOTIONAL RAINDROP TECHNIQUE: Use as often as dictated by the case and the individual animal. See Emotional Use of Blends for more information.

Single Oils:
Bergamot, Roman Chamomile, German Chamomile, Geranium, Lavender, Lemon, Melissa, Palo Santo, Patchouli, Rose, Spruce, Vetiver, Ylang Ylang

Blends:
Acceptance, Forgiveness, Hope, Purification, Release, Trauma Life, White Angelica

EPILEPSY
(See SEIZURES)

EPULIS - DENTAL
(See also DENTAL DISEASE)

An Epulis is generally a benign overgrowth of gum tissue in the mouth of a dog. Boxer dogs are particularly prone to this disorder, however it occurs in many breeds. They are difficult to resolve once they are present, but healing after resection and prevention of future occurrence are prime objectives.

FIRST LINE RECOMMENDATIONS:
Use recommendations for Dental Disease as well as:
SUPPLEMENTS: Longevity Softgels, Omega Blue, Essentialzyme, Sulfurzyme, NingXia Red
TOPICAL: Frankincense can be applied alone or mixed into Thieves Toothpaste or Mouthwash for application.

Single Oils:
Copaiba, Frankincense, Helichrysum, Myrrh

Blends:
Citrus Fresh, Exodus II, Thieves

Supplements & Products:
Essentialzyme, Longevity Softgels, MightyZyme, Omega Blue, Sulfurzyme

EYE CONDITIONS
(See also CORNEA, DRY EYE)

In general, any eye condition can benefit from good nutrition and a broad spectrum use of essential oils The Lavender Eye Spritzer does provide a huge amount of benefits to any eye condition, and is a general starting recommendation.

FIRST LINE RECOMMENDATIONS:
WATER MISTING: Lavender Eye Spritzer. See Essential Oils & Eyes for more information.
TOPICAL: Rose Ointment
WATER DIFFUSION: Any suggested oil diffused via tenting will contact the cornea and eye tissues during diffusion. This is an easy delivery of essential oils to all eye tissues, and generally any essential oil could be considered for use in this way. For an eye infection, Purification or Thieves could be diffused to permeate the area.

Single Oils:
Frankincense, Helichrysum, Lavender

Supplements & Products:
Animal Scents Ointment, Longevity Softgels, NingXia Red, Ningxia Wolfberries, Omega Blue, Rose Ointment

FALSE PREGNANCY
(See also EQUINE HORMONAL CONDITIONS)

FIRST LINE RECOMMENDATIONS:
ORAL: Clary Sage
PETTING: Clary Sage, Dorado Azul, or SclarEssence
DIFFUSION: Ylang Ylang

Single Oils:
Clary Sage, Dorado Azul, Geranium, Myrtle, Vetiver, Ylang Ylang

Blends:
Acceptance, Dragon Time, EndoFlex, Gentle Baby, Harmony, Joy, Lady Sclareol, SclarEssence

Supplements & Products:
Dragon Time Massage Oil, EndoGize, Estro, FemiGen, PD 80/20

FLEAS

Fleas are one of the most difficult parasites to eliminate. Often many multiple layers of prevention are needed. All animals in the household must be treated for fleas, not just one or two.

FIRST LINE RECOMMENDATIONS:
DIFFUSION: See the description for Pepper (Black), for directions for a household Flea Bomb Recipe.
RAINDROP TECHNIQUE: Apply up to once a day in severe situations, and at least weekly for maintenance. Frequency of application can be based on the response and needs of the individual animal. Modifications can be made by inserting additional insect repelling oils. Fleas dislike many of the Raindrop Technique oils, and the technique also strengthens the immune system which makes dogs less attractive to flea infestation.
PETTING: Purification. Kitty Raindrop Technique Solution is also wonderful to apply for flea repellency.
BATHING: Bathe with Thieves Household Cleaner, additional Purification oil can be added to the bathing mixture.
CLEANING: Cleaning, laundering, and spraying with Thieves Household Cleaner indoors and out is suggested.
SUPPLEMENTS: Healthier dogs are less attractive to fleas and other insects. Longevity is a highly recommended supplement, followed by NingXia Red, Omega Blue, and MultiGreens.

Single Oils:
Citronella, Eucalyptus Blue, Lavender, Lemongrass, Melaleuca Alternifolia, Melissa, Orange, Oregano, Palo Santo, Pepper (Black,) Peppermint, Rosemary, Tansy (Idaho)

Blends:
Exodus II, ImmuPower, Kitty Raindrop Solution, Longevity, Melrose, Purification, Thieves

Supplements & Products:
Animal Scents Ointment, ClaraDerm, Detoxzyme, Essentialzymes-4, ImmuPro, JuvaPower, JuvaSpice, JuvaTone, Longevity Softgels, LavaDerm Cooling Mist, MightyZyme, Mineral Essence, Omega

Blue, Ortho Ease Massage Oil, Ortho Sport Massage Oil, ParaFree, Rehemogen, Sulfurzyme, Thieves Household Cleaner, True Source

FLU
(See VIRAL CONDITIONS)

FOREIGN BODY - GASTROINTESTINAL

Veterinary attention is very important when a foreign object is suspected within the gastrointestinal system. These suggestions can decrease inflammation and allow the intestinal tract to function more effectively, however should never replace surgery when truly indicated. After a surgical procedure, use of the oils can aid in healing and return to function sooner.

FIRST LINE RECOMMENDATIONS:
PETTING: Di-Gize, Vetiver
DIFFUSION: Release
ORAL: Di-Gize

Single Oils:
Helichrysum, Lavender, Marjoram, Peppermint, Vetiver

Blends:
Di-Gize, M-Grain, Release, Trauma Life

Supplements & Products:
Life 5, MightyZyme, Power Meal, Sulfurzyme

GALL BLADDER

FIRST LINE RECOMMENDATIONS:
PETTING: Juva Cleanse or any of the recommended oils.
ORAL: GLF
DRINKING WATER: Citrus Fresh
SUPPLEMENTS: Digest + Cleanse, JuvaTone

Single Oils:
Geranium, Goldenrod, Helichrysum, Ledum, Lemon, Peppermint, Sage, Spearmint

ANIMAL DESK REFERENCE: CANINE

Blends:
Citrus Fresh, Deep Relief Roll-On, Di-Gize, GLF, Juva Cleanse, Juva Flex

Supplements & Products:
Detoxzyme, Digest + Cleanse, Essentialzymes-4, JuvaPower, JuvaSpice, JuvaTone, Life 5, Longevity Softgels, MightyZyme, NingXia Red

GASTRIC ULCERS

FIRST LINE RECOMMENDATIONS:
ORAL: Copaiba
PETTING: Di-Gize
SUPPLEMENTS: MightyZyme

Single Oils:
Copaiba, Clove, Helichrysum, Nutmeg, Peppermint

Blends:
Deep Relief Roll-On, Di-Gize, Longevity

Supplements & Products:
Digest + Cleanse, Life 5, MightyZyme

GASTRODILITATION VOLVULUS

This is an incredibly serious condition and requires immediate and emergency veterinary attention. Use of the recommendations can aid in supporting the patient, increase circulation to damaged tissues, and speed healing times from surgical procedures. Prevention of the disorder focuses on feeding wet and soaked foods, and providing support and nutrition towards healthy ligaments and connective tissues.

FIRST LINE RECOMMENDATIONS:
During an Emergency Situation:
INHALATION: Rose (or Joy) and Frankincense as life force enhancing oils.
PETTING: Rose, Frankincense, Helichrysum

For Post-Surgical Healing:
PETTING: Helichrysum, Palo Santo
ORAL: See also Pain Management

For Prevention Measures:
SUPPLEMENTS: BLM Capsules, Sulfurzyme
PETTING: Palo Santo

Single Oils:
Copaiba, Cypress, Frankincense, Helichrysum, Lavender, Lemongrass, Palo Santo, Rose, Tarragon

Blends:
Di-Gize, Joy

Supplements & Products:
BLM Capsules, Sulfurzyme

GDV
(See GASTRODILITATION VOLVULUS)

GIARDIA
(See also DIARRHEA)

FIRST LINE RECOMMENDATIONS:
SUPPLEMENTS: Inner Defense, Life 5
ORAL: Thieves, Clove
DRINKING WATER: Thieves Fresh Essence Mouthwash

Single Oils:
Clove, Lemon, Melaleuca Alternifolia, Mountain Savory, Nutmeg, Ocotea, Oregano, Peppermint, Tarragon, Thyme, Vetiver

Blends:
Abundance, Di-Gize, Exodus II, ImmuPower, Longevity, Melrose, Purification, Thieves

Supplements & Products:
ComforTone, Digest + Cleanse, Essentialzymes-4, Inner Defense, ICP, ImmuPro, Inner Defense, Life 5, Longevity Softgels, MightyZyme, ParaFree, Super B, Thieves Mouthwash, Thieves Household Cleaner

GLAUCOMA

(See also EYE CONDITIONS)

FIRST LINE RECOMMENDATIONS:
WATER MISTING: Therapeutic Eye Spritzer to general eye area, 2-3 times a day or as needed for individual animal.
PETTING: With any of the suggested oils.

Single Oils:
Copaiba, Helichrysum, Lavender, Ledum

Blends:
Juva Cleanse, Longevity, M-Grain

Supplements & Products:
JuvaTone, K&B Tincture, Longevity Softgels, NingXia Red, Ningxia Wolfberries, Omega Blue, Relaxation Massage Oil

HEAD TILT

(See VESTIBULAR DISEASE, NEUROLOGIC CONDITIONS)

HEART DISEASE

FIRST LINE RECOMMENDATIONS:
SUPPLEMENTS: Super B, Omega Blue, NingXia Red, Essentialzymes-4, CardiaCare
PETTING: Aroma Life, Helichrysum
DIFFUSION: Aroma Life
ORAL: Copaiba

Single Oils:
Copaiba, Cinnamon, Clove, Goldenrod, Helichrysum, Marjoram, Nutmeg, Ocotea, Orange, Rose, Spikenard, Tansy (Idaho), Thyme, Wintergreen, Ylang Ylang

Blends:
　　Abundance, Aroma Life, Longevity, Thieves

Supplements & Products:
　　BLM Capsules, CardiaCare, Essentialzymes-4, Longevity Softgels, MightyZyme, NingXia Red, Ningxia Wolfberries, Omega Blue, PD 80/20, Super B

HEARTWORM PREVENTION

FIRST LINE RECOMMENDATIONS:
　　SUPPLEMENTS: ParaFree, Longevity Softgels
　　PETTING or TOPICAL: Purification for insect repelling activity.
　　WATER MISTING: With insect repelling oils added to water or with various bug spray recipes.

Single Oils:
　　Nutmeg, Ocotea, Tarragon

Blends:
　　Di-Gize, Longevity, Purification

Supplements & Products:
　　Longevity Softgels, Ortho Ease Massage Oil, Ortho Sport Massage Oil, ParaFree

HEARTWORM DISEASE
　　(See also HEART DISEASE)

The following protocol is based off of a very well documented case where essential oils were used to eradicate severe heartworm infection from a dog. The documentation, from a University Veterinary Teaching Hospital, included thorough testing and evaluation, including an echocardiogram. The University had established a very guarded prognosis, where the dog would likely die with or without surgical removal of the heartworms. The dog went home, and proceeded to use the following protocol. A negative heartworm status was achieved by this dog, and considering the severe nature of the infection, the protocol was far superior than traditional heartworm treatment. Long term use (4-6 months) of this protocol is likely to be necessary, and conversion to a negative heartworm test is also not expected for 4-6 months, although it can occur sooner. Slowly killing the heartworm is important. My current recommendation is to use a similar protocol, with no parts being omitted. Careful monitoring with a veterinarian is important, and screening and monitoring for microfilaria (baby heartworm) within the blood stream during treatment, is suggested to be coordinated with a veterinarian.

FIRST LINE RECOMMENDATIONS:

The following recommendations would be used for most sized dogs. The one exception is with ParaFree, where doubling the dosage may be necessary in dogs over 50 pounds (23 kg). Adjustments to doses need to be considered based on individual responses and needs.

SUPPLEMENTS: ParaFree 1 capsule four times a day for 2 weeks, then 1 capsule twice a day for 2 weeks. Then 1-2 capsules per day for the remainder of the treatment (until negative status is achieved). This amount may need to be adjusted based on if the dog can tolerate the administration as well. CardiaCare (or similar replacement) as directed. MightyZyme 1 tablet daily, or with each meal. NingXia Red as suggested for body weight.

ORAL: Helichrysum 1 drop, three to four times per day (this may be placed directly into the mouth, especially in severe situations). Longevity 5 drops per day, mixed with Oregano 2 drops per day. The Longevity and Oregano are generally given together within a capsule. The dose can be split up into several administrations. These oral administrations can generally be reduced after 2-4 weeks, based on how the dog is doing and how severe the symptoms of heartworm are. See individual oil descriptions for more information on dosing.

RAINDROP TECHNIQUE: Is recommended weekly to monthly for general support and healing. This was not included in the original case protocol, however would be a helpful addition.

PETTING, ORAL, or DIFFUSION: Aroma Life and Copaiba used in these manners, are also additions to the original protocol, but are highly suggested.

Single Oils:

Cinnamon, Clove, Copaiba, Helichrysum, Ocotea, Oregano, Spikenard, Tansy (Idaho), Tarragon, Wintergreen, Ylang Ylang

Blends:
   Abundance, Aroma Life, Di-Gize, ImmuPower, Longevity

Supplements & Products:
   Essentialzymes-4, Longevity Softgels, MightyZyme, NingXia Red, Omega Blue, ParaFree

HEAT STROKE
(See HYPERTHERMIA)

HEMANGIOSARCOMA
(See CANCER – SPLEEN, HEMORRHAGE - INTERNAL)

HEMOABDOMEN
(See HEMORRHAGE - INTERNAL)

HEMORRHAGE - INTERNAL

FIRST LINE RECOMMENDATIONS:
   ORAL: Cistus

Single Oils:
   Cistus, Geranium, Helichrysum

Blends:
   ImmuPower

Caution:
   Avoidance of oils such as Cinnamon, Clove, Nutmeg, Wintergreen, Abundance, Exodus II, Thieves – that have anticoagulant effects, may be wise.

HISTIOCYTOMA

FIRST LINE RECOMMENDATIONS:
TOPICAL: Frankincense, Copaiba, and Peppermint applied to the lump, usually neat. Tumors may look worse before better. Some dogs may require dilution. Apply as frequently as tolerated and indicated by the individual. Usually between every 1-7 days. If the tumor responds well to one application, spacing apart the applications is more likely.
DRINKING WATER: Citrus Fresh
PETTING: Frankincense
SUPPLEMENTS: Inner Defense (if lesions are infected), NingXia Red, Omega Blue

HORNER'S SYNDROME
(See BELL'S PALSY)

HOT SPOTS
(See also ALLERGIES, SKIN INFECTIONS)

The use of ointments is often discouraged with Hot Spots as they are a moist condition in need of drying. Clipping the wound and using techniques that allow the tissues to dry out is suggested.

FIRST LINE RECOMMENDATIONS:
WATER MISTER: Skin Spray Recipe – Add 8 drops of Copaiba, 14 drops of Lavender, and 10 drops of Melaleuca Alternifolia to 4 ounces (120 mL) of distilled water, in a glass spray bottle. Shake well and spray skin as needed, generally 1-4 times a day.
TOPICAL: Thieves Waterless Hand Purifier in an emergency can be quite effective.
BATHING: Wash the area thoroughly with Thieves Household Cleaner.
SUPPLEMENTS: Inner Defense, Omega Blue, Sulfurzyme

HYPERADRENOCORTICISM
(See CUSHING'S DISEASE)

HYPERTHERMIA – EXERCISE INDUCED, HEAT STROKE

FIRST LINE RECOMMENDATIONS:
TOPICAL: Peppermint to ear flaps, foot pads, feet, and over femoral artery. Repeat as needed in severe situations.
ORAL: Peppermint directly into the mouth if needed.
DIFFUSION: Peppermint
DRINKING WATER: Peppermint

Single Oils:
Frankincense, Helichrysum, Lavender, Peppermint

Blends:
Deep Relief Roll-On, ImmuPower, Longevity, PanAway

HYPOGLYCEMIA

FIRST LINE RECOMMENDATIONS:
Give NingXia Red every 10-15 minutes or as needed to stabilize blood sugar. Make sure the dog can swallow adequately and seek medical attention.

Single Oils:
Frankincense, Peppermint, Rose

Blends:
En-R-Gee

Supplements & Products:
MightyZyme, NingXia Red, Power Meal

HYPOTHYROIDISM

Elimination of household chemicals and of the drinking of common tap water is highly recommended in cases of Hypothyroidism. Monitoring with a veterinarian is important, and adjustments of doses based on response is recommended.

FIRST LINE RECOMMENDATIONS:
SUPPLEMENTS: Thyromin
PETTING: EndoFlex and Myrtle over thyroid area at least daily.
DRINKING WATER: Spearmint or Citrus Fresh

Single Oils:
Lemongrass, Myrrh, Myrtle, Spearmint

Blends:
EndoFlex, Juva Cleanse, Juva Flex

Supplements & Products:
EndoGize, Essentialzymes-4, MightyZyme, Mineral Essence, Omega Blue, PD 80/20, Sulfurzyme, Thieves Household Cleaner, Thyromin

IBD
(See INFLAMMATORY BOWEL DISEASE)

IMHA
(See IMMUNE MEDIATED HEMOLYTIC ANEMIA)

IMMUNE MEDIATED HEMOLYTIC ANEMIA
(See also AUTOIMMUNE CONDITIONS)

FIRST LINE RECOMMENDATIONS:
Use the recommendations for Autoimmune Conditions, as well as these specific suggestions.
RAINDROP TECHNIQUE: Modify by inserting Pine and Spruce for added cortisone-like benefits, also insert Helichrysum. Apply up to daily, based on response and need.
SUPPLEMENTS: Rehemogen

Single Oils:
Cistus, Helichrysum, Pine, Spruce

Blends:
ImmuPower

Supplements & Products:
Longevity Softgels, PD 80/20, Rehemogen, Sulfurzyme

INCONTINENCE - URINARY

FIRST LINE RECOMMENDATIONS:
ORAL: Copaiba
PETTING: Copaiba, Palo Santo
SUPPLEMENTS: BLM Capsules, Sulfurzyme, FemiGen, MightyZyme, NingXia Red

Single Oils:
Copaiba, Helichrysum, Juniper, Lemongrass, Marjoram, Palo Santo, Sage, Tsuga

Blends:
EndoFlex, Longevity, SclarEssence

Supplements & Products:
BLM Capsules, Dragon Time Massage Oil, EndoGize, Essentialzymes-4, Estro, FemiGen, K&B Tincture, Longevity Softgels, MightyZyme, Mineral Essence, PD 80/20, Sulfurzyme

INFLAMMATORY BOWEL DISEASE
(See also DIARRHEA)

FIRST LINE RECOMMENDATIONS:
SUPPLEMENTS: Essentialzymes-4, Life 5, Super B, Omega Blue
ORAL: Thieves or Inner Defense if needed for severe bacterial overgrowth or painful bowels.
DRINKING WATER: Thieves Fresh Essence Mouthwash
PETTING: Di-Gize

Single Oils:
Helichrysum, Lemon, Nutmeg, Peppermint, Spruce, Tansy (Blue), Tarragon, Vetiver

Blends:
Di-Gize, GLF, Longevity, PanAway, Thieves

Supplements & Products:
ComforTone, Detoxzyme, Digest + Cleanse, Essentialzyme, Essentialzymes-4, ICP, Inner Defense, Life 5, Longevity Softgels, MightyZyme, Omega Blue, ParaFree, Sulfurzyme, Super B, Thieves Fresh Essence Mouthwash

INFLUENZA
(See VIRAL CONDITIONS)

INTERNAL HEMORRHAGE
(See HEMORRHAGE - INTERNAL)

IVDD
(See INTERVERTEBRAL DISC DISEASE)

INTERVERTEBRAL DISC DISEASE
(See also PAIN MANAGEMENT)

FIRST LINE RECOMMENDATIONS:
RAINDROP TECHNIQUE: Modified by inserting Helichrysum, RutaVaLa, and Copaiba. Apply up to daily as indicated by the response and individual.
ORAL: See Pain Management for techniques for severe pain. Copaiba is recommended for general use.
SUPPLEMENTS: BLM Capsules, Sulfurzyme, NingXia Red, Omega Blue, Longevity Softgels

Single Oils:
Chamomile (Roman), Copaiba, Helichrysum, Juniper, Laurus Nobilis, Lavender, Lemongrass, Marjoram, Mountain Savory, Nutmeg, Palo Santo, Peppermint, Spruce, Wintergreen

Blends:
Aroma Siez, Deep Relief Roll-On, M-Grain, PanAway, Relieve It, RutaVaLa

Supplements & Products:
BLM Capsules, Longevity Softgels, Omega Blue, Ortho Ease Massage Oil, Ortho Sport Massage Oil, PD 80/20, Regenolone Moisturizing Cream, Relaxation Massage Oil, Sulfurzyme

INTESTINAL CONDITIONS
(See also DIARRHEA, VOMITING, DEWORMING, INFLAMMATORY BOWEL DISEASE)

KCS
(See DRY EYE)

KENNEL COUGH

FIRST LINE RECOMMENDATIONS:
WATER DIFFUSION: With tenting or caging, diffuse 4 drops of Thieves and 1 drop of Eucalyptus Blue for 20 minutes, 4 times a day. Adjust as needed for individuals.
DIFFUSION: Open Room; up to 24 hours a day with Thieves, Purification, or other selected oils for general disinfecting and reduction of transmission.
SUPPLEMENTS: Inner Defense
CLEANING: Thieves Household Cleaner
RAINDROP TECHNIQUE: Up to daily, or as needed. Modifications with the insertion of ImmuPower, R.C., and Copaiba are suggested.

Single Oils:
Eucalyptus Blue, Eucalyptus Radiata, Hyssop, Laurus Nobilis, Lavender, Lemon, Lemongrass, Marjoram, Melaleuca Alternifolia, Melaleuca Ericifolia, Melissa, Mountain Savory, Myrtle, Oregano, Palo Santo, Peppermint, Rosemary, Spruce, Tsuga

Blends:
Aroma Siez, Breathe Again Roll-On, Egyptian Gold, Exodus II, Hope, ImmuPower, M-Grain, Melrose, Purification, Raven, R.C., Thieves

Supplements & Products:
Inner Defense, MultiGreens, ParaFree, Thieves Household Cleaner

KERATOCONJUNCTIVITIS SICCA
(See DRY EYE)

KIDNEY DISEASE

FIRST LINE RECOMMENDATIONS:
SUPPLEMENTS: K&B Tincture
DRINKING WATER: Citrus Fresh
PETTING: Over Kidney area; Juniper, Helichrysum, or any suggested oil.
ORAL: Helichrysum or other suggested oils in severe situations.

Single Oils:
Grapefruit, Helichrysum, Juniper, Ledum, Lemongrass, Tsuga

Blends:
Citrus Fresh, GLF, Juva Cleanse, Juva Flex

Supplements & Products:
K&B Tincture, Omega Blue, Thieves Household Cleaner

KNEE CAP
(See PATELLA - LUXATING)

LACERATIONS

FIRST LINE RECOMMENDATIONS:
TOPICAL: Animal Scents Ointment with Helichrysum mixed into it. This mixture can be applied directly into lacerations and also next to or over-top of stitched wounds. Melrose and/or Helichrysum can also be dripped directly into lacerations. When stitches are present, direct application of neat oils to the stitch material is generally avoided.

Single Oils:
Cistus, Frankincense, Geranium, Helichrysum, Lavender, Melaleuca Alternifolia, Myrrh

Blends:
Melrose, PanAway, Purification, Thieves

CANINE CONDITIONS

Supplements & Products:
Animal Scents Ointment, Rose Ointment, Sulfurzyme, Thieves Household Cleaner

LACTATION

FIRST LINE RECOMMENDATIONS:
PETTING: With any of the suggested oils, although Fennel is a primary selection. This can begin prior to birthing, or be used when increases in milk supply is desired.
DIFFUSION: SclarEssence
ORAL: Fennel can also be added to foods to increase milk supply.

Single Oils:
Celery Seed, Fennel, Spruce

Blends:
Abundance, EndoFlex, Juva Cleanse, SclarEssence

Supplements & Products:
Animal Scents Ointment, MightyZyme, Omega Blue, Power Meal, Sulfurzyme, True Source

LARYNGEAL PARALYSIS
(See also COUGH, NEUROLOGIC CONDITIONS)

FIRST LINE RECOMMENDATIONS:
SUPPLEMENTS: PD 80/20, Super B, Longevity
PETTING: Helichrysum, Roman Chamomile over throat area daily.
NEURO AURICULAR TECHNIQUE: See Advanced Techniques.

Single Oils:
Chamomile (Roman), Helichrysum, Juniper, Laurus Nobilis, Lemongrass, Marjoram

Blends:
M-Grain

Supplements & Products:
BLM Capsules, Longevity Softgels, MightyZyme, PD 80/20, Sulfurzyme, Super B

LENTICULAR SCLEROSIS
(See also CATARACTS, EYE CONDITIONS)

FIRST LINE RECOMMENDATIONS:
SUPPLEMENTS: NingXia Red, Omega Blue, Longevity, Essentialzymes-4. Generally all of these supplements should be given for best results, sometimes in quite high quantities.
WATER MISTING: Therapeutic Eye Spritzer; mist face area daily to twice a day. It is not important that this solution contact the inner eye or cornea. Petting applications may be substituted.

Single Oils:
Frankincense, Helichrysum

Blends:
GLF, Longevity

Supplements & Products:
Detoxzyme, JuvaPower, JuvaSpice, JuvaTone, Longevity Softgels, MightyVites, MightyZyme, MultiGreens, NingXia Red, Ningxia Wolfberries, Omega Blue, Sulfurzyme, True Source

LICK GRANULOMA
(See also ALLERGIES, SKIN INFECTIONS)

These lesions are incredibly frustrating and can have a variety of reasons for their occurrence. Deep infections (both bacterial or fungal), neuralgia (nerve pain), injury, cancer, arthritis, and many other conditions can promote this disorder. Trying a variety of essential oils to see which provide the best responses is recommended. Generally, oils can be applied to lesions in their neat form. Mixing with Animal Scents Ointment can be helpful when applied sparingly, however some animals enjoy the flavor, so if licking is increased with this product, discontinue its use.

CANINE CONDITIONS

FIRST LINE RECOMMENDATIONS:
TOPICAL: Spikenard, Helichrysum, and any other suggested oil to the lesion 1-4 times a day or as needed. The Ear Spray Recipe featured in Ear Infections is also a wonderful spray for these lesions.
SUPPLEMENTS: Super B, Sulfurzyme, BLM Capsules, NingXia Red, Essentialzymes-4, Inner Defense
RAINDROP TECHNIQUE: Apply as needed for the individual. Modifications and insertions can be made, rotation of oils is suggested.

Single Oils:
Chamomile (Roman), Frankincense, Geranium, Helichrysum, Juniper, Laurus Nobilis, Lavender, Lemongrass, Marjoram, Melaleuca Alternifolia, Melaleuca Ericifolia, Melissa, Mountain Savory, Myrrh, Nutmeg, Ocotea, Oregano, Palo Santo, Patchouli, Rose, Spikenard, Spruce, Tansy (Blue), Valerian, Vetiver, Wintergreen, Ylang Ylang

Blends:
Deep Relief Roll-On, Exodus II, GLF, Juva Cleanse, Juva Flex, Hope, Longevity, M-Grain, Melrose, PanAway, Purification, Relieve It, Thieves, 3 Wise Men

Supplements & Products:
Animal Scents Ointment, BLM Capsules, ClaraDerm, Detoxzyme, Digest + Cleanse, Essentialzymes-4, ImmuPro, Inner Defense, JuvaPower, JuvaSpice, JuvaTone, LavaDerm Cooling Mist, Life 5, Longevity Softgels, MightyVites, MightyZyme, Mineral Essence, MultiGreens, NingXia Red, Ningxia Wolfberries, Omega Blue, Ortho Ease Massage Oil, Ortho Sport Massage Oil, PD 80/20, Regenolone Moisturizing Cream, Relaxation Massage Oil, Rose Ointment, Sulfurzyme, Thieves Household Cleaner, Thieves Spray, True Source

LIPOMA

FIRST LINE RECOMMENDATIONS:
TOPICAL: Massage the lump daily to four times a day with Cel-Lite Magic Massage Oil. The addition of Frankincense, Lemon, and Lemongrass to the massage oil is suggested. Gradually build

up in the concentration of oils added to the massage oil based on tolerance. Some owners shave the lump for ease of application. This is a long term problem, and shrinkage of the lump is not expected for several months.
SUPPLEMENTS: Essentialzymes-4
DRINKING WATER: Citrus Fresh

Single Oils:
Frankincense, Grapefruit, Ledum, Lemon, Lemongrass, Orange, Tangerine

Blends:
Citrus Fresh

Supplements & Products:
Cel-Lite Magic Massage Oil, Essentialzymes-4, JuvaPower, JuvaSpice, JuvaTone, Longevity Softgels, MightyZyme, Omega Blue, True Source

LIVER DISEASE

FIRST LINE RECOMMENDATIONS:
ORAL: Helichrysum, Juva Cleanse
DRINKING WATER: Citrus Fresh
PETTING: Juva Cleanse, Juva Flex, Ledum
SUPPLEMENTS: NingXia Red, Omega Blue

Single Oils:
Chamomile (German), Chamomile (Roman), Geranium, Goldenrod, Grapefruit, Helichrysum, Juniper, Ledum, Myrrh, Myrtle, Nutmeg, Ocotea, Rosemary, Sage, Spearmint, Tangerine

Blends:
Citrus Fresh, GLF, Juva Cleanse, Juva Flex

Supplements & Products:
Detoxzyme, Digest + Cleanse, JuvaPower, JuvaSpice, JuvaTone, Longevity Softgels, MightyZyme, NingXia Red, Ningxia Wolfberries, Omega Blue, ParaFree, Super B, Thieves Household Cleaner

LIVER SHUNT
(See also LIVER DISEASE)

FIRST LINE RECOMMENDATIONS:
SUPPLEMENTS: NingXia Red, Omega Blue, MightyZyme
PETTING: Helichrysum, Aroma Life
DRINKING WATER: Citrus Fresh
ORAL: Helichrysum

Single Oils:
Chamomile (Roman), Chamomile (German), Geranium, Goldenrod, Grapefruit, Helichrysum, Juniper, Ledum, Lemongrass, Myrtle, Nutmeg, Rosemary, Sage, Spearmint, Tangerine

Blends:
Aroma Life, Citrus Fresh, GLF, Juva Cleanse, Juva Flex

Supplements & Products:
Detoxzyme, Digest + Cleanse, JuvaPower, JuvaSpice, JuvaTone, MightyZyme, NingXia Red, Omega Blue, Thieves Household Cleaner

LUPUS
(See AUTOIMMUNE CONDITIONS)

LUXATING PATELLA
(See PATELLA - LUXATING)

LYME DISEASE
(See TICK BORNE DISEASE)

ANIMAL DESK REFERENCE: CANINE

LYMPH NODES - LYMPHADENOPATHY
(See also CANCER - LYMPHOSARCOMA)

FIRST LINE RECOMMENDATIONS:
RAINDROP TECHNIQUE: Apply up to once a day, possibly including application to the Lymph Nodes. Modifications with inserting oils such as Grapefruit, Frankincense, and Juva Flex can also be performed.
TOPICAL: Cel-Lite Magic Massage Oil
PETTING: With any selected oils.

Single Oils:
Frankincense, Grapefruit, Lemon, Lemongrass, Palo Santo

Blends:
Aroma Life, Citrus Fresh, Forgiveness, ImmuPower, Juva Flex, Thieves, 3 Wise Men

Supplements & Products:
Cel-Lite Magic Massage Oil, Essentialzyme, Essentialzymes-4, ImmuPro, Longevity Softgels, MightyZyme, NingXia Red, Omega Blue

LYMPHOMA
(See CANCER - LYMPHOSARCOMA)

LYMPHOSARCOMA
(See CANCER - LYMPHOSARCOMA)

MALDIGESTION
(See also DIARRHEA, INFLAMMATORY BOWEL DISEASE, VOMITING, PANCREATIC INSUFFICIENCY)

FIRST LINE RECOMMENDATIONS:
SUPPLEMENTS: Essentialzymes-4
ORAL: Di-Gize
DRINKING WATER: Citrus Fresh

Single Oils:
   Geranium, Helichrysum, Juniper, Lemon, Ocotea, Tangerine, Tarragon

Blends:
   Citrus Fresh, Di-Gize, GLF, Juva Cleanse, Juva Flex

Supplements & Products:
   Carbozyme, ComforTone, Detoxzyme, Digest + Cleanse, Essentialzymes-4, ICP, JuvaPower, JuvaSpice, JuvaTone, Life 5, MightyZyme, Mineral Essence, NingXia Red, ParaFree, Power Meal, Super B, True Source

MAST CELL TUMORS
(See also CANCER)

FIRST LINE RECOMMENDATIONS:
TOPICAL: Neat application of Frankincense to Mast Cell Tumors has been very helpful. Some dogs may require dilution or lesser applications if they are very sensitive. Tumors often look worse before they look better.
ORAL: Melissa essential oil can be used for antihistamine effects.
RAINDROP TECHNIQUE: Apply as indicated for the individual, usually once a week or more. Insertion of any other indicated oils is suggested, and rotation of oils inserted is also recommended.

Single Oils:
   Frankincense, Grapefruit, Helichrysum, Lavender, Lemon, Melissa, Ocotea, Orange, Palo Santo, Sandalwood, Tangerine

Blends:
   Brain Power, Citrus Fresh, Forgiveness, Hope, ImmuPower, Juva Cleanse, 3 Wise Men

Supplements & Products:
   Animal Scents Ointment, Digest + Cleanse, Essentialzymes-4, ImmuPro, Inner Defense, JuvaTone, Longevity Softgels, MightyZyme, MultiGreens, NingXia Red, Ningxia Wolfberries, Omega Blue, ParaFree, PD 80/20

MASTICATORY MUSCLE MYOSITIS
(See also AUTOIMMUNE CONDITIONS)

FIRST LINE RECOMMENDATIONS:
RAINDROP TECHNIQUE: Daily for 7 days, then every other day for 10 days, then gradually reduce the frequency of applications based on how the individual responds. Inserting oils such as Aroma Siez, Lavender, and Copaiba are suggested.
SUPPLEMENTS: BLM Capsules, Sulfurzyme, Omega Blue, Essentialzymes-4, Longevity

Single Oils:
Copaiba, Frankincense, Helichrysum, Lavender, Marjoram, Spruce, Vetiver, Wintergreen

Blends:
Aroma Siez, Deep Relief Roll-On, ImmuPower, Juva Cleanse, Longevity, M-Grain, PanAway, Relieve It

Supplements & Products:
BLM Capsules, Essentialzymes-4, Longevity Softgels, MightyZyme, Mineral Essence, NingXia Red, Ningxia Wolfberries, Omega Blue, Ortho Ease Massage Oil, Ortho Sport Massage Oil, PD 80/20, Power Meal, Regenolone Moisturizing Cream, Relaxation Massage Oil, Sulfurzyme

MASTITIS

FIRST LINE RECOMMENDATIONS:
TOPICAL: Add 1 drop of Oregano, 3 drops of Melrose, and 3 drops of Helichrysum (or any other selected oils) to Animal Scents Ointment and massage into mammary area 1-4 times a day.
ORAL: Oregano and/or Thieves can be given orally for antibiotic action if needed.
SUPPLEMENTS: Inner Defense can be used if oral oils are not being utilized for antibiotic purposes.

Single Oils:
Geranium, Helichrysum, Lavender, Melaleuca Alternifolia, Melaleuca Ericifolia, Mountain Savory, Myrrh, Oregano

Blends:
　Melrose, Purification, Thieves

Supplements & Products:
　Animal Scents Ointment, ClaraDerm, Inner Defense, LavaDerm Cooling Mist, Longevity Softgels, NingXia Red, Ortho Ease Massage Oil, Ortho Sport Massage Oil

MEGAESOPHAGUS

(See also RESPIRATORY INFECTIONS, COUGH)

FIRST LINE RECOMMENDATIONS:
SUPPLEMENTS: Essentialzymes-4, Mineral Essence, Omega Blue, Longevity, NingXia Red, Super B
RAINDROP TECHNIQUE: Modify by inserting Roman Chamomile, Helichrysum, Laurus Nobilis or other selected oils on a rotational basis. Apply as frequently as indicated by the individual, usually weekly to monthly in maintenance situations.
NEURO AURICULAR TECHNIQUE: See Advanced Techniques.

Single Oils:
　Chamomile (Roman), Helichrysum, Juniper, Laurus Nobilis, Lavender, Marjoram, Peppermint, Tarragon

Blends:
　Di-Gize, Juva Cleanse, Longevity, M-Grain

Supplements & Products:
　BLM Capsules, Digest + Cleanse, Essentialzymes-4, Life 5, Longevity Softgels, MightyZyme, Mineral Essence, NingXia Red, Omega Blue, PD 80/20, Power Meal, Sulfurzyme, Super B, True Source

MUSCLE WASTING

Muscle Wasting or Sarcopenia, is common in older dogs and consists of the loss of muscle and condition. Some cases are caused by lack of innervation or from reduced use of the muscles due to pain. Most commonly, dogs experience this condition through chronic lack of digestive enzymes, resulting in nutritional deficiency. Digestive enzymes are the pinnacle of the repair of this condition.

FIRST LINE RECOMMENDATIONS:
SUPPLEMENTS: Essentialzymes-4, MightyZyme, NingXia Red, Power Meal, BLM Capsules
PETTING: Lavender, Marjoram

Single Oils:
Lavender, Marjoram

Blends:
Aroma Siez

Supplements & Products:
BLM Capsules, Essentialzymes-4, Life 5, Longevity Softgels, MightyZyme, Mineral Essence, MultiGreens, NingXia Red, Ningxia Wolfberries, Omega Blue, Ortho Ease Massage Oil, Ortho Sport Massage Oil, ParaFree, PD 80/20, Power Meal, Regenolone Moisturizing Cream, Sulfurzyme, True Source

NEUROLOGIC CONDITIONS

FIRST LINE RECOMMENDATIONS:
TOPICAL: Valor to ears and brainstem.
NEURO AURICULAR TECHNIQUE: See Advanced Techniques
RAINDROP TECHNIQUE: Insert oils such as Helichrysum, Roman Chamomile, and Laurus Nobilis.
SUPPLEMENTS: Super B, Omega Blue, Longevity, Mineral Essence

Single Oils:
Chamomile (Roman), Copaiba, Frankincense, Helichrysum, Juniper, Laurus Nobilis, Lavender, Nutmeg, Palo Santo

Physical Blends:
Brain Power, Deep Relief Roll-On, Forgiveness, Juva Cleanse

Supplements & Products:
Longevity Softgels, Mineral Essence, MultiGreens, NingXia Red, Omega Blue, Sulfurzyme, Super B

OBESITY

Obesity can be caused by a lack of nutrients being perceived by the body. When a body perceives that nutrition is lacking, it tried to hold onto any spare energy source (fat) that it can in case of emergency. Digestive enzymes, especially lipase, are also required to "digest away" the fat that is desired to be lost. When animals are in an enzyme deficient state, which is likely occurring in all animals, weight loss is almost impossible to occur.

FIRST LINE RECOMMENDATIONS:
SUPPLEMENTS: Essentialzymes-4, NingXia Red, MultiGreens, Stevia Extract, Omega Blue
DRINKING WATER: Citrus Fresh, Slique Essence
PETTING: EndoFlex

Single Oils:
Pepper (Black), Peppermint, Spearmint, Tangerine

Blends:
Abundance, Citrus Fresh, Di-Gize, EndoFlex, GLF, Juva Cleanse, Juva Flex, Slique Essence

Supplements & Products:
Allerzyme, Detoxzyme, EndoGize, Essentialzymes-4, Life 5, Longevity Softgels, MightyVites, MightyZyme, NingXia Red, Ningxia Wolfberries, Omega Blue, ParaFree, Stevia Extract, Thyromin, True Source

OCD
(See BEHAVIORAL CONDITIONS)

ORCHITIS
(See TESTICULAR INFLAMMATION)

OSTEOSARCOMA
(See CANCER - BONE)

PAIN MANAGEMENT

Pain is an important item to address. The presence of pain is not only uncomfortable for an animal, but it will actually suppress the immune system and inhibit healing. All of the recommendations can be used alongside of traditional medications when they are being used. Careful monitoring and care with a veterinarian is recommended to make sure that adequate control of pain is always met.

FIRST LINE RECOMMENDATIONS:
ORAL: Helichrysum, Copaiba, and Myrrh combination. See oil descriptions for dosing information.
PETTING: With any oil suggested, as needed.

Single Oils:
Copaiba, Helichrysum, Lavender, Marjoram, Myrrh, Palo Santo, Peppermint, Tansy (Blue), Wintergreen

Blends:
Deep Relief Roll-On, M-Grain, PanAway, Relieve It

Supplements & Products:
BLM Capsules, NingXia Red, Omega Blue, Ortho Ease Massage Oil, Ortho Sport Massage Oil, Sulfurzyme

PANCREATIC INSUFFICIENCY
(See also MALDIGESTION)

This disorder is mainly corrected through the supplementation of digestive enzymes. Supporting pancreatic function and the endocrine system in beneficial, as well as is addressing intestinal upset and other underlying issues or conditions.

FIRST LINE RECOMMENDATIONS:
SUPPLEMENTS: Digestive Enzymes are required, sometimes in very high amounts, with every meal. Giving multiple enzyme products is helpful for many dogs, and experimenting with which enzymes and also which amounts are needed for an individual is usually necessary. Every dog is unique, and one version or amount of an enzyme may work better than another.

PETTING: Di-Gize

Single Oils:
Geranium, Helichrysum, Ocotea, Peppermint, Spearmint, Tarragon

Blends:
Citrus Fresh, Di-Gize, GLF, Juva Cleanse, Juva Flex

Supplements & Products:
Allerzyme, Detoxzyme, Digest + Cleanse, Essentialzyme, Essentialzymes-4, Life 5, MightyZyme, Power Meal, True Source

PANCREATITIS
(See also DIARRHEA, PAIN MANAGEMENT, VOMITING)

Pancreatitis is often a severe situation that requires hospital care. Many times dietary change, getting into the garbage, a high fat meal, etc…can cause the pancreas to go into overload, and excrete too many enzymes. The inflammation caused by the enzymes of the pancreas escaping its organ – causes sometimes excruciating pain as the animal's own insides are digested.

FIRST LINE RECOMMENDATIONS:
PETTING: Copaiba, Di-Gize
ORAL: Di-Gize, Copaiba, Ginger
SUPPLEMENTS: Essentialzymes-4
RAINDROP TECHNIQUE: Can be used as needed based on response. Insertion of oils such as Helichrysum, Copaiba, and Patchouli is suggested.

Single Oils:
Copaiba, Geranium, Ginger, Helichrysum, Peppermint, Lavender, Myrrh, Ocotea, Patchouli, Peppermint, Pine, Spruce, Tansy (Blue), Tarragon, Wintergreen

Blends:
Deep Relief Roll-On, Di-Gize, GLF, Juva Cleanse, Juva Flex, PanAway, Raindrop Technique, Relieve It, Thieves

Supplements & Products:
Although not used while fasting or severe vomiting and diarrhea is occurring, supplements are an important part of getting a dog back to health. Enzymes are incredibly important, as the pancreas is unable to respond normally to the body's enzyme needs. As soon as foods are being offered start adding in supplements. Start with very small amounts (generally enzymes first) and gradually build up, making sure not to cause a relapse in the condition.

Detoxzyme, Digest + Cleanse, Essentialzymes-4, ICP, ImmuPro, Life 5, Longevity Softgels, MightyZyme, MultiGreens, NingXia Red

PANNUS
(See AUTOIMMUNE CONDITIONS, EYE CONDITIONS)

PANOSTEITIS
(See also BONE CONDITIONS, PAIN MANAGEMENT)

FIRST LINE RECOMMENDATIONS:
PETTING: Idaho Balsam Fir, Helichrysum, Wintergreen over affected area, as needed.
RAINDROP TECHNIQUE: As needed based on response. Insertion of additional oils is possible as well.
SUPPLEMENTS: BLM Capsules, Sulfurzyme, Omega Blue, NingXia Red
ORAL: Copaiba

Single Oils:
Balsam Fir (Idaho), Helichrysum, Lemongrass, Palo Santo, Peppermint, Pine, Spruce, Tansy (Blue), Wintergreen

Blends:
Deep Relief Roll-On, PanAway, Relieve It

Supplements & Products:
BLM Capsules, Essentialzymes-4, Longevity Softgels, MightyZyme, Omega Blue, Ortho Ease Massage Oil, Ortho Sport Massage Oil, PD 80/20, Regenolone Moisturizing Cream, Sulfurzyme

PAPILLOMA
(See WARTS)

PARASITES - INTERNAL
(See DEWORMING)

PARVO
(See DIARRHEA, VIRAL CONDITIONS, VOMITING)

Parvo is a virus that causes bloody diarrhea and vomiting, mainly in puppies. Dogs over 1 year of age, generally develop natural immunity. The virus can live in the environment for a very long time, and is resistant to many environmental disinfectants. Parvo often requires hospitalization with intense veterinary care. Do not abandon traditional veterinary treatments, however add in essential oil therapies to increase your outcome. Prevention with these same measures would be wise.

FIRST LINE RECOMMENDATIONS:
RAINDROP TECHNIQUE: Modified by inserting Eucalyptus Blue, ImmuPower, and Melissa (diluted). Apply daily or as indicated by patient.
DIFFUSION: Thieves with Eucalyptus Blue diffused up to 24 hours a day.
CLEANING: Thieves Household Cleaner.
PETTING: With any selected oils, 1-4 times daily.

Single Oils:
Eucalyptus Blue, Eucalyptus Radiata, Ginger, Hyssop, Lemon, Melaleuca Alternifolia, Melissa, Mountain Savory, Oregano, Patchouli, Peppermint, Tarragon, Thyme

Blends:
DiGize, Exodus II, Forgiveness, Hope, ImmuPower, Melrose, Purification, Thieves

Supplements & Products:
Although not used while severe vomiting and diarrhea is occurring, supplements can be an important part of getting a dog back to health. As soon as foods are being offered start adding in

supplements. Start with very small amounts and gradually build up.

Detoxzyme, Digest + Cleanse, Essentialzymes-4, ImmuPro, Inner Defense, Life 5, Longevity Softgels, MightyZyme, MultiGreens, NingXia Red, Omega Blue, Power Meal, Super B, Thieves Household Cleaner, True Source

PATELLA - LUXATING

With this condition, the knee cap slips off of its normal position on top of the knee, resulting in abnormal gaits, arthritic pains, as well as degradation of the bone and cartilage. This condition cannot often be reversed from its severe form, due to loss of boney material. However, post-surgical healing is greatly enhanced by the use of supplements and essential oils. In low grades of luxation, muscles, ligaments, cartilage, and tendons can be improved resulting in less degradation of the condition and less pain. Even though this condition is not often perceived as painful, I can assure you that inflammation and discomfort are present, and should be addressed.

FIRST LINE RECOMMENDATIONS:
 ORAL: Copaiba
 SUPPLEMENTS: BLM Capsules, Sulfurzyme, Omega Blue
 PETTING: Idaho Balsam Fir, Palo Santo, Helichrysum, Aroma Siez

Single Oils:
Balsam Fir (Idaho), Frankincense, Helichrysum, Lavender, Lemongrass, Marjoram, Palo Santo, Peppermint, Spruce, Wintergreen

Blends:
Aroma Siez, Deep Relief Roll-On, PanAway, Relieve It

Supplements & Products:
Animal Scents Ointment, BLM Capsules, NingXia Red, Omega Blue, Ortho Ease Massage Oil, Ortho Sport Massage Oil, Regenolone Moisturizing Cream, Sulfurzyme

PEMPHIGUS
(See AUTOIMMUNE CONDITIONS)

PNEUMONIA
(See RESPIRATORY INFECTIONS)

PREGNANCY & DELIVERY

FIRST LINE RECOMMENDATIONS:
WATER DIFFUSION: Gentle Baby can be diffused in an open room situation from the time of conception until after birth.
PETTING: En-R-Gee and Gentle Baby during delivery.
SUPPLEMENTS: NingXia Red during delivery gives increased stamina.

If painful or stressful birthing occurs, Lavender can be diffused or applied via Petting to relax and reduce stress. After delivery, Frankincense is often used to anoint puppies. See the individual oil description for more information. Myrrh can be applied to umbilical cords as well.

Single Oils:
Frankincense, Geranium, Helichrysum, Lavender, Myrrh, Rose, Vetiver

Blends:
En-R-Gee, Gentle Baby

Supplements & Products:
Animal Scents Ointment, ClaraDerm, MightyZyme, MultiGreens, NingXia Red, Ningxia Wolfberries, Omega Blue, ParaFree, Power Meal, Relaxation Massage Oil, Sulfurzyme, Thieves Household Cleaner, True Source

PROSTATE CONDITIONS

FIRST LINE RECOMMENDATIONS:
RAINDROP TECHNIQUE: Modify by inserting Copaiba, Mister, and Sage.
PETTING: Mister, Sage
ORAL: Copaiba
RECTAL: See Rectal Instillation for more information. Any selected oils could be used in this manner.

SUPPLEMENTS: Longevity, Essentialzymes-4, Prostate Health, Omega Blue

Single Oils:
Clary Sage, Sage, Frankincense, Helichrysum, Lavender, Mountain Savory, Myrtle, Oregano, Sage, Ylang Ylang

Blends:
EndoFlex, ImmuPower, Mister, SclarEssence, Thieves, 3 Wise Men

Supplements & Products:
Detoxzyme, EndoGize, Essentialzyme, Essentialzyme 4, ImmuPro, Life 5, Longevity Softgels, MightyZyme, MultiGreens, NingXia Red, Omega Blue, PD 80/20, Prostate Health, Protec

PROSTATITIS

(See PROSTATE CONDITIONS)

Prostatitis is an inflammation of the prostate in male dogs. There are several causes for this condition including bacteria, virus, sexually transmitted diseases, cancer, benign prostatic hyperplasia, and more. If infection is suspected, Inner Defense can be utilized as an antibiotic.

PYOMETRA

Pyometra is a serious bacterial infection of the uterus, that can turn fatal. It is a risk in all unspayed females, especially those who have not given birth. A common form of pyometra is a closed cervix situation, where pus cannot escape the body, and therefore the dog is very ill. The uterus can become very damaged and fragile from the bacterial infection leading to rupture. In an open cervix pyometra, pus can be seen draining from the vulva. The pus can vary in consistency, color, and texture. In most cases, it is very important for the infected uterus to be surgically removed. Only in valuable breeding dogs, are attempts to save the uterus made – often with great difficulty, expense, and poor outcome.

FIRST LINE RECOMMENDATIONS:
RAINDROP TECHNIQUE: Modify by inserting ImmuPower, Myrrh, and Hyssop.
SUPPLEMENTS: Inner Defense

Single Oils:
Cistus, Eucalyptus Radiata, Frankincense, Geranium, Helichrysum, Hyssop, Laurus Nobilis, Lavender, Lemon, Lemongrass, Melaleuca Alternifolia, Mountain Savory, Myrrh, Myrtle, Oregano, Sage, Thyme

Blends:
Di-Gize, Dragon Time, Egyptian Gold, EndoFlex, Exodus II, ImmuPower, Lady Sclareol, Melrose, Mister, Purification, SclarEssence, Thieves

Supplements & Products:
Detoxzyme, Dragon Time Massage Oil, EndoGize, Essentialzyme, Essentialzymes-4, Estro, FemiGen, Inner Defense, K&B Tincture, Life 5, Longevity Softgels, MightyZyme, Omega Blue, PD 80/20

RABIES
(See also VACCINOSIS, VIRAL CONDITIONS)

An entire book could certainly be written on the subject of Rabies, Rabies vaccinations, and the holistic approach to all of these subjects. In brief, we are often held to legal requirements within our communities as to whether or not we are obligated to vaccinate our animals. There are more and more holistic veterinarians consenting to the fact that vaccinations are less and less necessary. When health concerns are noted, many holistic veterinarians will now write a letter of recommendation to your community heads, that future vaccinations (of all sorts) are no longer recommended for your animal.

Certainly the decision has to be a personal one. However, if vaccination is deemed necessary, support of the body and detoxification from the vaccination is important. The use of a vaccination which is Thimerosal-free (Merial IMRAB 3 TF) is highly recommended.

For animals who are not vaccinated for Rabies, the focus would be creating a competent and healthy immune system. Good nutrition, regular exposure to essential oils, quality supplementation, and regular Raindrop Technique is recommended.

Symptomatic forms of Rabies will not be discussed due to the controversial nature of the disease, and the nearly almost fatal implications to both animals and humans. What can be said is what I would do for a suspected exposure to Rabies in an animal, or for an animal who was placed under a quarantine situation.

FIRST LINE RECOMMENDATIONS:
For suspected Rabies Exposure:
- RAINDROP TECHNIQUE: With Spikenard, Melissa, and Copaiba inserted up to daily. Rotational insertion of the other indicated oils is also recommended. Depending on the time frame of the quarantine, weekly rotation of the 3 inserted oils would be suggested.
- SUPPLEMENTS: NingXia Red, MultiGreens, Omega Blue, Longevity given orally every day.

Single Oils:
Copaiba, Frankincense, Helichrysum, Hyssop, Melissa, Mountain Savory, Ravintsara, Spikenard

Blends:
Brain Power, Forgiveness, ImmuPower, Exodus II, Hope, Raven

Supplements & Products:
Essentialzymes-4, ImmuPro, Longevity Softgels, MightyZyme, MultiGreens, NingXia Red, Omega Blue, Thieves Household Cleaner

RESPIRATORY INFECTIONS
(See also KENNEL COUGH, MEGAESOPHAGUS)

Respiratory infections can have many causes – bacterial, fungal, viral. Even allergies, parasitic infections, and cancer can cause the appearance of a lung infection. Having an accurate diagnosis is important in addressing the specific cause of a lung condition. However, the most assuring fact is that a holistic approach to health will truly benefit any lung condition, regardless of the cause.

FIRST LINE RECOMMENDATIONS:
    RAINDROP TECHNIQUE: Insert ImmuPower, Pine, and R.C. or other suggested oils. Apply up to daily as needed by the individual.
    SUPPLEMENTS: Inner Defense
    DIFFUSION: Thieves or Purification up to 24 hours a day. Tenting and caging methods can also be utilized with Water Diffusion.

Single Oils:
    Balsam Fir (Idaho), Eucalyptus Blue, Eucalyptus Radiata, Hyssop, Laurus Nobilis, Lavender, Lemon, Lemongrass, Marjoram, Melaleuca Alternifolia, Melaleuca Ericifolia, Mountain Savory, Myrtle, Oregano, Palo Santo, Pine, Rosemary, Spruce, Thyme

Blends:
    Breathe Again Roll-On, Egyptian Gold, Exodus II, ImmuPower, Melrose, Purification, Raven, R.C., Thieves

Supplements & Products:
    Detoxzyme, Essentialzymes-4, ImmuPro, Inner Defense, NingXia Red, MightyZyme, MultiGreens, NingXia Red, Omega Blue, Thieves Household Cleaner

RINGWORM

FIRST LINE RECOMMENDATIONS:
    TOPICAL: Neat Lavender, R.C., or Ocotea applied to lesions once to twice a day. Oils can also be mixed into Animal Scents Ointment for application.
    BATHING: With Thieves Household Cleaner at least weekly.
    RAINDROP TECHNIQUE: Apply at least weekly, insert other oils as desired.
    CLEANING: Wash bedding and other areas and materials in contact with infected individuals often with Thieves Household Cleaner.

Single Oils:
    Eucalyptus Radiata, Geranium, Lavender, Lemongrass, Marjoram, Melaleuca Alternifolia, Melaleuca Ericifolia, Mountain Savory, Myrrh, Ocotea, Oregano, Palo Santo, Rosemary, Thyme

ANIMAL DESK REFERENCE: CANINE

Blends:
Melrose, Purification, R.C., Thieves

Supplements & Products:
Animal Scents Ointment, LavaDerm Cooling Mist, Omega Blue, Ortho Ease Massage Oil, Ortho Sport Massage Oil, Thieves Household Cleaner, Thieves Spray

ROCKY MOUNTAIN SPOTTED FEVER
(See TICK BORNE DISEASE)

SARCOPTIC MANGE
(See also SKIN INFECTIONS)

Sarcoptic Mange is a contagious mite that lives in the skin of dogs. It is often very itchy, and can have secondary skin infections present. Traditional treatments with injectable Ivermectin are often quite effective, and are not associated with as many side effects as the high dose treatments used for Demodex Mange. Dips and other various forms of treatment are highly toxic, and are not recommended at all. All dogs in contact with an affected dog should be treated, whether or not they show symptoms.

FIRST LINE RECOMMENDATIONS:
RAINDROP TECHNIQUE: Insert Purification and Pine. Apply at least weekly.
BATHING: Thieves Household Cleaner with Purification added.
PETTING: Purification, daily.
SUPPLEMENTS: ParaFree may or may not be effective for this form of mange. Some reports claim effects, while others do not.

Single Oils:
Citronella, Geranium, Helichrysum, Lavender, Palo Santo, Pine, Tansy (Idaho)

Blends:
Purification, Thieves

Supplements & Products:
Animal Scents Ointment, ClaraDerm, LavaDerm Cooling Mist, Omega Blue, ParaFree, Thieves Household Cleaner, Thieves Spray

SEBACEOUS CYSTS

FIRST LINE RECOMMENDATIONS:
RAINDROP TECHNIQUE: Apply at least weekly. Oils may be dripped onto large cysts as well, or the Kitty Raindrop Solution may be applied to the cysts.

Single Oils:
Elemi, Frankincense, Geranium, Grapefruit, Lavender, Lemon, Myrtle, Orange, Palmarosa, Vetiver

Blends:
Citrus Fresh, GLF, Juva Cleanse, Juva Flex, Kitty Raindrop Solution

Supplements & Products:
Detoxzyme, Digest + Cleanse, Essentialzymes-4, JuvaPower, JuvaSpice, JuvaTone, Longevity Softgels, MightyZyme, Omega Blue

SEBORRHEA - OLEOSA

FIRST LINE RECOMMENDATIONS:
BATHING: Animal Scents Shampoo or Thieves Household Cleaner. Additional oils may be added to the bathing solution, especially Lavender, Lemon, and other selections that reduce sebum.
SUPPLEMENTS: Essentialzymes-4, Omega Blue

Single Oils:
Elemi, Geranium, Grapefruit, Lavender, Lemon, Myrtle, Orange, Palmarosa, Vetiver

Blends:
Citrus Fresh, GLF, Juva Cleanse, Juva Flex

Supplements & Products:
Animal Scents Shampoo, Detoxzyme, Digest + Cleanse, Essentialzymes-4, JuvaPower, JuvaSpice, JuvaTone, Longevity Softgels, MightyZyme, Omega Blue, Stevia Extract, Thieves Household Cleaner, True Source

SEIZURES

FIRST LINE RECOMMENDATIONS:
DIFFUSION: Idaho Balsam Fir, Jasmine up to 24 hours a day.
ORAL: Lavender, RutaVaLa, Valerian, or Roman Chamomile during a seizure.
PETTING: Frankincense, Idaho Balsam Fir, and Jasmine daily.
SUPPLEMENTS: Essentialzymes-4, Omega Blue, NingXia Red

Single Oils:
Balsam Fir (Idaho), Chamomile (Roman), Frankincense, Helichrysum, Jasmine, Juniper, Laurus Nobilis, Lavender, Melissa, Valerian

Blends:
Brain Power, Forgiveness, GLF, Hope, Juva Cleanse, Juva Flex, Peace & Calming, RutaVaLa, Valor

CAUTIONS:
These oils have general recommendations to avoid in people with epilepsy. Please see the single oil comments for more information: Basil, Fennel, Hyssop, Sage, Tarragon, Wintergreen.

Supplements & Products:
Essentialzymes-4, JuvaPower, JuvaSpice, JuvaTone, Longevity Softgels, MightyZyme, Mineral Essence, MultiGreens, NingXia Red, Ningxia Wolfberries, Omega Blue, Relaxation Massage Oil, Sulfurzyme, Super B, Thieves Household Cleaner

SENILITY
(See COGNITIVE DYSFUNCTION)

SKIN INFECTIONS
(See also ALLERGIES, HOT SPOTS)

FIRST LINE RECOMMENDATIONS:
TOPICAL: The Ear Spray Recipe can be used on yeast feet infections and other sites of need. See Ear Infections.
ORAL: Thieves, Oregano
SUPPLEMENTS: Inner Defense, Omega Blue
PETTING: Melrose, Lavender, Laurus Nobilis

CANINE CONDITIONS

BATHING: Animal Scents Shampoo mixed with Thieves Household Cleaner.

Single Oils:
Laurus Nobilis, Lavender, Lemongrass, Marjoram, Melaleuca Alternifolia, Melaleuca Ericifolia, Mountain Savory, Myrrh, Myrtle, Ocotea, Oregano, Palo Santo, Patchouli, Spikenard, Tansy (Blue)

Blends:
GLF, Juva Cleanse, Juva Flex, Melrose, Purification, Thieves

Supplements & Products:
Animal Scents Ointment, ClaraDerm, Detoxzyme, Digest + Cleanse, Essentialzymes-4, Inner Defense, JuvaPower, JuvaSpice, JuvaTone, LavaDerm Cooling Mist, Longevity Softgels, MightyZyme, Omega Blue, Stevia Extract, Thieves Household Cleaner, Thieves Spray, Thieves Waterless Hand Purifier, Thieves Wipes

SKIN TAGS

FIRST LINE RECOMMENDATIONS:
TOPICAL: Oregano applied neat to the skin tag, up to multiple times daily or as tolerated. The skin tag will look worse and may become crusty and scabbed prior to falling off.
SUPPLEMENTS: Addressing liver health is helpful in reducing the formation of skin tags.

Single Oils:
Oregano, Palo Santo

Blends:
GLF, Juva Cleanse, Juva Flex, Thieves

Supplements & Products:
Detoxzyme, Digest + Cleanse, Essentialzymes-4, JuvaPower, JuvaSpice, JuvaTone, Longevity Softgels, MightyZyme, Omega Blue, True Source

SPINAL CONDITIONS
(See also INTERVERTEBRAL DISC DISEASE)

FIRST LINE RECOMMENDATIONS:
PETTING: Spruce, Valor
RAINDROP TECHNIQUE: Apply as needed for individual.

Single Oils:
Helichrysum, Juniper, Laurus Nobilis, Lavender, Lemongrass, Marjoram, Mountain Savory, Palo Santo, Peppermint, Pine, Spruce, Wintergreen

Blends:
Aroma Siez, Deep Relief Roll-On, Harmony, M-Grain, PanAway, Relieve It, Valor

Supplements & Products:
BLM Capsules, Longevity Softgels, MightyZyme, Omega Blue, Ortho Ease Massage Oil, Ortho Sport Massage Oil, PD 80/20, Regenolone Moisturizing Cream, Relaxation Massage Oil, Sulfurzyme

SPLEEN
(See also CANCER - SPLEEN)

SPONDYLOSIS
(See also SPINAL CONDITIONS, ARTHRITIS)

FIRST LINE RECOMMENDATIONS:
RAINDROP TECHNIQUE: Apply as often as indicated by response, usually weekly. Insert Idaho Balsam Fir, Spruce, R.C., and Copaiba.
PETTING: Valor, Relieve It
TOPICAL: R.C. has been shown to dissolve bone spurs, as this condition also creates an accumulation of bone material, applying R.C. over the affected spinal area is suggested.

CANINE CONDITIONS

Single Oils:
Balsam Fir (Idaho), Copaiba, Helichrysum, Juniper, Laurus Nobilis, Lavender, Lemongrass, Marjoram, Mountain Savory, Myrrh, Nutmeg, Palo Santo, Peppermint, Pine, Spruce, Wintergreen

Blends:
Aroma Siez, Deep Relief Roll-On, M-Grain, PanAway, R.C., Relieve It, Valor

Supplements & Products:
BLM Capsules, Essentialzymes-4, Longevity Softgels, MightyZyme, Omega Blue, Ortho Ease Massage Oil, Ortho Sport Massage Oil, PD 80/20, Regenolone Moisturizing Cream, Relaxation Massage Oil, Sulfurzyme

STAPH INFECTIONS
(See SKIN INFECTIONS)

STEROIDS - REPLACEMENT

When steroids have been indicated or are being used for a condition, I have most commonly found that the Raindrop Technique can replace the use of, or reduce the use of these harmful drugs. Starting with a higher frequency of administration (often daily) and gradually reducing to every other day, every third day, every week, every month, and so forth is suggested. The administration must be adjusted to the individual response and needs of the animal.

FIRST LINE RECOMMENDATIONS:
RAINDROP TECHNIQUE: Apply as needed, inserting oils such as Pine, Spruce, and Copaiba may be helpful.

Single Oils:
Pine, Spruce, Tansy (Blue)

Blends:
Kitty Raindrop Technique Solution

Supplements & Products:
BLM Capsules, Longevity Softgels, Omega Blue, PD 80/20, Sulfurzyme

STOOL EATING
(See COPROPHAGIA)

SYSTEMIC LUPUS ERYTHEMATOSIS
(See AUTOIMMUNE CONDITIONS)

TAIL CHASING
(See BEHAVIORAL CONDITIONS)

TESTICULAR INFLAMMATION

FIRST LINE RECOMMENDATIONS:
ORAL: Copaiba
RAINDROP TECHNIQUE: Up to daily or as needed.
TOPICAL: LavaDerm Cooling Mist

Single Oils:
Copaiba, Frankincense, Helichrysum, Lavender, Spruce, Tansy (Blue)

Blends:
Relieve It

Supplements & Products:
Animal Scents Ointment, ClaraDerm, LavaDerm Cooling Mist, Longevity Softgels, NingXia Red, Omega Blue, Ortho Ease Massage Oil, Ortho Sport Massage Oil, Regenolone Moisturizing Cream, Sulfurzyme

TESTICLE - UNDESCENDED

FIRST LINE RECOMMENDATIONS:
SUPPLEMENTS: BLM Capsules, Ultra Young + Oral Spray with DHEA
PETTING: Mister, EndoFlex

Single Oils:
Lemongrass, Marjoram, Palo Santo

Blends:
EndoFlex, Mister

Supplements & Products:
BLM Capsules, EndoGize, Mineral Essence, Omega Blue, Sulfurzyme, True Source, Ultra Young + Oral Spray with DHEA

THROMBOCYTOPENIA
(See AUTOIMMUNE CONDITIONS)

THYROID - LOW
(See HYPOTHYROIDISM)

TICK BITES

FIRST LINE RECOMMENDATIONS:
TOPICAL: Apply any essential oil to a tick bite as soon as possible. Suggested oils are Purification or Thieves, but any oil should be used if the oils listed below are not available. Continue to apply neat oils to the site several times.

Single Oils:
Hyssop, Lavender, Melaleuca Alternifolia, Mountain Savory, Oregano, Thyme

Blends:
Egyptian Gold, Exodus II, ImmuPower, Melrose, Purification, Thieves

Supplements & Products:
Animal Scents Ointment, Inner Defense, Longevity Softgels, Ortho Ease Massage Oil, Thieves Spray

TICK BORNE DISEASE

FIRST LINE RECOMMENDATIONS:
ORAL: Ocotea, Oregano, Mountain Savory, or Thieves
SUPPLEMENTS: Inner Defense, Detoxzyme, Life 5, ParaFree, NingXia Red, Longevity, Omega Blue, Sulfurzyme

ANIMAL DESK REFERENCE: CANINE

RAINDROP TECHNIQUE: Daily to every other day depending on response of individual. Inserting ImmuPower and Copaiba is suggested.

Single Oils:
Helichrysum, Hyssop, Mountain Savory, Ocotea, Oregano, Thyme

Blends:
Exodus II, ImmuPower, Longevity, Thieves

Supplements & Products:
Inner Defense, Longevity Softgels, NingXia Red, Rehemogen, Sulfurzyme

TICK PARALYSIS
(See also TICK BORNE DISEASE)

FIRST LINE RECOMMENDATIONS:
ORAL: Helichrysum
RAINDROP TECHNIQUE: Up to daily, insert Helichrysum and Hyssop.
SUPPLEMENTS: NingXia Red, Sulfurzyme

Single Oils:
Copaiba, Helichrysum, Hyssop, Juniper, Mountain Savory, Oregano, Thyme

Blends:
Egyptian Gold, Exodus II, GLF, ImmuPower, Juva Cleanse, Longevity, Thieves

Supplements & Products:
Longevity Softgels, Inner Defense, Longevity Softgels, Mineral Essence, Omega Blue, PD 80/20, Sulfurzyme, Super B

ULCERS - GASTRIC
(See GASTRIC ULCERS)

URINARY INCONTINENCE
(See INCONTINENCE - URINARY)

CANINE CONDITIONS

VACCINATION
(See VACCINOSIS)

VACCINOSIS

FIRST LINE RECOMMENDATIONS:
RAINDROP TECHNIQUE: At least monthly, insert Tsuga, Juva Cleanse, and Ledum. Rotation through inserted oils is suggested.
SUPPLEMENTS: Rehemogen
ORAL: Juva Cleanse

Single Oils:
Chamomile (Roman), Geranium, Grapefruit, Helichrysum, Hyssop, Juniper, Ledum, Lemon, Tsuga

Blends:
Citrus Fresh, GLF, Juva Cleanse, Juva Flex, Longevity

Supplements & Products:
Detoxzyme, Digest + Cleanse, JuvaPower, JuvaSpice, JuvaTone, K&B Tincture, Longevity Softgels, NingXia Red, Ningxia Wolfberries, Omega Blue, Rehemogen

VAGINITIS

FIRST LINE RECOMMENDATIONS:
RAINDROP TECHNIQUE: Apply weekly or as indicated by the individual response.
PETTING: Dragon Time
SUPPLEMENTS: FemiGen, Inner Defense (if antibiotic action is indicated), Life 5
TOPICAL: ClaraDerm

Single Oils:
Clary Sage, Eucalyptus Radiata, Helichrysum, Laurus Nobilis, Lavender, Lemon, Lemongrass, Melaleuca Alternifolia, Melaleuca Ericifolia, Mountain Savory, Myrtle, Oregano, Sage, Thyme

Blends:
Dragon Time, EndoFlex, ImmuPower, Juva Cleanse, Longevity, Melrose, Mister, Purification, R.C., SclarEssence, Thieves

Supplements & Products:
ClaraDerm, Dragon Time Massage Oil, EndoGize, Essentialzymes-4, Estro, FemiGen, ImmuPro, Inner Defense, JuvaTone, K&B Tincture, LavaDerm Cooling Mist, Life 5, Longevity Softgels, Mineral Essence, NingXia Red, Ningxia Wolfberries, Omega Blue, Prenolone Plus Body Cream, Progessence Plus Serum, Thieves Household Cleaner

VERTIGO
(See VESTIBULAR DISEASE)

VESTIBULAR DISEASE
(See also NEUROLOGIC CONDITIONS)

FIRST LINE RECOMMENDATIONS:
NEURO AURICULAR TECHNIQUE: See Advanced Techniques. Apply up to daily.
SUPPLEMENTS: Super B, Longevity Softgels
PETTING: Helichrysum

Single Oils:
Chamomile (Roman), Frankincense, Helichrysum, Juniper, Laurus Nobilis, Lavender, Melissa, Petitgrain, Valerian

Blends:
Brain Power, Common Sense, Hope, Juva Cleanse, Longevity

Supplements & Products:
Essentialzymes-4, JuvaTone, K&B Tincture, Longevity Softgels, Mineral Essence, MultiGreens, NingXia Red, Omega Blue, ParaFree, PD 80/20, Relaxation Massage Oil, Sulfurzyme, Super B

CANINE CONDITIONS

VIRAL CONDITIONS

FIRST LINE RECOMMENDATIONS:
RAINDROP TECHNIQUE: Apply up to daily. Insertion of other antiviral oils is also suggested, especially Melissa (diluted), ImmuPower, and Ravintsara.
SUPPLEMENTS: MultiGreens
DIFFUSION: Thieves, Exodus II, Raven
PETTING: Ravintsara, Raven
CLEANING: Thieves Household Cleaner
ORAL: Melissa, Thieves

Single Oils:
Eucalyptus Globulus, Geranium, Helichrysum, Hyssop, Laurus Nobilis, Melissa, Mountain Savory, Oregano, Peppermint, Ravintsara, Sandalwood, Thyme

Blends:
Exodus II, Forgiveness, Hope, ImmuPower, Longevity, Raven, Thieves, 3 Wise Men

Supplements & Products:
ImmuPro, Longevity Softgels, Mineral Essence, MultiGreens, NingXia Red, Omega Blue, Thieves Household Cleaner

VOMITING
(See also DIARRHEA)

An accurate diagnosis with a veterinarian is mandatory for cases of vomiting. Using recommendations specific to the cause of the vomiting is advised. Fasting during the initial phases of vomiting is important, and often water will have to be withheld as well. Consult with a veterinarian to determine if fasting is appropriate for your situation, and for how long. See the description within Diarrhea for more information regarding fasting.

FIRST LINE RECOMMENDATIONS:
PETTING: Di-Gize, Peppermint, Ginger
ORAL: Ginger, Di-Gize
DRINKING WATER: Peppermint

ANIMAL DESK REFERENCE: CANINE

Single Oils:
Ginger, Helichrysum, Laurus Nobilis, Lemon, Marjoram, Nutmeg, Patchouli, Peppermint, Spearmint, Tarragon

Blends:
Citrus Fresh, Di-Gize, GLF, Juva Cleanse, M-Grain

Supplements & Products:
Detoxzyme, Digest + Cleanse, Life 5, MightyZyme, ParaFree

WARTS

FIRST LINE RECOMMENDATIONS:
TOPICAL: Clove or Oregano, up to daily depending on how the dog tolerates it. Neat application is often used. Warts may look worse before resolving.
SUPPLEMENTS: MultiGreens, Longevity, Omega Blue
ORAL: Melissa

Single Oils:
Cinnamon, Clove, Melissa, Oregano, Mountain Savory, Palo Santo, Peppermint, Sandalwood

Blends:
Abundance, Brain Power, Exodus II, Forgiveness, Hope, ImmuPower, Longevity, Thieves, 3 Wise Men

Supplements & Products:
ImmuPro, JuvaTone, Longevity Softgels, Mineral Essence, MultiGreens, NingXia Red, Ningxia Wolfberries, Omega Blue

WORMS - INTESTINAL
(See DEWORMING)

YEAST INFECTIONS
(See SKIN INFECTIONS)

EQUINE RAINDROP

There are as many ways to give a Raindrop Technique, as there are people using Essential Oils! Here is a method for a "down and dirty" Raindrop application that gets the oils on the horse quickly and effectively. I have found that when using essential oils for health concerns in my veterinary patients, that if I required the owner to do a procedure that took 40-60 minutes per day to perform – that it was unlikely to get done. If you have the time, and you want to enjoy the full process of a Raindrop Technique with your horse – by all means – please complete the entire process. There are many references available that demonstrate giving a Raindrop Technique.

The most important thing to remember is that ANY oils are better than no oils at all. So, if you are pressed for time – your horse will benefit more from just getting sprinkled with oils, than not having any applied at all. I find that so many people feel that if they do it wrong – they will somehow go to "Raindrop Jail" or scar their horse for life! WRONG! Relax and let your horse show you that even standing in a puddle with oils floating on top of the surface – can in fact be beneficial!

In the application, the chosen oils are dripped from tail to head, from a distance of about 3-6 inches from the spine. Combined with specialized strokes and reflexology techniques (called Vita Flex), Raindrop Technique can be a powerful tool that anyone can use.

When administering a Raindrop Technique to a horse who has never had one before – I may start out conservatively and use less drops of each oil. However, in a horse with a severe medical concern – using the full amounts of oils may be needed. Some horses may also "show" that they need fewer drops of oils applied or pre-diluted oils applied to them. The most common reason for this adjustment is for horses that "welt" from the application of oils.

There are several reasons why the welts may appear. Generally, I find the welts to occur in horses that are more "toxic" in general. They usually have more health concerns, have been on traditional medications, or are typically "over" vaccinated. Most horses will gradually welt less and less as the detoxification occurs. Over time, it is found that these same horses that welted severely when first getting a Raindrop, will not welt in the future. However, this may take many months of exposure to essential oils to completely detoxify them.

There are several schools of thought about what to do when a horse welts from a Raindrop. For me, it depends on the severity of the health concern – for how I will exactly proceed. If it is a life threatening situation, as in Strangles, then I will continue to give the Raindrop Technique daily if needed – even applying the full amount of drops. However, I will dilute the area with V-6 after the application of neat oils to make it more comfortable for the horse. Some horses are not uncomfortable at all with the welts, and may not need the V-6 applied. Other horses have rolled on the ground with irritation. Creating this level of irritation in any animal is never warranted. Diluting the oils before application, applying less oils at a time, applying V-6 after neat application, or even omitting certain oils from the Raindrop Technique is just fine.

Another horse owner I know was giving her horse a Raindrop application for a lameness issue. The horse had Raindrop applications previously, and had not welted. However, with this health condition – he proceeded to welt severely from the same exact technique. In this owner's eyes, this was a good sign of things being "cleared up". She continued to perform the Raindrop daily for this horse, and chose to aggressively deal with the problem. As a result, his lameness resolved in record time – at the same time that the welts stopped occurring!

Sometimes oils can be given orally instead of topically for severe cases. Any exposure to essential oils can help "detox" an animal – so changing the route of administration can make gradual detoxification more comfortable. Diffusing oils, adding oils to drinking water, applying "gentle" oils topically, or giving oils orally or in foods can aid in a slower more comfortable detox.

DiGize and Longevity are often oils chosen to give orally to horses that welt up. Giving 5-10 drops of each oil – DiGize in the morning and Longevity at night – can aid a horse.

Other oils have anti-histamine activity, and can be given orally to horses that are irritated with their welts. Melissa, Ocotea, and Basil oils have anti-histamine activity. Starting with 3-5 drops orally and evaluating the response is a good starting point. The number of drops given can certainly be increased as well. Mixing more expensive oils like Melissa with an equal amount of Copaiba (a magnifier oil) – can reduce the amount of oil that must be given. Copaiba is also very anti-inflammatory – so can add its own benefits into the regimen.

Equine Raindrop Technique (without hoof application):

Please refer to the information on Raindrop Technique within the EODR – this will help you understand the various steps. The following steps are for a regular sized horse – so you may want to scale down the amount of drops for a small pony, miniature horse, or foal.

- Balancing: Placing 3-6 drops of Valor into both hands, place your hands behind the ears on the top of the neck. Stand in a safe location of course, and always be mindful that you are working on a large animal, that could injure you. For horses that do not tolerate this, you can balance at the withers instead. For horses that seem to need more balancing or really enjoy the Valor oil, balancing at the poll and at the withers is just fine as well. Place another 3-6 drops of Valor into each hand, and balance over the pelvic area or sacrum. With severe time constraints or with animals that will not allow balancing of any sort – omit the balancing steps.
- If Hoof Application of Oils is desired, insert here. See the following description for more details. Hoof application is not 100% necessary, but is encouraged for any hoof or lameness concern.
- Applying the Raindrop Oils: Start by dripping approximately 6 drops of Oregano from the tail to the top of the neck. Generally, try to hold the bottle approximately 6 inches above the back as you drip them. This is due to the electrical field that we all have surrounding our bodies. As we drip the oils through this field, the natural frequency of the oil provides benefits to the energy field.

  Be careful not to get oils onto the face or near the eyes of the horse. As with the human Raindrop Technique the oils are stroked into the back with your fingers. Alternately, you may rub the oils into the back, with a clockwise circular action. Repeat either of these methods one to three times – from tail to head. Oregano is a "hot" oil, and you could see a horse develop discomfort from it. Dilute the area with V-6 if you see signs of irritation. Then, for future

Raindrop Techniques you may want to use fewer drops of Oregano or dilute it with V-6 before the application. There are some thoughts that diluting the oils will negate or greatly lessen the effects of the Raindrop Technique. I have not found this to be true. If horses are greatly irritated from an oil, it is less likely that the owner can give the horse a Raindrop at all, and this event will truly eliminate any benefits.

- Next, drip 6 drops of Thyme in the same manner as the Oregano. Rubbing or stroking the oils into the back, between one to three times, from the tail to the head. Thyme is also "hot", and is probably the most common oil that I see skin irritation and welts from. I try to stagger the "drip site" of this oil from where the Oregano oil "fell". This way, the skin will not be getting oils applied in only one location, over and over again.
- After the application of Oregano and Thyme – I almost always apply V-6 Enhanced Vegetable Oil Complex along the spine area. Depending on the horse and how they appear to be tolerating the procedure, I may apply more or less V-6 to the back. Rub and massage the oil into the spine area – three times is not important for this step – nor is the method of the rubbing. However, I do find that if the horse enjoys each step – this is a good way to encourage "easy" Raindrops in the future. So if there is a style of rubbing that the horse enjoys, please try to provide it!
- Next, you will apply 6 drops of Basil in the same exact manner. Although each oil can have a different amount of drops – I find it beneficial to my horse owners to just keep each oil at the same amount of drops at first. It is much easier to remember. In the future, as you become more comfortable with "tweaking" the Raindrop, you can apply more or less of particular oils, if it was indicated for a certain condition. For example, I may apply more Basil oil when the horse was indicating a need for an antihistamine.
- Continue to apply the remaining oils in the same way: Apply 6 drops of Cypress oil. This oil increases circulation, so occasionally in a sensitive horse, the increase in circulation can bring a more intense irritation to them. At any point in the Raindrop application, you can always apply more V-6 whenever needed. You can also reduce the amount of oils you are applying, or even stop the Raindrop if you are concerned that the horse is not doing well.
- Wintergreen oil is next. Apply 6 drops of this oil. Wintergreen is an anti-inflammatory oil. There are occasional animals that this appears to be a "hot" oil for – so keep this in mind.

- **Optional**: If you wanted to modify a Raindrop Technique by inserting additional oils – this is generally the location to do it. Don't worry – if you forget and insert oils before Wintergreen or after Marjoram – the Raindrop will still be effective. Usually I will not insert more than 1-3 different oils into the Raindrop Technique.
- Marjoram oil is the next oil. Apply 6-12 drops of this oil. Again, you can keep the amount at 6 drops at first for easy memorizing. This oil is very good for all muscular conditions and so is generally applied on the muscles up both sides of the spine. You can continue the basic rubbing in that we did for all of the oils, but this is also a step where doing more of a muscular massage would be great. At first, it is just fine to keep all of the steps the same. I find if I give too many instructions or variations to my clients, they can become overwhelmed.
- **Optional: Copaiba Oil** – although not a part of the "true Raindrop" I often insert Copaiba oil here. I know I said that I insert most other oils behind Wintergreen, but Copaiba oil is an exception for me. Since this oil is a magnifier oil, I will often apply it after almost every other oil is applied, the exception being Peppermint, which is explained below. Not only will the Copaiba oil make every other oils' actions "stronger", it also has its own health benefits. It is the highest powered anti-inflammatory in the essential oil world and also has gastro-protective properties. Something most horses will almost always benefit from. Although Copaiba magnifies the other oils, I have not found that it increases the "hotness" or welts caused by other oils. It seems that only the health benefits are amplified! For some horses, this can be an easy way to be able to use less oils, and get the same results.
- Peppermint oil is "always" the last oil. It is a driving oil, which means that it will help "drive" the Copaiba and the rest of the oils deeper into the tissues. So being the last oil – just "drives the other oils home". The main reason I may omit this oil is in the dead of winter. This is a "cold" oil, so it could cause some animals to become chilled more than is comfortable for them.
- When possible, the application of oils is followed by the Vita Flex procedure. For horses, we often use our entire hand and fingers to perform the Vita Flex, walking both hands up the sides of the spine, gradually inching forward after every repetition. Think of an inchworm, gradually inching its way up the back. Go from tail to head, and repeat this up to three times as well. If a horse will not allow this step to happen, I omit it.

Raindrop Technique – Hoof Application:

With conditions involving the hoof, lameness, or for a true "full" Raindrop Technique – applying oils to the hooves is definitely beneficial. Without this step, there are still significant medical benefits to the technique. Alternately, you could also administer the Hoof Application alone when pressed for time, or when dealing with a hoof or lameness issue.

Generally, oils are applied to the hooves after the Valor balancing steps described previously. Some people apply Valor to the hooves before the "body" balancing, and some people apply the "body" balancing before applying the Valor to the hooves. I have not found it to matter either way. I tend to want to deal with the hooves all at once, so will balance the head and rump first, and then move onto the entire hoof protocol.

The rest of the "spinal" Raindrop is generally administered after the hoof application.

- Most people start with the Right Front Hoof, and apply 3-6 drops of Valor to the bulb area. Then move to the Right Rear Hoof, and apply the Valor the same. Then the Left Rear Leg, and ending at the Left Front Leg. Again, if pressed for time, or when dealing with an uncooperative horse, I may omit this step, especially when the condition is not structural. However, almost any hoof issue will affect the way the horse will carry themselves, and Valor can be quite beneficial.
- Next you will apply the Raindrop Oils to the legs/hooves. Again there are many variations here as well. Firstly, some people only apply the "Raindrop" oils to the rear legs, however, I will often include the front legs in conditions that affect the front legs. For instance if the horse is having a lameness issue in the front leg, or has an abscess in a front hoof, I am certainly going to apply the raindrop oils to the those legs as well. If all four legs are to have the oils applied, generally people also start at the Right Front Leg, and circle back to the Left Front Leg, as described for the Valor. Most commonly, the oils are applied to the coronet band area, but may be applied on the leg itself as well.
    - Variations can include applying Oregano, Thyme, Basil, Cypress, Wintergreen, Marjoram, and Peppermint to the first leg, then moving to the second leg and applying all of the oils, and so forth.

- o My favorite technique tends to be to apply the Oregano to the Right Front Leg, then the Right Rear Leg, then the Left Rear Leg, then the Left Front Leg. Once completing this, I move onto the Thyme application, then Basil, and so forth. Again, I have not found a huge difference in benefits from choosing one way over the other, so I allow for the human to pick which way suits them best. Depending on if I have a helper during the Raindrop administration or not, will often determine how I will apply the oils. If I have to grab and open each individual bottle of oil, I am more likely to play "ring around the horsey" and apply the oils one at a time, to each leg.
- o The other main difference in application, is the location in which the oils are applied to the legs. Sometimes oils are applied only to the coronet area, and other times they are also applied to the leg itself. Oregano and Thyme are sometimes applied only to the coronet band area, as these are "hotter" oils. However, true to form, I have applied these oils to the leg area when there has been a tendon infection or a joint that would benefit from having the oils applied over the area. Many times the legs are more sensitive than the coronet band – and so dilution may be necessary.
- For ease of administration, I often suggest that all legs are treated with application being to the coronet band only. This way, the procedure does not become too confusing. You will start by applying Oregano oil, generally placing 3 drops into the palm of your non-dominant hand. Circle your fingertips into the oil puddle, then Vita Flex the oil into the coronet band. Start at the front center of the coronet band, and Vita Flex outward toward the rear of the hoof. Dip your fingers into the oil for each round of Vita Flex. Repeat this three times, on each side of the coronet band. When you move to the next leg, you may need to add another 3 drops of essential oil into your hand, and repeat the entire procedure.
- Repeat the application with Thyme, Basil, Cypress, Wintergreen, Marjoram, and Peppermint.
- If application to the leg itself is indicated or desired, the oils are generally applied to the inner surface of the rear legs, from the knee (stifle) down the leg. I will generally let the condition decide on where the oils need to be applied, and may apply to both areas (coronet and leg) if I think it will be beneficial. If the front legs are to receive oils, then they can be applied to either the coronet band or to

the area needing the application. Again, you will circle your fingertips into the oil, and Vita Flex the oil down the leg, three times.

- The Raindrop Technique for the hooves can also be modified by the insertion of various oils, just as described for the spinal portion of the application.
- Once you have applied the oils to the legs and locations you have chosen – now proceed to applying the spinal portion of the Raindrop Technique.

It is easy to see how confusing a Raindrop Technique can become for someone who has never facilitated one before. Creating as simple of a Raindrop Technique as possible, is often easier to learn and is very effective. Giving a Raindrop Technique every day can take up a considerable amount of time, and all of the different variations can cause stress for the owner of an already ill horse. Many will just shut down, and choose to not apply any oils at all to their horse. This is the last thing that is needed, so if a procedure needs to be simplified for the first few weeks, then that is what is best for the horse and owner.

EQUINE CONDITIONS

ABSCESS
(See also STRANGLES, HOOF ABSCESS)

An abscess in a horse can have many different causes and many different locations; from a contagious bacteria which causes "Strangles" to an abscess related to a snake bite wound. No matter what the cause, the basic care of these pus filled pockets can be addressed in a similar manner.

It is important to note, that there are forms of sterile abscesses as well – which are not related to bacterial infection at all. No matter what, the body is still "misbehaving" and the immune system is attempting to "eject" a substance from the body. Essential oils can be tremendously helpful as they support multiple levels of health; providing antibacterial, antifungal, and antiviral actions, immune system support, and aiding in tissue healing and regeneration. Accurate diagnosis can aide in supporting animals with a more exact approach to the origin of the condition.

FIRST LINE RECOMMENDATIONS:
TOPICAL: Apply Thieves, Purification, or Exodus II neat to the abscess head, up to twice a day. Hot pack the abscess with a very warm, damp wash cloth to help bring the abscess to a "head" or to drain. Once the "head" has opened and drainage is occurring, flush the wound with diluted Thieves Household Cleaner.
ORAL: Thieves, Oregano, or Exodus II
RAINDROP TECHNIQUE: Apply up to once per day. The Raindrop oils can also be applied to the abscess itself.

Single Oils:
Cassia, Cinnamon, Laurus Nobilis, Lavender, Lemon, Lemongrass, Melaleuca Alternifolia, Mountain Savory, Oregano, Spikenard, Thyme

Blends:
  Abundance, Egyptian Gold, Exodus II, Longevity, PanAway, Purification, Thieves

Supplements & Products:
  Animal Scents Ointment, Animal Scents Shampoo, Longevity, NingXia Red, Sulfurzyme, Thieves Household Cleaner, Thieves Spray

ANESTHESIA DETOXIFICATION

FIRST LINE RECOMMENDATIONS:
  RAINDROP TECHNIQUE: Applied up to once per day.
  PETTING: DiGize
  ORAL: DiGize, Longevity

Single Oils:
  Chamomile (Roman), Geranium, Grapefruit, Helichrysum, Hyssop, Juniper, Ledum, Lemon, Peppermint, Tsuga

Blends:
  Citrus Fresh, DiGize, GLF, Longevity, Juva Cleanse, Juva Flex

Supplements & Products:
  NingXia Red, Rehemogen

ARTHRITIS

(See also LAMENESS, NAVICULAR DISEASE)

Arthritis is an inflammatory condition of the joint by definition. However many owners will describe general stiffness, gait abnormalities, and other related changes as arthritis. Holistically we focus on supporting joint health, decreasing inflammation, and supporting health. With this approach, no matter what the cause of the perceived arthritis, the body will generally benefit and improvements will be seen. When possible, an accurate veterinary diagnosis is important.

FIRST LINE RECOMMENDATIONS:
ORAL: Copaiba, Longevity
SUPPLEMENTS: NingXia Red, Sulfurzyme.
PETTING: Any selected oil.
RAINDROP TECHNIQUE: Apply up to once per day.
WATER MISTING: Add 20 drops of desired essential oil(s) to 4 ounces of distilled water. Shake well, mist over arthritic area.

Single Oils:
Balsam Fir, Clove, Copaiba, Frankincense, Helichrysum, Lavender, Lemongrass, Marjoram, Myrrh, Nutmeg, Palo Santo, Pepper (Black), Peppermint, Pine, Spruce, Tansy (Blue), Tansy (Idaho), Vetiver, Wintergreen

Blends:
Aroma Siez, Deep Relief Roll-On, GLF, Juva Cleanse, Juva Flex, Kitty Raindrop Solution, Longevity, M-Grain, PanAway, Relieve It

Supplements & Products:
Longevity, NingXia Red, Omega Blue, Ortho Ease Massage Oil, Ortho Sport Massage Oil, PD 80/20, Sulfurzyme

AUTOIMMUNE DISORDERS

Any condition in which the immune system is malfunctioning can benefit from the following suggestions. Whether the immune system is overactive or underactive, the same supportive measures will allow the immune system to function appropriately.

FIRST LINE RECOMMENDATIONS:
RAINDROP TECHNIQUE: Modify by inserting ImmuPower, Frankincense, and Copaiba. Apply up to once a day.
ORAL: Longevity 3 drops or more twice a day.
SUPPLEMENTS: NingXia Red, Sulfurzyme.

Single Oils:
Balsam Fir, Copaiba, Frankincense, Helichrysum

Blends:
ImmuPower, Longevity, Raindrop Technique

Supplements & Products:
Longevity, NingXia Red, PD 80/20, Sulfurzyme, Thieves Household Cleaner

BACK, SPINAL CONDITIONS
(See also ARTHRITIS)

There can be many situations in which a condition is considered back related in a horse. Arthritis will also relate to many conditions that feature back discomfort. An accurate diagnosis is important with a qualified veterinarian as something as simple as a poor fitting saddle – to something as severe as a fracture – could fall into the category of a "back problem". The methods below are indicated and helpful for any form of back discomfort. It is important to keep in mind that a kidney infection (which is widely unrelated to the spine itself) can manifest as a back condition.

FIRST LINE RECOMMENDATIONS:
RAINDROP TECHNIQUE, up to once a day. Ensure use of Valor. Modify with insertions of Copaiba, Idaho Balsam Fir, Helichrysum.
ORAL: Copaiba
SUPPLEMENTS: NingXia Red, Sulfurzyme.
TOPICAL: Valor
PETTING: With any selected oil, up to multiple times daily.
SPRAYING: 20 drops or more of essential oil(s) can be added to 4 ounces of distilled water or V6 to be misted over the back area. Ortho Ease or Ortho Sport can also be misted over the spinal area for easy, wide spread application.

Single Oils:
Balsam Fir (Idaho), Bergamot, Copaiba, Frankincense, Helichrysum, Juniper, Laurus Nobilis, Lavender, Lemongrass, Marjoram, Mountain Savory, Palo Santo, Peppermint, Pine, Spruce, Vetiver, Wintergreen

Blends:
Aroma Siez, Deep Relief Roll-On, Grounding, Harmony, M-Grain, Ortho Ease, Ortho Sport, PanAway, Relieve It, Valor

Supplements & Products:
BLM Capsules, Longevity, NingXia Red, Ortho Ease Massage Oil, Ortho Sport Massage Oil, Relaxation Massage Oil, Sulfurzyme

BEHAVIORAL CONDITIONS
(See also HORMONAL CONDITIONS)

FIRST LINE RECOMMENDATIONS:
See Emotional Work with Oils and Emotional Use of Blends.
EMOTIONAL RAINDROP TECHNIQUE: Apply selected oils as described.
SUPPLEMENTS: Mineral Essence
PETTING: Any selected oil, multiple times a day or as needed.

Single Oils:
Bergamot, Chamomile (German), Chamomile (Roman), Clary Sage, Geranium, Grapefruit, Lavender, Lemon, Marjoram, Melissa, Myrtle, Orange, Palo Santo, Patchouli, Pine, Rose, Spikenard, Spruce, Tangerine, Valerian, Vetiver, Ylang Ylang

Blends:
Acceptance, Brain Power, Citrus Fresh, Dragon Time, Forgiveness, Harmony, Hope, Joy, Lady Sclareol, M-Grain, Mister, Release, SclarEssence, 3 Wise Men, Trauma Life

Supplements & Products:
Mineral Essence, NingXia Red, Omega Blue, Relaxation Massage Oil

BIRTHING AND DELIVERY

FIRST LINE RECOMMENDATIONS:
DIFFUSION: Gentle Baby
PETTING: En-R-Gee, Gentle Baby, Frankincense
SUPPLEMENTS: NingXia Red

Single Oils:
Chamomile (Roman), Frankincense, Geranium, Lavender, Marjoram, Myrrh, Orange, Rose, Vetiver

Blends:
Citrus Fresh, En-R-Gee, Gentle Baby

Supplements & Products:
ClaraDerm, NingXia Red, ParaFree, Relaxation Massage Oil, Thieves Household Cleaner

BONE CONDITIONS

FIRST LINE RECOMMENDATIONS:
PETTING: With any selected oil, multiple times per day.

Single Oils:
Balsam Fir (Idaho), Palo Santo, Pine, Spruce

Blends:
Believe, Deep Relief Roll-On, PanAway, Relieve It

Supplements & Products:
BLM, NingXia Red, Ortho Ease Massage Oil, Ortho Sport Massage Oil, Sulfurzyme

BOWED TENDON
(See TENDON CONDITIONS)

BRUISED SOLES

Also known as Corns, the condition is the bruising of the bottom of the horse hoof. This is a condition mainly caused by improper trimming or shoeing of the horse. Generally the heel is found to be too long and/or horse shoes too small. Although the recommendations can aid in healing, the underlying issue that caused the bruising to begin with needs to be addressed first and foremost.

FIRST LINE RECOMMENDATIONS:
TOPICAL: Direct neat application of PanAway, Idaho Balsam Fir, Helichrysum, and/or Cypress to the bruised area. Several drops, multiple times a day can be applied.

Single Oils:
Cypress, Helichrysum, Idaho Balsam Fir, Frankincense, Geranium

Blends:
Deep Relief Roll-On, PanAway, Valor, Raindrop Technique, Relieve It

BRUISING

Any trauma can result in a bruising of tissues, from surgery to a kick by another horse. All bruising will respond to these general methods. An important note is that certain essential oils carry blood thinning or anti-coagulant properties. If bruising continues, does not improve, or worsens – omitting the oral use or excessive topical use of oils such as Cinnamon, Clove, and Wintergreen is recommended. Remembering, that they are also contained within various blends such as Thieves, Longevity, and PanAway.

FIRST LINE RECOMMENDATIONS:
TOPICAL: Direct application or Petting of PanAway, Idaho Balsam Fir, Helichrysum, and/or Cypress to the bruised area, up to several times a day. The method chosen may depend more on location and size of the injury.
WATER MISTING: Place 20 or more drops of the selected essential oil(s) into 4 ounces (120 mL) of distilled water or V6 and mist onto bruised area.
ANIMAL SCENTS OINTMENT: Mix desired essential oil(s) into ointment and massage onto location.

Single Oils:
Cypress, Helichrysum, Idaho Balsam Fir, Frankincense, Geranium, Lavender

Blends:
PanAway, Valor

Supplements & Products:
NingXia Red, Sulfurzyme

CANCER

(See also CANCER in Feline and Canine descriptions)

It is very important in conditions such as cancer, to incorporate as many layers of care as possible. This is one situation, where starting with small amounts of items, in low amounts, but building up to using many, many items and in relatively high amounts (sometimes quickly) is fully warranted.

FIRST LINE RECOMMENDATIONS:
DIET: Eliminate items such as sweet feed, corn, or high carbohydrate diets. Purified or spring water should be provided if possible.
ELIMINATE TOXINS: For horses this often consists of cleaners, bug sprays, or shampoos.
SUPPLEMENTS: NingXia Red, Longevity.
DIFFUSION: Rotational diffusion of emotional oils is recommended. See also the chapter on Emotional Use of Blends for more information. Diffuse any anti-cancer oils up to 24 hours a day. Rotation through a variety of oils is recommended.
RAINDROP TECHNIQUE: Modify by inserting Frankincense, Copaiba, and ImmuPower to the mixture. Apply up to once a day, and at least weekly. Each time a Raindrop is given, you can rotate through which recommended oils are inserted. I strongly recommend a weekly Raindrop Technique for the owner as well.
RAINDROP TECHNIQUE – EMOTIONAL: It is very important to address emotional cleansing with Cancer. See Emotional Work with Oils and Emotional Use of Blends. I strongly recommend emotional work and cleansing for the owner as well.
PETTING: Applying any essential oil you desire up to twice a day or more.
ORAL: Frankincense and Longevity. Frankincense is commonly given orally in quite high doses for cancer. Usually, limits on the amount of Frankincense given, are placed due to budget constraints, and not due to giving "too much."
DRINKING WATER: Frankincense, Citrus Fresh, Orange, Tangerine, or other desired oil.

Single Oils:
Frankincense, Grapefruit, Lemon, Orange, Palo Santo, Sandalwood, Palo Santo, Sandalwood, Tangerine

Blends:
Brain Power, Citrus Fresh, Forgiveness, Hope, ImmuPower, Longevity, 3 Wise Men

Supplements & Products:
NingXia Red, ParaFree, Sulfurzyme, Thieves Household Cleaner

CANKER

Canker is a horrible condition which acts somewhat like a cancerous wart-like tumor in horses. Affecting the foot of the horse, it has resulted in permanent lameness and club foot deformities in many horses. Often a condition of the "well-kept horse" there are many cases documented of profound response to the use of essential oils. Traditionally, this condition is treated with various forms of surgery, all which are quite bloody in nature. It is not surprising that treatment with essential oils, also brings forth some bleeding in this condition.

Supporting the immune system and providing for good nutritional support is also vital in this condition. Outlined below are recommendations for the canker lesion itself - care of the immune system is an important layer as well.

FIRST LINE RECOMMENDATIONS:
TOPICAL: Neat application of Oregano, Thieves, Frankincense, and Copaiba essential oils to the canker. Bleeding may start or increase temporarily, due to the "cauterizing" sort of action we desire on this lesion. Repeat several times per day.

Single Oils:
Cassia, Cinnamon, Clove, Copaiba, Frankincense, Copaiba, Lemongrass, Oregano, Thyme

Blends:
Abundance, Exodus II, ImmuPower, Longevity, Raindrop Technique, Thieves

Supplements & Products:
BLM Capsules, Longevity, NingXia Red, Sulfurzyme, Thieves Household Cleaner

CASTRATION
(See also PAIN MANAGEMENT)

FIRST LINE RECOMMENDATIONS:
TOPICAL: Myrrh applied to castration site prior to the surgical procedure is helpful. The Myrrh can be diluted in V-6 for easier application, and rubbed into the scrotal area with your hand.
ANIMAL SCENTS OINTMENT: Selected oils can be mixed into the ointment and applied to the site of the castration as needed.
SURGICAL SCRUB: Cleansing the castration site with Thieves Household Cleaner prior to surgery is suggested.
WATER MISTING: 10-20 drops of Helichrysum, Myrrh, Melrose or other desired oil(s), can be added to 4 ounces (120 mL) of distilled water and misted onto the castration site several times a day, or as needed.

Single Oils:
Helichrysum, Laurus Nobilis, Lavender, Lemon, Melaleuca Alternifolia, Myrrh

Blends:
Deep Relief Roll-On, Melrose, PanAway, Purification, Thieves

Supplements & Products:
Animal Scents Ointment, ClaraDerm, LavaDerm Cooling Mist, NingXia Red, Sulfurzyme, Thieves Household Cleaner

CHOKE

FIRST LINE RECOMMENDATIONS:
PETTING: Apply 20 drops of Peace & Calming over the esophagus area.
ORAL: Give 20 drops of Peace & Calming and/or Peppermint into the bottom lip. Repeat if needed.

Single Oils:
Marjoram, Peppermint, Vetiver, Wintergreen, Ylang Ylang

Blends:
Aroma Siez, Deep Relief Roll-On, Di-Gize, M-Grain, PanAway, Peace & Calming, RutaVaLa

Supplements & Products:
Relaxation Massage Oil

CHRONIC OBSTRUCTIVE PULMONARY DISEASE
(See HEAVES)

CLUB FOOT

Club foot is a crippling condition in which contraction of the tendons and ligaments surrounding the hoof and foot are tight and result in abnormal structure of the foot of the horse. The condition can arise secondary to injury, infection, surgery or other forms of trauma. A proactive preventive approach to this condition is ideal, as once the condition has set in, it is very difficult to correct. A natural, barefoot farrier with experience in the condition is mandatory. This condition has commonly occurred after Canker surgery in many horses.

FIRST LINE RECOMMENDATIONS:
TOPICAL: Valor as well as other suggested oils can be applied to the affected leg up to multiple times per day.

Single Oils:
Balsam Fir (Idaho), Copaiba, Lavender, Lemongrass, Marjoram, Palo Santo, Pine, Spruce, Wintergreen

Blends:
Aroma Siez, Deep Relief Roll-On, PanAway, Release, Relieve It, Valor

Supplements & Products:
BLM, Ortho Ease Massage Oil, Ortho Sport Massage Oil, Relaxation Massage Oil, Sulfurzyme

COLD & FLU

(See also EQUINE HERPES VIRUS, RESPIRATORY CONDITIONS, STRANGLES, HEAVES)

Cold and flu-like symptoms can have many causes in horses. From viral infections such as Equine Herpes Virus, bacterial infections such as Strangles, inflammatory conditions such as Heaves, many conditions affect the respiratory system of horses. Although it is ideal to be able to use essential oils that are specifically directed toward viruses or bacteria – the broad spectrum activity of essential oils, as well as their tremendous support to the immune system and body as a whole – we are often able to effectively benefit the entire respiratory system when an exact contributing factor has not been identified.

FIRST LINE RECOMMENDATIONS:
RAINDROP TECHNIQUE: Insert ImmuPower, apply up to daily.
ORAL: Thieves
DIFFUSION: Thieves

Single Oils:
Eucalyptus Blue, Eucalyptus Globulus, Hyssop, Laurus Nobilis, Lavender, Lemon, Marjoram, Melissa, Mountain Savory, Myrtle, Peppermint, Pine, Ravintsara, Rosemary, Sandalwood, Spruce

Blends:
Breathe Again Roll-On, Egyptian Gold, Exodus II, Forgiveness, Hope, ImmuPower, Longevity, M-Grain, Purification, Raven, R.C., 3 Wise Men, Thieves

Supplements & Products:
NingXia Red, Thieves Household Cleaner

EQUINE CONDITIONS

COLIC

Colic is the leading cause of death in horses. It is defined as any condition that causes intestinal or abdominal pain or discomfort in a horse or equid. There are many causes for the condition including impaction of intestinal material, parasites, twisted intestinal tracts, tumors and more. Symptoms of colic can vary from just being "off" to pawing at the ground, kicking at the belly, sweating, going off feed, and also full out rolling on the ground. This situation is certainly an emergency, and an accurate diagnosis from a veterinarian is imperative to accurately deal with the cause of the colic.

It is recommended that you call your equine veterinarian first, but while they are on their way – you use the following recommendations to support your horse. It is not uncommon that you will not need your veterinarian once they arrive to your farm.

FIRST LINE RECOMMENDATIONS:

The following recommendations are for an average sized horse. Smaller amounts may be indicated for miniature horses, ponies, or smaller equids. First - call your veterinarian.

PETTING: Calm the horse and owner by petting 3 or more drops of RutaVaLa, (Peace & Calming or Lavender may also be used) onto the muzzle area of the horse and onto the belly. Repeat this step every 20 minutes or as needed.

ORAL: Administer 20 drops of Di-Gize and 20 drops of Peppermint oil orally. It does not matter which oil is given first, but often times a preference toward using Di-Gize before the Peppermint is felt. Placing these oils into a 2 mL Essential Oil Sample Bottle is a great way to have a pre-measured and convenient way to dispense the oils into the mouth. Having several of these small bottles ready and waiting in your equine emergency kit is wise.

TOPICAL: Next apply 20 drops of Di-Gize to the abdomen, in the location near the umbilicus. Then, apply 20 drops of Peppermint to the abdomen in the same location. A preference is placed on applying the Di-Gize first and the Peppermint second, although the most important aspect is to actually apply the oils, and not to worry about which order they are applied in.

Repeat the calming, oral, and topical applications every 20 minutes until symptoms have improved. There has not appeared to be a maximum dose reached at this point, and many horses have consumed entire bottles of Di-Gize during difficult colic situations. If the colic does not respond within 1 hours' time, generally it is found that the colic situation will require surgery.

Single Oils:
Copaiba, Frankincense, Helichrysum, Lavender, Marjoram, Peppermint, Tarragon, Valerian, Vetiver, Ylang Ylang

Blends:
Aroma Siez, Deep Relief Roll-On, Di-Gize, M-Grain, Peace & Calming, RutaVaLa, Tranquil

Supplements & Products:
Relaxation Massage Oil

COLIC, IMPACTION

This protocol was created by Sara Kenney and is described in her book *Natural Health Care For Your Four-Legged Friends*.

FIRST LINE RECOMMENDATIONS:
RECTAL INSTILLATION: Mix 20 drops of Di-Gize, 20 drops of Peppermint, and 6-10 capsules of Detoxzyme into 4 cups of warm water. This solution is inserted rectally and/or orally every 15 minutes for 4 doses. A Turkey Baster or large syringe can be used for the rectal enema.

ORAL: The same solution can be given orally as well.

Single Oils:
Juniper, Lavender, Marjoram, Peppermint, Valerian, Tarragon, Valerian, Vetiver, Ylang Ylang

Blends:
Aroma Siez, Deep Relief Roll-On, Di-Gize, M-Grain, Peace & Calming, Release, RutaVaLa, Tranquil

Supplements & Products:
Detoxzyme

CONTRACTED TENDONS
(See also CLUB FOOT)

FIRST LINE RECOMMENDATIONS:
TOPICAL: Mix multiple recommended oils into Animal Scents Ointment and massage onto tendon area multiple times per day.
PETTING: Release

Single Oils:
Lavender, Lemongrass, Marjoram, Palo Santo

Blends:
Aroma Siez, Deep Relief Roll-On, M-Grain, PanAway, Release, Relieve It, Valor

Supplements & Products:
Animal Scents Ointment, Ortho Ease Massage Oil, Ortho Sport Massage Oil, Relaxation Massage Oil, Sulfurzyme

COPD
(See HEAVES)

CORNEA
(See CORNEA in CANINE CONDITIONS)

CORNS
(See BRUISED SOLES)

COUGH
(See HEAVES, RESPIRATORY CONDITIONS, COLD & FLU)

CRIBBING
(See also BEHAVIORAL CONDITIONS)

FIRST LINE RECOMMENDATIONS:
SUPPLEMENTS: Mineral Essence, NingXia Red
PETTING: With any selected oil.
DIFFUSION: With any selected oil.

EMOTIONAL RAINDROP TECHNIQUE: See Emotional Use of Blends for more information.

Single Oils:
Bergamot, Roman Chamomile, Geranium, Grapefruit, Lavender, Lemon, Melissa, Orange, Palo Santo, Patchouli, Spikenard, Spruce, Tangerine, Valerian, Vetiver, Ylang Ylang

Blends:
Acceptance, Citrus Fresh, Di-Gize, Forgiveness, Hope, Peace & Calming, 3 Wise Men, Tranquil Roll-On, Trauma Life

Supplements & Products:
Mineral Essence, NingXia Red, Omega Blue, Relaxation Massage Oil

CUSHING'S

FIRST LINE RECOMMENDATIONS:
PETTING: Nutmeg, Clove, Rosemary over adrenal gland area, up to twice a day or as needed. EndoFlex on the neck area. Cedarwood to the brainstem. Frankincense. Any suggested oil may be used.
ORAL: Idaho Balsam Fir and Lavender in the evening to reduce cortisol levels. Ocotea, Dill, or Fennel for blood sugar handling.
SUPPLEMENTS: NingXia Red

Single Oils:
Balsam Fir (Idaho), Cedarwood, Cinnamon, Clove, Copaiba, Coriander, Dill, Fennel, Frankincense, Helichrysum, Lavender, Ledum, Lemon, Nutmeg, Ocotea, Rosemary

Blends:
EndoFlex, Exodus II, GLF, ImmuPower, Juva Cleanse, Thieves

Supplements & Products:
EndoGize, NingXia Red, PD 80/20, Sulfurzyme

CUTS
(See LACERATIONS)

EQUINE CONDITIONS

CYSTIC OVARY
(See LARGE ANIMAL CONDITIONS)

DEWORMING
(See also PARASITES, GASTROINTESTINAL CONDITIONS, DIARRHEA)

Deworming holistically is a frustrating predicament for many veterinarians. On one hand, a protocol will have complete success when even traditional remedies have failed, and then for the next animal – we will see no response at all. This is the way of the parasite. They are incredibly deceptive and have a strong will to live and survive in their host. It is important to recognize that no "one" remedy will be effective for every situation, and screening and checking stool samples with a veterinarian will often be helpful in determining the results of your efforts.

FIRST LINE RECOMMENDATIONS:
SUPPLEMENTS: See ParaFree for descriptions and use of the Large Animal Parasite Blend.
ORAL: Tarragon, Ocotea, Di-Gize, Longevity

Single Oils:
Eucalyptus Globulus, Hyssop, Lemon, Lemongrass, Melaleuca Alternifolia, Mountain Savory, Nutmeg, Ocotea, Peppermint, Tarragon, Thyme, Ylang Ylang

Blends:
Di-Gize, Longevity

Supplements & Products:
ParaFree

DIARRHEA
(See also DEWORMING, GASTROINTESTINAL CONDITIONS)

FIRST LINE RECOMMENDATIONS:
ORAL: Di-Gize, Ocotea, Thieves, Copaiba, Peppermint
ORAL: For severe diarrhea Oregano, Clove, Mountain Savory, Ginger
PETTING: Di-Gize, Ocotea, Thieves, Copaiba, Peppermint

RAINDROP TECHNIQUE: Up to daily or as needed.
SUPPLEMENTS: Life 5

Single Oils:
Clove, Copaiba, Ginger, Lemon, Lemongrass, Melaleuca Alternifolia, Melissa, Mountain Savory, Ocotea, Oregano, Peppermint, Tarragon, Thyme, Vetiver

Blends:
Di-Gize, Exodus II, Hope, ImmuPower, Melrose, Purification, Thieves

Supplements & Products:
Life 5, ParaFree, Thieves Household Cleaner

EDEMA, PERIPHERAL

FIRST LINE RECOMMENDATIONS:
PETTING: Cypress
RAINDROP TECHNIQUE: Up to daily or as needed.
DRINKING WATER: Citrus Fresh
SUPPLEMENTS: NingXia Red

Single Oils:
Cypress, Pine, Tangerine

Blends:
Aroma Life, Citrus Fresh, GLF, Juva Cleanse, Juva Flex

Supplements & Products:
Cel-Lite Magic Massage Oil, K&B Tincture, NingXia Red

EHRLICHIA
(See TICK BORNE DISEASES)

EHV
(See EQUINE HERPES VIRUS)

ENCEPHALITIS
(See also WEST NILE VIRUS, VIRAL CONDITIONS)

FIRST LINE RECOMMENDATIONS:
RAINDROP TECHNIQUE: Modify by inserting Roman Chamomile, Helichrysum, and Copaiba. Apply up to daily.
TOPICAL: RutaVaLa to Brainstem
PETTING: With any indicated oil.

Single Oils:
Chamomile (Roman), Helichrysum, Juniper, Laurus Nobilis

Blends:
Brain Power, Juva Cleanse, RutaVaLa

Supplements & Products:
NingXia Red

EPM
(See EQUINE PROTOZOAL MYELOENCEPHALITIS)

EQUINE HERPES VIRUS
(See also VIRAL CONDITIONS)

FIRST LINE RECOMMENDATIONS:
RAINDROP TECHNIQUE: Modify by inserting ImmuPower, Ravintsara, and Melissa
ORAL: Thieves
SUPPLEMENTS: NingXia Red

Single Oils:
Geranium, Helichrysum, Laurus Nobilis, Marjoram, Melaleuca Ericifolia, Melissa, Mountain Savory, Peppermint, Ravintsara, Rose, Sandalwood, Thyme

Blends:
3 Wise Men, Forgiveness, Exodus II, Hope, ImmuPower, Thieves

Supplements & Products:
MultiGreens, NingXia Red, Thieves Household Cleaner

EQUINE PROTOZOAL MYELOENCEPHALITIS

FIRST LINE RECOMMENDATIONS:
RAINDROP TECHNIQUE: Modify by inserting Helichrysum, ImmuPower, Thieves. Apply up to daily, rotation of inserted oils is suggested.
ORAL: Thieves, Exodus II
PETTING: Brain Power over brain stem area.
SUPPLEMENTS: NingXia Red

Single Oils:
Chamomile (Roman), Helichrysum, Juniper, Laurus Nobilis, Thyme

Blends:
Brain Power, Exodus II, ImmuPower, Thieves

Supplements & Products:
NingXia Red, ParaFree, Thieves Household Cleaner

EYE CONDITIONS
(See also UVEITIS)

FIRST LINE RECOMMENDATIONS:
TOPICAL: Rose Ointment
WATER MISTING: Lavender or Therapeutic Eye Spritzer
SUPPLEMENTS: NingXia Red
ORAL: Longevity

Single Oils:
Frankincense, Helichrysum, Lavender

Blends:
Longevity

Supplements & Products:
Animal Scents Ointment, NingXia Red, Omega Blue, Rose Ointment

FEVER

FIRST LINE RECOMMENDATIONS:
RAINDROP TECHNIQUE: Apply as needed, up to once a day.
PETTING: Peppermint
ORAL: Peppermint, Thieves
DRINKING WATER: Peppermint
DIFFUSION: Any selected oil

Single Oils:
Eucalyptus Globulus, Helichrysum, Lavender, Melaleuca Alternifolia, Melissa, Mountain Savory, Oregano, Palo Santo, Peppermint, Thyme

Blends:
Deep Relief Roll-On, Exodus II, Hope, ImmuPower, Longevity, Melrose, PanAway, Thieves

Supplements & Products:
NingXia Red, ParaFree, Thieves Household Cleaner

FLOAT RIDES
(See TRANSPORTATION)

FLU
(See COLD & FLU, RESPIRATORY CONDITIONS)

FOUNDER
(See LAMINITIS)

GASTRIC ULCERS
(See ULCERS, GASTRIC)

GELDING
(See CASTRATION)

GIRTH GALLS
(See SADDLE SORES)

GREASY HEEL
(See SCRATCHES, SKIN CONDITIONS)

HEAVES
(See also RESPIRATORY CONDITIONS)

FIRST LINE RECOMMENDATIONS:
DIFFUSION: Thieves, Raven
ORAL: Oregano
TOPICAL: Oregano or other selected oils to throat and chest area, multiple times a day.
RAINDROP TECHNIQUE: Apply as needed. Insert oils as desired.
SUPPLEMENTS: NingXia Red

Single Oils:
Cedarwood, Dorado Azul, Eucalyptus Blue, Eucalyptus Globulus, Hyssop, Laurus Nobilis, Lavender, Lemon, Lemongrass, Marjoram, Melissa, Myrtle, Oregano, Peppermint, Pine, Rosemary, Spruce, Tsuga

Blends:
Aroma Siez, Breathe Again Roll-On, Egyptian Gold, Exodus II, Hope, Juva Cleanse, Longevity, Melrose, Raven, R.C., Thieves

Supplements & Products:
NingXia Red, ParaFree, PD 80/20, Thieves Household Cleaner

HENDRA VIRUS
(See also VIRAL CONDITIONS)

FIRST LINE RECOMMENDATIONS:
DRINKING WATER: Thieves Household Cleaner, Thieves
RAINDROP TECHNQUE: Weekly to monthly for prevention. Up to daily for at risk horses or symptomatic horses. Insert Melissa, Spikenard, Eucalyptus Blue, Hyssop.
ORAL: Spikenard, Copaiba, Melissa, Longevity

CLEANING: Thieves Household Cleaner
SUPPLEMENTS: NingXia Red

Single Oils:
Clove, Copaiba, Cypress (Blue), Eucalyptus Blue, Frankincense, Helichrysum, Hyssop, Laurus Nobilis, Melissa, Ravintsara, Spikenard

Blends:
ImmuPower, Longevity, Thieves

Supplements & Products:
Thieves Household Cleaner

HIVES

FIRST LINE RECOMMENDATIONS:
ORAL: Di-Gize 10 drops in the morning. Longevity 10 drops in the evening.
ORAL: Basil or Ocotea for antihistamine actions.

Single Oils:
Basil, Geranium, Patchouli, Lavender, Melissa, Myrrh, Ocotea, Pine, Spruce, Tansy (Blue)

Blends:
Di-Gize, GLF, Hope, Juva Cleanse, Juva Flex, Longevity, Purification, R.C.

Supplements & Products:
Animal Scents Ointment, ClaraDerm, LavaDerm Cooling Mist, NingXia Red, PD 80/20, Rehemogen

HOOF ABSCESS
(See also PAIN MANAGEMENT)

FIRST LINE RECOMMENDATIONS:
TOPICAL: Thieves applied neat to the abscess area or hoof three or more times a day.
ORAL: Clove

RAINDROP TECHNIQUE: As needed, can be applied to abscess area and affected hoof and leg as well.

Single Oils:
Cassia, Cinnamon, Clove, Helichrysum, Laurus Nobilis, Lavender, Lemongrass, Melaleuca Alternifolia, Oregano, Thyme

Blends:
Abundance, Deep Relief Roll-On, Exodus II, Longevity, PanAway, Purification, Relieve It, Thieves

Supplements & Products:
NingXia Red, Ortho Ease Massage Oil, Ortho Sport Massage Oil, Thieves Household Cleaner, Thieves Spray

HORMONAL CONDITIONS

FIRST LINE RECOMMENDATIONS:
ORAL: Clary Sage
DIFFUSION: Ylang Ylang
PETTING: Progessence Plus

Single Oils:
Clary Sage, Geranium, Lavender, Marjoram, Myrrh, Myrtle, Sage, Spikenard, Spruce, Tansy (Blue), Tarragon, Vetiver, Ylang Ylang

Blends:
Dragon Time, EndoFlex, Gentle Baby, Lady Sclareol, Mister, Peace & Calming, Progessence Plus, SARA, SclarEssence, White Angelica

Supplements & Products:
Dragon Time Massage Oil, EndoGize, Estro, FemiGen, NingXia Red, PD 80/20,

HYPERADRENOCORTISICM
(See CUSHING'S)

IMPACTION COLIC
(See COLIC, IMPACTION)

INSECT BITES

FIRST LINE RECOMMENDATIONS:
TOPICAL: Animal Scents Ointment with Purification and other insect repelling oils mixed in. Apply to areas being bitten.

Single Oils:
Eucalyptus Globulus, Geranium, Hyssop, Lavender, Lemongrass, Melissa, Ocotea, Patchouli, Peppermint, Tansy (Blue), Tansy (Idaho)

Blends:
Hope, Longevity, Purification, R.C., Thieves

Supplements & Products:
Animal Scents Ointment, ClaraDerm, LavaDerm Cooling Mist, Ortho Ease Massage Oil, Ortho Sport Massage Oil, Thieves Household Cleaner

INSULIN RESISTANCE
(See also METABOLIC SYNDROME, CUSHING'S)

FIRST LINE RECOMMENDATIONS:
ORAL: Ocotea, Dill, Fennel
SUPPLEMENTS: NingXia Red

Single Oils:
Cinnamon, Ocotea, Pepper (Black), Ylang Ylang

Blends:
EndoFlex, Exodus II

Supplements & Products:
EndoGize, NingXia Red

KIDNEY CONDITIONS

FIRST LINE RECOMMENDATIONS:
TOPICAL: Juniper, Geranium over the Kidney area.
SUPPLEMENTS: NingXia Red

Single Oils:
Geranium, Grapefruit, Helichrysum, Juniper, Ledum, Marjoram, Tsuga

Blends:
Citrus Fresh, GLF, Juva Cleanse

Supplements & Products:
K&B Tincture, NingXia Red

LACERATIONS

FIRST LINE RECOMMENDATIONS:
TOPICAL: Mix Thieves, Melrose, and Helichrysum into Animal Scents Ointment (approximately 5 drops of each into 1 tablespoon) and fill laceration with the ointment mixture. Repeat as needed, generally once or twice a day.

Single Oils:
Helichrysum, Lavender, Melaleuca Alternifolia, Myrrh

Blends:
Melrose, PanAway, Purification, Thieves

Supplements & Products:
Animal Scents Ointment, Sulfurzyme Thieves Household Cleaner

LAMINITIS
(See also PAIN MANAGEMENT)

FIRST LINE RECOMMENDATIONS:
RAINDROP TECHNIQUE: Up to once a day, including legs and hooves.
TOPICAL: Wintergreen applied at the heels for vasodilation.
ORAL: Clove
SUPPLEMENTS: NingXia Red

Single Oils:
Clove, Helichrysum, Lavender, Lemongrass, Marjoram, Palo Santo, Peppermint, Pine, Spruce, Tansy (Blue), Wintergreen, Ylang Ylang

Blends:
Aroma Life, Aroma Siez, Deep Relief Roll-On, Di-Gize, Juva Cleanse, Longevity, M-Grain, PanAway, Relieve It, Thieves

Supplements & Products:
Life 5, NingXia Red, Ortho Ease Massage Oil, Ortho Sport Massage Oil, Sulfurzyme

LICE
(See also INSECT BITES)

FIRST LINE RECOMMENDATIONS:
BATHING: With Thieves Household Cleaner, additional oils may be added.
OIL SPRITZER: Mix large amounts (20 or more drops each) of Ocotea, Purification, Peppermint, Clove, and Di-Gize per 1 ounce (30 mL) of Ortho Ease or Ortho Sport Massage Oil and spray heavily. Repeat daily or as needed.

Single Oils:
Clove, Eucalyptus Globulus, Geranium, Lavender, Lemon, Lemongrass, Ocotea, Orange, Oregano, Peppermint, Pine, Tansy (Blue), Tansy (Idaho)

Blends:
Abundance, Di-Gize, Exodus II, Longevity, Melrose, Purification, Thieves

Supplements & Products:
Ortho Ease Massage Oil, Ortho Sport Massage Oil, Thieves Household Cleaner

LIVER DISEASE

FIRST LINE RECOMMENDATIONS:
ORAL: Helichrysum, Juva Cleanse
DRINKING WATER: Citrus Fresh
SUPPLEMENTS: NingXia Red
PETTING: Ledum

Single Oils:
Celery Seed, Chamomile (German), Geranium, Goldenrod, Grapefruit, Helichrysum, Juniper, Ledum, Myrrh, Myrtle, Nutmeg, Ravintsara, Rosemary, Sage, Spearmint, Tangerine

Blends:
Citrus Fresh, GLF, Juva Cleanse, Juva Flex

Supplements & Products:
JuvaPower, JuvaSpice, JuvaTone, NingXia Red

LYME DISEASE
(See TICK BORNE DISEASE)

MANGE
(See also INSECT BITES, SKIN CONDITIONS)

FIRST LINE RECOMMENDATIONS:
BATHING: Purification and Melrose added to Animal Scents Shampoo and/or Thieves Household Cleaner.
TOPICAL: Helichrysum, Patchouli
ORAL: Copaiba for inflammation. Melissa, Ocotea, or Basil for antihistamine action. Vetiver for severe itching.

Single Oils:
Basil, Chamomile (Roman), Eucalyptus Globulus, Geranium, Helichrysum, Lavender, Melissa, Myrrh, Ocotea, Patchouli, Peppermint, Pine, Tansy (Blue), Tansy (Idaho)

Blends:
Juva Flex, Longevity, Melrose, Purification, R.C., Relieve It, Thieves

Supplements & Products:
Animal Scents Ointment, ClaraDerm, LavaDerm Cooling Mist, Thieves Household Cleaner, Thieves Spray

EQUINE CONDITIONS

METABOLIC SYNDROME
(See also CUSHING'S, INSULIN RESISTANCE)

FIRST LINE RECOMMENDATIONS:
Use recommendations for Cushing's and Insulin Resistance.

Single Oils:
Cinnamon, Geranium, Grapefruit, Lavender, Ledum, Myrrh, Myrtle, Nutmeg, Ocotea, Pepper (Black), Spearmint, Ylang Ylang

Blends:
Abundance, Brain Power, Citrus Fresh, EndoFlex, Exodus II, GLF, Juva Cleanse, Juva Flex, Longevity

Supplements & Products:
EndoGize, Mineral Essence, NingXia Red

MITES
(See MANGE)

MOON BLINDNESS
(See UVEITIS, EYE CONDITIONS)

MUSCULAR CONDITIONS

FIRST LINE RECOMMENDATIONS:
PETTING: Marjoram, Lavender, Aroma Siez
RAINDROP TECHNIQUE: Applied at least weekly.
SUPPLEMENTS: NingXia Red, 4 ounces per day.

Single Oils:
Cedarwood, Cypress, Helichrysum, Lavender, Lemongrass, Marjoram, Pepper (Black), Peppermint, Wintergreen

Blends:
Aroma Siez, Deep Relief Roll-On, Longevity, M-Grain, PanAway, Relieve It

Supplements & Products:
NingXia Red, Ortho Ease Massage Oil, Ortho Sport Massage Oil, Relaxation Massage Oil, Sulfurzyme

NAVICULAR DISEASE

FIRST LINE RECOMMENDATIONS:
RAINDROP TECHNIQUE: Up to daily, including legs and hooves. Insert additional oils as desired.
ORAL: Clove, generally in larger amounts. Copaiba.
PETTING: Any recommended oils as needed, usually 3-4 times a day for severe cases. Lemongrass is suggested.
SUPPLEMENTS: NingXia Red, Sulfurzyme

Single Oils:
Balsam Fir (Idaho), Clove, Helichrysum, Lavender, Lemongrass, Marjoram, Palo Santo, Peppermint, Pine, Spruce, Tansy (Blue), Wintergreen

Blends:
Aroma Siez, Deep Relief Roll-On, Longevity, M-Grain, PanAway, Relieve It, Thieves

Supplements & Products:
NingXia Red, Ortho Ease Massage Oil, Ortho Sport Massage Oil, Sulfurzyme

NEUROLOGIC CONDITIONS

FIRST LINE RECOMMENDATIONS:
RAINDROP TECHNIQUE: Insert Helichrysum, Copaiba, Frankincense.
PETTING: RutaVaLa, Brain Power, Helichrysum to brain stem area 3 times a day or as needed.
SUPPLEMENTS: NingXia Red, Mineral Essence

Single Oils:
Chamomile (Roman), Copaiba, Frankincense, Helichrysum, Juniper, Laurus Nobilis, Nutmeg, Valerian, Wintergreen

Blends:
   Brain Power, Juva Cleanse, PanAway, RutaVaLa

Supplements & Products:
   Mineral Essence, NingXia Red, Sulfurzyme

OBSCESSIVE COMPULSIVE CONDITIONS
   (See BEHAVIORAL CONDITIONS, CRIBBING)

OCD
   (See BEHAVIORAL CONDITIONS, CRIBBING)

PAIN MANAGEMENT

   FIRST LINE RECOMMENDATIONS:
   ORAL: Clove, Copaiba, Helichrysum, and Myrrh 5 drops of each, repeat as needed.
   PETTING: Ortho Sport, or any indicated oils.

   Single Oils:
   Balsam Fir (Idaho), Clove, Copaiba, Helichrysum, Myrrh, Peppermint, Valerian, Vetiver, Wintergreen

   Blends:
   Deep Relief Roll-On, M-Grain, PanAway, Relieve It

   Supplements & Products:
   NingXia Red, Ortho Ease Massage Oil, Ortho Sport Massage Oil, Sulfurzyme

PAPILLOMA VIRUS
   (See WARTS)

PARASITES
   (See DEWORMING, LICE, INSECT BITES, MANGE)

PERFORMANCE TESTING
(See WINTERGREEN)

Please see the discussion of essential oils and performance testing within the Single Essential Oils chapter, under Wintergreen.

PHOTOSENSITIVITY
(See also LIVER DISEASE)

Causes of Photosensitivity often include ingestion of plants such as Alsike Clover, Vetch, Alfalfa, or St. John's Wort. Liver Disease and the use of medications such as Tetracycline can also cause this disorder. Sunburns are not a normal occurrence for horses, no matter how white or fair skinned they are, and veterinary diagnosis should always be explored.

FIRST LINE RECOMMENDATIONS:
TOPICAL: Myrrh, Helichrysum, Patchouli, Lavender added to Coconut Oil and applied topically.

Single Oils:
Chamomile (Roman), Geranium, Helichrysum, Lavender, Ledum, Myrrh, Patchouli

Blends:
GLF, Juva Cleanse, Juva Flex

Supplements & Products:
ClaraDerm, LavaDerm Cooling Mist, NingXia Red

PIGEON FEVER
(See STRANGLES)

Pigeon Fever is similar in nature to Strangles infection. The recommendations for this disease are the same as for Strangles.

POTOMAC FEVER
(See also UVEITIS)

FIRST LINE RECOMMENDATIONS:
RAINDROP TECHNIQUE: Apply up to daily. Insertion of ImmuPower is suggested.
ORAL: Thieves, Longevity

Single Oils:
Helichrysum, Mountain Savory, Oregano, Thyme

Blends:
Exodus II, ImmuPower, Longevity, Thieves

Supplements & Products:
NingXia Red

PROUD FLESH

FIRST LINE RECOMMENDATIONS:
TOPICAL: Helichrysum, Melrose. Apply various oils via Water Misting or by mixing into Animal Scents Ointment.
SUPPLEMENTS: NingXia Red, Sulfurzyme

Single Oils:
Chamomile (Roman), Geranium, Helichrysum, Lavender, Melaleuca Alternifolia, Melaleuca Ericifolia, Myrrh, Patchouli, Rose, Sandalwood, Spikenard

Blends:
Aroma Life, ClaraDerm, Juva Cleanse, Juva Flex, Longevity, Melrose, Purification, Rose Ointment, Thieves

Supplements & Products:
Animal Scents Ointment, ClaraDerm, LavaDerm Cooling Mist, NingXia Red, Omega Blue, Stevia Extract, Sulfurzyme, Thieves Household Cleaner, Thieves Spray

QUEENSLAND ITCH (QLD ITCH)
(See SUMMER ITCH, INSECT BITES)

RABIES
(See RABIES in CANINE CONDITIONS)

RAIN ROT
(See also SKIN CONDITIONS)

FIRST LINE RECOMMENDATIONS:
BATHING: With Thieves Household Cleaner

Single Oils:
Eucalyptus Globulus, Geranium, Helichrysum, Laurus Nobilis, Lavender, Lemongrass, Marjoram, Melaleuca Alternifolia, Melaleuca Ericifolia, Mountain Savory, Myrrh, Ocotea, Oregano, Patchouli, Rose, Rosemary, Sandalwood, Spikenard, Thyme

Blends:
Juva Flex, Melrose, Purification, R.C., Relieve It, Thieves

Supplements & Products:
ClaraDerm, LavaDerm Cooling Mist, NingXia Red, Omega Blue, Ortho Ease Massage Oil, Ortho Sport Massage Oil, Sulfurzyme, Thieves Household Cleaner, Thieves Spray

RAINDROP WELTS

Generally when these occur it is best to just apply additional V-6 to the sites, and leave the welts alone. They will generally resolve in around 24 hours. The majority of these welts are not irritating to the horse.

FIRST LINE RECOMMENDATIONS:
TOPICAL: V-6
ORAL: Longevity, NingXia Red

Single Oils:
Lavender, Melissa, Myrrh, Ocotea, Patchouli

Blends:
Di-Gize, Hope, Juva Cleanse, Longevity

Supplements & Products:
ClaraDerm, LavaDerm Cooling Mist, NingXia Red, Sulfurzyme

RASHES
(See SKIN CONDITIONS)

RESPIRATORY CONDITIONS
(See also HEAVES)

FIRST LINE RECOMMENDATIONS:
DIFFUSION: Any selected oil. Tenting can be achieved by hanging a piece of painting plastic over the stall door or shelter entrance, for severe situations.
RAINDROP TECHNIQUE: Apply up to daily.
PETTING: With any indicated oil, up to multiple times per day.

Single Oils:
Dorado Azul, Eucalyptus Blue, Eucalyptus Globulus, Hyssop, Laurus Nobilis, Lavender, Lemon, Lemongrass, Marjoram, Melaleuca Alternifolia, Melaleuca Ericifolia, Mountain Savory, Myrtle, Oregano, Palo Santo, Peppermint, Pine, Ravintsara, Rosemary, Spruce, Tsuga

Blends:
Aroma Siez, Breathe Again Roll-On, Egyptian Gold, Exodus II, ImmuPower, M-Grain, Melrose, Purification, Raven, R.C., Thieves

Supplements & Products:
NingXia Red, Thieves Household Cleaner

RETAINED PLACENTA

FIRST LINE RECOMMENDATIONS:
INSTILLATION: Place 20-30 drops each of Thieves, Myrrh, and Copaiba into a syringe with 30-60 mL of water or V-6. Instill into uterus.

Single Oils:
Copaiba, Lavender, Marjoram, Myrrh, Sage

Blends:
EndoFlex, Thieves

Supplements & Products:
ClaraDerm, NingXia Red, Thieves Household Cleaner

RHINO
(See EQUINE HERPES VIRUS, VIRAL CONDITIONS)

RHODOCOCCAL PNEUMONIA
(See also RESPIRATORY CONDITIONS)

Rhodococcus equi is a bacteria that causes pneumonia in immune compromised and susceptible foals, generally between 3 weeks and 6 months of age.

FIRST LINE RECOMMENDATIONS:
DIFFUSION: Thieves
RAINDROP TECHNIQUE: Up to daily.
ORAL: Thieves and or Oregano

Single Oils:
Laurus Nobilis, Lavender, Lemongrass, Marjoram, Melaleuca Alternifolia, Melaleuca Ericifolia, Mountain Savory, Myrtle, Oregano, Peppermint, Pine, Ravintsara, Rosemary, Spruce, Thyme, Tsuga

Blends:
Exodus II, ImmuPower, Melrose, Purification, R.C., Thieves

Supplements & Products:
NingXia Red, Thieves Household Cleaner

RINGBONE
(See also PAIN MANAGEMENT)

FIRST LINE RECOMMENDATIONS:
TOPICAL: Any of the indicated oils, especially Idaho Balsam Fir, R.C., Lemongrass, and PanAway applied neat multiple times per day.
RAINDROP TECHNIQUE: Apply to spine as well as to frog and bulb area up to daily.
ORAL: Idaho Balsam Fir and Clove

Single Oils:
Balsam Fir (Idaho), Clove, Copaiba, Frankincense, Helichrysum, Lemongrass, Myrrh, Oregano, Palo Santo, Peppermint, Pine, Spruce, Thyme, Wintergreen

Blends:
Deep Relief Roll-On, Longevity, PanAway, R.C.

Supplements & Products:
NingXia Red, Ortho Ease Massage Oil, Ortho Sport Massage Oil, Sulfurzyme

RINGWORM

FIRST LINE RECOMMENDATIONS:
BATHING: Thieves Household Cleaner
TOPICAL: Neat oils such as Lavender, Thieves, R.C., Ocotea, or any selected oil to the lesion multiple times per day.
ANIMAL SCENTS OINTMENT: Mix several indicated oils into the ointment. This can be made very strong in concentration. Apply to lesions as needed, usually 1-2 times per day.

Single Oils:
Geranium, Laurus Nobilis, Lavender, Lemongrass, Marjoram, Melaleuca Alternifolia, Melaleuca Ericifolia, Mountain Savory, Myrrh, Ocotea, Oregano, Pepper (Black), Peppermint, Rosemary, Thyme

Blends:
Melrose, Purification, R.C., Thieves

Supplements & Products:
Animal Scents Ointment, LavaDerm Cooling Mist, NingXia Red, Ortho Ease Massage Oil, Ortho Sport Massage Oil, Thieves Household Cleaner, Thieves Spray

ROTAVIRUS DIARRHEA

FIRST LINE RECOMMENDATIONS:
ORAL: Di-Gize, Thieves, Exodus II, Ravintsara, Peppermint
RAINDROP TECHNIQUE: Apply up to daily. Insert oils such as Ravintsara, Thieves, ImmuPower
DIFFUSION: Thieves
CLEANING: Thieves Household Cleaner

Single Oils:
Melissa, Mountain Savory, Oregano, Peppermint, Ravintsara, Tarragon, Thyme

Blends:
Di-Gize, Exodus II, Hope, ImmuPower, Longevity, Purification, Thieves

Supplements & Products:
Life 5, NingXia Red, Thieves Household Cleaner

SADDLE SORES

FIRST LINE RECOMMENDATIONS:
TOPICAL: Melrose, Idaho Balsam Fir several drops applied generally neat per day.
ANIMAL SCENTS OINTMENT: Various indicated oils can be mixed into the ointment and applied once to twice per day.

SUPPLEMENTS: Sulfurzyme

Single Oils:
Balsam Fir (Idaho), Chamomile (Roman), Geranium, Helichrysum, Lavender, Myrrh, Patchouli, Rose, Sandalwood, Spikenard

Blends:
Melrose, Purification, 3 Wise Men

Supplements & Products:
Animal Scents Ointment, Ortho Ease Massage Oil, Ortho Sport Massage Oil, Rose Ointment, Sulfurzyme

SARCOIDS

FIRST LINE RECOMMENDATIONS:
RAINDROP TECHNIQUE: Up to daily, and including application to the sarcoid when possible and tolerated. Insert oils such as Sandalwood, Frankincense, and Copaiba.
DIFFUSION: Longevity, Believe
TOPICAL: Oregano, Frankincense applied to sarcoid neat several times a day. Other oils may be applied as well, selections should be based on responses. Usually, the sarcoid will look much worse and crusty before getting better.
SUPPLEMENTS: NingXia Red, Sulfurzyme
ORAL: Longevity, Frankincense

Single Oils:
Clove, Frankincense, Grapefruit, Helichrysum, Lavender, Melissa, Mountain Savory, Orange, Oregano, Palo Santo, Peppermint, Ravintsara, Sandalwood, Tangerine, Thyme

Blends:
Australian Blue, Believe, Brain Power, Citrus Fresh, Exodus II, Forgiveness, Hope, ImmuPower, Longevity, Thieves, 3 Wise Men

Supplements & Products:
Animal Scents Ointment, MultiGreens, NingXia Red, PD 80/20, Sulfurzyme, Thieves Household Cleaner

SCRATCHES

FIRST LINE RECOMMENDATIONS:
Clip the area if necessary.
BATHING: Wash the area gently but thoroughly with Thieves Household Cleaner. Additional oils may be added to this wash solution as well.
TOPICAL: Thieves Toothpaste is a wonderful poultice to apply to the washed and dried area. Additional oils such as Melaleuca Alternifolia, Helichrysum, and Copaiba may be mixed into the toothpaste for additional function.

Single Oils:
Copaiba, Geranium, Helichrysum, Lavender, Ledum, Lemongrass, Marjoram, Melaleuca Alternifolia, Melaleuca Ericifolia, Mountain Savory, Myrrh, Ocotea, Oregano, Patchouli, Rosemary, Thyme

Blends:
GLF, Juva Cleanse, Juva Flex, Melrose, Purification, Thieves

Supplements & Products:
ClaraDerm, LavaDerm Cooling Mist, NingXia Red, Sulfurzyme, Thieves Dentarome Toothpastes, Thieves Household Cleaner, Thieves Spray, Thieves Waterless Hand Purifier, Thieves Wipes

SEEDY TOE
(See WHITE LINE DISEASE)

SKIN CONDITIONS

FIRST LINE RECOMMENDATIONS:
BATHING: With Animal Scents Shampoo or Thieves Household Cleaner.
WATER MISTING: This can be helpful to apply oils to a broad area. Place 10-20 drops of any selected oil into 4 ounces (120 mL) of distilled water and mist the area of concern several times a day or as needed.
TOPICAL: Oils can also be added to LavaDerm Cooling Mist or Animal Scents Ointment for additional care and support.
ORAL: If needed for infections, Thieves or Oregano can be given for antibacterial action.

Single Oils:
Chamomile (Roman), Geranium, Helichrysum, Juniper, Lavender, Ledum, Lemon, Lemongrass, Melaleuca Alternifolia, Melaleuca Ericifolia, Myrrh, Palo Santo, Patchouli, Rose, Rosemary, Sandalwood, Spikenard, Tsuga, Vetiver

Blends:
GLF, Juva Cleanse, Juva Flex, Melrose, Purification, Thieves

Supplements & Products:
Animal Scents Ointment, ClaraDerm, LavaDerm Cooling Mist, NingXia Red, Omega Blue, Stevia Extract, Sulfurzyme, Thieves Dentarome Toothpastes, Thieves Household Cleaner, Thieves Spray, Thieves Waterless Hand Purifier, Thieves Wipes

SPLINTS
(See also BONE CONDITIONS)

FIRST LINE RECOMMENDATIONS:
TOPICAL: Idaho Balsam Fir and Helichrysum (or other indicated oils) can be applied neat over the splint area, at least daily.
RAINDROP TECHNIQUE: This can be helpful as well, and should be given to include the affected legs. Raindrop oils can be applied directly over the splint area.
SUPPLEMENTS: BLM, Sulfurzyme

Single Oils:
Balsam Fir (Idaho), Frankincense, Helichrysum, Palo Santo, Peppermint, Pine, Spruce, Wintergreen

Blends:
Deep Relief Roll-On, PanAway, Relieve It

Supplements & Products:
Animal Scents Ointment, BLM, NingXia Red, Ortho Ease Massage Oil, Ortho Sport Massage Oil, Sulfurzyme

STOCKING UP
(See EDEMA, PERIPHERAL)

STRANGLES

FIRST LINE RECOMMENDATIONS:
See the information in ABSCESS as well.
CLEANING: See Thieves Household Cleaner for many recommendations on disinfecting.
RAINDROP TECHNIQUE: Applied daily. Oils can also be applied to large abscesses if they are in locations that are amenable to it.
ORAL: Exodus II, Longevity daily to twice a day.
TOPICAL: Any of the suggested oils applied up to 4 times per day to the abscess.
SUPPLEMENTS: NingXia Red

Single Oils:
Cassia, Cinnamon, Helichrysum, Laurus Nobilis, Lavender, Lemongrass, Melaleuca Alternifolia, Mountain Savory, Oregano, Ravintsara, Thyme

Blends:
Abundance, Exodus II, ImmuPower, Longevity, Thieves

Supplements & Products:
Animal Scents Ointment, NingXia Red, Thieves Household Cleaner

STREPTOCOCCUS EQUI
(See STRANGLES)

SUMMER ITCH
(See also INSECT BITES)

FIRST LINE RECOMMENDATIONS:
RAINDROP TECHNIQUE: Use caution around irritated skin, however many insects dislike the Raindrop Oils. Apply as often as indicated by the individual.
PETTING: With Purification or other indicated oils to repel insects.
OIL SPRITZER: Adding additional oils such as Oregano, Idaho Tansy, and Purification into Ortho Ease or Ortho Sport Massage Oil and using as a bug spray works well.

CLEANING: Treating the area for bugs with Thieves Household Cleaner is helpful to reduce insects. See the product description for more information.
ORAL: Longevity

Single Oils:
Basil, Chamomile (Roman), Citronella, Copaiba, Eucalyptus Blue, Eucalyptus Globulus, Geranium, Helichrysum, Lavender, Lemongrass, Melissa, Myrrh, Ocotea, Orange, Oregano, Palo Santo, Patchouli, Tansy (Blue), Tansy (Idaho), Vetiver

Blends:
GLF, Hope, Juva Cleanse, Juva Flex, Longevity, Purification, R.C., Thieves

Supplements & Products:
Animal Scents Ointment, ClaraDerm, LavaDerm Cooling Mist, NingXia Red, Ortho Ease Massage Oil, Ortho Sport Massage Oil, Sulfurzyme, Thieves Household Cleaner

SUNBURN
(See PHOTOSENSITIVITY)

SWABBING
(See PERFORMANCE TESTING)

SWEET ITCH
(See SUMMER ITCH, INSECT BITES)

TENDON CONDITIONS

FIRST LINE RECOMMENDATIONS:
PETTING: Apply Palo Santo to the tendon area up to 4 times a day.
ANIMAL SCENTS OINTMENT: Mix any selected oils into the ointment and rub into the tendon area for a long lasting application.

Single Oils:
Helichrysum, Lavender, Lemongrass, Marjoram, Palo Santo

Blends:
Aroma Siez, Deep Relief Roll-On, M-Grain, PanAway, Relieve It

Supplements & Products:
Animal Scents Ointment, NingXia Red, Ortho Ease Massage Oil, Ortho Sport Massage Oil, Sulfurzyme

TETANUS
(See LARGE ANIMAL CONDITIONS)

THRUSH

FIRST LINE RECOMMENDATIONS:
TOPICAL: Apply Thieves neat to the affected hoof area, 2-4 times a day or as needed.

Single Oils:
Cassia, Cinnamon, Eucalyptus Globulus, Lavender, Lemongrass, Marjoram, Melaleuca Alternifolia, Mountain Savory, Ocotea, Oregano, Pepper (Black), Thyme

Blends:
Abundance, Exodus II, Melrose, Purification, R.C., Thieves

Supplements & Products:
Thieves Household Cleaner, Thieves Spray

TICK BITES

FIRST LINE RECOMMENDATIONS:
TOPICAL: As soon as a bite is detected or a tick is removed, apply any of the recommended oils to the bite site. Neat application is generally tolerated, but based more on the location of the bite.
RAINDROP TECHNIQUE: Applying a Raindrop Technique for prevention of transmission of tick borne disease is a good idea.

Single Oils:
Hyssop, Lavender, Melaleuca Alternifolia, Mountain Savory, Oregano, Thyme

Blends:
Exodus II, Longevity, Melrose, Purification, Thieves

Supplements & Products:
Animal Scents Ointment, Ortho Ease Massage Oil, Ortho Sport Massage Oil, Thieves Spray

TICK BORNE DISEASE

FIRST LINE RECOMMENDATIONS:
ORAL: Oregano or Thieves
SUPPLEMENTS: NingXia Red
RAINDROP TECHNIQUE: Daily to every other day depending on response of individual. Inserting ImmuPower and Copaiba is suggested.

Single Oils:
Helichrysum, Melaleuca Alternifolia, Mountain Savory, Ocotea, Oregano, Thyme

Blends:
Exodus II, GLF, ImmuPower, Longevity, Melrose, Thieves

Supplements & Products:
NingXia Red

TRAILER RIDES
(See TRANSPORTING)

TRANSPORTING

FIRST LINE RECOMMENDATIONS:
PETTING: Peace & Calming, Grounding
INDIRECT DIFFUSION: Drip oils such as Lavender into the manger or other area where the horse can inhale them.

ORAL: Di-Gize can prevent motion sickness and keep the intestinal tract happy and healthy while traveling.

Single Oils:
Cedarwood, Chamomile (Roman), Lavender, Palo Santo, Valerian, Vetiver, Ylang Ylang

Blends:
Aroma Siez, Di-Gize, Grounding

Supplements & Products:
Animal Scents Ointment, NingXia Red, Ortho Ease Massage Oil, Ortho Sport Massage Oil, Relaxation Massage Oil, Sulfurzyme, Thieves Household Cleaner

TUMORS
(See CANCER, CANKER, PROUD FLESH, SARCOIDS, WARTS)

TYING UP
(See also MUSCULAR CONDITIONS)

FIRST LINE RECOMMENDATIONS:
TOPICAL: Release, Idaho Balsam Fir, Aroma Siez applied by Petting or any other technique.
ORAL: Idaho Balsam Fir, Cypress, Lavender
SUPPLEMENTS: NingXia Red, Sulfurzyme
DIFFUSION: Idaho Balsam Fir, Cypress, Aroma Siez, Lavender, and/or Marjoram on a rotational schedule.

Single Oils:
Balsam Fir (Idaho), Cedarwood, Cypress, Frankincense, Helichrysum, Lavender, Lemongrass, Marjoram, Nutmeg, Peppermint, Valerian, Vetiver, Wintergreen, Ylang Ylang

Blends:
Aroma Siez, Deep Relief Roll-On, Longevity, M-Grain, PanAway, Release, Relieve It

Supplements & Products:
Mineral Essence, NingXia Red, Omega Blue, Ortho Ease Massage Oil, Ortho Sport Massage Oil, Relaxation Massage Oil, Sulfurzyme

ULCERS, GASTRIC

FIRST LINE RECOMMENDATIONS:
ORAL: Copaiba, Di-Gize
DIFFUSION: Oils to reduce stress such as Lavender or Peace & Calming.

Single Oils:
Copaiba, Clove, Helichrysum, Melissa, Nutmeg, Patchouli, Peppermint, Rose, Valerian, Ylang Ylang

Blends:
Di-Gize

Supplements & Products:
Thieves Fresh Essence Mouthwash, Thieves Household Cleaner

UMBILICAL INFECTION

FIRST LINE RECOMMENDATIONS:
TOPICAL: Oils such as Myrrh, Exodus II or other indicated oils can be applied directly to the site of infection several times a day.
RAINDROP TECHNIQUE: Apply up to daily as needed.
ORAL: Thieves or Oregano

Single Oils:
Cassia, Cinnamon, Laurus Nobilis, Lavender, Lemon, Lemongrass, Melaleuca Alternifolia, Mountain Savory, Myrrh, Oregano, Thyme

Blends:
Abundance, Exodus II, ImmuPower, Melrose, Purification, Thieves

Supplements & Products:
Animal Scents Ointment, Thieves Household Cleaner, Thieves Spray

UVEITIS

FIRST LINE RECOMMENDATIONS:
SUPPLEMENTS: Sulfurzyme: 1 heaping tablespoon twice a day. NingXia Red: 3-4 ounces per day.
RAINDROP TECHNIQUE: With ImmuPower inserted, apply up to daily or as needed.
WATER MISTING: With Therapeutic Eye Spritzer twice a day. This spray does not need to contact the cornea, the presence of the oils around the eye area is beneficial.

Single Oils:
Copaiba, Frankincense, Helichrysum, Lavender

Blends:
ImmuPower, M-Grain, PanAway

Supplements & Products:
NingXia Red, PD 80/20, Sulfurzyme

VACCINATION DETOXIFICATION

FIRST LINE RECOMMENDATIONS:
RAINDROP TECHNIQUE: Given on a regular basis, weekly to monthly depending on need. Insertion of Ledum and Tsuga is suggested.
ORAL: Longevity or Juva Cleanse
SUPPLEMENTS: NingXia Red, Rehemogen
DRINKING WATER: Citrus Fresh

Single Oils:
Chamomile (Roman), Geranium, Grapefruit, Helichrysum, Hyssop, Juniper, Ledum, Lemon, Ocotea, Tsuga

Blends:
Citrus Fresh, GLF, Juva Cleanse, Juva Flex, Longevity

Supplements & Products:
K&B Tincture, NingXia Red, Rehemogen

VIRAL CONDITIONS

FIRST LINE RECOMMENDATIONS:
RAINDROP TECHNIQUE: Up to daily with oils such as ImmuPower, Melissa, and Ravintsara inserted.
ORAL: Thieves or Exodus II
SUPPLEMENTS: NingXia Red
DIFFUSION: Thieves
CLEANING: Thieves Household Cleaner

Single Oils:
Geranium, Helichrysum, Hyssop, Laurus Nobilis, Melaleuca Ericifolia, Melissa, Mountain Savory, Oregano, Peppermint, Ravintsara, Rose, Sandalwood, Thyme

Blends:
Exodus II, Forgiveness, Hope, ImmuPower, Raven, Thieves, 3 Wise Men

Supplements & Products:
Mineral Essence, MultiGreens, NingXia Red, Thieves Household Cleaner

WARTS

FIRST LINE RECOMMENDATIONS:
RAINDROP TECHNIQUE: Weekly with ImmuPower and Clove inserted.
TOPICAL: Clove or Oregano applied neat, directly to warts located in areas that can tolerate it.
ORAL: Longevity
SUPPLEMENTS: NingXia Red

Single Oils:
Cinnamon, Clove, Lemon, Melissa, Mountain Savory, Oregano, Peppermint, Ravintsara, Sandalwood, Thyme

Blends:
Abundance, Brain Power, Exodus II, Forgiveness, Hope, ImmuPower, Longevity, Thieves

Supplements & Products:
Mineral Essence, MultiGreens, NingXia Red, Thieves Household Cleaner

WEST NILE VIRUS
(See VIRAL CONDITIONS, ENCEPHALITIS)

FIRST LINE RECOMMENDATIONS:
ORAL: Oregano and ImmuPower
RAINDROP TECHNIQUE: Apply up to twice a day for severe situations. Modify with insertion of ImmuPower, Helichrysum, and Copaiba. Balancing with Valor is recommended.
TOPICAL: Valor, Helichrysum to brain stem area, once or more per day.
PETTING: With any of the selected oils, multiple times a day.
SUPPLEMENTS: NingXia Red, Super C

Single Oils:
Chamomile (Roman), Helichrysum, Hyssop, Melissa, Mountain Savory, Oregano, Ravintsara, Thyme

Blends:
Exodus II, Hope, ImmuPower, RutaVaLa, Thieves, Valor

Supplements & Products:
Mineral Essence, MultiGreens, NingXia Red, Super C, Thieves Household Cleaner

WHITE LINE DISEASE

FIRST LINE RECOMMENDATIONS:
TOPICAL: Apply 3-4 drops of Thieves directly to the hoof wall 3-4 times a day. Hoof wall resection is not necessary, however if a small groove has been made for diagnosis, drip the oil directly into the area. Treatment for 2 or more weeks is recommended, until confirmation of the condition being resolved.

Single Oils:
Eucalyptus Globulus, Lavender, Lemongrass, Melaleuca Alternifolia, Mountain Savory, Ocotea, Oregano, Thyme

Blends:
   Abundance, Exodus II, Melrose, Purification, R.C., Thieves

Supplements & Products:
   Thieves Household Cleaner, Thieves Spray

WINDGALLS

FIRST LINE RECOMMENDATIONS:
   SUPPLEMENTS: Sulfurzyme
   RAINDROP TECHNIQUE: Apply approximately weekly, including leg applications.
   TOPICAL: Any of the suggested oils can be applied as needed.

Single Oils:
   Balsam Fir (Idaho), Basil, Cypress, Helichrysum, Lemongrass, Palo Santo, Pine, Spruce, Wintergreen

Blends:
   Believe, Sacred Mountain

Supplements & Products:
   Animal Scents Ointment, Ortho Ease Massage Oil, Ortho Sport Massage Oil, Sulfurzyme

WOUNDS
   (See LARGE ANIMAL CONDITIONS)

LARGE ANIMAL TECHNIQUES

For the majority of Large Animals, the techniques and application methods will be similar to those used for dogs and for horses. Animals such as goats and pigs, tend to follow the dog recommendations. And larger animals such as Cattle, Alpaca, Llama, and other hoof stock, tend to follow the horse recommendations. Raindrop Technique for these animals should follow the descriptions and recommendations made within the dog and horse section.

ABSCESS
(See discussion in EQUINE CONDITIONS)

ARTHRITIS
(See discussion in EQUINE CONDITIONS)

BIRTHING & DELIVERY
(See also discussion in EQUINE CONDITIONS)

FIRST LINE RECOMMENDATIONS:
TOPICAL: Apply Myrrh or other essential oils to the umbilical cord upon birth.
DIFFUSION: Gentle Baby
PETTING: Gentle Baby, En-R-Gee

Single Oils:
Frankincense, Geranium, Lavender, Marjoram, Myrrh, Orange, Rose

Blends:
Citrus Fresh, En-R-Gee, Gentle Baby

Supplements & Products:
ClaraDerm, NingXia Red, ParaFree, Relaxation Massage Oil, Thieves Household Cleaner

BLOAT

FIRST LINE RECOMMENDATIONS:
ORAL: Tarragon for its anti-fermentation action. Also Di-Gize and Peppermint may be given.
TOPICAL: Apply Di-Gize to abdomen area.
PETTING: Any suggested oils, multiple times per day or as needed.

Single Oils:
Juniper, Lavender, Marjoram, Peppermint, Tarragon, Vetiver, Ylang Ylang

Blends:
Aroma Siez, Deep Relief Roll-On, Di-Gize, Peace & Calming, RutaVaLa

Supplements & Products:
Relaxation Massage Oil

CAE
(See CAPRINE ARTHRITIS ENCEPHALITIS)

CANCER
(See discussion in EQUINE CONDITIONS)

CAPRINE ARTHRITIS ENCEPHALITIS
(See also MASTITIS, and VIRAL CONDITIONS in EQUINE)

Caprine Arthritis Encephalitis is caused by an RNA virus and affects goats. Symptoms include arthritis, encephalitis, hard udder, mastitis, poor milk production, pneumonia, and weight loss.

FIRST LINE RECOMMENDATIONS:
RAINDROP TECHNIQUE: Apply up to daily. Insertion of oils such as Mountain Savory, Ravintsara, Melissa, ImmuPower are recommended.
ORAL: ImmuPower, Exodus II, and/or Longevity. Use of multiple oils may be required for some cases, start with one and

add additional oils if needed. Giving small amounts frequently throughout the day is often suggested.
SUPPLEMENTS: MultiGreens, NingXia Red
DIFFUSION: Thieves

Single Oils:
Helichrysum, Laurus Nobilis, Lavender, Melissa, Mountain Savory, Oregano, Ravintsara, Thyme

Blends:
Brain Power, Exodus II, Hope, ImmuPower, Longevity, Raven, Thieves

Supplements & Products:
MultiGreens, NingXia Red, Sulfurzyme, Thieves Household Cleaner

CASEOUS LYMPHADENITIS

Caseous Lymphadenitis is also known as CLA, Cheesy Gland, Lympho, or Thin Ewe Syndrome. It is caused by the bacteria Corynebacterium pseudotuberculosis, and affects sheep and goats. The bacteria can survive for several months in the environment. The bacteria has a think lipid wall, making essential oils a perfect tool to penetrate and destroy the otherwise difficult bacteria.

FIRST LINE RECOMMENDATIONS:
CLEANING: Spray farm, especially shady areas, with Thieves Household Cleaner.
RAINDROP TECHNIQUE: Apply up to once a day, drip oils onto the abscess sites when possible. Insert oils such as ImmuPower.
ORAL: Longevity, Thieves, and/or Oregano

Single Oils:
Grapefruit, Laurus Nobilis, Lavender, Lemon, Lemongrass, Mountain Savory, Oregano, Pine, Rosemary, Thyme

Blends:
Aroma Life, Exodus II, ImmuPower, Juva Flex, Longevity, Purification, Thieves

LARGE ANIMAL CONDITIONS

Supplements & Products:
Animal Scents Ointment, NingXia Red, Thieves Household Cleaner

CASTRATION
(See discussion in EQUINE CONDITIONS)

CLA
(See CASEOUS LYMPHADENITIS)

COCCIDIA
(See also DIARRHEA)

FIRST LINE RECOMMENDATIONS:
SUPPLEMENTS: ParaFree
ORAL: Thieves, Oregano
RAINDROP TECHNIQUE: Applied as needed, at least weekly. Insert ImmuPower, Di-Gize.

Single Oils:
Lemon, Melaleuca Alternifolia, Mountain Savory, Nutmeg, Ocotea, Oregano, Tarragon, Thyme

Blends:
Di-Gize, ImmuPower, Longevity, Melrose, Purification, Thieves

Supplements & Products:
Life 5, ParaFree, Thieves Household Cleaner

CRYPTOSPORIDIA

FIRST LINE RECOMMENDATIONS:
ORAL: Oregano up to four times per day.
RAINDROP TECHNIQUE: Apply as needed, up to once per day in severe situations. Insert oils such as ImmuPower, Di-Gize.
DRINKING WATER: Thieves Household Cleaner, Thieves

Single Oils:
Lemon, Lemongrass, Melaleuca Alternifolia, Mountain Savory, Oregano, Patchouli, Tarragon, Thyme

Blends:
   Di-Gize, Exodus II, ImmuPower, Longevity, Melrose, Purification, Thieves

Supplements & Products:
   Inner Defense, Life 5, Thieves Household Cleaner

CYSTIC OVARY

FIRST LINE RECOMMENDATIONS:
   RAINDROP TECHNIQUE: Apply as needed, weekly or more often. Insert oils such as Clary Sage, Frankincense, and Myrrh.
   INSTILLATION: Add 1-4 drops each of Myrrh, Lavender, Frankincense, and Myrtle to 5 mL of V-6. Instill into the uterus, twice a day for 5-7 days.

Single Oils:
   Clary Sage, Copaiba, Frankincense, Lavender, Marjoram, Myrrh, Myrtle, Orange, Sage, Tansy (Blue)

Blends:
   Citrus Fresh, EndoFlex, Lady Sclareol, Mister, PanAway, SclarEssence

Supplements & Products:
   EndoGize, Estro, FemiGen, NingXia Red

DEHORNING
(See also PAIN MANAGEMENT in EQUINE CONDITIONS)

FIRST LINE RECOMMENDATIONS:
   TOPICAL: Apply any essential oil to the site of dehorning immediately. Mix oils into Animal Scents Ointment for longer lasting applications.
   PETTING: Trauma Life

Single Oils:
   Geranium, Helichrysum, Lavender, Lemongrass, Melaleuca Alternifolia, Palo Santo, Valerian

Blends:
  Acceptance, Deep Relief Roll-On, Forgiveness, Melrose, PanAway, Peace & Calming, Purification, RutaVaLa, Thieves Tranquil, Trauma Life, Valor

Supplements & Products:
  Animal Scents Ointment, Thieves Household Cleaner

DEWORMING
  (See discussion in EQUINE CONDITIONS)

DIARRHEA

  FIRST LINE RECOMMENDATIONS:
    ORAL: Di-Gize, Peppermint
    RAINDROP TECHNIQUE: Apply as needed.
    PETTING: Di-Gize, Peppermint

  Single Oils:
    Lemon, Lemongrass, Melaleuca Alternifolia, Melissa, Mountain Savory, Oregano, Peppermint, Tarragon, Thyme, Vetiver, Ylang Ylang

  Blends:
    Di-Gize, Exodus II, Hope, ImmuPower, Melrose, Purification, Thieves

  Supplements & Products:
    Life 5, ParaFree, Thieves Household Cleaner

LICE
  (See discussion in EQUINE CONDITIONS)

LIVER DISEASE
  (See discussion in EQUINE CONDITIONS)

MANGE
  (See discussion in EQUINE CONDITIONS)

MASTITIS

FIRST LINE RECOMMENDATIONS:
ORAL: Oregano and Melrose
TOPICAL: Oregano and Melrose can be added to Animal Scents Ointment or massage oils to be applied to the udder. Many oils can be incorporated into an "udder rub", and the solution can be made very strong, as neat oils can often be applied to the udder.

Single Oils:
Cypress, Helichrysum, Laurus Nobilis, Lavender, Lemongrass, Melaleuca Alternifolia, Melaleuca Ericifolia, Mountain Savory, Oregano, Thyme

Blends:
Melrose, Purification, Thieves

Supplements & Products:
Animal Scents Ointment, ClaraDerm, LavaDerm Cooling Mist, Ortho Ease Massage Oil, Ortho Sport Massage Oil, Thieves Household Cleaner

MILK PRODUCTION

FIRST LINE RECOMMENDATIONS:
ORAL: Fennel
PETTING: Fennel

Single Oils:
Fennel, Celery Seed

Blends:
Abundance, EndoFlex, SclarEssence

Supplements & Products:
Animal Scents Ointment

PAIN MANAGEMENT
(See discussion in EQUINE CONDITIONS)

POLIOENCEPHALOMYELITIS

FIRST LINE RECOMMENDATIONS:
SUPPLEMENTS: NingXia Red, Super B
RAINDROP TECHNIQUE: Apply as needed.
PETTING: Helichrysum

Single Oils:
Helichrysum, Juniper, Laurus Nobilis

Blends:
Brain Power, Longevity, Valor

Supplements & Products:
Mineral Essence, NingXia Red, Super B

RINGWORM
(See discussion in EQUINE CONDITIONS)

SCOURS
(See DIARRHEA)

SCRAPIE
(See also VIRAL CONDITIONS, NEUROLOGIC CONDITIONS in EQUINE CONDITIONS)

Scrapie is a condition mainly of sheep, and rarely of goats, which is similar in nature to Mad Cow Disease, and caused by a prion. It affects the central nervous system and is a reportable disease. Positive animals are quarantined and often destroyed. Protocols will mainly focus on prevention of the disease. It is unknown if the disease can be cleared, as most positive animals are slaughtered. Certainly, the protocols could be used more aggressively in attempts to clear positive animals, however cooperation with your state and government agencies regarding this disease, must be followed.

FIRST LINE RECOMMENDATIONS:
RAINDROP TECHNIQUE: Apply up to daily or as needed. Insertion of oils such as ImmuPower, Melissa, and Hyssop are suggested.
ORAL: Exodus II, Longevity

Single Oils:
Helichrysum, Hyssop, Melissa, Oregano, Ravintsara, Thyme

Blends:
Brain Power, Egyptian Gold, Exodus II, Hope, ImmuPower, Longevity, Raven, Thieves

Supplements & Products:
Mineral Essence, MultiGreens, NingXia Red, Super B, Thieves Household Cleaner

TEAT DIP, TEAT WASH

FIRST LINE RECOMMENDATIONS:
Use Thieves Household Cleaner to make a teat wash solution. The addition of Vegetable Glycerin to the solution can help to condition the skin. Additional oils may be added to the wash solution to create custom benefits or preventive measures. For example, cows prone to mastitis could have Oregano and Melrose added to their teat wash, to be regularly exposed to their effects. The addition of Fennel, can be an easy way to increase milk supply through absorption within the teat wash or dip.

Udder Wash Recipe: Add approximately ½ capful of Thieves Household Cleaner to ½ gallon of water. Add 1 tablespoon or more of Vegetable Glycerin. Adjust according to skin responses or dilute further if a tacky residue is left on the udder.

After milking, the use of a natural and therapeutic teat dip is strongly suggested. My favorite is to use the Animal Scents Ointment applied by hand. Additional oils can likewise be added to the ointment.

For those who like a more liquid teat dip, various essential oils can be added to V-6 or massage oils, and these solutions can be applied via a teat dip cup.

Single Oils:
Fennel, Frankincense, Geranium, Lavender, Melaleuca Alternifolia, Melaleuca Ericifolia, Mountain Savory, Oregano

Blends:
Dragon Time, Melrose, Purification, Thieves

Supplements & Products:
Animal Scents Ointment, ClaraDerm, Ortho Ease Massage Oil, Ortho Sport Massage Oil, Thieves Household Cleaner

TETANUS
(See also NEUROLOGIC CONDITIONS in EQUINE CONDITIONS)

FIRST LINE RECOMMENDATIONS:
Prevention of Tetanus is the wisest approach. Application of ANY essential oil to any wound or surgical site should occur immediately. Selection of any antibacterial essential oil can be applied neat, diluted, or within Animal Scents Ointment.

ORAL: For active infection and symptoms: Copaiba, Laurus Nobilis, and Spikenard are given orally. Give 3 drops of each oil by mouth, 6 times per day.

Single Oils:
Copaiba, Helichrysum, Juniper, Laurus Nobilis, Lavender, Melaleuca Alternifolia, Mountain Savory, Spikenard

Blends:
Brain Power, Exodus II, ImmuPower, Longevity, Purification, Thieves,

Supplements & Products:
Mineral Essence, NingXia Red, Thieves Household Cleaner

WOUNDS

FIRST LINE RECOMMENDATIONS:
TOPICAL: Mix Thieves, Melrose, and Helichrysum into Animal Scents Ointment (approximately 5 drops of each into 1 tablespoon) and apply to wound. Repeat as needed, generally once or twice a day. Neat oils can also be applied to wounds.

WATER MISTING: Selected essential oils can easily be applied over a larger area via misting. Generally this can be a fairly strong concentration, 20 or more drops of each oil added to 4 ounces (120 mL) of distilled water. Apply multiple times a day or according to response.

Single Oils:
Geranium, Helichrysum, Lavender, Lemongrass, Melaleuca Alternifolia, Melaleuca Ericifolia, Myrrh, Palmarosa, Spikenard, Tansy (Idaho)

Blends:
Melrose, PanAway, Purification, Thieves

Supplements & Products:
Animal Scents Ointment, LavaDerm Cooling Mist, Stevia Extract, Sulfurzyme, Thieves Household Cleaner

LARGE ANIMAL CONDITIONS

INDEX

3 Wise Men	201	Aria	28
Abscess, canine	376	Aroma Life	177
Abscess, equine	471	Aroma Siez	178
Abscess, feline	327	Arthritis, avian	255
Abscess, hoof	493	Arthritis, canine	384
Abundance	177	Arthritis, equine	472
Acceptance	177	Arthritis, feline	331
Acne, feline	328	Ascites	384
Acupuncture, use of oils with	75	Asian Beetles	146
Addison's Disease	377	Aspergillosis	256
Adrenal tumors, ferrets	289	Asthma, feline	331
Advanced Techniques	72	Atopy	See Allergies
Agave	209	Aural Hematoma	385
AlkaLime	205	Auricular Adjustment	73
Allergies, canine	378	Australian Blue	178
Allergies, feline	328	Autoimmune, canine	386
Allerzyme	206	Autoimmune, equine	473
Alopecia X	379	Autoimmune, feline	331
Amphibians	303	Awaken	178
Amyloidosis	380	Back conditions, equine	474
Anal Glands	381	Bacteria, resistant	117
Anaplasma	See Tick Borne Disease	Bag balm	207
Anemia, feline	329	Balance Complete	208
Angelica	77	Balancing	61
Animal Scents Ointment	206	Balsam Fir, Idaho	77
Animal Scents Shampoo	207	Basil	78
Anise	77	Bath & Shower Gel	208
Anorexia, canine	382	Bay Laurel	111
Anorexia, feline	330	Behavior, canine	387
Antihistamine	382	Behavior, equine	475
Anxiety, canine	383	Behavior, feline	332
Aortic Thromboembolism ..See Saddle Thrombus		Behavior, hormonal equine	494
Application, frequency	58	Behavioral conditions, avian	256
Application, quantity	58	Believe	178
Aquariums	46, 307	Bell's Palsy	387

INDEX

Benign Prostatic Hypertrophy ...... *See* Prostate
Bergamot 79
Bilious Vomiting 388
Birthing, equine 475
Birthing, large animals 522
Black Pepper 140
Bladder infection, canine 389
Bladder infections .... *See* Urinary
Bladder stones, canine 389
Blastomycosis 390
Bleeding, avian 257
Blends, Essential Oil 177
Blends, mixing 68
BLM Capsules 208
BLM Powder 209
Bloat, canine 416
Bloat, large animals 523
Blocked, feline 333
Blood clot .... *See* Saddle Thrombus
Blood feather 258
Blue Agave Nectar 209
Blue Cypress 90
Blue Tansy 155
Bone, broken 391
Bone, conditions 392
Bones, broken avian 258
Bones, equine 476
Borna Virus 259
Box Elder Bugs 146
BPH .... *See* Prostate
Brain Power 178
Breathe Again 178
Breeding 21
Breeding, rabbits 294
Brucella Canis 392
Brucellosis 392
Bruised sole, equine 476
Bruising, equine 477
Bumblefoot 259
Butterflies 311
CAE 523
Callus 393
Cancer, avian 260
Cancer, bone 396
Cancer, canine 394

Cancer, equine 478
Cancer, feline 334
Cancer, liver 396
Cancer, lung 396
Cancer, lymph 397
Cancer, mammary 397
Cancer, spleen 397
Canine Influenza .... *See* Virus, canine
Canker 479
Caprine Arthritis Encephalitis 523
Carbozyme 209
Cardamom 79
CardiaCare 210
Cardiomyopathy, canine 398
Cardiomyopathy, feline .... *See* Heart Disease
Carrot Seed 79
Caseous Lymphadenitis 524
Cassia 80
Castration, large animal 480
Cataract 398
Cats 321
Cats, exotic 304
Cats, large 304
Cavity .... *See* Feline Odontoclastic Resorptive Lesion
Cedar, Western Red 80
Cedarwood 80
Celery Seed 80
Cel-Lite Magic Massage Oil 210
Cervical Line, feline .... *See* Feline Odontoclastic Resorptive Lesion
Chamomile, German 81
Chamomile, Roman 81
Cheesy Gland 524
Cheyletiella 296
Chinchillas 305
Choke 480
Christmas Spirit 179
Chronic Obstructive Pulmonary Disease .... *See* Heaves
Cinnamon Bark 82
Cistus 83
Citronella 84
Citrus Fresh 179
CLA 524

535

ClaraDerm	210	Declaw, feline	338
Clarity	179	Deep Relief Roll-On	179
Clary Sage	84	Dehorning	526
Clove	85	Demodex	406
Club foot	481	Dental Disease, canine	407
Coccidia	525	Dental Disease, feline	339
Cognitive dysfunction	399	Dentarome toothpastes	241
Cold and flu, equine	482	Detoxification	See Vaccinosis
Colic	483	Detoxification, anesthesia	472
Colic, impaction	484	Detoxification, equine	518
Collapsing Trachea	400	Detoxzyme	211
ComforTone	210	Deworming, canine	408
Common Sense	179	Deworming, equine	487
Competition testing	166	Deworming, feline	340
Conjunctivitis, feline	337	Deworming, recipe	231
Constipation	402	Diabetes, canine	408
Contracted tendons	485	Diabetes, feline	341
Copaiba	87	Diarrhea, avian	262
Copal	87	Diarrhea, canine	409
COPD	492	Diarrhea, equine	487
Coprophagia	403	Diarrhea, feline	341
Coriander	89	Diarrhea, ferrets	289
Cornea	403	Diarrhea, large animal	527
Corns, canine	393	Diarrhea, rabbits	295
Corns, equine	476	Diarrhea, Rotavirus	508
CortiStop – Women's	211	Diffusion	28
Corynebacterium	524	Diffusion, air	31
Cougars	304	Diffusion, caging	30
Cough, canine	404	Diffusion, cats	323
Cribbing	485	Diffusion, open room	30
Crop infection	261	Diffusion, tenting	30
Crop stasis	262	Diffusion, water-based	28
Cruciate injury	405	Digest + Cleanse	212
Cryptorchid	See Testicle, undescended	Digestive enzymes	204
Cryptosporidia	525	Di-Gize	180
Crystals, feline	See Urinary, feline	Dill	91
Cumin	90	Direct application	41
Cushing's, canine	406	Disc, spinal	426
Cushing's, equine	486	Distemper, feline	See Viral, feline
Cuterebra	296	Dorado Azul	92
Cuts	See Laceration	Dragon Time	181
Cypress	90	Dragon Time Massage Oil	212
Cypress, Blue	90	Dream Catcher	182
Cystic ovary	526	Drinking water, adding oils	32
Cystitis, feline	See FLUTD	Dry Eye	409
Cytochrome p450	322	Dystocia	See Pregnancy & Delivery

INDEX

Ear infections 410
Ear Mites, feline 342
Ear Spray Recipe 54, 246
Ears, applying oils to 42
Ears, use of essential oils 52
Edema, equine 488
Egg binding 263
Egg laying, excessive 263
Egg laying, inadequate 264
Egyptian Gold 182
Ehrlichia .... *See* Tick Borne Disease
EHV 489
Elemi 93
Elephants 306
Elimination, inappropriate 354
Emotional Cleansing 411
Emotional Raindrop Technique 70, 172
Emotional use of blends 171
Emotional work with oils 67
Emotions 171
Encephalitis, equine 489
EndoFlex 182
EndoGize 213
En-R-Gee 182
Envision 182
EPA 228
Epilepsy .... *See* Seizures
EPM 490
Epulis 412
Equine Herpes Virus 489
Equine Protozoal Myeloencephalitis
  490
Essential Oil Blends 177
Essentialzyme 213
Essentialzymes-4 214
Estro 214
Eucalyptus Blue 93
Eucalyptus Globulus 94
Eucalyptus Polybractea 95
Eucalyptus Radiata 95
Exodus II 183
Eye spritzer, therapeutic 51
Eyes, canine 412
Eyes, equine 490
Eyes, use of essential oils 49

Fading Kitten Syndrome 342
Fairies 307
False pregnancy 413
Fatty Liver Disease, feline 343
Fatty Liver Disease, avian 265
Fatty tumor 431
Feather loss 265
Feather picking 266
Feather Spray Recipe 251
Feet, applying oils to 43
Feline Acne 328
Feline Infectious Peritonitis 344
Feline Leukemia .... *See* Viral, feline
Feline Odontoclastic Resorptive
  Lesions 345
FELV .... *See* Viral, feline
FemiGen 215
Fennel 96
Ferrets 288
Fever, equine 491
Fever, feline 346
FIP 344
Fish 307
Fistula 197
FIV .... *See* Viral, feline
Flea Bomb Recipe 140
Fleas, canine 414
Fleas, feline 347
Float rides 515
Flu .... *See* Virus
Flu, equine 482
FLUTD 348
Foods, adding oils to 36
Foreign body, canine 415
Forgiveness 183
FORL 345
Founder 496
Frankincense 97
Frankincense, carteri 97
Frankincense, Sacred 101
Frequency of application 58
Frogs 303
FUO .... *See* Fever, feline
Galbanum 101
Gall Bladder 415
Gastric ulcers, canine 416

537

Gastrodilatation Volvulus 416
Gastrointestinal, avian 268
Gathering 184
GDV 416
Gelding .... See Castration
Gentle Baby 184
Geranium 101
Gerbils 315
German Chamomile 81
Giardia, avian 268
Giardia, canine 417
Ginger 103
Girth Galls .... See Saddle Sores
Glaucoma, canine 418
GLF 184
Goldenrod 104
Gout, avian 269
Grapefruit 105
Grapefruit, and medications 105
Grass scald, urine 205
Gratitude 185
Greasy Heel 510
Grounding 185
Guinea Pigs 308
Hair follicles 23
Hair loss, from essential oils 158
Hair, embedded 198
Hairballs, feline 349
Hamsters 315
Harmony 185
Head tilt, canine 460
Head trauma, avian 269
Heart disease, canine 418
Heart disease, feline 350
Heartworm disease 419
Heartworm prevention 233, 419
Heat stroke .... See Hyperthermia
Heaves 492
Heavy metals, avian 270
Hedgehogs 309
Helichrysum 106
Helicobacter, ferrets 289
Hemangiosarcoma 397
Hemorrhage, internal 421
Hendra Virus 245, 492
Hermit Crabs 311

Herpes, feline 350
Highest Potential 186
Hippopotamus 310
Histiocytoma 422
Hit by car 351
Hives, equine 493
Honey Bees 311
Hoof abscess 493
Hope 186
Hormonal conditions, avian 271
Hormones, equine 494
Horner's Syndrome 352
Hot Spots 422
Humility 186
Hyperesthesia 352
Hypertension 353
Hyperthermia 423
Hyperthyroidism 353
Hypoglycemia 423
Hypothyroid 423
Hyssop 109
IBD 425
IBD, feline 355
IBF (Idaho Balsam Fir) 77
ICP 215
Idaho Balsam Fir 77
Idaho Tansy 156
IMHA 424
Immune Mediated Anemia 424
ImmuPower 186
ImmuPro 215
Incontinence, urinary 425
Indirect application 48
Inflammatory Bowel Disease 425
Inflammatory Bowel, feline 355
Influenza, canine .... See Virus, canine
Injections of oils 76
Inner Child 187
Inner Defense 216
Insect bites, equine 495
Insects, pets 311
Inspiration 187
Insulin resistance, equine 495
Insulinoma, ferrets 290
Intervertebral Disc Disease 426
Into the Future 187

INDEX

Intravenous, use of oils 76
IVDD 426
Jasmine 110
Joy 188
Juniper 111
Juva Cleanse 188
Juva Flex 189
JuvaPower 217
JuvaSpice 217
JuvaTone 217
K&B Tincture 218
Kennel Cough 427
Kenney, Sara 246
Kidney disease, avian 272
Kidney, canine 428
Kidney, equine 495
Kidney, feline 356
KidScents MightyVites 222
KidScents MightyZyme 222
Kitty Cocktail Deworming Recipe 231
Kitty Raindrop Technique 325
Knee injury, canine 405
Koi 307
KRDT 325
Labdanum 83
Lacerations, canine 428
Lacerations, equine 496
Lactation 21
Lactation, canine 429
Lady Sclareol 189
Laminitis 496
Large Animals 522
Laryngeal paralysis 429
Laurus Nobilis 111
LavaDerm 219
Lavender 113
Lavender Eye Spritzer 51
LC 72
Lead poisoning .... See Heavy Metals
Ledum 114
Lemon 115
Lemon Balm 123
Lemongrass 117
Lenticular sclerosis 430
Lice 497
Lick granuloma 430

Life 5 220
Life force oils 145
Limping Kitten Syndrome 356
Lions 304
Lipoma 431
Lipozyme 221
Litter box, not using 354
Litteroma 323
Live with Passion 190
Liver disease, avian 273
Liver metabolism, cats 322
Liver shunt 433
Liver, canine 432
Liver, equine 497
Liver, feline 357
Lizards 313
Locus Ceruleus 72
Longevity 190
Longevity Softgels 221
Lozenges, Thieves 243
Lupus .... See Autoimmune
Luxating Patella .... See Patella
Lyme Disease .... See Tick Borne Disease
Lymph nodes, canine 434
Lympho 524
Lymphoma, ferrets 291
Lymphosarcoma 397
Macaw Wasting Disease .... See
    Proventricular Dilatation Disease
Magnify Your Purpose 191
Maldigestion, canine 434
Malnutrition, avian 273
Mange, equine 498
Mange, sarcoptic 450
Marjoram 118
Mast Cell Tumors 435
Master Formula HERS 221
Master Formula HIS 221
Masticatory Muscle Myositis 436
Mastitis, canine 436
Mastitis, large animal 528
MegaCal 222
Megaesophagus 437
Melaleuca Alternifolia 120
Melaleuca Ericifolia 122
Melaleuca Quinquenervia 122

539

Melaleuca, cats 321
Melatonin 215, 237, 379
Melissa 123
Melrose 191
Metabolic Bone Disease 313
Metabolic syndrome, equine 499
Methicillin Resistant Staph. aureus
 .... 117, 197
Methyl Salicylate 166
M-Grain 191
Mice 315
MightyVites 222
MightyZyme 222
Milk production 528
Mineral Essence 223
Mister 191
Mites, demodex 406
Mites, equine 498
Mites, rabbits 296
Mites, sarcoptic 450
Monkeys 312
Moon Blindness 518
Motivation 192
Mountain Savory 125
Mouthwash, Thieves 242
MQV 122
MRSA 117, 197
MSM 238
MultiGreens 224
Muscle Wasting 437
Muscular conditions, equine 499
Mutilation, avian 274
Myrrh 125
Myrtle 128
NAT 72
Navicular disease 500
Neroli 129
Neuro Auricular Technique 72
Neurologic conditions, avian 276
Neurologic, canine 438
Neurologic, equine 500
Neurologic, feline 357
Newts 303
Niaouli 122
NingXia Red 225
Ningxia Wolfberries 227

Nutmeg 129
Obesity, canine 439
OCD .... *See* Behavior, *See* Behavior
Ocotea 130
Octopus 316
Odor Eliminating Spray 355
Oil Misting 47
Ointment, adding oils to 46
Omega Blue 228
Oral use of oils 39
Orange essential oil 133
Orchitis .... *See* Testicle
Oregano 134
Ortho Ease Massage Oil 229
Ortho Sport Massage Oil 230
Osteosarcoma .... *See* Cancer, bone
Ovary, cystic 526
Pain control, feline 358
Pain management, avian 276
Pain, canine 440
Pain, equine 501
Palmarosa 136
Palo Santo 137
PanAway 192
Pancreatic insufficiency 440
Pancreatitis 359
Pancreatitis, canine 441
Pannus .... *See* Autoimmune
Panosteitis, canine 442
Papilloma, avian 277
Papilloma, canine 462
Papilloma, rabbits 301
ParaFree 230
Parasite Blend 231
Parasite Blend, Large Animal 231
Parasites .... *See* Deworming
Parasites, rabbits 296
Parrot Fever .... *See* Psittacosis
Parvo, canine 443
Pasteurella, rabbits 297
Patchouli 138
Patella, luxating 444
PBFD ..... *See* Psittacine Beak and Feather
 Disease
PD 80/20 233

INDEX

PDD .... *See* Proventricular Dilatation Disease
Peace & Calming 192
Pemphigus .... *See* Autoimmune
Pepper, Black 140
Peppermint 141
Performance testing 166
Petitgrain 143
Petting 42
Petting, cats 324
Photosensitivity 502
Physical use of blends 174
Pigeon Fever 502
Pillow Paw ...... *See* Autoimmune, feline
Pine 144
Placenta, retained 506
Pneumonia .... *See* Respiratory
Pneumonia, aspiration .... *See* Cough
Polioencephalomyelitis 529
Polyzyme 234
Ponds 46, 307
Potomac Fever 503
Poultry 254
Power Meal 234
Pregnancy 21
Pregnancy & Delivery, canine 445
Pregnancy, feline 360
Prenolone Body Cream 234
Present Time 193
Primates 312
Probiotic 220
Products 203
Progessence Plus Serum 235
Prostate Health 235
Prostate, canine 445
Prostate, ferrets 292
Prostatitis, canine 446
Protec 235
Proud flesh 503
Proventricular Dilatation Disease . 278
Psittacine Beak and Feather Disease 280
Psittacosis 281
Pulmonary contusions 107
Pure Protein Complete 235
Purification 193

Purifier, hand 247
Pyometra 446
Queensland Itch 512
R.C. 194
Rabbits 294
Rabies 447
Rain Rot 504
Raindrop Technique, avian 252
Raindrop Technique, canine 373
Raindrop Technique, cats 325
Raindrop Technique, Emotional 70
Raindrop Technique, equine 463
Raindrop Technique, ferrets 293
Raindrop Technique, general 60
Raindrop Technique, modifications 65
Raindrop Technique, rabbits 298
Raindrop Technique, reptiles 313
Raindrop Technique, rodent 315
Rats 315
Raven 194
Ravintsara 145
Rectal, use of oils 56
Regenolone Moisturizing Cream .. 236
Regurgitation, avian 281
Rehemogen 236
Relaxation Massage Oil 237
Release 194
Relieve It 194
Reptiles 313
Respiratory infections, canine 448
Respiratory, avian 282
Respiratory, equine 505
Rhino 489
Rhodococcus equi 506
Ringbone 507
Ringworm, canine 449
Ringworm, feline 361
Ringworm, large animal 507
Rock Rose 83
Rocky Mountain Spotted Fever .... *See* Tick Borne Disease
Rodents 315
Roman Chamomile 81
Rose 145
Rose of Sharon 83

541

Rose Ointment	237	Soaking water	46
Rosemary	146	Spearmint	150
Rotavirus	508	Spikenard	151
RutaVaLa	195	Spinal, equine	474
RutaVaLa Roll-On	195	Spine, canine	454
Sacred Frankincense	101	Splints, equine	511
Sacred Mountain	195	Spondylosis	454
Saddle sores	508	Spritzers	43
Saddle Thrombus	362	Spruce	153
Safety	18	Squamous Cell Carcinoma	365
Sage	148	Squid	316
Salamanders	303	Staph infections	*See* Skin Infections
Sandalwood	149	Steroids	455
SARA	195	Stevia Extract	238
Sara Kenney	246	Stocking up, equine	488
Sarcoids	509	Stomatitis	366
Sarcoma, feline	363	Stool eating	*See* Coprophagia
Sarcoma, vaccine	363	Strangles	512
Sarcoptic mange	450	Streptococcus equi	512
Scaly face mites	283	Stress Away Roll-On	196
SclarEssence	196	Sugar Gliders	316
Scrapie	529	Sulfurzyme	238
Scratches	510	Summer Itch	512
Sebaceous cysts	451	Sunburn	*See* Photosensitivity
Seborrhea	451	Super B	239
Seedy Toe	520	Super C	240
Seizures, avian	284	Super C Chewable	240
Seizures, canine	452	Super Cal	241
Seizures, feline	364	Supplements	203
Self-mutilation, avian	274	Suppositories	56
Senility	*See* Cognitive dysfunction	Surrender	197
Sensation	196	Swabbing	*See* Wintergreen
Sensation Massage Oil	237	Sweet Itch	512
Shampoo, adding oils to	46	Swimming pools	46
Shampoos, human	211, 220	Syphilis, rabbits	299
Shope Papilloma, rabbits	301	Tangerine	154
Sinus infection, avian	285	Tansy, Blue	155
Skin conditions, equine	510	Tansy, Idaho	156
Skin infections, canine	452	Tarantulas	311
Skin tags	453	Tarragon	157
Sleep Essence	237	Tea Tree Oil	120
Slique Essence	196	Tea Tree Oil, cats	321
Slique Tea	238	Teat dip	530
Smell, sense of	23	Teat wash	530
Snakes	313	Tender Tush	241
Snuffles, rabbits	297	Tendons, equine	513

INDEX

Testicle, inflammation 456
Testicle, undescended 456
Tetanus 531
The Gift 197
Therapeutic Eye Spritzer 51
TheraPro Premium Diffuser 31
Thieves 197
Thieves Foaming Hand Soap 242
Thieves Household Cleaner 243
Thieves Lozenges 243
Thieves Mouthwash 242
Thieves Spray 246
Thieves toothpastes 241
Thieves Waterless Hand Purifier .. 247
Thieves Wipes 247
Thin Ewe Syndrome 524
Thrombocytopenia .... See Autoimmune
Thrush 514
Thyme 158
Thyromin 247
Tick bites, canine 457
Tick bites, equine 514
Tick Borne Disease, canine 457
Tick Borne Disease, equine 515
Tick Paralysis 458
Tigers 304
Toads 303
Toothpastes 241
Topical application 41
Torticollis, rabbits 297
Tortoises 318
Toxoplasmosis 367
Trailer rides 515
Tranquil Roll-On 201
Transformation 201
Transporting 515
Trauma Life 201
Treponema, rabbits 299
Tritrichomonas 367
True Source 247
Tsuga 161
Tumor, canine 388
Tumor, fatty 431
Turtles 319
Tying up 516
Udder care 530

Ulcers, canine gastric 416
Ulcers, equine 517
Ultra Young + Oral Spray 248
Umbilical infection, large animal .. 517
Unicorns 307
Upper Respiratory Infections 368
Urethra, blocked 333
URI, feline 368
Urinary, feline 369
Urine pH 205
Urine, grass scald 205
Uveitis, equine 518
V-6 248
Vaccination detox, feline 370
Vaccine detox, equine 518
Vaccinosis 459
Vaginitis 459
Valerian 162
Valor 202
Valor Roll-On 202
Vent, rabbits 299
Vertigo 460
Vestibular disease 460
Vetiver 163
Viral, feline 371
Virus, canine 461
Virus, equine 519
Vita Flex 74
Vomiting, canine 461
Vomiting, feline 372
Warts, avian .... See Papillomatosis
Warts, canine 462
Warts, equine 519
Warts, rabbits 301
Wasting Disease, avian .... See Proventricular Dilatation Disease
Water misting 43
Water, adding oils to 32
Welts, equine 504
Welts, horses 463
Welts, Raindrop 463, 504
West Nile Virus 520
Western Red Cedar 80
White Angelica 202
White Line Disease 520
Windgalls 521

543

Wintergreen	165
Wipes, Thieves	247
WNV	520
Worms	*See* Deworming
Wounds, avian	287
Wounds, large animal	532
Wry Neck, rabbits	297
Xylitol	205, 208, 209, 222
Yacon syrup	249
Yeast infections	*See* Skin infections
Ylang Ylang	168
Yogurt, Life 5	317
Zinc Poisoning, avian	*See* Heavy Metals
Zoo Animals	319

Made in the USA
Lexington, KY
07 August 2014